THE COMPANION GUIDE TO

WALES

COMPANION GUIDES

First published 2005

Companion Guides

ISBN 1 900639 43 2

*The publishers and author have done their best to ensure
the accuracy and currency of all the information in
The Companion Guide to Wales.
However, they can accept no responsibility for any loss, injury,
or inconvenience sustained by any traveller as a result
of information or advice contained in the guide.*

Companion Guides is an imprint of Boydell & Brewer Ltd.
PO Box 9, Woodbridge, Suffolk IP12 3DF, UK
and of Boydell & Brewer Inc.
668 Mt. Hope Avenue, Rochester, NY 14620, USA
website: www.companionguides.com

A BIC catalogue record for this book is available
from the British Library

Printed and bound in Finland by WS Bookwell

Contents

Illustrations

Introduction

Introduction

The task I was set by my publisher was to produce a single volume *Companion Guide to Wales* to replace the two volumes, long out of print, by Elizabeth Beazley and Peter Howells. The publication of these volumes coincided, more or less, with my appointment to a teaching position in Aberystwyth and the purchase of my first car. They subsequently guided me about Wales on innumerable excursions, their enthusiasm for the then neglected Victorian era in church architecture a revelation. The other book that I would take with me on my wanderings, either on foot or by car, was Bill Condry's *Exploring Wales* (1970). Altogether less detailed, it gave greater prominence to natural history and deepened my understanding of a landscape with which I had grown enchanted on youthful hiking holidays in north Wales. It seemed a necessary complement to Beazley and Howells. The missing ingredient in both was cultural. George Borrow had learned some Welsh, from a stable boy at Newmarket, before he ventured on his celebrated pedestrian tour of *Wild Wales* (1862) a century before. He used his knowledge, or claimed so to do, to gain insight into a culture that he knew to be distinctive. 'Very nice pub', runs the recommendation in a well-regarded Guide to one of the hostelries near my home, 'but very Welsh'. It has always been difficult for me to imagine the mind-set that would approach a visit to Wales in that spirit. Certainly my aim from the outset has been to enable the visitor to share as much as possible of this exceptional country from the inside: its history, its landscape and its culture. Of course, not every visitor has time to learn Welsh before visiting the country but a brief acquaintance with the Welsh alphabet (largely a phonetic system) and the key elements to be found in place-names will add immeasurably to an appreciation of the visit. Both are supplied as Appendices.

The most difficult part of my task has been keeping within the strict word length necessitated by the current economics of travel publishing. My first draft was a third as long again, and cutting it down to size, whilst improving the final product in many ways – 'less is usually best', as every graduate student has been told by his supervisor – has nevertheless been painful. It seems no accident to me that the first attempt to write a *Companion Guide to Wales* produced two volumes, just as John Davies's celebrated *History of Wales* (1993) overran his publisher's commission three times over. The question posed to me by a prospective American visitor – 'What is there to see?' – is not susceptible of a short, or quick, answer. For the delights of Wales are cumulative and understated: a succession of small country churches rather than great city cathedrals, a labyrinth of byways away from the few highways, details of vernacular architecture rather than grand edifices, the thirteenth-century Edwardian castles being the exception that proves this rule. Even our mountains are often no more than hills. '*Mon Dieu*, but the Almighty has forgotten to put the tops on them!' exclaimed Jean Charlet, as he passed through the country, far from his native Switzerland, on his way to work as groom for squire Lewis Lloyd of Nantgwyllt in Radnorshire, a house that now lies beneath the waters of Birmingham's Elan Valley reservoir. A cultural tradition rooted in the austerity and erudition of the Celtic saints, a tradition more confirmed than repudiated by the Reformation, is best appreciated by lovers of small things. Wales is a country where small is beautiful. The juggernaut of globalisation may be threatening the Welsh way of life with extinction; appropriately, Welsh poetry has a fine tradition both of elegy and lament, sentiments frequently in evidence here. There have scarcely ever been more than a million Welsh speakers on the planet at any one time, yet the depth and vitality of the Welsh cultural tradition is remarkable. In the words of the popular folk anthem composed by Dafydd Iwan, the singing politician who was elected president of Plaid Cymru in 2003, 'In spite of everything, we're still here':

> *Yma o hyd*
> *Er gwaetha pawb a phopeth*
> *ryn yma o hyd!*

The aim of approaching Wales from within accounts for the organisation of the book, which begins and ends deep inside the country, with successive chapters devoted to the historic counties of Wales. Late twentieth-century local government reorganisation has made little impact on the old loyalties that are celebrated here; our politicians ignore maps of the heart at their peril. In a country of strong local loyalties, numerous sins of omission have been committed and for these I beg forbearance. Friends and colleagues have generously read over sections of the book and have saved me from numerous mistakes and infelicities. Whilst retaining full responsibility for all remaining errors, I would like to thank in particular: Sir Rees Davies, Richard Davies, Muriel Bowen Evans, R. Alun Evans, John Harris, R. Elwyn Hughes, Glyn Tegai Hughes, Gwilym Hughes, Ray Howell, Brian Ll. James, Terry John, Brian and Margaret Mitchell, Gerald Morgan, Keith Parker, Edward Parry, Liz Pitman, Geraint Tudur and Geoffrey Veysey. My membership of *Cymdeithas Edward Lhuyd*, the Society of Welsh Naturalists that organises interpretative walks for its members in various parts of Wales on every Saturday of the year, continues to surprise and delight me by revealing fresh experiences with astonishing regularity. Last but certainly not least, my wife, Ilona, has been ever supportive. Not only has she tolerated my lack of attention to her, the house and the garden, for two whole years but she has prepared the Index and, in what were a series of memorable family expeditions around the country, also took the photographs. John Davies ended his *tour de force* with an optimistic assertion that his *History of Wales* had been written 'in the faith and confidence that the nation in its fullness is yet to be.' It is an optimism one yearns to share and, in that spirit, the book is dedicated not only to my wife but also to our daughter, Margarita.

David Barnes, St David's Day 2005

For

Ilona and Margarita

Croeso i Gymru

The historic Welsh counties, 1543–1974.

I
Mid Wales

1

Ceredigion

THE MEDIAEVAL PRINCIPALITY OF CEREDIGION, a political unit with its origins in the fifth century survived as the county of Cardiganshire from 1284 until local government reform in 1974, when the three counties of south and west Wales – Cardiganshire, Carmarthenshire and Pembrokeshire – were uneasily united as Dyfed. In 1996, they reverted to separate unitary authorities, with Cardiganshire readopting its ancient name. Essential to any understanding of Ceredigion and its people, therefore, is its longevity as a self-contained territory with clear boundaries and a strong sense of its distinctive identity. The boundaries are: the sea to the west; the high, empty moorland of Pumlumon to the east, the Afon Teifi to the south and the Dyfi estuary and its tributary, the Llyfnant, to the north. As to particularities, Ceredigion has its own distinctive dialect of southern Welsh, the linguistic frontier coinciding with the northern county boundary where the Llyfnant joins the Dyfi. Its inhabitants, known as *Cardis*, have a reputation in the rest of Wales for tightness of the purse strings. Cardiganshire sent many of its sons and daughters to London as dairymen, whence originated those oft-repeated stories of *Cardi* milkmen taking off their hats as a mark of respect whenever they passed a water-pump; *Cardis* have been the backbone of the London Welsh ever since. The county town of Ceredigion today is Aberystwyth but Quarter Sessions magistrates in the eighteenth century also met in Tregaron and Lampeter, as well as in what was then the county town of Cardigan. Today the county council meets more conveniently (or, as

3

often in Wales, equally inconveniently) just outside the Regency new town of Aberaeron.

The Cambrian Coast Line from Shrewsbury crosses the Llyfnant into Ceredigion after Dyfi Junction – a stage-set in waiting for a Welsh version of *Waiting for Godot* – where it branches south for Borth and Aberystwyth. It was the building of an embankment for the Cambrian Railway (as this line was formerly known) over the quayside at **Glandyfi** that finally killed off the shipping in that once busy little port. Iron ore was imported here for the **Furnace** that is such an impressive sight in the village that bears its name, on a bend in the coast road south from Machynlleth. In the care of Cadw, this charcoal furnace with its giant water-wheel has been meticulously conserved. The parish church of St Mary's at **Eglwys-fach** was in the care of the poet R.S. Thomas (1913–2000) in the 1970s; it was his idea to paint so much of the interior black. A keen ornithologist, he was attracted to the Dyfi estuary by its teeming wildfowl, becoming a close friend of the naturalist Bill Condry (1918–1998) who lived at Ynys Edwin and was founder warden of the magnificent RSPB nature reserve at **Ynys-hir** as well a regular country diary contributor to *The Guardian*.

The Clettwr is now bridged conveniently but unattractively at **Tre'r-ddôl** but the older bridge in the by-passed village has period charm. This village by-pass typically succeeds in opening up those parts of the village best hidden from the public gaze whilst concealing the parts that were designed to be seen. In the village itself is the former Wesleyan chapel of Soar, epicentre of the 1859 Welsh Revival that followed the return to the village of his birth of the Revd. Humphrey Jones (1832–1895) from the 'Burned Over District' of up-state New York. In 1961 the lexicographer R.J. Thomas (1908–1976) bought the Old Chapel to house his collection of bygones, leaving the collection to the National Museum (NMGW) when he died in 1976. The National Museum removed the bygones to Cardiff and replaced them with a display on Welsh religious history but the new museum failed to survive the financial cuts of the 1980s. Above **Taliesin** are the sadly mutilated remains of Bedd Taliesin, a kerb cairn with a massive capstone that Romantic antiquarians have associated with the sixth-century poet. A walk in the direction of the Afon Clettwr brings spectacular views over the Dyfi estuary to Aberdyfi. The entire estuary acquired World Biosphere status in 1977.

Immediately below lies **Cors Fochno**, a raised peat bog that formed when the waters of the Afon Leri were cut off from the sea by the lengthening sand-spit which ends at Ynys-las. At its russet-hued best in the autumn, it is now managed as a national nature reserve. An oracular toad was reputed to inhabit its centre and an ancient practice of burning the bog back at the end of winter was associated with the belief that the bog carried the ague, as malaria was then known. An old witch, *Yr Hen Wrach*, was said to come off the bog at night and infect people as they slept. Today the bog is a sanctuary for rare flora, including bog mosses, bladderworts and sundews. In 2004, a mediaeval trackway across the bog was discovered preserved in the peat. The last three kilometres of the Leri were canalised in 1824 as part of an act of enclosure to reclaim bogland for agricultural use.

A succession of dunes at **Ynys-las** encroached on an area of woodland – pine, birch, elder and oak – the remains of which can be seen at low tide as submerged tree stumps and are now part of the Dyfi National Nature Reserve. The water between Cerrig-y-Penrhyn and Aberdyfi is one of the most ancient ferry crossings in Wales, used by such famous personages as Lord Rhys, Gerald of Wales and Dafydd ap Gwilym. The remains of a refuge tower associated with the ferry crossing can still be seen on the Twyni Bach. The estuarine sands exposed at low tide are named after Maelgwn, a sixth-century prince who sought to unite the western Welsh against the Saxon advance from the east. He demonstrated his fitness to undertake this mission as king of Gwynedd at a gathering of princes on the seashore. Leadership of the Welsh was to be given to whoever remained seated on their chairs as the tide raced in; Maelgwn alone was carried above the waves by a chair of waxed birds' wings, made for him by his adviser Maeldaf Hen. This ceremony is re-enacted annually at the Borth Carnival.

Borth is a former fishing village overgrown to seaside resort with the coming of the railway adjacent to this fine stretch of beach. The Revd. Edward Thring, headmaster of Uppingham, evacuated his school here for the years 1876 and 1877 to escape epidemic sickness in Rutlandshire. Two inscribed slate seats on the 'Uppingham Path' record the gratitude of staff and pupils. The evacuation of University College, London, to Borth during the Second World War continued this tradition. A coastal footpath, following the cliff south to Aberystwyth, is the first stage of the Ceredigion Coastal Path that continues south to link with the Pembrokeshire Coastal Path at St Dogmaels, making over 100 kilometres of this magnificent coastline, much of it designated Heritage Coast, available to walkers.

At Wallog, an unusual shingle ridge, **Sarn Cynfelyn** juts out into Cardigan Bay. A striking feature at spring tides, it is said to denote the southern limit of the sunken commote of Cantre'r Gwaelod. **Clarach Bay** is disfigured by caravans, but a kilometre upstream, on a glacial morraine at **Llangorwen**, is an interesting Tractarian church, an unlikely find in this part of the country. It was built in 1841 on land provided by the Revd. Isaac Williams (1802–1865), a Tractarian poet and theologian who had been born in the Georgian mansion of Cwmcynfelyn; he had befriended Newman and Keble during his Oxford days. Keble donated the lectern and Newman the chandeliers for the church.

Talybont has declined in importance as a market centre, its former woollen mills now silent. An attractive square has two public houses and a striking mural on the wall of the original premises of *Y Lolfa*, a successful modern Welsh publisher that has now taken over the former police station in the village. Opposite, the adjacent Independent and Baptist chapels, Bethel and Tabernacl – the latter now a soap factory – bear eloquent testimony to the fierce interdenominational rivalry of the nineteenth century. To the east of Talybont at **Bont-goch** (**Elerch**) is another Tractarian church. It was built by the Revd. Lewis Gilbertson, Vice-Principal of Jesus College, Oxford, who was vicar of Llangorwen from 1841 to 1852. As at Llangorwen, the architect employed was William Butterfield; his work carries conviction.

To experience the hinterland of Talybont, take the more northerly route east into the hills on the lonely road that passes the **Nant-y-Moch** reservoir on its way to Ponterwyd. The retreat of agriculture and the death of lead mining have emptied these hills of all but sheep. The reservoirs were constructed in 1964 as part of a local hydroelectric scheme that utilizes the waters of the Rheidol. Sir John Rhys (1840–1915), the Celtic scholar, was born in the tiny cottage of Aberceiro-fach on the Nant-y-Moch road at **Ponterwyd**. A centennial memorial plaque was unveiled at this humble abode in 1940 and the village primary school, opened in 1953, bears his name. The A44 runs through the village, by-passing a splendid single-arch eighteenth-centruy bridge, so it is possible to turn back west towards Aberystwyth or head east towards Llangurig. Continuing south with the Rheidol, the intriguing church of **Ysbyty Cynfyn** appears to have been built within a prehistoric stone circle, now incorporated in the churchyard wall, although the antiquity of the stone circle is much disputed. A path leads over Parson's Bridge to **Ystumtuen**, one of the many former lead-mining villages of north Cardiganshire.

Aberystwyth, the largest town in the county, was described in Edwardian guidebooks as 'the Athens of Cardigan Bay'. It is certainly a bookish place, thanks to the presence of the university library and the National Library on Penglais, the hill that rises steeply behind the town. The best entry into the town, from a scenic point of view, is from the north on the road from Machynlleth, with the whole compass of Cardigan Bay opening up as the descent of Penglais into the town begins. The National Library was opened in the town in 1911 after its founding librarian, Sir John Ballinger, had seen off stiff competition from Cardiff. It is one of Britain's five copyright libraries and offers both permanent and temporary exhibitions of art and manuscripts in dignified surroundings. Anyone with even the slightest interest in Welsh culture would profit from a visit, with the view over the town and bay from the grandiose entrance steps an added bonus. The Penglais campus of the university is the result of the expansion – many in Wales would say over-expansion – of the university in the 1960s and 1970s. The Great Hall was opened in 1970 and a small but attractive *Theatr y Werin* followed two years later to celebrate the university's centenary. Together comprising the **Aberystwyth Arts Centre**, they are an invaluable resource to town and gown but architecturally the ensemble has not lasted well. A more enduring vista lies beyond the Rheidol to the south-west, the impressive ramparts of Pen Dinas iron age hillfort, adorned with the Wellington Monument, erected in 1852.

The **Old College** is located on the Edwardian seafront. Intended as a hotel by Thomas Savin, the railway entrepreneur who brought the Cambrian Railway to the town from Machynlleth, he employed the architect J.P. Seddon for this hastily constructed neo-Gothic confection. When the hotel failed, it was purchased in order to establish the new University College of Wales, the first of the federal colleges of the national university. It is a much-loved building, with its gable mosaic of Archimedes receiving emblems of modern science and industry and its fine *porte-cochère* in King Street. In these premises a fine tradition of scholarship was inaugurated that has attracted generations of distinguished scholars to the town. Funding from the Llandinam estate of David Davies gave Aberystwyth the world's first Department of International Politics; established in 1919, it is soon to have a new departmental building on the Penglais campus. Occupying the same site as the Old College is another building that started life as a hotel, the former Theological College of the Calvinistic Methodists that closed in 2002. For counterpoint, return up Penglais to see the confident new Parry-Williams building, opened in 2000, of the Department of Theatre, Film and Television Studies. The last quarter of the twentieth century saw an entire generation of Welsh youth transfer its ambitions from the pulpit to the TV studio, possibly not as great a contradiction as might at first be thought.

A delightful Edwardian **Promenade** runs the length of the seafront. The traditional walk along its length involves 'kicking the bar' at either end. The rusty pier, originally 200 meters long, was truncated during a storm in 1938. It accommodates a flock of starlings whose spectacular nightly roosting manoeuvres always attract attention from passers-by. The sweep of the bay to the north-east is very satisfying with its ensemble of down-at-heel guest houses and student hostels culminating in the dilapidated remains of Alexandra Hall, now happily under restoration. This hostel for female students was opened by Princess Alexandra in 1896 and placed as far away from the Old College as possible although it should be remembered that the University of Wales was one of the first universities in Britain to award degrees to its female students. Behind the hostel, a funicular railway, in operation since 1896, can be taken to the Camera Obscura on top of Constitution Hill, where the coastal path from Borth arrives. The hill is flood-lit at night to resemble a huge slab of liver.

Pier Street has several good town houses and, to the south, Laura Place has the best surviving Georgian buildings in the town. St Michael's church, built in 1890 in uncompromisingly English style continues to flourish, its once attractive graveyard cleared to create a commodious and lucrative car park. In New Street, a plaque on the wall of the diminutive, and now disused, Unitarian chapel commemorates David Ivon Jones (1883–1924), a key figure in the history of the civil rights movement and the Africa National Congress in South Africa, who worshipped here as a young man. South Beach is attractive and the inevitable marina has, on balance, probably served to tidy up the old harbour without too much loss of character. Other noteworthy examples of conservation, both of which may cause eyebrows to rise, are the transformation of both the railway station (point of departure for the Vale of Rheidol Railway) and St Paul's Welsh Wesleyan chapel into public houses. The town's largest chapel – Y Tabernacl of the Calvinistic Methodists with its magnificent organ – closed at the beginning of this century but there are plans to turn it into a museum of Welsh emigration.

The street pattern of Aberystwyth retains the grid pattern of the thirteenth-century Edwardian borough with Eastgate, Northgate and Southgate serving as reminders of the former points of entry into what was built as a walled town. The castle ruins, on a 'perilous rock' overlooking South Beach, are impressive and cry out for systematic excavation and improved interpretation. One of the group of new castles built by Edward I following his conquest of Wales in 1282, it was famously captured by Owain Glyn Dŵr in 1404. For a brief period, from 1637 to 1643, it housed a royal mint, taking advantage of local supplies of silver. A royalist stronghold during the Civil War, the castle succumbed to a five-month siege by Cromwellian forces in April 1646. In the years that followed the siege, the castle was reduced to it present ruinous state, with local people making ready use of the supplies of high quality building stone. The impressive war memorial, designed by Mario Rutelli, was unveiled in 1923.

In the immediate vicinity of Aberystwyth, the ancient church of St Padarn at **Llanbadarn Fawr** was built on the site of the *clas* (a Celtic monastic site), famous for its scholarship, established by Padarn in the sixth century. The church dates from the thirteenth century and consists of a large aisleless nave and transepts with a central tower, monastic in scale. A permanent exhibition in the south transept displays two Early Christian crosses formerly in the churchyard and provides information on Padarn, Sulien, the eleventh-century cleric and his son Rhygyfarch, author of a celebrated life of St David, as well as on William Morgan, the translator of the Bible into Welsh, who ministered here. It was designed by Peter Lord and opened on St Padarn's Day, 15 April 1988. There are memorials to the Pryse family of Gogerddan and the Powells of Nanteos in the chancel of Llanbadarn church, together with one to Lewis Morris (1701–1765, Llywelyn Ddu o Fôn). The Thanksgiving Window was designed by John Petts and donated by the composer Ian Parrott, who loved the church's acoustic. A congregation at mass in the church is memorably evoked in *Merched Llanbadarn* (Girls of Llanbadarn) by one of the greatest European poets of the fourteenth century, Dafydd ap Gwilym (c.1320–1370). A large slate plaque commemorates his birthplace at Brogynin, two kilometres east of **Penrhyn-coch**. The unattractive contemporary bungalow now occupying the plot has been named Tŷ Dafydd. The small-scale church, a Victorian oddity by R.J. Withers, contains further memorials to the Pryses of **Plas Gogerddan**, a dull mansion that now houses the Institute of Grassland and Environmental Research (IGER).

The old tollgate at Southgate, built in 1772, was moved to St Fagans in 1968 and is now a popular feature at the Museum of Welsh Life (MWL). From this point, south of Aberystwyth, several important routes radiate inland. The old turnpike road linking Aberystwyth with Kington on the

English border can be followed through Capel Seion to **Devil's Bridge**. This part of north Ceredigion was formerly lead-mining country. The Vale of Rheidol Railway, a narrow-gauge line that runs down the south side of the Rheidol valley from Devil's Bridge was completed in 1902 to transport lead ore and timber down to the harbour at Aberystwyth. The railway quickly established itself as a tourist attraction and, until privatised in 1989, was the last steam railway operated by British Rail. Its popularity ensured the continued use of the wholly inappropriate English version of the Welsh name of the village, Pontarfynach. The original mediaeval bridge spanning the dramatic Mynach falls survives beneath a second bridge constructed in the mid-eighteenth century. An iron bridge was further superimposed in 1901. All three can be seen from the dramatic turnstile walk that has provided revenue for the Hafod Arms Hotel for over a century. This attractive hotel was built around 1830 by the Duke of Newcastle who had acquired the Hafod estate following the death of Thomas Johnes. It's a good walk, in spite of its commercialisation, and even the tea-room, strategically situated at the exit turnstile, can be a welcome sight. From Devil's Bridge, the old coach road passes under the Jubilee Arch, built by Johnes to celebrate the Jubilee of George III, and on through the lead-mining village of **Cwmystwyth,** where the eerie remains of lead extraction will fascinate anyone with a penchant for industrial archaeology. Experienced cavers come here to explore the underground workings whilst hang-gliders and the local red kites look down on this unique landscape from the skies above. The road continues into Radnorshire past Hillgate, where, in 1843, an elderly female gatekeeper was shot in the face during the Rebecca Riots. At 406 metres, the road crosses the watershed between the upper reaches of the Ystwyth and the Elan before skirting the reservoir and dropping down into Rhayader, with Gwynllyn lying prettily in the valley below.

A newer, less precipitous route linking Rhayader with Aberystwyth via Eisteddfa Gurig was in use by coaches by the 1830s. It's a long lonely road through the empty moorland of **Pumlumon** (anglicised as Plynlimon), the highest point of which, an Ordovician outcrop rising to 752 metres through the surrounding Silurian deposits, can be reached from **Eisteddfa Gurig**, presumably named after the saint who rested here on his peregrination. Although the summit is not dramatic, it provides exceptional views over vast tracts of both north and south Wales. As befits a territory where the sources of both Severn and Wye are located, not to mention lesser rivers like Clywedog or Rheidol, Pumlumon has historically been a repository of Welsh folk tale and memory.

From Southgate, the B4575, known locally as *Y Ffordd Ganol* (the middle road), cuts a south-easterly diagonal in the direction of the ancient abbey of Strata Florida. At **New Cross**, the grave of Caradoc Evans (David Evans, 1878–1945), in the burial ground of Horeb, serves as a reminder that all this natural beauty can conceal darker social realities. His short stories, exploring the themes of lust, greed and a degraded Nonconformity brought him notoriety in his home country. A couple of kilometres to the east, attractively hidden in a hollow in the hills, sits the village of **Llanfihangel-y-Creuddyn**. St Michael's church has a massive fourteenth-century tower, as though the original architects had envisaged a building on the same scale as Llanbadarn. The interior has an intriguing oak reredos, carved in 1919 by a Belgian artist, Jules Bernaerts, who had been commissioned to commemorate the end of the Great War by Dr Roberts, Penwern. He is said to have found his models for the scene of the Last Supper on the promenade at Aberystwyth: 'Look at Matthew the rate collector', he suggested, 'the very type of a Welsh miser!' A new west window cheerfully celebrates local rural life.

From Aberystwyth, two famous houses of the gentry present themselves along *Y Ffordd Ganol*. **Nanteos**, home to the Powells, is the finest example of Georgian architecture in this part of Wales. Overlooking Nant Paith, it was promoted as the repository of the Nanteos Cup, one of only two mediaeval mazer bowls extant in Wales but alleged, in the early twentieth century, to be none other than the Holy Grail. This fantasy drew sustenance from the fact that 'gentle' George Powell (1842–1882), an aesthete out of sympathy with the local hunting set, had befriended Richard Wagner, whose *Parsifal* incorporates this subject matter. Inconveniently for the myth-makers, *Parsifal* was written a decade before Wagner's visit to Britain, which may not have included a visit to Nanteos at all. **Trawsgoed** was the ancestral home of the Vaughans, elevated to an Irish peerage as Lords Lisburne in 1695. The house, known in translation as Crosswood, was taken over by the Ministry of Agriculture in 1947 and is now in the process of further conversion into luxury apartments. The grounds, in which the remains of a Roman fort lie, have magnificent displays of roses, azaleas and rhododendrons.

Departing from *Y Ffordd Ganol* at Pont Llanafan, a delightfully scenic minor road follows the Ystwyth to Pontrhydygroes with good forest walks on both sides of the valley. **Llanafan** has an undistinguished Victorian church that served as the estate church for Crosswood; inside there are memorials to the Vaughans and a colony of Natterer's bats. At **Pontrhydygroes**, another lead-mining village, the arrival of Cornish miners in the nineteenth century accounts for the grandeur of Bethel Wesleyan chapel, built in 1874 and now a private dwelling. In this Alpine setting, Thomas Johnes (1748–1816) set about creating a sylvan paradise at **Hafod**, planting deciduous and coniferous trees, encouraging agricultural improvement amongst his tenants and establishing a private press at the splendid house, designed for him by Thomas Baldwin of Bath in 1786. The house, together with its collection of precious Welsh manuscripts, housed in the library added by John

Nash in 1794, was destroyed by fire in 1807; for Hafod seems to have been cursed with tragedy. Mariamne, Thomas Johnes' frail but talented only daughter died in 1811, aged twenty-seven. Francis Chantrey's monument to her, in Eglwys Newydd church above Hafod, was in turn destroyed by fire in 1932 and the ruins of the subsequent property were demolished in 1962. The enthusiastic Friends of Hafod have successfully restored the estate walks: the Lady's Walk, incorporating the Bedford Monument – commemorating Francis the 5th Duke, 'the most judicious and munificent promoter of the National Agriculture' – together with the reconstructed Alpine Bridge and the longer Gentleman's Walk. There are plans to restore both Mrs Johnes' and Mariamne's gardens.

Ysbyty Ystwyth shares with Tre'r-ddôl the honour of lighting the fires of revival in Wales in 1859, for the Revd. Dafydd Morgan (1814–1883), its joint leader, was brought up in the village and was raised to the ministry there. His Calvinistic Methodist chapel, Maesglas, is adjacent to the old church. The more recent church, built higher up, has good views of the Ystwyth valley. The more recent Methodist chapel failed to survive into the twenty-first century and is now for sale as a building plot. The name of the village reminds us of the proximity of Strata Florida abbey, for a monastic hospice was once located here; Rhydygroes (Ford of the Holy Cross) and Rhydfendigaid (Ford of the Blessed Virgin) share these monastic origins, their bridges were built later and added to the village names.

Y Ffordd Ganol leaves the Ystwyth dramatically by climbing the steep south bank of the Ystwyth at Trefriw. **Ystrad Meurig** has a Norman motte, controlling the upper reaches of the Teifi, and the former St John's College, a grammar school made famous by its Augustan headmaster, the scholarly Edward Richard (1714–1777). It is said that locals once waited expectantly at the roadside for hours to see an M.A. (Oxon.) pass by on his way to the college. That was before the arrival of the Manchester and Milford Railway Company: an ambitious project to construct a railway though the Welsh heartland from Milford Haven to Manchester, with the objective of expediting the importation of cotton to the textile mills of northern England. The railway reached Ystrad Meurig from Milford Haven via Carmarthen – having changed from Brunel's broad gauge to standard gauge at Pencader – but was then defeated by Welsh topography. The intended link from Ystrad Meurig to Llanidloes proved beyond the capacities of the engineers and a right angle was made with the result that Aberystwyth became the final destination. Thus was the much-loved and, since Beeching, long-lamented Carmarthen to Aberystwyth railway born. Its trains travelled so slowly that it was said that students returning home from college had time to vacate the carriages and gather floral bouquets for their mothers as the train progressed. In 1965, the pre-eminent Welsh dramatist of the twentieth century, Saunders Lewis (1893–1985), wrote a play about it, *Yn y Trên*. Constructing the line over Cors Caron was a significant engineering achievement, with sacks of wool being used to provide a foundation for the track on top of the peat bog. Remnants of Strata Florida station are still visible at Ystrad Meurig and Tecwyn Ifan, Baptist minister in Pontrhydfendigaid in the 1980s, has recorded a nostalgic folk-song in its memory.

Pontrhydfendigaid, another lead-mining village, is chiefly visited for Strata Florida abbey, which lies in rare tranquillity on the banks of the Teifi to the east of the village. The village has a noteworthy humpback bridge, the opening of which in 1760 was commemorated in verse by Edward Richard. There is a good Calvinistic Methodist chapel in the centre of the village and a prominent war memorial on what passes for a village green. The cavernous eisteddfod hall, currently under restoration after fire damage, was provided by Sir David James, Pantyfedwen, a local boy who made his fortune in London; his shameless monument beside St David's church at Strata Florida fails to mar the atmosphere of sanctity of this ancient burial place. Close to Sir David James, by way of reprimand, lies an Osborne-Jones family grave whose memorial inscription has adapted Ceiriog's modest epitaph: *Dyma eu bedd a dim lol* (Here is their grave and no pretension). The severely pruned yew tree next to St David's church has a plaque commemorating Dafydd ap Gwilym, traditionally believed to be interred at the abbey. There are two other curiosities. Beside the church is a grave containing the left leg and thigh of Henry Hughes, who suffered an agricultural accident in the summer of 1756 and subsequently emigrated to America, where the greater part of his remains are interred. By the north wall of the graveyard lies the body of an unidentified traveller, found frozen to death after a snow-storm in the vicinity of the Teifi Pools in the winter of 1929.

Strata Florida Abbey (Cadw) has inspired so much poetry in both national languages that it is high time that someone compiled an anthology. T. Gwynn Jones memorably concludes his elegy to the abbey,

> *Pan rhodiwyf ddaear Ystrad Fflur*
> *O'm dolur ymdawelaf.*
>
> (Strolling the grounds of Strata Florida
> is balm for my troubled soul.)

The physical remains are tantalisingly scant. The Abbey's great west door, with its pastoral motif, invariably attracts attention, as does the collection of original mediaeval tiles in the chapels of the south transept. The hold of this place on the nation's memory, however, can scarcely be over-stated. In the middle ages the princes of Wales were buried here – a collection of grave-slabs lie outside the south transept – and the annals of the nation, *Brut y Tywysogion*, are thought in large part to have been compiled here. A Cistercian foundation, dating back to 1164 – the original site of the monastery is at Hen Fynachlog, a few kilometres to the south – the foundation was taken over by Lord Rhys, the powerful prince of Deheubarth, in the following year. Crucially, what had initially been encountered as the alien force of Norman monasticism now came to be viewed favourably, as Cistercian simplicity and poverty formed a bridgehead to the austerity and erudition of the native Celtic monastic tradition. By 1238, the monastery had established itself as a centre of Welsh culture and influence, such that it was the natural choice of venue for Llywelyn Fawr when he assembled the princes of Wales to swear allegiance to his son, Dafydd. Strata Florida never fully recovered from the Glyn Dŵr Rising; at its dissolution in 1538, it housed an abbot and seven monks, one of whom stood accused of counterfeiting coinage. From the monastic masonry, a mansion house was constructed beside the former abbey for the Stedman family, secular beneficiaries of the Dissolution. This fine property, Abbey Farm, is one of only two pre-seventeenth century houses in the county.

The Teifi, the longest river in the county, has marked the boundary of a Welsh province, a Norman lordship and subsequently of the county, a continuous frontier over many centuries. It has its source above the abbey in a hauntingly beautiful glaciated landscape where a group of natural lakes are together known as the **Teifi Pools**. The largest of these is Llyn Teifi, where the river has its source. A narrow mountain road leads out to the pools from **Ffair Rhos**, an ancient settlement of smallholdings that takes its name from the former monastic fair. Subsequently, it was renowned for its annual horse fair on 16 September, *Gŵyl y Grog*. The lead mines at Esgair Mwyn, the extensive remains of which still dominate the landscape to the north-east, also provided employment. The village was a notable nest of *beirdd gwlad* – skilled country poets who extol the virtues of their own locality – providing a popular Archdruid in recent times, Elerydd (W.J. Gruffydd). He is the author of the much-loved tales of those archetypal *Cardis, Tomos a Marged* which recreate the rural world of Ffair Rhos in the middle years of the twentieth century, in what now seems a bygone age.

Looking south and west from the Teifi Pools there are extraordinary views over **Cors Caron**, with the sun glistening on the flashes of the Teifi as it meanders through the largest area of raised peat bog in southern Britain. Once extensively worked for its peat, this activity had ceased by the 1960s. In 1955 some 789 hectares of the bog were designated a National Nature Reserve. Trails have been carefully constructed to reveal a wide variety of habitats for the bog's distinctive fauna and flora. Water voles and otters inhabit the bog throughout the year, with polecats coming down onto the bog from the surrounding hills in the summer months. Whooper swans winter regularly on the flashes, as do mallard, teal and wigeon. The once endangered red kite is now a common enough sight in the skies above the bog but no less magnificent for that. Willow scrub, bog asphodel, bog rosemary and crowberry are among the many plants that thrive in this unique habitat. The Teifi itself is celebrated for its salmon, brown trout and sea trout, the national fish of Wales known by its Welsh name, *sewin*. In winter the bog can turn a wonderful shade of russet red, its dying sedges splendid when lit by the setting sun. Locally, the bog is known as *Cors-goch Glan Teifi*, the red mire on the banks of the Teifi.

To the south of the bog, with its parish church of St Caron crowning a terminal moraine, lies the market town of **Tregaron**, well described by a contemporary Welsh historian as 'a black knarled knuckle of a drovers' town in a crook of the moors'. For Tregaron was a droving centre, where cattle and other livestock were assembled in readiness for the annual trek to Barnet fair where they were fattened and sold in exchange for the ready cash that gave this part of Britain some of its first provincial banks. The Aberystwyth and Tregaron Bank, founded in 1810, was known in Welsh as *Banc y Ddafad Ddu* (The Black Sheep Bank) because its notes were engraved with a drawing of one sheep for every pound they represented. Once asked by a television reporter where Tregaron was, a local farmer replied, philosophically, that it was outside the Talbot, *Tu fâs i'r Talbot!* The square outside the Talbot Hotel is dominated by a statue of Henry Richard (1812–1888), the 'Apostle of Peace'. A local Independent minister of radical views, he became MP for Merthyr Tydfil in the pivotal election of 1868 that followed the extension of the franchise to urban workingmen in the previous year. A pioneer of structures for international peace, he occupies a distinguished place in the Welsh internationalist and pacifist tradition. Today, Henry Richard presides over an art gallery, a craft centre and a jewellery manufacturer, the latter using Welsh gold for innovative Celtic designs. To the east, it is possible to follow the drovers' trail through the Green Desert of Wales along the narrow mountain road to Abergwesyn in Breconshire.

The biggest chapel in Tregaron is that of the Calvinistic Methodists, the slate-hung Bwlch-gwynt, for this had been Methodist country since revival broke out in the 1730s at that denomination's Mecca of **Llangeitho**, some five kilometres to the west. A stern-looking statue of the powerful revivalist preacher Daniel Rowland (1713–1790) stands outside his 'New Church' in the village, Capel Gwynfil. A victim of his own success as a preacher, he was deprived of his curacy of the parish church in 1763. For contrast, high on the mountain road to Llyn Brianne stands **Soar-y-Mynydd**, an iconic chapel for the whole of Welsh Nonconformity that has become a place of pilgrimage for its Sunday afternoon services in the summer season. Founded by Ebenezer Richard, father of the 'Apostle of Peace', this homely chapel served a scattered pastoral community. The pulpit stands between tall, rounded Georgian windows with a stenciled Biblical text rising from it: *Duw Cariad Yw*, God is Love.

Following the Teifi south, another massively defensive Norman church on a hill can be found at **Llanddewibrefi**. To explain the hill, it is said that when St David preached here at a synod in AD570, the crowd was so great that the Almighty caused the ground to rise up under the saint's feet so that all could see and hear him. An attractive village, thoroughly Welsh until recently, it now has an English-speaking majority. From **Llanfair Clydogau** an interesting section of the Roman road known as Sarn Helen crosses the ridge over to Cwm Twrch before running down into Carmarthenshire. It is still possible to locate the ruins of Llanfair Manor, a Johnes family property. It was the marriage of Thomas Johnes, senior, to Jane Herbert, heiress of Hafod, which served as the prelude to the drama of that upland estate. The floor of the vestry of the church at **Silian** incorporates an Early Christian inscribed stone, with a simple cross, superimposed on an earlier inscription. In the churchyard is the grave of Julian Cayo-Evans (1937–1995), horse breeder and leader of the Free Wales Army, who served a gaol sentence in the latter capacity at the time of the investiture of Prince Charles in 1969. Across the river at **Cellan**, Caeronnen Unitarian chapel and Capel yr Erw for the Independents testify to heated theological controversies remote from a twenty-first century cast of mind. The village is thus part of *Y Smotyn Du* (The Black Spot), a unique cluster of rural Unitarian chapels that flourished in the Teifi valley in the nineteenth century. Doctrinally progressive Principals of the Presbyterian Academy at Carmarthen were the well-springs of Cardiganshire Unitarianism, a faith famously described by Erasmus Darwin as 'a feather bed on which to catch a falling Christian'. Fittingly, the literary historian G.J. Williams (1892–1963), pioneer biographer of Iolo Morganwg, was born here, the son of the local blacksmith. So too was Moses Williams (1685–1742), the antiquarian and scholar, at Glaslwyn.

Lampeter appears thoroughly orthodox. St David's College, founded by Bishop Burgess in 1827 for the training of ordinands, was built in Oxbridge collegiate style and the town now appears to be clustered around the college buildings, although the former obviously preceded the latter. The Founder's Library, opened in 1827 and designed by Charles Robert Cockerell (1788–1863), has a notable tract collection from the seventeenth and eighteenth centuries. The college chapel has portraits of early college Principals. The town war memorial, honouring the men of Lampeter and Nurse Richards who died in the Great War, was designed by Sir William Goscombe John (1860–1952) and unveiled in 1921. Work by this prolific sculptor, the son of a Cardiff woodcarver who had studied under Burges in Cardiff and Rodin in Paris, enhances public areas throughout Wales. The college has its own war memorial designed by William Douglas Caröe (1857–1938), the Victorian restorer of Danish ancestry, who did his best work in Wales.

From Lampeter the A482 crosses over into the Aeron valley at **Felinfach**, where a community theatre has flourished for over 30 years, and heads west to the coastal town of Aberaeron. Neuadd-lwyd was the site of a flourishing Nonconformist academy in the early nineteenth century that nurtured a band of missionaries who took the Protestant faith to Madagascar. The Black Spot spread out towards it with Unitarian chapels at Llwynygroes, Rhydygwin, Tynygwndwn, Llwyd Jack and Cribyn; at the latter, Thomas Emlyn Williams, the minister, was the leader of his community at the time of the Rebecca Riots. **Llanerchaeron** (NT) is a traditional rural estate that was bequeathed to the National Trust in 1989. The house is a well-preserved example of the early work of the Regency architect, John Nash. The house, stables, farm buildings and walled garden are all open to the public, as is the controversial new Visitor Centre, visually jarring in corrugated iron but ecologically innovative. St Non's, the estate church, was restored by John Nash in 1798; his attractive and unusual lead dome on the tower was replaced with a fibreglass replica in the 1960s.

Aberaeron is a Regency new town, created by the vision of one man, the Revd. Alban Thomas Jones (1751–1819), to whom was bequeathed the name and fortune of the Gwynnes of Mynachdy, a substantial property a few kilometres to the east of the town above a tributary of the Arth. In 1808, he had obtained a Parliamentary bill to enable him to build a new pier, and the new town was born. His name is commemorated in Alban Square, east of the main road. The town has uniformity of architectural style within a compact area, its colourful town houses neatly arranged around its small stone-walled harbour that once exported herrings, butter and oats in exchange for coal, lime and slates. Sloops were built at Aberaeron from the 1830s, the last being the *Cadwgan*, built in 1883 and named after a local earthwork long since claimed by the sea. Today the harbour is popular with yachtsmen and artists and has attracted distinguished residents like the opera singer Sir Geraint Evans (1922–1992) who lived in retirement in the town and served as a volunteer coastguard.

From Aberystwyth, the coast road south to Cardigan reaches Aberaeron through an attractive section of country. At St Bridget's church, **Llansannffraid**, recent repairs have revealed sections of the former chancel screen. The church has a sturdy tower and the exterior walls are hung with slates. On the seaward side of the village, it is worth exploring the distinctive field strips, known as *slangiau*, at Morfa Esgob. Corn marigolds and knapweed here help sustain goldfinches, wheatears and stonechats. The ruins of Capel Non, behind the Post Office in **Llan-non**, testify to mediaeval veneration of the mother of St David. Between

Llan-non and Aber-arth, the road climbs steeply to over 100 metres where a parking place affords the chance of magnificent views out to sea. On a clear day, Bardsey, Mynydd y Rhiw, Carn Fadryn and Yr Eifl in distant Llŷn are visible on the horizon, a sign of impending rain. At low tide ancient fish-traps known as *coredi* are visible, crescent-shaped walls of stone that were set in the shallows to catch fish when the tide receded. Similar features, known in Gaelic as *caraidh*, are found around the shores of the Hebrides.

Inland lies a remote upland territory known as **Mynydd Bach**, celebrated for *Rhyfel y Sais Bach*, The Little English-man's War. The Englishman in question was Augustus Brackenbury whose attempts to enclose common land on the mountain at the end of the Napoleonic Wars were frustrated by the local inhabitants who burnt down his house. The remains of the replacement property, with its defensive moat, still survive as Little Englishman's House in **Trefenter**. The Aeron has its source in Llynnoedd Fanod and Eiddwen, before flowing down through Llangeitho and Ystrad Aeron to the sea; it is a delightful valley to explore. The road joins the Ystwyth valley at **Llanilar**, a church thought to be dedicated either to Hilary of Poitiers or to a sixth-century Celtic saint. It occupies an ancient site; indeed, a bronze age cemetery was discovered close by in 1980.

South of Lampeter, the Teifi marks a frontier with Carmarthenshire. The A475 leaves Lampeter near the remains of **Peterwell**, vibrant in the folk memory of the county for a dastardly deed perpetrated by its notorious squire, Sir Herbert Lloyd. Local lore insists that the squire Lloyd falsely incriminated his neighbour, Siôn Philip, by lowering a black ram down the chimney of his neighbour's cottage and then marshalling the full might of the law to have poor Siôn hanged for theft. All this, so that the view from the squire's mansion should not be marred by the sight of Siôn Philip's humble abode which was subsequently demolished. The story made a fine subject for an opera by Ian Parrott, first staged in Aberystwyth in 1966.

South of Llanwnnen on the banks of the Teifi is the delightful Unitarian chapel of **Alltyblaca**, founded in 1740 as a result of the work of the Arminian minister, Jenkin Jones. The high, battlemented tower of St Gwenog's church at **Llanwenog**, one of the most attractive churches in the county, is a conspicuous local landmark. The Norman font has robust carvings of twelve faces around its rim and the ends of the pews have been finely carved to the designs of Mrs Davies-Evans of Highmead, by a Belgian refugee from the First World War, Joseph Reubens from Bruges. Beneath the tower lie the mortal remains of Dafydd Dafis (1745–1827) who translated Gray's *Elegy on a Country Churchyard* into Welsh and is sometimes paid the compliment of having improved upon the original. As progressive in theology as he was corpulent in body, he ran a distinguished school at **Castellhywel** in premises now used by a food wholesaler.

Llwynrhydowen, the handsomely Palladian chapel that is so striking a feature on the hill slope at **Rhydowen**, opened in 1733 under the ministry of Jenkin Jones. It was the first Arminian chapel to be opened in Wales. In an echo of the original ejection of clergy from their livings two centuries earlier, William Thomas (Gwilym Marles, 1834–1879), the great-uncle of the poet Dylan Thomas (1914–1953), and his congregation were evicted from their chapel in 1876. Their landlord, the squire of Alltyrodyn, would no longer tolerate the minister's liberal preaching. Anna Lloyd Jones, mother of Frank Lloyd Wright, was a member of this congregation. The architect's maternal grandparents had farmed at Blaenalltddu nearby before emigrating from New Quay in 1844. A plaque on the farmhouse wall commemorates the birthplace of Jenkin Lloyd Jones (1843–1916), Frank Lloyd Wright's uncle, the celebrated Unitarian preacher in

Chicago where his nephew was to build his early master-piece, the Unity Temple. To the west, at Esgair Wen in the Cerdin valley, a centennial tree was planted in 1938 at the birthplace of another preacher, Christmas Evans (1766–1838). A clutch of Welsh Nonconformists from within so small a compass.

The Clettwr can be followed south, through **Capel Dewi**, where its waters power the woollen factory at Rock Mill. Built in 1890 by the great grandfather of the present owner, this is the last working woollen mill in Wales still driven by water power. **Llandysul**, huddled on the west bank of a big meander in the river, is a delightfully old-fashioned place. It still celebrates New Year's Day in the parish church of St Tysul according to the Julian calendar, that is on 12 January, with a special Sunday School service known as *Codi Pwnc*. This was designed by the Revd. Enoch Jones in 1833 to promote knowledge of Holy Scripture and stamp out the more boisterous traditional celebrations of *Hen Galan*. The interior of the church contains a number of Early Christian inscribed stones. One of these, known from its Roman capitals as the Velvor Stone, is incorporated into the north wall.

The Teifi has one of its finest stretches in the vicinity of **Henllan**, where it flows through a deep gorge before passing under the graceful, three-arched bridge built by Edward Ellis in 1789. From 1943 to 1946, Henllan Bridge prisoner of war camp held Italian prisoners captured during the North African campaign. Their chapel, with its fresco of the Last Supper, has survived in one of the huts and has now been restored as a symbol of friendship and reconciliation. The prisoners had arrived by train on a branch line from Pencader that closed to passenger traffic in 1952 and to freight in 1973. In 1986, the Teifi Valley Railway Society reopened a section of the line from Henllan to **Llandyfrïog**, where, in the well-kept church-yard, lies the grave of the victim of the last fatal duel to be fought in Wales, that between Beynon and Heslop in 1814. Over a drink at the Salutation Inn in Newcastle Emlyn, Beynon had questioned the chastity of the barmaid whereupon Heslop gallantly chose to defend her honour by challenging Beynon to the duel that he subsequently lost. His grave says it all: 'Alas, poor Heslop.'

Cardigan in Welsh is Aberteifi, the mouth of the Teifi, its English name deriving from a forlorn English attempt to pronounce Ceredigion, for which it was the county town. Its castle, established by the Normans in 1093 after a long struggle, has recently passed from private ownership into the care of the local authority and much-needed restoration work is under way. By 1171, it had passed into the hands of the Lord Rhys, who organised a memorable eisteddfod in the town five years later, the first such event to be organised nationally. The town is a knot of narrow streets beside the quay, full of interesting buildings. A regular market is still held in the covered market under the Guildhall, one of R.J. Withers finest creations built in 1858. There are good chapels: the homely Capel Mair for the Independents, the grandly classical Bethania for the Baptists and a suitably respectable Tabernacl for the Calvinistic Methodists. A lively arts centre has been established as Theatr Mwldan in a former nineteenth-century abattoir.

The five-arched bridge over the river dates from 1726; needless to say, it is more graceful than the new by-pass bridge built in 1991, although the latter has reduced traffic congestion in the town centre. Another example of modern architecture is the Catholic Church, at the northern edge of town. It opened in 1970, with its shrine reviving the cult of Our Lady of the Taper that, in the Middle Ages, was focused on the Benedictine Priory. The Priory became a private residence following the Dissolution, at one time home to 'the matchless Orinda', Katherine Philipps (1631–1664), who had married the High Sheriff of the county. Beside the

Priory is the fourteenth-century parish church of St Mary that has suffered an undignified redevelopment of its graveyard; the inscriptions on the headstones, now lined up against the wall, bear testimony to the town's maritime past. This subject can be further explored in the excellent Heritage Centre that has been developed in the former Teifi Wharf, an eighteenth-century building that once housed a sail loft and granary. The former Custom House in St Mary's Street, now a craft shop and gallery, was built in 1815 to control shipping from Fishguard to Aberaeron. There were once as many as 300 ships registered in the harbour, ship-building was an established local craft and many emigrants left Wales from the Teifi estuary for the New World, as is evidenced by the township of Cardigan in Nova Scotia. Their last sight of their native county would be **Cardigan Island**, now a nature reserve stocked with Soay sheep, with a backward glance at Traeth-y-Mwnt where the lowly, whitewashed church of the Holy Cross shelters from the gales behind the hill from which **Mwnt** takes its name. Steam, in ships and on the railways, put an end to Cardigan's age of sail as elsewhere in Cardigan Bay.

It was a similar story in **New Quay**, although as its name implies the harbour here was of more recent construction. A Harbour Act authorised the construction of the pier in 1835 and the original table of tolls is still prominently displayed. Dylan Thomas stayed here at the end of the Second World War and the town may have inspired his *Under Milk Wood*. There is an attractive Independent chapel at the top of the town and a lifeboat station above the beach. At Penrhiwgaled, the former Independent chapel is now a honey farm, with excellent interpretive displays and a variety of honey products on sale. Following the coast road in the direction of Aberaeron, **Llanarth** straddles its valley handsomely, with Georgian houses and a striking church with a fifteenth-century tower. Y Wern, a house of character with fine interior plastering, is reputed to have accommodated

Henry Tudor and his retinue on their way from Milford Haven to Bosworth Field. Beyond the coast road lies **Banc Siôn Cwilt**, a district named after an eighteenth-century smuggler who had colourful patches on his coat, is celebrated in the poetry of Thomas Jacob Thomas (Sarnicol, 1873–1945) who was born at Capel Cynon. A contemporary Welsh master of the art of *cynghanedd*, the poet Donald Evans has also drawn inspiration from this part of the country. He lives at **Talgarreg** and has vivid memories of David Emrys James (Dewi Emrys, 1881–1952), emerging like an eagle from the cottage his friends had rented for him in the village when the revered poet had fallen on hard times. Dewi Emrys lies in the burial ground of Pisgah chapel to the west of the village, his prominent memorial inscribed with his own poignant epitaph:

> *Melys hedd wedi aml siom*
> *Distawrwydd wedi storom*
>
> (Sweet peace after many disappointments,
> calm after the storm)

Beyond Ffostrasol on the Synod Inn to Llandysul road is the attractive village of **Rhydlewis**, with its lovely Independent chapel, Hawen, where Caradoc Evans forged his love-hate relationship with Welsh Nonconformity. Twrgwyn chapel, in the same parish to the north, was an early Calvinistic Methodist cause. Both date from the 1740s.

A glorious stretch of coastline, mostly in the care of the National Trust, runs between New Quay with Llangrannog. Craig-yr-Adar (Birds Rock), the high cliff face at **New Quay Head**, has the largest colony of Atlantic seabirds in the county. **Cwmtydu** is a tiny cove with caves and wonderful displays of flowers in the spring, the yellow ragwort attracting a profusion of cinnabar moths. The iron age hillfort of Gaer Wen precedes Pen Moel-ciliau, which, at 216 metres, offers remarkably complete views over Cardigan Bay. It's an inspirational landscape. The farm of Ciliau has nurtured a brood of country poets over several generations, known collectively as *Bois y Cilie*, and **Ynys Lochtyn**, the headland that shelters Llangrannog from the north, inspired the English composer, Elgar, to compose his *Introduction and Allegro for Strings*. This is a good place to look for choughs and peregrine falcons.

Llangrannog, a most attractive former fishing village, is known throughout Wales for its youth camp, run by *Urdd Gobaith Cymru*. This little cove can be reached from the coast road along a narrow winding road. Its church, along with that at Gwbert on the Teifi estuary, is dedicated to Carannog. As with so many of the churches along the coast of Cardigan Bay, its grave inscriptions tell of a time when lives revolved around the maritime trades. Sarah Jane Rees, Cranogwen (1839–1916), the formidable poet and editor who had spent her younger years at sea with her father, is buried in the churchyard of her native village, an elegant obelisk marking the spot. The burial ground of Capel-y-Wig has the grave of Jeremiah Jones, patriarch of the Ciliau family. The name of the village of **Penbryn** 'was celebrated all the way from Holyhead to Newport' when a Nonconformist was forced to sell his family Bible to pay the vicar's tithes in the summer of 1842. Anne Adaliza Puddicombe (1836–1908), the best-selling author who wrote under the pseudonym of Allen Raine, is buried in the churchyard. Her best romances are set in the small coastal villages of Cardigan Bay, including *Queen of the Rushes*, a tale of the 1904 Welsh Revival that began in **Blaenannerch**. The contemporary Welsh poet, Dic Jones, worked the family farm here until his recent retirement. Now his son, the talented rock musician Brychan Llŷr, has diversified, creating a Sioux-style tepee village for tourists. Such are the strategies for survival now being employed in Welsh Wales.

2

Montgomeryshire

A GENTLE, kindly place is how the Welsh came to regard Montgomeryshire: *Mwynder Maldwyn*. It is also the only Welsh county to span the width of Wales, a mere 57 kilometres as the crow flies from Offa's Dyke in the east to Cardigan Bay in the west. This tranquil hill country is where Wales is at its narrowest and most vulnerable. Writing in his peaceful study whilst a priest at Manafon in the middle of the county, the poet R.S. Thomas detected 'strife in the strung woods, vibrant with sped arrows' and 'spilled blood that went into the making of the wild sky'. An ancient east-west thoroughfare followed the upper reaches of the Severn westward from Shrewsbury over the Talerddig Pass and down into the Dyfi valley. It is a route that has been followed by a succession of would-be conquerors. The Romans may have passed this way, en route from Wroxeter (Viroconium). They were followed by the Normans and the English each encountering the Welsh hill country that here forms so visible a natural frontier: the Breiddens to the north, then the steep flank of Long Mountain followed by the Kerry Hills to the south. The Cambrian Railway also came this way: the railway cutting at Talerddig, the deepest in the world when completed in 1861, enabled excursion trains to carry holidaymakers for the more peaceful purpose of savouring the delights of Cardigan Bay. From east to west, this delightfully gentle and sparsely populated county runs the gamut from conspicuously English to stubbornly Welsh.

There is nowhere better to start our exploration than in the town that subsequently gave this county its name.

Visiting **Montgomery** is like calling to see a much-loved uncle, long retired from a senior position in the civil service, and now well into his anecdotage: an encounter with the well-mannered civility of a bygone age. It is difficult to believe that Montgomery was the county town for some four and a half centuries: only in 1974 did Welshpool take over its district functions within the new county of Powys. The town takes its English name from the Norman Marcher baron Roger de Montgomery, whose origins were in Sainte Foy de Montgomery in the Calvados district of Normandy. Following 1066, this valiant knight found himself raised to the rank of Earl of Shrewsbury by William the Conqueror. With the help of his energetic son Arnulf, he drove a wedge of eight mottes into Wales, starting with Hen Domen at Montgomery and finishing with a flourish at Moat Lane near Caersŵs. Hen Domen, built around the year 1073, was the first castle to be built in the county. Its remains can still be traced in a field about a mile west of the town. Montgomery's Welsh name, Trefaldwyn, is taken from the castle's subsequent Norman owner, Baldwin de Boulers. The Marcher barons, the Cossacks of British history, were given a large measure of autonomy in return for securing and advancing the frontier of an expanding realm. Their names, Mortimers, Charltons and the famous William Marshal reverberate along the highways and byways of mediaeval Welsh history. Naturally, they met resistance: the first recorded use of the longbow, the deadliest weapon in mediaeval armoury, was in 1120, when Welsh archers ambushed King Henry II's men as they approached Powys through the Vale of Montgomery. The remains of Hen Domen's successor, the New Castle (Cadw), built in stone by Henry III in 1224, to guard the English frontier against Llywelyn ab Iorwerth, can be reached by a footpath that starts behind the Town Hall. The New Castle subsequently passed into the hands of the Mortimers and then the Herberts, names that recur frequently in these parts. It was partially demolished in 1649, having been unsuccessfully held by the royalists. A walk up to this historic vantage-point is worth the effort for the wonderful views over the town and along the straight approach roads from England beyond. Some of the best stretches of Offa's Dyke are clearly visible beyond the lakes in Lymore Park, still marking the border with England after more than a thousand years.

The town itself follows the street plan of a mediaeval English borough. Broad Street has a fine ensemble of Georgian frontages and recently restored cobbled pavements including Montgomeryshire's last surviving Georgian Town Hall, built in 1748 and extended for meetings of Quarter Sessions in 1828. The former County Gaol was built in 1830 by Thomas Penson (1791–1859), County Surveyor and distinguished member of a clan of local architects. The Montgomery Civic Society has made good use of a former inn, the Old Bell in Arthur Street, to house an excellent local history collection and its historical plaques around the town keep the observant visitor informed. The mediaeval church of St Nicholas contains a fine fifteenth-century roof, a double rood screen of Welsh and English origins and the Elizabethan canopied tomb of Richard and his wife Magdalen Herbert. They were the parents of George Herbert (1593–1633), another renowned Welsh priest-poet. Magdalen Herbert was the friend and patron of the poet John Donne and Lord Herbert of Chirbury (1583–1648), the celebrated philosopher, was George Herbert's eldest brother. The raised churchyard has spectacular views towards Shropshire; Geraint Goodwin (1903–1941), whose stories finely evoke early-twentieth century Welsh life in border country, is buried there.

The pre-eminence of the Herbert family, that dominated this county for over 300 years, dates to the part played in the Tudor settlement by Richard Herbert who was later knighted for his efforts on behalf of the new Welsh dynasty. The Herberts acquired **Powis Castle** (NT), a mile south-west of Welshpool, when Sir Edward Herbert, younger son of the Earl of Pembroke, bought the castle in 1587. His son William was created Baron Powis in 1629 and defended the castle for the royalist cause in the Civil War. The Glorious Revolution in 1688 saw the Catholic Herberts briefly relinquish their hold on the castle, but the family was reinstated in 1722 following the Hanoverian settlement. In 1784, when the male line of the Herberts failed – an occurrence that was replicated to an unusual degree across Wales in the eighteenth century – Henrietta Herbert married Edward Clive, the son of Clive of India, who was created Earl of Powis in 1804. It is their descendants who still live in the castle, now a National Trust property.

Powis Castle is deservedly famous both for its gardens and for its interior. The grandiose gardens and Italianate terraces were laid out by William Winde, a gentleman architect who had spent his formative years with royalist exiles in Holland at the end of the seventeenth century. His boldness in setting immense yews, long borders and an orangery beneath the red walls of the mediaeval castle is as remarkable as the views obtained in the spring or autumn, the seasons when the gardens are at their best. As a contrast to formality, a circular walk through a woodland wilderness has been created providing good views back to the castle. An early nineteenth-century ice-house, some twenty feet deep, is a curiosity worth seeking out. Inside, a superb chronological sequence of furnished rooms illustrates styles from the sixteenth to the nineteenth centuries. Parts of the present massive red sandstone structure – in Welsh, the castle is known as Castell Coch – may date back to the eleventh-century Welsh princes of Powys. Today the place is very English in feel, with a room dedicated to Clive of India. There are good specimens from the English school of portraiture, including works by Reynolds, Gainsborough and Romney.

The dominance of the Herbert family also has much to do with the reputed Englishness of **Welshpool**, known until recently as the 'Tory headquarters' for Wales. Its English name was first recorded in the fifteenth century; following the town's incorporation under the 1835 Municipal Corporations Act, it served to distinguish it from Poole in Dorset. The earlier form Pool derived from the pools, locally known as 'pills' (W. pyllau), that characterised the Severn flood plain on which the town is situated. The town's Welsh name, Y Trallwng, may derive from the name of a lake near the castle. **Pool Quay**, three miles north-east of the town, was the limit of navigation on the Severn, one of England's principal mediaeval thoroughfares. Geographically and commercially therefore the town's orientation was eastward. All that remained of the town's wharf was washed away in the great flood of 1881. It had seen little use for over a century following the arrival in the town centre of the Montgomeryshire Canal, which was planned as a feeder to the Ellesmere Canal linking the Severn at Shrewsbury with the Dee at Chester and the Mersey at Netherpool. Work on the canal began in 1794 and its arrival at Garthmyl three years later briefly stimulated the flannel trade in the town before the baton of industry passed to Newtown following the canal's extension there in 1821. Unused for half a century, the canal is being lovingly brought back to life through the efforts of the Montgomeryshire Waterway Restoration Trust, founded in 1980. The towpath walks are delectable, with picturesque locks, cottages and lift-bridges, the latter to be found as the canal approaches Welshpool from Pool Quay. The award-winning Powysland Museum, that occupies former Canal Company offices and warehouse on Canal Wharf, is a splendid place to discover more of the town's past.

Within the space of a generation, the railway followed the canal to Welshpool. The splendid railway station, built in 1866 in the style of a French château, was abandoned to make way for a by-pass in 1997, and now accommodates shops selling 'craft' goods to tourists. Fortunately, the canal was not filled in as part of the same scheme as was proposed at one stage. Indeed, we should perhaps be thankful for the by-pass. Its construction revealed the bronze age timber circle at Sarn-y-bryn-caled that has since been replicated at the Museum of Welsh Life and an imaginative nature reserve was created at Llyn Coed y Dinas from the gravel pit excavated when the new road was constructed. Christ Church was built in 1840 to commemorate the coming of age of an heir to Powis Castle. The mediaeval church of St Mary's contains the Jacobean tomb of Sir Edward Herbert and many interesting Victorian fitments. Broad Street and Severn Street have good Georgian town houses and there is a rare example of a surviving cockpit, last used in 1849, in New Street.

A second railway station in Welshpool, no longer on its original site, is the eastern terminus of the **Welshpool and Llanfair Light Railway** that opened in 1902 to link the surrounding country districts more closely with the market town. Its narrow gauge steam trains follow an idyllically scenic route of some 16 kilometres along the Sylfaen brook into the valley of the Banwy at Llanfair Caereinion. The journey is pure nostalgia. As with every experience on one of the 'Great Little Trains' of Wales there is something touchingly innocent in the eager enthusiasm of the volunteer staff who wave their flags and blow their whistles at every opportunity. Leaving Welshpool, the train battles up the notoriously steep Golfa Bank, the sounds of the locomotive echoing in the surrounding hills. Breaking the journey at **Castle Caereinion**, the halfway point, brings mixed blessings. Disappointment at the levelling and reseeding of the churchyard by a government-funded job creation scheme, but exhilaration at Cadw's imaginative restoration of an aisled hall dating from 1460 that was discovered inside a later structure in 1971. Robert Roberts,

'Y Sgolor Mawr' (The Great Scholar), was the village schoolmaster in the mid-nineteenth century. His autobiography, written after his emigration to Australia, provided evidence of the westward retreat of the Welsh language. He described Castle Caereinion as a linguistic frontier, with Welsh and English spoken in the upper and lower parts of the village respectively.

On arrival at the end of the line, the town of **Llanfair Caereinion** is reached from the station by crossing a contemporary wooden bridge over the rushing Banwy. Not having received a charter, Llanfair never became one of the Montgomeryshire boroughs, but it reckons itself a town nonetheless. Regular fairs were held here and the town recovered from a disastrous fire in 1758 to be briefly active in flannel manufacture. The foundations of the original twelfth-century church were uncovered in 1993 as the foundations for an extension to the church were being dug. A fourteenth-century effigy of a Welsh knight survives inside the church, but otherwise the church should be appreciated for its magnificent situation high above the Banwy. A path leads down to the restored Ffynnon Fair, St Mary's Well, much frequented in the middle ages for its healing properties and for the protection its waters afforded against the curses of witchcraft. The Calvinistic Methodist chapel has an imposing tower, paid for by David Davies, Llandinam (1818–1890), the railway king and coal tycoon, whose wife came from Llanfair.

The parish church at **Llanerfyl**, further upstream, has on display an Early Christian memorial to a thirteen-year-old girl, discovered in the churchyard. It serves to remind us that in the Celtic lands of Britain along the western seaways Christianity flourished after the barbarians had overrun most of the former Roman territories. In Wales, as in Ireland, therefore, historians do not speak of the Dark Ages but proudly of the Early Christian period. In the churchyard at **Llangadfan** lies William Jones (1726–1795) who succeeded in influencing the political development of his country by promoting the ideas of Voltaire in Welsh. He supported the ideas underlying the French Revolution and anticipated Samuel Roberts, Llanbryn-mair, by over a century in denouncing the steward of Wynnstay and encouraging emigration from this area to the United States. He was born in Dôl-hywel.

South of Llangadfan, a solitary road crosses the open moorland of Nant yr Eira in the direction of Llanbrynmair. R.S. Thomas comments on the empty farmsteads here in his *Welsh Hill Country*. To the north of Llangadfan lies the reservoir of **Lake Vyrnwy** (Efyrnwy, in Welsh). After a century, the intrusive civic stonework of Liverpool Corporation is beginning to mellow and the deep reservoir that supplies Liverpool with up to 59 million gallons a day of drinking water is now home to breeding goosanders and other waterfowl. The RSPB nature reserve and information centre here is open all year round. The twelve-mile shoreline of the lake provides that real Welsh rarebit: a long, flat, circular road, ideal for cycling. The journey around the lake has been enlivened by the creation of a sculpture trail along its banks. A hotel at the lake's eastern edge overlooks the drowned village of Llanwddyn; nearby, the grim church, built by Liverpool Corporation to replace the mediaeval one that now lies beneath the lake, contains the lectern from the original church, providing some continuity with the past. In Wales, reservoirs are ambivalent places.

South-east of the reservoir is *plygain* country, the Welshspeaking heartland of the county, at least until recently. Plygain, a word deriving from the Latin for cock crow, *pulli cantio*, was a service held in the early hours of Christmas Day in which traditional carols were sung by individuals and family groups. Originating in the pre-Reformation church, this traditional *a cappella* singing has survived both the sceptical puritanism of the Dissenters and the moral disapproval of the Methodists to enrich contemporary

Welsh culture with some fine solo folk singers, like Siân James, and folk groups like *Plethyn*. Most *plygain* services are now held early in the New Year in local churches and chapels culminating in the Plygain Fawr at **Llanfihangel-yng-Ngwynfa**. The church of St Michael-in-Paradise, to give it its English name, is a dull mid-nineteenth century replacement for the earlier mediaeval building that once stood on this exposed hilltop. The rebuilding by Benjamin Lay in 1867 was of such poor quality that structural work had to be undertaken in 1987 to make the building safe. The church contains some mediaeval sepulchral slabs but is most visited for the graveyard monument to Ann Griffiths (1776–1805), the mystic Methodist hymn-writer who died shortly after the birth of her first child at the age of twenty-nine, never having strayed far from her native parish. There is irony to savour in all this. The supremely influential Anglican squire, Sir Watkin Williams-Wynn of Wynnstay strongly disapproved of Nonconformity in general and Methodism in particular. He exerted his territorial prerogative to ensure that, although nine chapels were registered for public worship in this parish, none was built less than a mile from the village centre. Yet it is the legacy of Ann Griffiths that has endured long after the pomp and splendour of the nabob of Wynnstay has faded into oblivion. For a classic account of life in the confines of this very special parish some two generations back, read the sociological masterpiece by Alwyn Rees, *Life in a Welsh Countryside*, which is based on his detailed observation of life as lived here in the 1940s and the follow-up study published by a village group in 2003.

Dolanog is a small hamlet lying at the throat of a narrow gorge on the Vyrnwy where Liverpool Corporation once proposed to build its dam. In the eighteenth century, the antiquary and naturalist Thomas Pennant (1726–1798) described this river as abounding in fish. He noted grayling, minnow, perch, ruffe, carp, tench, roach, dace, gudgeon,

bleak chub, loach, bullhead, shad, eel, lamphrey and floun-
der, the latter not totally impossible, as sea fish are period-
ically reported far up the Severn. It remains a most
attractive stretch of river with dramatic waterfalls following
periods of heavy rain. Away from the river we can continue
the story of dissension between Anglicans and Methodists
by taking a stroll around the village. In the Anglican corner
we have **Plas Dolanog**, a seventeenth-century timber-framed
house, which was one of Sir Watkin's country retreats. For
the Methodists, close by, there is **Dolwar Fach**, former
home of Ann Griffiths. The Anglican tradition has St John's
church, designed in 1853 by R.K. Penson (1816–1886), the
son of Thomas Penson, and paid for by the Wynnstay
estate. The Methodists have their equally austere Ann
Griffiths Memorial Chapel. Built by national subscription
and completed in 1905, it is an unusual example of work
from the Arts and Crafts movement in rural Wales. Look
out for the corbel heads of Ann Griffiths, the Reverends
John Hughes and Robert Roberts, together with that of
David Davies, deacon of the former chapel, Salem. Strongly
influenced by the *plygain* tradition, Ann Griffths did not
write down any of her own hymns. They were memorised
in her lifetime by her servant Ruth Evans who later married
the Revd. John Hughes whose chapel, built in 1800, can
be seen in the beautifully situated village of **Pontrobert**.
He transcribed her hymns in addition to his own extensive
writings and is buried opposite the chapel. John Davies
(1772–1855), the Calvinistic Methodist missionary to
Tahiti, was also a member of this congregation. He produced a dictionary and grammar of the Tahitian language
and the first translations of portions of the New Testament
and Psalms into it. The chapel closed in 1865 but reopened
in 1995 as a nondenominational Centre for Christian Unity
and Renewal.

A mile to the south-east of this village is the Quaker meeting house of **Dolobran** where the famous Montgomeryshire

Lloyd family (as in Lloyds Bank) worshipped. The interior fittings of this meeting house have been transported to Pennsylvania but the exterior continues to bear witness to the austere faith of this most radical dissenting group. A fragment of the Lloyds family home, Dolobran Hall, can be inspected nearby. Thomas Lloyd (1640–1694) became William Penn's deputy as Governor of Pennsylvania. Racing down from the hills through Dolanog and Pont Robert, the Vyrnwy flows more sedately through the wide valley of Dyffryn Meifod. **Meifod**, the village after which this valley is named, has a spacious feel, comfortable with its prospect of fertile meadows. An important religious centre for Powys in the early middle ages, the village itself has good Georgian buildings along the main road. A sepulchral slab of one of the princes of Powys is a possible explanation for the incised stone monument to be found inside the largely nineteenth-century parish church. Three dedications are recorded inside this nine-acre churchyard, to Saints Tysilio, Gwyddfarch and Mary. The fact that the mortal remains of the princes of Powys were laid to rest here testifies to the importance of the site. They may well have resided at nearby **Mathrafal**, where a motte marks the spot. Between Meifod and Mathrafal, Dyffryn Hall occupies a commanding position in the valley. It was the home of Clement Davies (1884–1962), leader of the British Liberal Party from 1945 to 1956. He was born at Globe House, Llanfyllin, and lies buried in the churchyard at Meifod.

Llanfyllin lies on the Cain, a tributary of the Vyrnwy, and it goes without saying in a land so rich in Biblical allusion that the smaller stream flowing in from the south is called the Abel. The town received its market charter from Llywelyn ap Gruffudd, making it a distinctly Welsh borough. What strikes today's visitor is the quantity and quality of the eighteenth-century red-brick architecture in the town, for bricks were manufactured here from the beginning of that century. The parish church, rebuilt in brick in 1706, is an early example of this style and has a fine acoustic, should you be fortunate enough to catch a concert there. Otherwise the interior has suffered the depredations of Victorian improvers. Pendref Independent Chapel, at the west end of town, has a history as colourful as its brickwork. The first members of this congregation were led by the Welsh Puritan leader, Vavasor Powell (1617–1670); their first chapel building was destroyed by the Jacobites in 1715 and re-erected at government expense. The only part of that structure that survived a subsequent rebuilding in 1829 was the cleverly incorporated memorial stone. Ann Griffiths was converted at an outdoor meeting organised by this congregation in 1795. On the eastern edge of the town the former Llanfyllin Union Workhouse has been preserved following a vigorous local and national campaign.

North-west of the town in the direction of the Berwyn Mountains lies the beautiful and romantic Tanat valley that Thomas Pennant also found to be rich in fish. The valley is a stronghold of Welsh culture, with a lively *plygain* tradition. In the eighteenth century, **Llangynog** was the largest centre of lead mining in Europe and the spoil still scars the landscape here as does that of the slate quarries. In neighbouring **Pen-y-bont-fawr** there is a commemorative plaque on the wall of Penybont, the farm where Nansi Richards (1888–1979) was born. She won the triple harp competition at the National Eisteddfod at the age of twenty and was henceforth known by her bardic title, *Telynores Maldwyn*, The Montgomeryshire Harpist. One of the last exponents of the Welsh folk harp tradition, she succeeded in her old age in passing that tradition on to a newly-interested younger generation. **Pennant Melangell** sits in the upper reaches of the Tanat valley that have a reputation as a sanctuary for wild creatures. According to legend, Saint Melangell gave shelter to a hunted hare beneath her skirts and succeeded with miraculous power in stopping both huntsmen and hounds in their tracks. The fact that the huntsman was said to be Brochwel, Prince of Powys adds to the drama. The church that commemorates her has a fifteenth-century screen on which the story is depicted. The original twelfth-century Romanesque shrine to the saint, sympathetically reassembled from 1989 to 1994, now occupies an east chapel, Cell y Bedd. The rarity of the shrine and the romantic story surrounding it makes this a lively place of pilgrimage and the associated commercialism, overwhelmingly English, is mercifully restrained.

The rivers Cain and Vyrnwy meet a couple of miles downstream at **Llansanffraid-ym-mechain** where the parish church, dedicated to St Bride, is full of such curiosities as the early nineteenth-century candelabra and a good late seventeenth-century brass memorial to the Revd. Griffith Lloyd. A stained glass window commemorates the parish's connection with William Morris Hughes, the former Prime Minister of Australia. The Victorian church of St Tysilio at **Llandysilio**, built in 1868 to replace a ruined mediaeval structure, has a pleasing round tower with conical belfry and an ornate interior with a fine stained glass window of Christ walking on the water, a memorial to local Welsh boys lost in the China Sea. From this tranquil spot, there are good views to the south-east of Breidden Hill and Moel y Golfa rising sharply on the far bank of the Severn, marking the English border. Breidden Hill has Rodney's Pillar, commemorating one of Admiral Rodney's (1719–1792) naval victories, marking its summit; Moel y Golfa has a simpler monument to the Romany leader, Ernest Burton. These igneous outcrops have been much frequented by botanists since Edward Lhuyd (1660–1709) recorded rock cinquefoil, spiked speedwell and sticky catchfly here in the seventeenth century. Lhuyd, scientist, antiquarian, philologist and towering Celtic scholar, who was appointed Keeper of the Ashmolean in Oxford in 1691, was born not far away at **Llanforda**, near Oswestry, in what was then a thoroughly Welsh part of Shropshire.

A couple of miles back west up the Cain valley is **Llanfechain**, where the parish church is dedicated to St Garmon, a missionary saint of the ninth century with a cluster of dedications in this part of Wales. The church is possibly the most complete Norman church in the county, well restored by John Douglas and R.K. Penson, even if its slender spire and red-tiled roof give it an incongruously Germanic feel. The village is the birthplace of Walter Davies (1761–1849), commonly known in Wales as Gwallter Mechain after his place of birth. He composed *plygain* carols as well as learned treatises on the state of Welsh agriculture.

Guilsfield lies a mile off this road but worth the detour. Behind the heavy oak entrance door of St Aelhaearn's parish church, a remarkably rich mediaeval interior is revealed. There is a magnificent panelled roof of fifteenth-century origin, a late Norman font and numerous fine memorials. The Welsh name of the village, Cegidfa, means place of hemlock. The modern village sits safely suburban in its sheltered valley but prehistoric peoples were attracted to the surrounding hills. There are some half a dozen iron age hill forts in the immediate vicinity of the village, the most extensive, Gaer Fawr, being managed by the Woodland Trust. The Guilsfield bronze age hoard, now at the National Museum in Cardiff, was unearthed at Crowther's Coppice.

In 1970, the Powysland Club – the senior county antiquarian society in Wales, founded in 1867 – commemorated the octocentenary of the foundation of **Strata Marcella** (Ystrad Marchell) by erecting a memorial stone to mark the spot where this most ruined of the Welsh Cistercian abbeys lies beneath the ground. It can be found between the road and the river a mile to the south of Pool Quay on the main road from Oswestry to Welshpool. One of its capitals is in use as a font in the parish church at nearby **Buttington**.

Leighton Hall, on the east bank of the Severn, is an opulent Victorian pile built by the Liverpool banker, John Naylor.

Naylor's *nouveau riche* spending power did leave a legacy of curiosities, including one of the finest stands of redwoods in the country. These were brought to Wales from California in pots in 1857 and can be admired from the B4388. He has the dubious honour of having propagated the original Leyland cypress on his estate, the shrub taking its name from his Liverpool bank. Such was his wealth, that, had Naylor had any Welsh interests, this remarkable estate might have become another Gregynog.

South from Welshpool in the direction of Newtown lies **Berriew,** just far enough off the main road to have preserved its tranquillity. An aqueduct carries the Montgomeryshire Canal over an approach road to the village. The village name is an eighteenth-century anglicisation for Aberriw, meaning the confluence of the Rhiw, the sparkling stream that runs through the village under the recently restored bridge and which contributes significantly to the village's chocolate box reputation. The village has good examples of timber-framed houses, the best being the seventeenth-century vicarage. The rather plain church is dedicated to the Celtic Saint Beuno, sometimes described as the patron saint of north Wales, who is supposed to have been born here. It contains monuments to scions of the local great houses: fine effigies of Arthur Price of Vaynor Park and his wives and a memorial to William Owen and Sir Arthur Davies Owen of Glansevern Hall. **Vaynor Park** is a much-renovated Elizabethan brick house; its chimneys have been imitated on nineteenth-century Vaynor estate cottages in the village. **Glansevern Hall,** by contrast, is a delectable Greek Revival villa built in the style of the Petit Trianon at Versailles by Joseph Bromfield who completed this project in 1807. The house has delightful gardens and a lakeside walk open to the public in the summer months.

Five miles up river from Berriew is **Manafon** where Gwallter Mechain was rector from 1807 to 1837 and R.S. Thomas from 1942 to 1954. The poet's early collection,

Song at the Year's Turning (1955) speaks of this landscape and its people, including this evocative description of the parish church here:

> The church stands, built from the river stone,
> Brittle with light, as though a breath could shatter
> Its slender frame, or spill the limpid water,
> Quiet as sunlight, cupped within the bone.

His initials can still be seen carved on roof timbers in the belfry. Continuing in the direction of Newtown, another church dedicated to St Beuno in **Betws Cedewain** contains the only pre-Reformation brass in the county, a memorial to John ap Meredith who built the church's perpendicular tower. To the east, in **Pentre Llifior**, is a Georgian English Wesleyan chapel, established in 1798 in the wake of John Wesley's evangelical campaigns in the district; it is a gem of chapel, the second oldest Wesleyan chapel in Wales still in use.

Abermule's principal claim to fame is the 1921 railway disaster when two trains on the Cambrian Railway collided head-on killing both drivers and nineteen passengers, including Lord Herbert Vane-Tempest, third son of the 5th Marquess of Londonderry, who was on his way from Plas Machynlleth to London. Following this accident procedures for single-track railways were altered throughout Britain. The road bridge over the Severn is one of Thomas Penson's (1791–1859) cast-iron bridges, completed in 1852. To the north of the village are to be found the dramatic remains of Llywelyn ap Gruffudd's castle of **Dolforwyn** (Cadw), opened to the public in 2002 after lengthy excavations. The castle, possibly by the same architect as Dinas Brân, was unfinished when besieged and captured by the English in 1277. Llywelyn had founded a town next to the castle; after the Edwardian conquest it was replaced by a new town five miles to the west that still bears the name of Newtown. This strategic site affords good prospects of the surrounding countryside, including the Kerry Hills to the south, famous for their distinctive breed of black-nosed sheep.

The parish church in the village of **Kerry** has the stone tower and timber belfry characteristic of the county, fitted with ghastly electronic chimes for the millennium. Inside, there is a reminder of Gerald of Wales' turbulent visit to the church when he was Archdeacon of Brecon in 1176. He successfully disrupted a service of rededication by the Bishop of St Asaph with the result that the church remained in the diocese of St Davids until it was amicably transferred to St Asaph in 1849. Thomas Burgess, Bishop of St Davids, unveiled the commemorative plaque to this event on the north wall in 1818. An adjacent plaque commemorates John Jenkins (Ifor Ceri, 1770–1829) who spent his life as vicar of this parish and worked with William Jenkins Rees (1772–1855), Cascob, to promote the provincial eisteddfodau. Continue along the road to the Anchor Inn for fine views over Clun and Shropshire or take to the hills in Clun Forest along the Kerry Ridgeway.

Gregynog, an imitation half-timber mansion set in beautiful countryside to the north of Newtown, was acquired in 1921 by Gwendoline and Margaret Davies, granddaughters of David Davies, Llandinam. David Davies, of whom more later, was the first native Welsh industrial tycoon. His income from coal in the nineteenth century, as with later twentieth-century revenues from oil, that newer form of black gold, placed him at the centre of a system of patronage that extended across central Wales. His granddaughters used their share of his industrial fortune to develop Gregynog as an arts and crafts centre for Wales, echoing the patronage of the mediaeval Welsh princes. Gregynog patronage was lubricated with tea rather than mead, however, since the Davies sisters inherited the family's strictly teetotal version of Calvinistic Methodism. Stanley Baldwin was dismayed to find that no scotch was allowed on the premises having accepted an offer of taking a summer break here in 1932. The Gwendoline and Margaret Davies collection of French impressionist and post-impressionist paintings, subsequently donated to the National Museum, remains the core of the Cardiff art collection. The Gregynog Press, established in 1923, one of the great private presses of Europe in its day, continues to produce sought-after fine editions. A summer music festival continues a tradition that saw the likes of Elgar, Holst and Vaughan Williams performing their own work here. The intimate Gregynog concert hall has a good organ and the legendary Gregynog kitchen supplies superlative cakes for interval teas. Gregynog was bequeathed to the University of Wales in 1960 and today a Director presides over a residential conference and study centre for its students for whom a basement bar has been discreetly installed.

There are extensive grounds including a remarkable golden yew ornamental hedge and sunken lawn at the front of the property. Viewed from the bridge that crosses the lawn, the house exudes suburban respectability. What appears at first sight to be a Jacobean timber house, turns out on closer inspection to be a fabrication: the black and white timbers having been painted onto moulded concrete. For the resident family member of the property in the mid-nineteenth century, before the Davies sisters, was one Henry Hanbury Tracy, a late-Victorian pioneer of industrial construction methods who may at least be given the credit, unusual with his ilk, for trying out the new methods on his own home.

The neighbouring village of **Tregynon** is the birthplace of Thomas Olivers (1725–1799), the powerful Wesleyan preacher and hymn-writer once described as John Wesley's 'bully-in-chief'. Both his autobiography and the hymns of Ann Griffiths have been handsomely published by Gwasg Gregynog. Tregynon has further examples of Hanbury Tracy's construction projects in the form of the Concrete Cottages. Although traditional-looking, these were some of the first buildings in the world to be made entirely of this new material; they housed the Gregynog estate workers. St Cynon's church occupies an ancient site but, needless to say, its interior was improved under the Tracys. The church contains some fine memorials, including a fitting epitaph to the kindly Arthur Blayney who died in 1795, the last of his line to reside in the original Gregynog as his forebears had done since the fifteenth century. An eccentric squire, much loved in the locality, his kindly treatment of his tenants earned him the sobriquet, 'The Father of Montgomeryshire'. His exquisitely designed memorial describes him as 'the last of a time-honoured race, a worthy scion of the kings of ancient Britain'.

The man who made the fortune underwriting the modern history of Gregynog was David Davies who was born in **Llandinam**, a village halfway between Newtown and Llanidloes. He started life as a sawyer (his earliest nickname was Top Sawyer), progressed to road and bridge builder, then won the contract to build the Cambrian Railway. He invested his earnings in the first deep pit to be sunk in the Rhondda, later building docks at Barry in the 1880s from which his coal was exported. By this time he was representing Cardigan Boroughs in Parliament as a Liberal and was popularly known as 'Davies the Ocean' after the Ocean Coal Company he had formed in 1887. There is a fine statue of him in the village replicating the one in Barry. It stands next to Thomas Penson's cast-iron bridge over the Severn that Davies had helped construct in 1846, the first iron bridge in the county. He had the house of **Broneirion** built for its prospect of the bridge and railway he had constructed and of the Calvinistic Methodist chapel where he worshipped regularly. The Lion Hotel, standing near the Methodist chapel, was strictly temperance. His grandson, who became Lord Davies of Llandinam in 1932, used the family fortune for philanthropic purposes in the county and elsewhere in Wales.

Returned unopposed as part of the 1906 Liberal landslide and a member of Lloyd George's 'kitchen cabinet', he devoted himself to the cause of international peace in the years following the Great War. A part-founder of the League of Nations Union, he also became a major benefactor of Welsh education endowing the Woodrow Wilson chair of international politics at the University of Wales, Aberystwyth, in 1919, the first of its kind in the world. He went on to endow chairs in music, Welsh, geography and extra-mural studies in the same institution. Lord Davies, elder brother of Gwendoline and Margaret Davies of Gregynog, resided at **Plas Dinam**, built in the 1870s in the mediaeval revival style. The Davies family graves are in the churchyard surrounded by railings.

Caersŵs, downstream from Llandinam, was an important intersection for the Romans who established a fort here: *caer* is a native Welsh word for the Latin *castra* meaning a fort, a word that occurs in English place-names as 'chester'. Their interest in Welsh hill country was strictly limited to mineral extraction: a Roman road from Caersŵs took lead ore to Pennal on the Dyfi where they had a port. More than a thousand years later, lead ore from Y Fan was brought to the Cambrian Railway at Caersŵs using a branch line built in 1871 by David Davies. Caersŵs station is still open and the outline of the Roman fort is clearly visible close to the railway line. The poet John Ceiriog Hughes (1832–1887), author of sentimental but, in his day, enormously popular verse, was stationmaster here after his stint at Llanidloes. The line from Llanidloes used to meet the Cambrian Railway close by at Moat Lane where the largest of Roger of Montgomery's sequence of earth works can be admired. Ceiriog is buried in the churchyard at **Llanwnog**, with a fitting memorial:

> Carodd eiriau cerddorol – carai feirdd
> Carai fyw'n naturiol

Carai gerdd yn angerddol
Dyma'i lwch, a dim lol

(He loved poets and lyrics
He loved the simple life
Poetry was his passion
Herein his remains, and no pretension)

The church walls contain blocks of red sandstone cobbled from the Roman fort at Caersŵs; inside, the fifteenth-century rood screen is one of Montgomeryshire's treasures. Ceiriog's red-brick house, marked with a plaque, lies beyond the railway on the road towards Trefeglwys.

To the north-west is **Carno**, situated on the river valley of the same name, where the parish church contains the fragment of an early Celtic cross discovered in use as a gatepost in 1960. Laura Ashley (1925–1985) is buried behind the parish church of St John the Baptist. Her textile company provided employment in the village for a generation of workers until the closure of the factory in 2004. The factory represented continuity of the county's historic industry: not only has the name Laura Ashley found its way into the Oxford English Dictionary but the word flannel itself is a rare example of a Welsh loan word in English, flannel being an anglicisation of the Welsh word for woollen cloth, *gwlanen*.

In 1279, Edward I granted a charter to Roger de Mortimer for a fair and market to be held at Llanfair-yng-Nghedewain. **Newtown** grew up alongside, with the new name displacing the old within a relatively short period. A loop of the Severn provided the borough with sufficient natural defence. The town's mediaeval church of St Mary, close by the river, was abandoned in the 1840s because of flooding but its graveyard should be visited for the memorial to Robert Owen (1771–1858) who is buried there. A figure of international importance in the development of socialist thought, Owen is regarded as a pioneer of the Co-operative Movement. He left Newtown at the age of ten and by an advantageous marriage came to run the New Lanark Mills on the banks of the Clyde in Scotland. This he did in a progressive manner uncharacteristic of his times, with controls on hours of work, strict attention to safety in the workplace and with a school that used progressive teaching methods for children who elsewhere would have found themselves at work on the factory floor. His communitarian colony at New Harmony in Indiana in the United States is generally counted a failure but his legacy endures in many a small Welsh town at the local Co-op. Another memorial to him is the informative Robert Owen Memorial Museum in Broad Street. The newer church of St David has the font from the old church and fragments from the late fifteenth-century rood screen of the so-called Newtown School. By the middle of the nineteenth century, first with its extended canal, then with the Cambrian Railway, Newtown had aspirations to become known as 'the Leeds of Wales'. Evidence of its historic flannel industry can be found in the conservation area of Penygloddfa north of the river in the parish of Llanllwchaearn. The brick houses in Commercial Street, for example, have large windows on their top floors to provide light for handloom weavers. There is a good Textile Museum, recently refurbished, in the same street. The hopes of a textile boom did not survive competition from the north-west of England and, following the Chartist disturbances of the 1830s, it fell to Pryce Pryce-Jones (1834–1920) to effect a change of direction by establishing the world's first mail order business in the town in 1859. Starting with flannel goods, his range of products widened and from his Royal Welsh Warehouse, built opposite the station in 1875, he served mail order customers throughout Britain and the Continent with a variety of goods that had been brought to Newtown by canal and railway. He was shrewd enough to mail goods to Queen Victoria and other crowned heads of Europe, hence both the royal arms and the vainglorious stained glass that can be viewed on the premises by today's bargain hunters. Subsequently knighted, Sir Pryce is buried at All Saints, Llanllwchaearn. Another commercial oddity to be savoured in Newtown is the branch of W.H. Smith's in High Street. The shop looks as it did when it first opened in 1927 and contains an upstairs museum celebrating over 200 years in the history of this high street retailer. A Mid-Wales Development Corporation was established in 1967 with a mission to expand the existing borough of Newtown. As a result, Newtown has doubled its population in twenty years, with results that are not always aesthetically pleasing. The exception that proves this rule is the splendid Davies Gallery, opened at The Park in 1967 with a mission to bring the best of contemporary Welsh art and crafts to this part of central Wales.

Newtown's partner in the textile boom of the mid-nineteenth century lay further up river at **Llanidloes,** the first settlement on the Severn after its race down from Pumlumon. The river powered the woollen mills that saw the town's population swell in the 1830s to over four thousand. It is difficult to imagine this peaceful and attractive town as a place of riot and commotion but so it was in 1839 when the town was in the grip of Chartist strikes and political agitation. To deal with the situation, the Home Secretary sent three London 'Bobbies' to Llanidloes to restore order. Ringleaders were identified and briefly incarcerated in the Trewythen Arms Hotel only to be liberated by angry working people. They controlled the town for five days, during which time shops were forced to sell staple goods at fair prices, a brief interval of moral economy before the Montgomeryshire Yeomanry restored the status quo. The subsequent show trial at Welshpool saw three men transported to New South Wales. The popular mid-twentieth century Welsh poet and Archdruid, Gwilym Tilsley (1911–1997), a minister with the Wesleyan Methodists who was born on the outskirts of the town at Ty-llwyd, wrote compassionate poems in honour of the industrial working-class, both coal miners and slate quarrymen.

No canal ever reached Llanidloes, but the town has a lively railway history. Indeed the imposing classical façade of the former station is one of the most striking buildings in the town. When the Llanidloes and Newtown Railway connected the town with the Shropshire Union in 1859, the town quickly became the focus of attention for several rival railway companies. The Mid Wales Railway made its way up from Brecon in 1864 and plans were advanced for the proposed Manchester to Milford line to pass through the town. The embodiment of these Victorian ambitions, the station was closed by Dr Beeching in 1962. To sample the distinctly tranquil reality of Llanidloes the railway town, read the pastoral verse of Ceiriog, its stationmaster a century earlier.

Today Llanidloes has reverted to a peaceful market town, its mediaeval street plan unchanged since 1280 when the town was granted its borough charter. Its two principal streets meet at the late sixteenth-century timber-framed Market Hall where a stone marks the spot from which John Wesley preached. There are some delightful shop-fronts: Siop-yr-Oen, with its hanging sign of a woolly sheep, the oldest surviving Laura Ashley shop in Great Oak Street and Pumlumon House with its conspicuous royal arms in Long Bridge Street. Sion Chapel, built in 1878, is a magnificent example of late nineteenth-century Nonconformist architecture, and is based on Morriston's Tabernacle. The parish church, on the banks of the Severn near Thomas Penson's fine three-arched bridge, dates from mediaeval times and is dedicated to the Celtic Saint Idloes. It has a beautiful thirteenth-century arcade, originally part of the abbey at Cwm-hir, and a magnificent hammer-beam timber roof. There is good late Victorian stained glass and a beautiful contemporary memorial window dedicated in millennium year.

To the west of Llanidloes the borders with Ceredigion and Radnorshire are approached near the village of

Llangurig situated 270 metres above sea level on the central Welsh plateau. Its historic associations are with the sixth-century Curig who established a *clas* here – a monastic settlement of the early Celtic church – having journeyed through Ceredigion. The mediaeval church was restored by Sir Gilbert Scott (1811–1878), the leading light of the Gothic revival in British architecture. It is also possible to trace cuttings and a bridge for the proposed Manchester and Milford railway in the vicinity of the village.

North-west of Llanidloes a mountain road winds its way up to the **Clywedog** reservoir. A circular route around the 250-hectare reservoir leads into the Hafren forestry plantation from which trails lead through Cwmbiga to a boggy tract where the source of the Severn is sign-posted. In this remote and difficult terrain Owain Glyn Dŵr won his first great victory in 1401 at the Battle of Hyddgen. The Clywedog dam was the highest in Britain when it was constructed in the mid-1960s. At the foot of the dam, the **Bryntail Lead Mine** (Cadw) has good on-site interpretation. The richest lead mines in Wales were close-by at **Y Fan** where 6,850 tonnes of lead ore were mined at the height of production in 1876. The mines closed in the depression years following the end of the Great War. **Dylife,** meaning 'place of floods', also has the remains of lead workings, once owned by the famous Victorian freetraders, Cobden and Bright. Continuing onward, upward and westward, there are wonderful views to be had as this mountain road rises to over 500 metres. At Glaslyn, the Montgomeryshire Wildlife Trust has its largest reserve, over 200 hectares of undulating heather moorland: it is a glorious sight in late summer, particularly when viewed from the slopes of Foel Fadian which, at 564 metres is the county's highest peak. Further on, a memorial to the late Wynford Vaughan Thomas (1908–1987), Broadcaster, Author, Traveller has been erected by the Council for the Protection of Rural Wales at one of his favourite vistas near Rhiw Fawr from which a good path leads down to Aberhosan.

Machynlleth is the most westerly of the ancient boroughs of Montgomeryshire. Its lively Wednesday market has been in continuous existence since a charter was granted in 1291 by Owain de la Pole (that is, from Welshpool). It attracts regular customers from Ceredigion and Gwynedd, two historically distinct divisions of Wales that border the town to the south and north respectively. Of all the Montgomeryshire boroughs it has traditionally been the most securely Welsh. Taken together these considerations may explain why Owain Glyn Dŵr chose this otherwise unremarkable place to hold one of his parliaments in 1404, to the lasting benefit of the local tourist trade. The Parliament House in Maengwyn Street continues to attract visitors although how much of the existing structure was contemporary with Glyn Dŵr is disputed. A stained glass memorial window in the adjoining Institute gives Owain Glyn Dŵr the face of Lord Davies of Llandinam.

Graig Independent Chapel (1824) in Heol Powys, is a good example of early Welsh Nonconformist architecture with its two entrance doors to either side of the pulpit. In front of the chapel entrance is the imposing tomb of the Revd. David Griffiths (1792–1863), pioneer missionary to Madagascar and translator of the Bible into Malagasy. Maengwyn Chapel was built for the Calvinistic Methodists in 1867 and, like the station, was built with stone from the Talerddig cutting. The Wesleyan Methodists built their neo-classical Tabernacl close by in 1880 and this building has been imaginatively restored as an arts centre and incorporated into the adjoining property which houses the Museum of Modern Art Wales. Its permanent collection includes works by Augustus John, Aneurin Jones, Peter Prendergast, Stanley Spencer, Catrin Webster, Kyffin Williams and Shani Rhys James. The Taliesin Mosaic, created with Gulbenkian funding in 1996, seems to be peripatetic, but should not be missed.

Celtica, a hi-tech exhibition on the Celts, has been opened as a tourist attraction in Plas Machynlleth, the former country seat of the Londonderry family to the south of the town. The Plas dominated the town from the mid-eighteenth century, its owners, the Edwards family, being the beneficiaries not only of rental from the surrounding farms but of the profits from the lead mines at Y Fan. In 1846 Mary Cornelia Edwards married George Vane-Tempest who became the 5th Marquess of Londonderry in 1872. The rococo Town Clock in the town centre was erected in 1874 for the coming of age the previous year of a Londonderry heir, Lord Castlereagh. Regrettably, the parish church of St Peter was the object of Londonderry largesse in 1894. A substantial mediaeval rood screen was swept away in the improvements and, as a substitute, we can now view a sequence of stained glass representations of the Londonderry family.

Beyond the station, restored to its original glory in 1996, a five-arched stone bridge (1805) across the Dyfi at its first bridging point marks the border with the old county of Merioneth, now part of Gwynedd. The Dyfi here is tidal and a prized fishery for salmon and *sewin*. Close by, an imaginatively designed cycle bridge, opened in 2001, leads to the internationally renowned **Centre for Alternative Technology** to which access is gained, appropriately, by water-powered funicular railway. This rises 50 metres to the disused slate quarry which houses the centre where visitors are informed, instructed and entertained on the subject of renewable energy.

Hugh Williams (1796–1874), the Carmarthen solicitor, prominent in the Rebecca and Chartist disturbances, was born at Gelli-goch on the road to **Derwenlas**, a few miles to the south-west of Machynlleth at the county border with Ceredigion, where this otherwise land-locked county had its only taste of salt water. His sister married Richard Cobden – hence the Cobden interest in the Dylife mines.

Before the arrival of the railway, lime and coal were imported and slate, oak and lead ore were exported from a quay beside the Dyfi. The last shipment of Dylife lead was exported from Derwenlas in 1863, the year the railway arrived. Slate was brought down from Aberllefenni and Corris by narrow-gauge railway. Cwm Llyfnant, the historic border with Ceredigion, remains deliciously unspoilt, for it is only really possible to explore it on foot. A good base is the tiny former chapel of the Independents at **Glaspwll**, which was erected in 1822. The river rises in the hill walker's paradise of Uwch Garreg, and quickly plunges at Pistyll-y-Llyn into the ravine that opens out into the Dyfi estuary. Dippers work their way upstream, diving into the water to feed while overhead the red kite circles majestically, all to the accompaniment of the tumbling waters of the Llyfnant.

A few miles east along the wide and fertile Dyfi valley out of Machynlleth lies **Penegoes**. Its slate-walled Victorian church has memorials to the father of British landscape painting Richard Wilson (1713–1782) who was born at the rectory. Opposite the church, the village's restored holy well can now be accessed but the nearby water wheel at Felin Crewi, lovingly restored to working order in the 1980s, is now sadly silent again.

Llanbryn-mair, where the three streams Rhiw Saeson, Twymyn and Iaen meet, was a centre of the flannel trade. The delightful parish church of St Mary is indeed situated on a hill in a place now known simply as **Llan**. With the coming of the railway, the old village of Llanbryn-mair migrated north. Once a busy market centre for scattered farms, today rural employment derives from less familiar sources. In 2002, a Museum of Mechanical Change opened here, its collection of automata the first of its kind in Wales. Llanbryn-mair's reputation derives from the Nonconformist tradition associated with the much-rebuilt Hen Gapel (Old Chapel). This Independent chapel lies just beyond the level crossing at Dol-fâch. It was first erected in 1739, the second dissenting meeting house to be built in Montgomeryshire after Pendref at Llanfyllin. Its distinguished succession of ministers includes Samuel Roberts, founder of *Y Cronicl,* a progressive mid-nineteenth century journal that campaigned for land and postal reform, free trade, the abolition of slavery and international peace. He led a local emigration to Tennessee in the United States to escape the oppression of landlordism. A more recent representative of this tradition was Iorwerth Peate (1901–1982), pacifist founder of the Folk Museum at St Fagans, now the Museum of Welsh Life. Whereas Samuel Roberts had campaigned for a railway as a necessary amenity for a rural district, Iorwerth Peate resented a great deal of what arrived through the Talerddig cutting. His Folk Museum was intended to preserve the memory of the culture he valued so highly lest it be lost forever. For neither Romans, Saxons, Normans nor even Victorian railway speculators, for all their monumental labours had inflicted wounds on the local Welsh-language culture to compare with those of television and the satellite dish in our own time.

3

Radnorshire

POWYS continues southwards into Radnorshire, the smallest and least populated of the old Welsh counties:

> *Radnorsheer, poor Radnorsheer*
> *Never a park, not even a deer*
> *Never a squire of five hundred a year*
> *But Richard Fowler of Abbey Cwmhir.*

This oft-quoted rhyme encapsulates a negative truth: Radnorshire has no really great houses. Its castles, usually built by a Mortimer or a de Braos, have tended to decay, so that we are more likely to encounter outline mounds mellowed into the landscape than splendid battlements. There are no large towns. As for scenery, although these green, Welsh hills rise on average to some 300 metres, they too are understated. Moated by the rivers Teme to the east and the Wye to the south-west and with the Eithon and Lugg winding their ways between, this smallest and least populated of the old Welsh counties contains an abundance of unpretentious and unspoilt small towns and villages set in incomparably tranquil countryside. During the famous Brecon and Radnor by-election of 1985, the BBC's political editor, John Cole, noted that there could be very few other constituencies in Britain where fine summer weather brought with it the threat of a low turnout. From time immemorial, fine summer weather has meant harvest time for the majority of the inhabitants of Radnorshire.

The county's Welsh name is Maesyfed, derived from Maes Hyfaidd, the territory of Hyfaidd, a sixth-century Welsh chieftain. Its historic border with England is **Offa's**

Dyke, that remarkable earthwork – Britain's longest archaeological monument – constructed by King Offa of Mercia in the eighth century to mark the boundary between such Welsh chieftains and his Saxon kingdom. To this day, a Welsh-speaker going to England crosses Offa's Dyke to the land of the Saxon, *mynd dros Glawdd Offa i wlad y Saeson*. **Knighton** is the largest town on Offa's Dyke, provided you do not count those at the coastal extremities, and is thus the natural location for the Offa's Dyke Centre which has a good exhibition, small library and information centre. Knighton is the only town where sections of the Dyke can be seen in the town itself, notably in a designated park where the 293-kilometre Offa's Dyke Path continues out of the town beside the Teme before cutting north towards the Clun Forest. It is here, to the north of the town that the best-preserved sections of this ninth-century boundary, in places up to eight metres high, are to be seen.

Knighton sits snugly in the Teme valley. There are good views up and down the valley from Bryn-y-Castell, a castle mound, which can be reached from Bowling Green Lane. Approaching Knighton on the long-distance footpath from the south, over Furrow and Hawthorn Hills, there are fine views over Radnor Forest to the west, and the Kerry Hills to the north with a last over-the-shoulder glimpse of the distant Black Mountains. To Welsh-speakers, Knighton is *Tref-y-clawdd*, the Town on the Dyke; in English the name refers to those knights of the march who kept the peace in Welsh border country. Welsh has not been spoken here for generations; the nearest superstores are in Ludlow, the meeting place of the Council in the Marches in the sixteenth and seventeenth centuries. Indeed, Knighton was originally a Saxon settlement subsequently overrun by the Welsh. Its railway station is in Shropshire and its parish church, like some others in the county, is in the diocese of Hereford. Although the town has been continuously settled since Norman times, it is nineteenth-century domestic architecture that now predominates in the huddle of streets in upper town, although it is worth seeking out the seventeenth-century George and Dragon in Broad Street. The church of St Edward (his only dedication in Wales) in lower town retains its fourteenth-century tower but was also subject to large-scale late nineteenth-century improvements.

The designation 'Radnor Forest' requires explanation. In Welsh, this area of high, lonely but magnificently heather-clad moorland between the rivers Teme and Wye, long renowned for the quality of its wool, was once only known as Clud, a name now barely surviving in isolated place-name elements. The word 'forest' here retains its original meaning of open country. It was unfortunate therefore, that when the Forestry Commission was at its most active in the mid-twentieth century, opposition to its inappropriate monocultural practices was muted by the false belief that the Radnor Forest was in some sense being restored. On the contrary, in 1565 a surveyor noted that the only woodland in the Forest was 'VIII acres of lowe shrubbes and bushes of small hazill and thornes' and that the tenant farmers had 'free common of pasture there tyme out of mind in the said forrest'. It remains great walking country with glorious views in all directions.

Heading south-west from Knighton by road, a ridge is crossed before the descent into the valley of the Lugg. Like many river names throughout Britain, this name is Celtic in origin, in this case from the Welsh *Llugwy*, signifying the brightness of the water. The largest Elizabethan house in the county is situated at **Monaughty**; as its name implies, it was originally the monastic grange of Abbey Cwm-hir. The wonderfully preserved mediaeval church of Our Lady at **Pilleth** is approached along a grassy track. To the west of the church, memorial trees have been planted to commemorate the battlefield on the lower slopes of Bryn Glas where Owain Glyn Dŵr defeated Edmund

Mortimer on 22 June 1402 and boosted his credibility as a national leader. The event is partially described by the Earl of Westmorland in Shakespeare's *Henry IV*, Part I:

> A post from Wales loaden with heavy news,
> Whose worst was, that the noble Mortimer,
> Leading the men of Herefordshire to fight
> Against the irregular and wild Glendower,
> Was by the rude hand of the Welshman taken,
> And a thousand of his people butchered,
> Upon whose dead corpse there was such misuse
> Such beastly, shameless, transformation
> By those Welsh women done, as may not be
> Without much shame, retold, or spoken of.

Many of the slain, it is said, lie buried beneath the mysterious mounds above the church where the remains of a motte and bailey, Castell Foel Allt, are also to be found. Sir Richard Green-Price (1803–1887), the local MP, planted four Wellingtonia to mark the Welsh burial mound and placed a slab in the churchyard to commemorate the fallen English. Pilleth church was a centre of pilgrimage in the middle ages, as it housed an image of the Virgin: the holy well beside the church dates from this period. A fire in 1894 did as much damage as the Glyn Dŵr Rising and the admirable Friends of Pilleth are undertaking urgent restoration work.

Nestling in the hills at the head of the Cas valley to the south is St Michael's church, **Cascob**. It has a collapsed tower, probably the result of damage sustained during the Glyn Dŵr Rising. It also has a plain early sixteenth-century screen, a monument to a former vicar of the church, the antiquary and cleric William Jenkins Rees and an intriguing abracadabra charm, dating from the seventeenth century and written out on a piece of paper now displayed on the south wall. The tie-beam roof, in Radnorshire style, was restored in 1895 when the church's late seventeenth-century pulpit migrated to the church of St David, in the neighbouring border village of **Whitton**. A little further downstream, the church of St Michael at **Discoed** has a much-admired bell-tower – the bell is dated 1675 – and an ancient yew tree by the north porch. Beyond the church is a wonderfully restored seventeenth-century timber-framed farmhouse, Upper House.

Presteigne is situated a couple of miles on the English side of Offa's Dyke, the Lugg which is bridged here marking the border between Wales and England. In the words of George Borrow, Presteigne is 'neither in Wales nor in England but simply in Radnorshire', which it served for centuries as both county town and assize town. The parish church is dedicated to St Andrew, hence the Welsh name for the town, Llanandras. It is a Saxon foundation and, although situated in Wales, belongs to the diocese of Hereford. It is full of architectural and ornamental interest ranging from Saxon to Victorian times, with a sixteenth-century Flemish tapestry and a Georgian chandelier among its treasures. The tapestry, depicting Christ's Entry into Jerusalem, is one of only two pre-Reformation tapestries still to be found inside a church in the United Kingdom. The faded colours of the Radnorshire Militia are a fascinating reminder that, even in this haven of tranquillity, Napoleon was perceived to be a menace.

A curfew bell has rung from the church tower each evening since 1565, when wealthy wool merchant John Beddoes made this a condition for the continuation of the town's grammar school that he founded in that year in Church Street. Originally on the coach road from London, Cheltenham and Gloucester to Aberystwyth, the town has several fine coaching inns: the Radnorshire Arms, with its secret hiding places; the Bull, formerly a site of bull-baiting; and the Duke's Arms with its galleried courtyard. Red House in Broad Street was the home of Rear Admiral Puget, after whom Puget Sound, south of Vancouver Island was named. The town owes its charm to having been by-passed in the early nineteenth century by a new road running through Kington. Even the branch line organised by the indefatigable Green-Price did little to disturb the peace of a town described as a 'sort of paradise' by Lord Chief Justice Campbell when he passed through in 1855. Pride of place in a particularly pleasing townscape must now be accorded to the well-preserved Shire Hall that ceased to accommodate visiting judges like Campbell as recently as 1970 and was finally left redundant when the public library vacated the building in 1996. An uncompromising restoration project by Powys County Council and Cadw transformed the building into a major tourist attraction, the Judge's Lodging, which boasts Britain's only working example of an open burner gasolier, a gas-powered chandelier. On the ground floor of the Judge's Lodging it is possible to inspect the original gravestone of Mary Morgan, who was hanged at age seventeen for the murder of her illegitimate baby, the last woman to be publicly executed in Wales. The headstone relates the poignant tale. A later memorial stone, still *in situ* in the churchyard bears the inscription: 'He that is without sin among you, let him first cast a stone at her.'

Although a branch line finally reached Presteigne in 1875, it was the Central Wales (now the **Heart of Wales**) Line running through Knighton that accelerated the growth of the latter town. Constructed in stages by four different companies between 1857 and 1868, the line remains open thanks to George Thomas, who, when Secretary of State for Wales in 1968, pointed out to a pre-election cabinet meeting that the line ran through six marginal constituencies. A journey from Shrewsbury to Swansea, along the line's entire length of 150 kilometres, makes an ideal introduction to the landscape of central Wales. Heading eastward out of the town in the direction of Llandrindod, the single-track line crosses the Teme on the thirteen-arched Knucklas Viaduct, a neo-gothic fancy dating from the railway's construction in 1863. There the Heart of

Wales Line continues on via Llanbister Road and Penybont stations to its mid-way point at Llandrindod Wells, where it makes use of the valley of the Eithon, one of the most beautiful of the many small rivers of Wales.

Knucklas has the outline of a Norman castle, almost entirely destroyed, like its sister castle at Knighton, by Llywelyn ap Gruffudd in 1262. Its lasting claim to fame is as the birthplace of Vavasor Powell, the founding father of Old Dissent in this county, in a tavern on the road to **Heyop**, where the admirably plain parish church of St David is worth a visit. **Brampton Bryan**, home of the Puritan squire Sir Robert Harley and his formidable wife Lady Brilliana, was the meeting place for the Welsh Puritan leaders Walter Cradoc, Vavasor Powell and Morgan Llwyd; as such, the 'Brampton Bryan enclave', as it is known, is a place of great significance for Welsh religious history, even though it lies just over the border in Shropshire. Close by, back in Wales, is **Stanage Park**, landscaped in the eighteenth century by the Johnes family that went on to create the Hafod estate in north Cardiganshire and rebuilt by Charles Rogers in the opening decades of the nineteenth.

Following the Teme upstream, there are good examples of bronze age tumuli and megaliths on the valley bottom. This tranquil river marks the often turbulent border between Wales and England. At **Beguildy**, the church of St Michael and All Angels still has a fine fifteenth-century screen with its original monochrome Tudor roses. It has suffered over the years but must once have rivaled those at Llananno and Old Radnor in its artistry. The church also contains an impressive thirteenth-century churchwardens' chest. Close by is the farmhouse of Bryndraenog, the most complete surviving timber-frame house in Wales, lauded by a mediaeval Welsh poet as a 'proud maiden of ash and lime'. Beguildy in Welsh is spelt Bugeildy, literally meaning 'shepherd's house', referring, presumably, to the predominantly pastoral occupations of the parishioners in a parish comprising some 7,000 hectares and containing more sheep than people. The anglicised spelling of the village name was occasioned by the opening of the village school: there were fears that the pupils would be called little bugs, or worse!

Some of Radnorshire's best small country churches are situated on the enchanting banks of the Eithon, a river much frequented by herons and kingfishers. **Llanbadarn Fynydd** has a remnant of its rood screen; a foretaste of delights to come. At **Llanbister**, prominently situated in its rounded churchyard, is the delightful church of St Cynllo with its surviving eighteenth-century singing-loft complete with musical instruments, a reminder of the days before pipe organs became universal. At **Llananno**, the outer walls of the church (like those of Llanbister) contain blocks of distinctive honey-coloured Grinshill stone that was brought by horse and cart some sixty miles from Grinshill, north of Shrewsbury, as building stone for the abbey at Cwm-hir. The Corbett family who owned the quarry were friends of Llywelyn Fawr who worked on enlargeing the abbey between 1228 and 1234. Stone culled from the abbey can be found over a wide radius from the abbey in these parts. It is a miracle that the church's rood screen survived both the sixteenth-century reformers' doctrinal hostility to the separation of the eucharist from the congregation and the attentions of nineteenth-century Victorian church improvers. Elsewhere, on both occasions, bonfires were made of these artistic treasures. The screen is an extraordinary example of fourteenth-century Welsh woodcarving: flowers, leaves, pomegranates and grapes on the vine issuing from the serpent's jaws. This is mediaeval theology exquisitely carved in native oak.

Cefnllys shares, with Llananno, not only a secluded location beside the river but another wonderful rood screen. A borough in mediaeval times, all that now remains at this evocative site is the church and the castle. The isolated church of St Michael has seventeenth-century box pews facing a fifteenth-century screen inside and is surrounded by a ring of ancient yews outside. Castell Cefnllys is the earthwork remains of a structure continuously defended from the iron age to the time of Owain Glyn Dŵr. The Eithon flows north in a great meander under Shakey Bridge and Alpine Bridge into the parish of **Llanbadarn Fawr**, not to be confused with its namesake in Ceredigion. Restored in 1894 by Stephen W. Williams, the outer walls contain Grinshill stone blocks and there are Abbey Cwm-hir pillar capitals to either side of the porch. Its church has one of only two Romanesque carved tympana to be found in Wales. The lions, trees and sun dial carved above the doorway suggest a twelfth-century origin and links with the school of craftsmanship that produced the masterpiece of St Mary's and St David's church at Kilpeck in Herefordshire. On the west bank of the Eithon, as the river again heads south, the simple church of **Llanfihangel Helygen**, St Michael in the Willows, was sympathetically restored by the Pilgrim Trust in 1956. Its seventeenth-century box pews and double-decker pulpit were brought from another church in the nineteenth century. Carpenters' assembly marks are visible on the fourteenth-century roof. The plain internal arrangements are vigorously Protestant, as befits the church where the Celtic antiquarian Thomas Price (Carnhuanawc, 1787–1848) served as curate.

There are interesting remains of a Roman fort on the riverbank at **Castell Collen**, just to the north of Llandrindod. A failure to recover trenchings after an excavation by Edwardian enthusiasts – shocking by today's archaeological standards – makes this a more interesting site to visit than others of its kind. The remains of a substantial bathhouse were more carefully uncovered by archaeologists in the 1950s and many finds from their excavation can be viewed at the museum in Llandrindod. Cae-bach Independent chapel at **Llanyre**, now on the northern outskirts of Llandrindod, is worth seeking out. Built in 1715 by the Revd. Thomas Jones, its eighteenth-century interior fittings are still intact. The painter Thomas Jones attended services here in his youth; there is a memorial to the painter and his family on the chapel wall. Further down the Eithon, beyond Llandrindod, **Disserth** has the wonderfully atmospheric church of St Cewydd. *Cewydd y Glaw*, Cewydd the Rain, is a weather saint with strong Radnorshire associations. The church is now celebrated for its atmospheric late seventeenth-century interior, just the type that the Victorians have tidied up all too frequently elsewhere. Many of the box pews have the names of their original proprietors carved on them, and there is a three-decker pulpit dated 1687. The church itself is a largely thirteenth-century structure, with a surviving bell of 1300, but the circular churchyard hints strongly of greater antiquity as does the name Disserth itself, meaning a desert place. Like a sister Irish place-name *Díseart*, it recalls the earliest eremetical tradition of Christianity in these islands, which was influenced by the teachings of the desert fathers. The riverside walk beside the Eithon is particularly fine here as it meanders westwards to its confluence with the Wye, a perfect spot for a contemplative picnic.

A couple of miles further to the west lies **Newbridge-on-Wye**, a crossroads that aspired to spa status following the arrival of the Mid Wales Railway in 1864. The glass porch of a former temperance hotel on the main road is a reminder of the time when clergymen flocked to such places for their summer vacations. The architecturally bland All Saints Church conforms to the village's other buildings. From here, the main road up the Wye valley to Rhayader soon passes **Doldowlod**, retirement home of James Watt (1736–1819), the inventor of the steam engine; subsequent generations of the Watt family made improvements to the property. Another property to seek out lies south of Newbridge: the mansion of **Pencerrig**, home of the landscape painter Thomas Jones (1742–1803). Born in Cefnllys, Thomas Jones' parents actually moved here to escape the hustle and bustle of Llandrindod Wells. A pupil of Richard Wilson, his painting of the house that he inherited in 1787, *Penkerrig*, can be seen in Birmingham City Art Gallery and his masterpiece, *The Bard*, in the National Museum in Cardiff. The lake beside the house was made for his daughter. Further south John Norton's fine Victorian restoration of the church of St Matthew over-looks the Wye at **Llanelwedd**, where Radnorshire meets Breconshire, and all Welsh farmers and everyone else inter-ested in Welsh country life meet for the annual Royal Welsh Agricultural Show at the end of July each year.

The main road east from Builth to New Radnor passes beneath the Carneddau – lovingly painted by Thomas Jones – where the prominence of Caer Einon iron age hill fort at some 400 metres affords wonderful views to the south over Breconshire. North of **Llanfihangel Nant Melan**, with its yew-encircled churchyard, is the pictur-esque waterfall known as **Water-break-its-neck**, where Llywelyn ap Gruffudd is said to have hid as a fugitive from the English. Its curious name appears to derive from the English pronunciation of the original Welsh name Cwm yr Heusor, the Valley of the Herdsman. Yr Heusor came to be pronounced locally as 'razor' and the fancy name for the waterfall followed quickly on the arrival of the first tourists. Serious hill-walkers might venture further north into the Forest to inspect the Three Riggles (from the Welsh *rhigol* for furrow), ancient earthworks of unknown purpose that run down the side of Great Rhos into Harley Dingle. The summit of the Great Rhos is the highest point in the county at 660 metres.

The road from Hundred House to Gladestry passes through David's country. **Glascwm** has a large mediaeval church dedicated to St David who is said to have founded the church on this site. Gerald of Wales passed this way on his journey through Wales and inspected the saint's miraculous handbell, known mysteriously as *Bangu*. This church has two daughter churches close by sharing the same dedication to the patron saint of Wales. The first, another gem of a country church, is at **Cregina** where the Clas Brook meets the Edw. Restored by the Pilgrim Trust, it contains a small rood screen of the Radnorshire School. The second church, upstream at **Rhulen**, has a pyramidal wooden belfry and combines rustic charm with whitewashed simplicity to effect a rare serenity somehow emblematic of the spirit of Radnorshire. Further upstream, at **Llanbadarn-y-Garreg**, there is another well-situated church of wondrous simplicity, this time dedicated to St Padarn. The altar rails and pulpit are seventeenth-century. Back on the Gladestry road lies **Colva**, its simple thirteenth-century church – another dedication to St David – remarkable for its high defensive site in the mountain pass between Colva Hill and Yr Allt.

From Builth, the Wye races south between the upland massif of Mynydd Epynt in Breconshire to the west and an equally rugged landscape, as attractive as it is anonymous, still in Radnorshire to the east. The confluence of the Edw with the Wye at **Aberedw** has strong associations with the last native Prince of Wales. The castle, the remains of which were bisected by the Mid Wales Railway Company in 1864, was the last refuge of Llywelyn ap Gruffudd before he rode out to final defeat at Cilmeri in 1282. Folk memory speaks of the traitors of Aberedw, but perhaps we should not delve too deeply into those troubled waters. St Cewydd's church, where Llywelyn may have received his last communion, has a late fourteenth-century screen of the Radnorshire School and a collection of musical instruments from a church orchestra. Cewydd's obit bell, a handbell rung at the head of a funeral procession, can now be viewed at the National Museum in Cardiff. Llywelyn's Cave, which overlooks the village, may originally have been St Cewydd's fifth-century cell. It is said that the saint would walk to Disserth – the only other Cewydd dedication in Wales – following the hill track over Aberedw Hill along which he is commemorated by the standing stone of Maengewydd. Upstream from Aberedw, it is worth visiting the churchyard at **Llanfaredd** for its magnificent yew, reputedly the largest in the county. **Llandeilo Graban** has the epitaph of the last dragon to be killed in Radnorshire; apparently, it was wont to sleep in the church tower where the memorial is located.

The road joins the valley of another delightful tributary of the Wye, the Bach Howey (from the Welsh, Bachawy). At **Llanbedr**, there is a pleasingly simple but spacious church with some good locally produced wall memorials. A simple white cross marks the burial place of the Revd. John Price (1810–1895), the learned but impoverished clergyman who lived here in squalor while ministering to his flock. His natural affinity with vagrants gave rise to his reputation as the "tramps' chaplain". The road continues with the Begwns to the south; here, there are good views from the appropriately named Roundabout over to the attractive village of **Painscastle**, once active as a gathering place for cattle drovers. There are extensive ruins of the Norman castle from which the settlement derives its name. It has had an eventful history. Most notable of several incidents of border skirmishing was the unsuccessful bid to storm this Norman stronghold in 1198 by Gwenwynwyn, Prince of Powys. Reinforcements were sent from England to dislodge him and in the fighting which followed some 3,000 men were slain, with the consequence that the Bach Howey is reputed to have run red with their blood. It is possible to turn off the main road here and follow the Arrow (from the Welsh, Arwy) east to **Michaelchurch-on-Arrow** to view the fifteenth-century rood screen in St Michael's church. In the springtime, a profusion of alder catkins turns the valley into a purple ribbon.

Glasbury is an important bridging point for the Hereford road. On first arrival the village seems pure

Herefordshire, with its nucleated settlement around a village green, unusual for upland Wales. There was once a monastic settlement of the Celtic Church here, however, as the Welsh name of the village, *Clas-ar-Wy* (the *clas* on the Wye) indicates and this accounts for the pattern of settlement. The village has one of the oldest vicarages in Wales near the river and an adjacent tithe barn. The principal source of interest in the village, however, is its collection of chapels. In 1818 Richard Hergest, a local farmer, underwent a religious experience during which he heard the voice of God, saying 'give that corner of the meadow to the Methodists and build a chapel'. As a consequence the village acquired a delightful Wesleyan chapel with a characteristically Radnorshire half-hipped roof. Treble Hill Baptist Chapel was built in the Temple style and its handsome pinewood pews can accommodate a congregation of 350. It has frosted glass windows, in part to protect the congregation from the distractions of nature but mainly as protection from the hostile and inquisitive gaze of members of rival denominations. A mile to the north is **Maesyronnen Independent Chapel**, one of the oldest surviving Nonconformist meeting houses in Wales. A seventeenth-century barn converted to a place of worship by local dissenters, it has been in continuous use ever since. It has box pews and other evocative fittings of the eighteenth and nineteenth centuries, and there are good views from the windows. As is the way with Nonconformist meeting houses, its doors are kept locked but it is well worth the journey up the lane to Ffynnon Gynydd to borrow the key. This original Welsh name for this village was Fynnon Gynidr, meaning Cynidr's Well. Cynidr was one of the sons of Brychan and his well, handsomely roofed in 1892 as a memorial to Walter de Winton of Maes-llwch, is on the right hand side on arrival at the village common from the chapel. Maes-llwch Castle itself was largely demolished in 1951.

St Meulig's church in **Llowes** contains an early font and an eleventh-century Celtic cross that once stood atop the Begwns. It also has something unusual for Radnorshire, a gravestone inscribed in Welsh commemorating one William Bevan who died in 1684; it can be located by the priest's door in the south wall of the church. **Clyro** has the remains of a Roman camp, a fourteenth-century Cistercian grange at Clyro Court Farm and the neo-Jacobean Clyro Court, built for Thomas Baskerville, where Sir Arthur Conan Doyle stayed to write *The Hound of the Baskervilles*. But the village is now principally celebrated as the place where the Revd. Francis Kilvert (1840–1879) wrote the greater part of his diary. Ashbrook House, where he lived while serving as a curate from 1865 to 1872, has a plaque in his memory. The charming collection of buildings in the village, framed by Clyro Hill and the delightful views to the south over the Wye to the Black Mountains beyond, powerfully conjure up his life and times. Reading Kilvert's lyrical diaries and following in his footsteps as he walks the hills of his parish to neighbouring Aberedw or Painscastle is to enter into a world now largely lost. Nevertheless, for those willing to take the time to linger appreciatively in this county, the slow pace and rural charm of Kilvert's world can still feel tantalisingly close.

Spectacular views over the Radnorshire hills can be obtained by walking along the whale back of Hergest Ridge on the Welsh border near Kington in Herefordshire. Hergest is a name celebrated in the history of Welsh literature since the Vaughans of **Hergest Court** preserved one of the most important mediaeval Welsh manuscripts, the Red Book of Hergest (*Llyfr Coch Hergest*), now conserved in the Bodleian Library. *The Hound of the Baskervilles* was based on legends surrounding this property. West of Kington, the main road into Wales heads to New Radnor past the steep cliffs of **Stanner Rocks**, well known to botanists for their semi-upland flora, with abundant displays of rockrose, rock stonecrop and the Radnorshire Lily, discovered here in the 1970s. Between **Walton** and **Evenjobb**, there are a number of megaliths and barrows dating from the late neolithic and bronze ages and associated flint chippings have been found in quantity hereabouts. Most famous are the Four Stones, the only Welsh example of a type of monument more usually associated with Scotland: the south-east stone has the characteristic 'cup marks' associated with such monuments as the Clava Cairns, near Inverness. Nearby **Burfa Camp**, which overlooks Offa's Dyke, is an excellent example of a multivallate iron age hill fort of which Radnorshire has several good examples.

Old Radnor, just off the main road from Walton, has one of Radnorshire's most celebrated churches. It contains an erratic dolerite boulder in use as a font, a fifteenth-century rood screen of the Gloucestershire School, an early sixteenth-century organ case which is the earliest of its kind in the British Isles together with good tombs, memorials and hatchments. The structure is largely fifteenth century, following the destruction of an earlier building in the Glyn Dŵr Rising, and sits in an ancient circular enclosure. Like St Andrew's in Presteigne, St Stephen's in Old Radnor also stayed in the diocese of Hereford after disestablishment in 1920. All this can be contemplated from the adjacent Harp Inn, restored by the Landmark Trust in 1971.

New Radnor, in spite of its borough status from 1562 to 1833, has never been more than a sleepy village. Traces of its intended grid plan can be seen from the remains of the Norman castle that overlooks the settlement, with some of the original plots still unoccupied. St Mary's church has been largely spoilt by renovation although two eroded effigies in the porch may be worth investigating. The Lewis Memorial at the entrance to the village commemorates the local MP, Sir George Cornewall Lewis, whose political career was cut short by an early death in 1864. He had reached the cabinet, was Chancellor of the

Exchequer from 1855 to 1858, as well as being editor of the *Edinburgh Review*.

Further west, at **Llandegley**, the substantially restored church of St Tecla was fortunate to retain its original rood screen. On a spur to the north of the main road between Llandegley and Penybont, it is well worth seeking out **The Pales Meeting House**. Erected by the local Quakers as a place of worship in 1717, it served a community that had first come into existence after George Fox had preached to a large crowd on Penybont Common in 1654. A succession of distinguished schoolmasters, including the American abolitionist Yardley Warner, served this community for generations. Today, it is the oldest Quaker meeting house in Wales still in use. There are beautiful views over the Eithon from the chapel's porch. **Penybont**, once noted for its fairs, is now celebrated in these parts for its annual trotting races.

Taking the Knighton road north-west from Penybont, **Bleddfa** has the attractive mediaeval church of St Mary Magdalene. Of the Montgomeryshire type, the church is said to have been founded by St Brendan. It has a number of interesting features: externally, there is an unusual clap-boarded bell-turret; internally, seventeenth-century altar rails and pulpit together with a large parish chest. An archaeological dig from 1962 to 1963 demonstrated that a prominent mound in the churchyard, reputed to be a bronze age round barrow, was in fact the remains of an earlier church tower. This had probably collapsed, like its counterpart at Cascob, after having been set on fire during the Glyn Dŵr Rising. The use of some stanzas from Alexander Pope on a prominent tomb near the churchyard entrance, speak eloquently of Anglican distaste for new-fangled Methodist enthusiasm; in 1808, John Phillips was proud to depart this life, 'a stranger to civil and religious rage'. Off the main road towards the south-west lies Llyn Gwyn, the largest natural lake in the county, a sobering thought to recall when viewing the Elan valley reservoirs.

Rhayader is an anglicisation of the Welsh for waterfall, the falls of the Wye being spectacular hereabouts. In Welsh, the town is *Rhaeadr Gwy*, the falls on the Wye. An ancient market town for the surrounding countryside, the high points of the trading year used to be the May and December Fairs, the latter known as Dom Fair from the Welsh word for mire, *domled*, and the October ram sales. The town's location on the A44 between Birmingham and the sea makes it an attractive place to stop for refreshment and there are numerous tea-rooms and public houses. Of the latter the seventeenth-century Cwmddeuddwr Arms is the town's oldest building but it sadly stopped tap for the last time recently and is now, of all things, a cycle shop. The town church, now dedicated to St Clement, was founded by St Cynllo, and is another example of Stephen W. Williams' restoration work. A riverside walk can be taken here to inspect the remains of a motte and bailey castle. There is another riverside walk on the east bank to the south of the town where the former Union Workhouse has been converted to a restaurant. It is an interesting survival of original New Poor Law architecture where the residents are now encouraged to ask for more. Close by at Gigrin Farm, a rich meat diet is made available each afternoon for the local red kites, an imperilled species a generation ago, but now thriving in this part of Wales.

Rhayader is a simple crossroads, the London to Aberystwyth coach road having run through the town and on over what is now marked as the mountain road to Cwmystwyth. This road is very attractive in fine weather, particularly on a fine early morning with the sun behind you. As the ascent is made leaving the town there is a good surviving stand of the native sessile oak on the mountainside before reaching the start of a track that leads to **Maen Serth**. This is an impressive megalith, situated on open moorland some 500 metres above sea level, onto which a Christian cross has been inscribed around the eighth century and a benchmark incised by the Ordnance Survey in the nineteenth.

Cwmdeuddwr, where the mountain road leaves Rhayader for the Elan valley reservoirs, is a contraction of the original Cwmwd Deuddŵr, the Commote of the Two Waters, that is Wye and Elan. The valley was flooded at the behest of Birmingham Corporation at the beginning of the twentieth century. During the century before Cwm Elan was flooded, its scenery had attracted romantic travellers. The young poet Shelley eloped to Nantgwyllt for a short time in 1810 with Harriet Westbrook. Four years later, she drowned herself in the Serpentine at the age of twenty as Shelley embarked with Mary Godwin on the Alpine tour that had been closed to him during the Napoleonic wars. Some fifty years later, the energetic daughter of the house, Miss Emmeline Lewis Lloyd, the eighth woman to ascend Mont Blanc, recruited her Swiss climbing instructor to work for her father. She was equally at ease as a pioneer female Alpinist as she was hunting the otter or casting for salmon along the banks of the Wye. The nearby church of St Bride's has a memorial tablet to her. Nantgwyllt later accommodated Birmingham Corporation's project engineer but was itself drowned beneath the reservoir when the scheme was completed in 1904. A special clause in the compulsory purchase order ensured that the house was not demolished, so it is possible to look for its roof appearing above the waters of the lowest reservoir in times of drought. Also beneath the water, ironically, is Dolau Baptist chapel, one of the final bastions of the Welsh language in the county. A moving account of the appearance of some members of its congregation before the Parliamentary Select Committee that was to approve the drowning of the valley can be found in the closing chapter of Elizabeth Clarke's charming memoir, *The Valley*. The model village that housed Birmingham Corporation's workers survives as **Elan Village** with stone cottages and a school. It is possible to view all four linked reservoirs on a circular drive from Rhayader during which time should be found to visit the nature trail in Cnwch Wood, an ancient oak woodland with a rich variety of plant and animal life.

An extension to this tour can be made to the more recent **Claerwen** reservoir which was completed in 1952; fortunately the fine Radnorshire long-house of Cilewent escaped drowning and can be viewed inside and out at the Museum of Welsh Life where it was re-erected in 1959. For the more energetic, it is possible to follow an ancient road which passes the top of the reservoir at Pont-ar-Elan as it connects the sister Cistercian abbeys of Strata Florida and Abbey Cwm-hir. The track is more clearly marked on the map than on the ground and in bad weather this stretch of Radnorshire moorland can be treacherous; nevertheless, there is something very moving about making this transit in the mediaeval footsteps of the white monks.

A new connecting road to Aberystwyth via Llangurig was built out of Rhayader in 1829 and this has carried the through traffic to Cardigan Bay ever since. From this road it is possible to explore the isolated Marteg valley, a notorious frost pocket, but containing a rich collection of bronze age barrows and megaliths. A restored Welsh long-house at Gilfach is now an information centre for an extensive nature reserve where native sessile oak and the botanical richness of unimproved pastures can be inspected at close hand. The church in the village of **St Harmon** is dedicated to St Garmon (St Germanus) whose mother church this probably was. There are fine bronze age burial mounds and standing stones in the vicinity. Gerald of Wales mentions a certain staff of St Curig that was kept in the church: it was covered in gold and silver and was sought after for the cure of glandular swellings. Kilvert was vicar here from 1876 to 1877.

We are now in the vicinity of one of the most romantic of Welsh historic monuments, the melancholy ruins of

Abbey Cwm-hir. The heart of the village is the church of St Mary, first built at the expense of the Fowler family in the seventeenth century but entirely rebuilt using Grinshill stone in 1866. Inspiration for the 20-metre tower, a wedding cake confection completely out of character for the area, apparently came from Normandy. Kilvert walked here in the company of Middleton Evans and his son when he was their guest at Lwynbarried Hall, Nantmel, in 1870. He viewed the church that had been completed four years previously and watched the workmen putting the finishing touches to Abbey Cwm-hir Hall, a large gabled house built above the church in the 1830s 'in the Elizabethan style', with a garden terrace overlooking the abbey ruins. Here Kilvert and party dined on cold mutton, bread and butter with sherry and 'some splendid Burton ale'. Opposite this attractive pair of Victorian buildings is the Happy Union public house with its splendidly cheerful old signboard showing a Welshman astride a goat, brandishing a glass of ale and sporting a leek.

Access to the abbey is through the entrance gate next to Home Farm a little further down the road. Given the importance of this site in Welsh history, it seems sadly in need both of conservation and interpretation to meet the needs of the steady stream of contemporary pilgrims. Like other Cistercian foundations its site seems to have been chosen for both seclusion and enchantment. The delightful monk's pool, adjacent to the ruins, serves as a reminder that Cistercian simplicity also encompassed their diet. At the height of his powers in the mid-thirteenth century Llywelyn Fawr intended the abbey church to become a national cathedral and began to build a nave the length of which was only exceeded in the British Isles by Winchester and Durham. But Llywelyn Fawr's grandson Llywelyn ap Gruffudd became Llywelyn Ein Llyw Olaf (Lywelyn our Last Leader) in 1282, a date as infamous to the Welsh as 1066 is to the English. '*Cofiwch 1282!*' (Remember 1282!) is a slogan not infrequently encountered, daubed on a wall, as you progress around Wales. The abbey may even be Llywelyn's burial place and an unpretentious slate memorial was placed in the nave in 1978. The destruction of the abbey, ironically, owes much to another Welsh national hero: it seems the abbey never fully recovered from the treatment it received at the hands of Owain Glyn Dŵr's retinue. By the time of the Dissolution, the abbey had only three monks and it passed into the hands of the Fowler family, the relatively prosperous squires in the rhyme that opened this chapter. The abbot's house and surviving abbey buildings served as a royalist stronghold in the Civil War until captured, with more destruction, by Cromwellian forces in 1644. The Fowlers' house at nearby **Devannor** still stands, a massive late seventeenth-century structure built of Grinshill stone. The house is occupied by the Griffiths family who have farmed the surrounding land for generations; early converts to Methodism, one room has served as a Methodist chapel since 1818. It is possible to join the main Newtown to Llandrindod road by following the Clywedog Brook a few miles downstream.

We have skirted around **Llandrindod Wells** and left it till last in order to heighten the impact of a first visit. The border towns of Radnorshire all date back to early mediaeval times as do the country villages and churches. By contrast, Llandod, as Llandrindod Wells is affectionately known locally, is a relatively new town situated in the middle of the county. With a population of over five thousand it is by far the largest town in Radnorshire. The town has a reputation as a spa that goes back to the eighteenth century: 'Let England boast Bath's crowded springs, Llandrindod happier Cambria sings', proclaimed the *Gentleman's Magazine*, ironically, in 1748. It owes its present appearance almost entirely to the railway that here celebrates its halfway point of transit across the Heart of Wales with a flourish of double track. Here the up and down trains meet and linger at the restored station. It was the railway companies, in an attempt to boost business, that added the English 'Wells' to so many of the places along this line, none more successfully than in Llandrindod. In its Victorian heyday this spa town was much frequented by respectable holidaymakers, especially clergymen and their families. Some came to hear the preaching of Kilsby Jones (1813–1889), the eccentric Independent minister whose red brick Capel y Drindod stands as his monument. When it opened in 1871 it had cost £1,700 to build, a considerable sum in those days; but Kilsby's eccentricities were well deployed in fund-raising. These Victorians strolled the lakeside paths, ventured out onto the boating lakes and took the waters at the Pump Room in Rock Park, there being a choice of chalybeate, from the Arlais brook, magnesium, saline or sulphur. The Victorians also set great store by the eye pool adjacent to the Pump Room. The town's villas are a sedate oasis of red Ruabon brick, brought by the railway, that initially shock the senses after the greys and greens of the surrounding Radnorshire countryside. Good examples are the Metropole and the Glenusk Hotels that continue to flourish on the conference trade, Llandrindod being a popular choice for national meetings for many Welsh organisations, presumably on the grounds that it is equally inaccessible to everyone. In the memorial gardens beside the Metropole an excellent small museum displays archaeological finds from the Castell Collen Roman fort situated half a mile to the north of the town.

Regrettably, the original Pump Room closed in 1971 and was subsequently demolished. The adjacent Pump House Hotel has been converted into the principal offices of Powys County Council, the recent renaissance of Llandrindod owing much to a decision to base the headquarters of the new county of Powys here in 1973. This new unitary authority has survived subsequent reorganisations and upheavals in local government so that the former counties of Montgomeryshire, Radnorshire and Breconshire all now look to Llandrindod for leadership in local government. Belatedly, but with commendable enthusiasm, the town has also understood the potential of celebrating its Victorian heritage. It is again possible to take the waters, and during Victorian Festival week each summer, to savour the nineteenth-century atmosphere of this celebrated Welsh spa.

Llandrindod is a good base for exploring the surrounding countryside by bicycle. The Heart of Wales Line is remarkably bicycle friendly with Llandrindod at the hub of the Welsh Cycle Network. The splendid art deco premises of the former Automobile Palace, that once sold aeroplanes, motor cars and bicycles, is now home to the National Cycle Exhibition with a display of over two hundred bicycles dating from 1810. These premises were opened by Tom Norton (1870–1955), transport pioneer and friend of Henry Ford: his was the first Ford agency in Wales and he organised the first bus service in the country, from Llandrindod to Newtown. He is buried in the old parish church above the lake where the Pentrosfa Mire nature reserve has sedgebeds that are home to a wealth of wildlife. From here, an extensive network of shaded footpaths links the Eithon to such evocative haunts as Lover's Leap and The Lake. At the latter, migratory toad crossing signs beside the road testify to the pace of life in twenty-first century Radnorshire.

4

Breconshire

BRECONSHIRE AND RADNORSHIRE were the only two of the former Welsh counties to be completely land-locked. Historically, Breconshire has also laboured under the cumbersome English name Brecknockshire but the derivation is the same in each case: Brychan, a semi-legendary ruler, is reputed to have founded his eponymous kingdom of Brycheiniog in the fifth century. He may have been Irish in origin: there are six Ogham stones in Breconshire that lie on an ancient route-way from Pembrokeshire to the Usk valley. Brychan also had a miraculously large progeny of saints, both sons and daughters, whose church dedications extend from Ireland in the west to Cornwall and Brittany in the south. It has been suggested that Brycheiniog was an early centre from which a distinctive Celtic Christianity, mingling Welsh and Irish influences, was diffused in the fifth and sixth centuries. Certainly, the county's rich Christian tradition will occupy much of our attention as we explore its highways and byways. The distinctive appearance of Breconshire derives from its old red sandstone soils, especially attractive when ploughed fields are suddenly illuminated with clear sunlight in a race of showers. The gentle hill country of Montgomery and Radnor here quickens its pace to a controlled crescendo in the forms of the Black Mountains to the east and the Brecon Beacons to the south. Established in 1957, the Brecon Beacons National Park was the first National Park in Wales.

Moving south from Radnorshire, the Wye is crossed at **Builth** by John Parry of The Hay's impressive six-arched stone bridge dating from 1799. Immediately on the east bank is the former Market Hall (1875), now transformed into the attractive and lively Wyeside Arts Centre. Appropriately the original terracotta medallions on the façade are of Shakespeare, Haydn and Mozart. The Lion (formerly the Royal Oak) opposite accommodated the three infamous education commissioners, Lingen, Symons and Vaughan Johnson while they finalised the report that the Welsh regarded as an act of treachery. The Report into the State of Education in Wales, published in 1847, caricatured the Welsh as ignorant and immoral and blamed this condition on the prevalence of the Welsh language. Fixed in popular memory as *Brad y Llyfrau Gleision* (The Treason of the Blue Books), the Report gave the Welsh an enormous chip on their shoulder. Throughout the next century Wales was to reinvent itself as a Land of Song, Temperance and White Gloves, the latter a reference to exceptionally low crime rates, as Assize Judges put on white gloves when there were no cases to try. The arrival of the Mid Wales Railway in 1864 prompted efforts to develop the town as a spa, but all three stations bearing the name of Builth were situated in Radnorshire, as though the town wished to keep a safe distance from this latest example of modernity. The fledgling spa never recovered from the Great War and subsequent years of depression and with the closure of the town station in 1962 Builth returned to its former name – a corruption of the Welsh form, Llanfair-ym-Muallt, Buallt being a distinctive territory in the Middle Ages.

Mediaeval Builth was destroyed by fire in 1691. One of the county's three chartered markets, its single one-way street now contains mainly Georgian buildings. St Mary's parish church has its original fourteenth-century tower and, in the porch, an effigy of a sixteenth-century 'ysquer to the bodye' of Elizabeth I. Capel Alpha, as its name implies, claims primacy in the early history of Calvinistic Methodism in Wales, having been built under the supervision of Howell

Harris in 1747. 'Howell Harris told his congregation last night in my hearing', reported an outraged Lewis Morris after passing though the town, 'that God had never been before in Llanvair. Most of the people here are drunk with religion.' There is a curiosity worth seeking out in Strand Street: the only Post Office in Britain to have been opened during the brief reign of the uncrowned Edward VIII, a rare instance of this sleepy town getting ahead of itself.

The Heart of Wales Line crosses into Breconshire from Builth Road on its way down from Llandrindod to stop at **Cilmeri**. Here every patriotic Welshman or woman will want to alight at least once (perhaps annually on 11 December for the wreath-laying ceremonies) for this is reputed to be the place and date where Llywelyn ap Gruffudd fell at the hands of the English in 1282. In 1952 a 5-metre high jagged monolith of Caernarfonshire granite was erected to commemorate this national calamity and was inaugurated with a rousing address by the serving Archdruid, Dyfnallt. Thirteen young oaks surround the monument representing each of the historic Welsh counties.

The next station, **Garth**, is the stop for Methodists. Garth House, on the banks of the Dulas, was the home of Marmaduke Gwynne (1694–1769), local squire and Justice of the Peace. At first irritated by the Methodists, like so many of his Anglican peers, he was won over by the preaching of Howell Harris and became his patron. The Wesleys stayed with Edward Phillips at neighbouring **Maesmynys** in the 1740s, John Wesley preaching in St David's church there. Charles Wesley fell in love with the squire's daughter, Sarah, and it was his brother John Wesley who joined them in matrimony at the nearby church of **Llanlleonfel** in 1749. This was to the chagrin of the squire of Maesmynys who had been eyeing her up himself. Understandably, he never came to share his neighbour's enthusiasm for Methodism. The church contains an ancient burial stone with a Latin inscription to two warriors and excellent stained glass by

John Petts. The ancient hilltop site of this church was beloved of Kilvert. He illustrates its then ruined state with a hilarious tale of a man arriving at the altar rail for his second marriage only to find a handkerchief left there by his first wife, his first marriage being the last time there had been a service in the church.

Llangamarch grew up on the banks of the Irfon, an exceptionally beautiful tributary of the Wye; the railway, which now bisects it, brought aspirations to spa status. This is a stop for Anglicans and Independents. St Cadmarch's church has two interesting memorials, both in English, one to Theophilus Jones (1759–1812), author of the pioneering county history, and the other to his grandfather Theophilus Evans (1693–1767), the Anglican controversialist who was vicar here from 1738 to 1763. He was the author of the Welsh classic *Drych y Prif Oesoedd*, an early attempt to interpret Welsh history that is now read as literature. He lived at Llwyn Einon, a fine gentleman's residence that can be seen from the train as it approaches the station. It is claimed, on flimsy evidence, that John Penry (1563–1593), one of the founders of Independency, was born nearby at **Cefn-brith** on the Epynt scarp. He advocated the preaching of the Gospel in Welsh but was put to death by those who had only recently achieved the right to preach the Gospel in English. It was David Williams (1779–1874), the indefatigable minister at Troedrhiwdalar, who made Cefn-brith a place of pilgrimage for Welsh Nonconformists. A classic Welsh long-house, Cefn-brith is the architectural embodiment of John Penry's courage and integrity.

Llanwrtyd Wells – pronounced La Naughty Dwells, as one of its hotels helpfully recommends in its brochure – is another ancient market centre that had a brief career as a spa town following the arrival of the railway. It was Theophilus Evans who publicised the stinking well, *Y Ffynnon Ddrewllyd*, that was to be the making of this spa;

he claimed it cured him of his 'radicated scurvy'. Once again, however, it was the railway that brought the visitors to fill the town's hotels along the banks of the Irfon. The well was claimed to be the most sulphurous in the Principality and it can be viewed and smelt about half a kilometre upstream in the grounds of Dolcoed Hotel, a scene of poignant dilapidation. Llanwrtyd Wells was a favoured resort of the clergy: the well-known rugby song *Sospan Fach* was composed by a ministerial student in 1895 at one of their weekly eisteddfodau in the Victoria Wells Pavilion. St James' church was built in the following year by David Jenkins; there is a good Edwardian Congregational chapel, while the red and yellow bricks and terracotta of the Baptist cause remind us of the role the railway played in bringing alien building materials into the country districts.

The parish church of St David, hastily restored by Buckeridge in 1862, is pleasantly situated in the original village of Llanwrtyd, formerly known as Pontrhydyfere, a kilometre to the north of the newer settlement. Here it is possible to view the memorial column erected by the friends of the Revd. Kilsby Jones. 'He being dead yet speaketh', is the chosen text, originally a reference to the Lord himself but here seeming to refer to the eminent divine. Kilsby had expressed the wish to be buried in the grounds of his unprepossessing yellow-bricked house, Glenview, where he had constructed a school to civilise the local children by teaching them in English. He was fortunate in his friends, however, and now lies buried in the churchyard. Glenview was renamed Kilsby in the 1970s. Since 1917, the Cambrian Mill has employed disabled servicemen in its woollen mill maintaining the local tradition of Esgair Moel, the former Llanwrtyd mill that now works in the grounds of the Museum of Welsh Life. Today the town wallows in its reputation as home to the annual World Bog-snorkelling championships that are held here each summer. From

Llanwrtyd, the railway crosses the county boundary into Carmarthenshire though a tunnel.

A circular return journey to Builth can be made from Llanwrtyd Wells via Newbridge. The Drovers' Road follows the upper reaches of the Irfon through romantic scenery to Abergwesyn and on to **Beulah**, a village named after its Independent chapel, replacing the earlier name of Dôlranell. As a counter to the strength of Nonconformity in the area, John Norton's Eglwys Oen Duw, the church of The Lamb of God, was built in 1866 under the patronage of the kindly and devout Clara Thomas, widow of Henry Thomas of Llwyn Madoc. The fonts from two earlier churches can be seen in the polychrome interior of this pretty Victorian church.

As the Newbridge road crosses the Dulas, the famous chapel of **Troedrhiwdalar** comes into view. One of the oldest dissenting congregations in the county it is possible that this cause was founded by John Penry himself; certainly Walter Cradoc and Vavasor Powell preached to the 'gathered church' between Rhayader and Builth. A chapel was erected on this site in 1714. Services in the chapel only went from Welsh to English in the 1950s. Inside St Michael's church at **Llanfihangel Brynpabuan** is a memorial to Thomas Huet who translated the Book of Revelation into Welsh in 1567. Plas Llysdinam on the banks of the Wye near Newbridge was the ancestral home of Kilvert's vicar at Clyro, the Revd. Richard Lister Venables. The Wye at Newbridge marks the boundary with Radnorshire. To return to Builth, follow the Wye downstream.

My preferred route to Brecon from Builth is the road over **Mynydd Epynt**. These high open moors, the haunts of the Welsh cattle drovers, combine magnificence and melancholy in a characteristically Welsh way: magnificence, for their wild scenery and for their population of wild ponies, the word Epynt deriving from the Brythonic form for 'place of horses'; melancholy, for the memory of the eviction of the Welsh-speaking community that farmed these hills by the Ministry of Defence in 1940 to make way for an army firing range. In the space of just a few months, a community with a heritage reaching back for centuries was obliterated. A Ministry of Defence information board boasts that the requisition of the Epynt has 'helped to preserve an extraordinary (sic) rich deserted landscape, untouched by modern agriculture', and that 'disused military installations are also now of considerable interest'. After a millennium of stewardship by a remarkable farming community, such sentiments are effrontery. It is possible to take your chance when the red flag of the firing range isn't hoisted, to seek out the site of Capel-y-Babell, once noted for its eisteddfod. The army rebuilt the chapel to use for target practice; a memorial stone was unveiled at this depressing spot by the Fellowship of Reconciliation in 2000.

The magnificent box hedges of **Castle Madoc** always catch the eye. This dignified property occupies an ancient site that has been home to the Powel family for centuries. Their original eleventh-century motte lies just north-east of the house. Charles Powel (1712–1796), the antiquarian, was the last in the male line of this family; a friend of Howell Harris, he was one of the founder members of the Breconshire Agricultural Society. He married Catherine Penry, the heiress of Cefn-brith. There are Powel memorials in the eighteenth-century church of St Michael's in Lower Chapel. In the church at **Llandefaelog Fach** is the Briamail Flou stone, a larger than life carving of an armed man with Celtic interlace decoration in an otherwise over-restored Victorian interior. The Epynt road descends into Brecon by the cathedral.

The Ysgir, running parallel to the Honddu to the west, can be followed upstream to **Merthyr Cynog**. The church has a massive tower and fourteenth-century screen. The circular churchyard is traditionally held to be the burial place of St Cynog, a 'holy fool' who was one of Brychan's sons. Downstream, **Aberyscir** has the remains of a large Roman fort, excavated by Sir Mortimer Wheeler in 1924–5. **Brecon Gaer Roman Fort** (Cadw) occupies a strategic and attractive site, commanding views of the Usk and Ysgir approaches. In the vicinity of the fort the rare dwarf elder flourishes, growing to several feet in height with attractive white flowers.

The other route from Builth to Brecon follows the west bank of the Wye, here marking the boundary with Radnorshire. The river is at its foaming best hereabouts, a favourite haunt of fishermen. In the church of St Mauritius at **Alltmawr**, there is a touching bronze memorial to Lord Trevethin who lost his life in pursuit of a salmon here in 1936 at the ripe old age of 92. From Erwood, a country lane leads to **Crickadarn**, where the sixteenth-century embattled tower of St Mary's beckons. This simple mediaeval church, sensitively restored by Clough Williams-Ellis (1883–1978) in 1910, has a fine seventeenth-century communion table and memorials. South of Crickadarn, beyond Nant Scithwen, is Wernos, where Howell Harris held his first *seiat*, or devotional meeting, in May 1737. 'Great was the crowd here', he reported in his diary. The house is revered in the Welsh Calvinistic Methodist tradition.

Returning to the main road, the luxury hotel of **Llangoed Hall** is delightfully situated on the banks of the Wye. This early domestic commission from Clough Williams-Ellis was completed in 1914, sympathetically incorporating the remains of the original Jacobean mansion. Its monumentally grand style has proved the perfect vehicle for Sir Bernard Ashley's country-house hotel. There are good riverside walks here both up and downstream. The A470 turns right at **Llyswen** to make for Brecon, passing the impressive and most welcome restoration of Trebarried, a fine Jacobean property that stood ruined for many years.

This section of the A470, connecting Cardiff with Brecon, follows the Tarell valley to the south-west. The A470 is the main conduit for vehicles between north and south Wales and has been the subject of poems and contemporary works of art; even the newsletter of the Welsh Academy is named after it. From **Libanus**, the **Brecon Beacons National Park Mountain Centre** at Mynydd Illtud is sign-posted; it provides copious information and refreshments. On the open moorland, so Theophilus Jones assures us, a cairn marks the ancient burial place of St Illtud, founder of the celebrated Celtic monastery of Llanilltud Fawr in the Vale of Glamorgan. Nearby, the abandoned church, dedicated to the same saint, occupies a large circular graveyard of great antiquity.

The main road continues to climb as it approaches **Storey Arms**. There would have been an inn of that name here at one time but the temperance cause put paid to that. All the weary traveller has to look forward to today is one of those depressing mobile tea vans that seem to be parasitic to Welsh beauty spots. Better to investigate Craig Cerrig-gleisiad that rises steeply to the west. It is home to rare arctic flora. From Storey Arms the easiest but least interesting ascent of **Pen-y-Fan** can be made and backpackers are usually in evidence. Corn Du is approached past an obelisk commemorating the death of Tommy Jones, the five-year-old son of a Rhondda miner, whose body was found there on 2 September 1900. He was staying with his grandparents in Llyn Cwm Llwch below and had failed to return after setting off for an evening walk up the mountain, a cautionary tale. My favourite point of departure for this climb is from the car park in Cwm Gwdi, a valley that can be reached by car from Llan-faes on the outskirts of Brecon. This walk follows the crest of a ridge, Cefn Cwm Llwch, to the summit. The *llwch* in these place-names comes from the earlier Celtic word for lake (as in loch or lough); Llwch Llyn is therefore tautologous. A sprinkling of

Irish place-name elements in this landscape should not surprise us in Brychan's country. The road to Merthyr then descends past a cascade of reservoirs built in the Taf Fawr: Beacons, Cantref and Llwyn-on, each with mock mediaeval battlements.

West of Brecon, the A40, the old coach road, follows the Usk valley to Sennybridge. A stop should be made at **Llanspyddid**, not because there is now a great deal to see inside St Cadog's church after Buckeridge tidied it up in 1870, but in order to pay our respects to Aulach, father of Brychan, whose commemorative pillar stone is located on the north side of the churchyard. **Sennybridge** developed at the expense of the older settlement of Defynnog that lies a mile upstream following the arrival of the Neath to Brecon Railway in 1872. It has a modern army base, servicing the Epynt artillery range, and the ruins of a Norman keep, Castell Du. **Defynnog** has more of interest. St Cynog's church has, on its font, the only runic inscription to have been found in Wales and, at the base of the tower, a pillar stone inscribed in Latin and Ogham. The church has some distinguished incumbents. The vicarage next to the church was built in 1721 for Moses Williams, the antiquarian who assisted the great Edward Lhuyd. Theophilus Evans began his clerical career here as Williams' curate.

The Usk is fortunate in its bridges. That at **Aberbran**, built by Joseph Parry in 1791, incorporates seats for pedestrians. There is another noteworthy bridge at **Pantysorn on Ngallog**, before one of the finest Norman mottes in Wales, crowned with beech trees, comes into view at **Trecastle**. An old Roman road runs west along the spine of Mynydd Bach Trecastell towards the site of two Roman marching camps at **Y Pigwn** to look out over neighbouring Carmarthenshire. The parish church for Trecastle is at **Llywel**, further along the A40 where it leaves the Usk to make for the narrow pass of Cwm Dwr. Llywel was a fifth-century disciple of St Teilo. The church has an Ogham-inscribed pillar stone and a replica of the extraordinary sixth-century Llywel Stone, with its rich collection of inscriptions, pictographs and figure drawings. Originally located at Capel Ilud in Crai, it is now housed in the British Museum. On the churchyard wall is a memorial to David Owen (1795–1866), Baptist, turned Independent, turned Anglican, more commonly known in Welsh by his *nom-de-plume*, Brutus. Editor of the Welsh Anglican journal *Yr Haul*, he used its pages to pour scourn on Nonconformist preachers as 'noisy, ill-mannered Jacks', to belittle the value of the Welsh language and to promote the values of English conservatism.

The county boundary with Carmarthenshire is at **Halfway** – between Trecastle and Llandovery on the A40, that is. Two miles beyond the boundary, in a lay-by on the left hand side of the road is an obelisk, erected in 1841, known as the Coachman's Cautionary. It details the events leading to the plunge of a speeding stagecoach into the nearby ravine under the direction of its inebriated driver.

Returning to Defynnog, it is possible to follow the Senni valley, a stronghold of the Welsh language in an increasingly anglicised county, south to its source in **Fforest Fawr**. The road rises steeply into the former royal hunting ground, then better known as the Great Forest of Brecknock, a vast area of moorland plateau rising to over 700 metres. 'Forest' is here used, as at Radnor Forest, in its original sense of open hunting terrain. Hence, Forest Lodge to the east of **Heol Senni**, a village celebrated as the birthplace of the only bishop to have played rugby for Wales. The Rt. Revd. W.T. Havard was capped in 1919 and later became Bishop of St Asaph and Bishop of St Davids. At **Ystradfellte**, the Mellte flows underground, briefly reappears, before disappearing finally into Porth-yr-Ogof, a cavern some 500 metres long. This spot regularly attracts cavers who follow the river underground but for walkers there are paths that lead to impressive views of three contrasting waterfalls rushing down the darkly wooded valley.

The Welsh for waterfall in this locality is *sgwd* and appears in the names of the many waterfalls in this limestone country. To return directly to Brecon, take the main road that marks the county boundary with Glamorgan from **Penderyn**, where Welsh whiskey is distilled, to join the A470 at the Beacons reservoir.

To return to Defynnog cross Fforest Fawr by following the Tawe upstream from **Ystradgynlais**, a surprising outpost of industrialisation in a rural county. It owes its appearance to the invention, by George Crane and David Thomas of the Ynyscedwyn ironworks in 1837, of a method of smelting iron ore using the local anthracite. David Thomas took the technique with him to Pennsylvania when he emigrated to the United States in 1839. The arches of the ironworks survive as their memorial. The decline of heavy industry in the last century and the failure of subsequent attempts at replacing lost jobs with light industry – an electric clock factory quickly became known as *Y Ffatri Tic-Toc* – has proved an almost impossible challenge for this resilient Welsh-speaking community. Its sterling qualities have been captured forever on the canvases of Josef Herman (1929–2000), the Polish artist who came to live here at the end of the Second World War and who made the town and its people the sympathetic subject of his art. The church, another Cynog dedication, has an Early Christian pillar stone with Latin inscription.

The architectural severity of **Craig-y-Nos** belies the romance of the place. Here, in 1878, Adelina Patti (1843–1919), considered by Verdi to be the finest soprano of her generation, arrived to set up home in a house originally built for Rhys Powell in 1842. Wales had spent half a century determinedly turning itself into a Land of Song and Madam Patti's arrival seemed a triumphant recognition of these efforts. The Diva and the nation revelled in mutual admiration: Madam Patti was the sensation of the 1889 National Eisteddfod held in Brecon, arriving theatrically late in her special train on the Neath to Brecon Railway. In 1891 she had a house theatre built, a miniature Bayreuth, and embarked on a series of concerts and opera performances. The house now accommodates the Opera School Wales which gives regular performances in the theatre and its gardens are a country park, the famous greenhouse having been moved to Victoria Park in Swansea, where, renamed the Patti Pavilion, it serves as a performance venue.

A little to the north is the cave complex of **Dan-yr-Ogof**, regrettably commercialised with lurid lighting and facetious names for the stalactites and stalagmites but worth a visit nonetheless. Children love it. There are two separate cave systems, discovered in 1912 and 1953 respectively, the latter containing the enormous Cathedral Cave. The lane to the north at Tafarn-y-Garreg, an old drovers' inn, leads past a bronze age stone circle and standing stones to Bwlch Cerrig Duon, the best place from which to ascend the **Carmarthen Fan**, one of the classic hill walks of Wales. The path leads onto the ridge that links Llyn-y-Fan Fach and Llyn-y-Fan Fawr, crossing the county boundary as it does so at 802 metres. The main road returns past the reservoir to Defynnog.

Through mountain and vale, all roads converge on the former county town of **Brecon** where, in 1923, the priory church of St John the Evangelist became a cathedral. The town is situated at the confluence of the rivers Usk, Tarell and Honddu, the latter giving the town its Welsh name of Aberhonddu. Wales was the first part of Britain to have state secondary education (in 1889) and comprehensive schools (in 1951) and the country has few 'public' schools, a confusing English usage meaning private school. One of its most celebrated public schools is **Christ College**, Brecon, a collegiate institution reformed as a public school in 1853, which vies with Llandovery College for Welsh rugby caps. Originally a Dominican friary, the buildings were lucky to suffer only a change of use at the Reformation. The Large and Small Hall are fine mediaeval structures with timber roofs. Prichard and Seddon restored the friary chapel where there is good stained glass and fine ecclesiastical monuments, the grandest of the latter commemorating the Lucy family. The Library, built in 1880, completes an ensemble of High Victorian architecture.

The majestic seven-arched bridge over the Usk into Brecon was improved in 1794 by Thomas Edwards, son of William Edwards who spanned the Taf at Pontypridd. The bridge can best be viewed from the gardens of the Castle Hotel that incorporates the remains of the eleventh-century Norman castle of Bernard de Neufmarché. The motte and ruined keep are in the Bishop's garden across the road from the hotel. There are only a few traces of the town walls left following their destruction during the Civil War; the best can be inspected along the promenade known as Captain's Walk.

Brecon became a county town when Henry VIII created Breconshire from the commotes of Builth, Blaenllynfi and The Hay. The Grecian Shire Hall (1842) is one of Wyatt's better efforts and, since the local government changes of 1974, when Breconshire was subsumed into Powys, now houses an excellent county museum and art gallery. The preservation of the historic Court Room as an assize court of 1880 is particularly successful. The museum also displays one of the finest Early Christian monuments from Powys, the tenth-century pillar cross from Maesmynys, and the dug-out canoe from Llangors Lake. St Mary's has been the town's parish church since the elevation of the priory church to cathedral status. It occupies an unusual position, literally at the centre of town, encircled by manoeuvring traffic. A statue of Wellington stands guard at the head of The Bulwark, a square containing good Georgian buildings, including the Wellington Hotel. Wellington has no particular Brecon connection, but the sculptor was a local boy, John Evan Thomas (1810–1873), a pupil of Chantrey.

Nearby are plaques to mark the birthplaces of Sarah Siddons (1755–1831), the actress, Theophilus Jones, the antiquarian, and Thomas Coke the Wesleyan Methodist. Sarah Siddons was the daughter of Roger Kemble and niece of John Ward, two eighteenth-century impresarios. Thomas Coke's Memorial chapel stood where the Co-op superstore stands today. Beside Watergate Baptist chapel, near the castle, is a charming curiosity: one of Penfold's hexagonal pillar-boxes. Bethel Calvinistic Methodist chapel, a fine building dating from 1852, survives as Boots the Chemist. The Plough Congregational chapel in Lion Street has its origins in a 'gathered church' at Aberllyfni. In 1699, a chapel was built on the site of a public house called The Plough and successive chapels on this site have retained the name. The former Congregational Memorial College at Camden Court, now sheltered accommodation, opened in 1869. An insecure, peripatetic institution, it had come to Brecon via Abergavenny, Oswestry, Wrexham, Llanfyllin, and Newtown. Its last Principal, the saintly Dr Pennar Davies (1911–1996), moved with the college to Swansea in 1959, sadly ending a distinguished chapter in the town's educational history.

The Watton, the main road to the east, has the South Wales Borderers Museum, with their barracks close by. As the 'Old 24th', they won the lasting affection of empire loyalists for their defence of Rorke's Drift in the 1879 Zulu War. The head of the Brecon and Monmouth Canal reached here in 1812 but was only commercially viable for a generation. By 1900, there was only one boat working the entire length of the canal from Newport to Brecon and that ceased to operate in 1933. Pleasure boat trips now operate from the wharf where, in 1997, an exciting new arts centre was opened for the town, Theatr Brycheiniog.

The architectural treasure of Brecon is its **Cathedral**, on the northern edge of the town beside the road to Upper Chapel. Bernard de Neufmarché, who founded the

Norman town, granted the 'Church of St John the Evangelist Without the Walls' to his confessor, Roger, a Benedictine monk from Battle Abbey in Sussex. (The village of Battle, named after the abbey, lies to the west on the banks of the Ysgir.) The hillside Priory was completed by the twelfth century. At the Reformation, the Prior's House passed into the hands of Sir John Price (1502–1555) who was one of those charged with oversight of the Dissolution of the monasteries and a church commissioner for Wales. One of the principal architects of Tudor Wales, he was responsible for the first book to be printed in Welsh, known by its opening phrase, *Yn y lhyvyr hwnn* (1547). The Priory became the parish church. Another Price, Sir Hugh (1495–1574) founded Jesus College, Oxford, in 1571. The fortunate consequence of the Reformation in Brecon, therefore, was the survival of an attractive group of conventual buildings that have since returned to something close to their original function, following the establishment of the Cathedral for the new Church in Wales diocese of Swansea and Brecon in 1923. The interior of the Cathedral, sensitively restored by Sir Gilbert Scott and W.D. Caroë, frees the eye to admire the chancel, a precious example of the Early English style of architecture. A series of chapels dedicated to mediaeval trades' guilds include fine monuments and works of art, including a memorial to Bishop Bevan by Goscombe John. There is also a Regimental Chapel of the South Wales Borderers.

Two kilometres to the northeast of Brecon, the village of **Llanddew** preserves shades of mediaeval Welsh ecclesiastical history. Here, the Bishop of St Davids had an occasional residence; all that remains is an arch, a wall and Bishop Gower's Well, a reminder of the holy well tradition, dating back to Celtic times, that was so effectively suppressed by the Reformation. Gerald of Wales, as Archdeacon of Brecon, came to live here in 1175. The glory of the village is its beautifully proportioned church, dedicated to St David. The interior suffers from recent over-pointing, but a Maltese cross reminds us that Archbishop Baldwin was Gerald's guest here when he was preaching the Third Crusade in 1188.

For good views, follow the lanes up to Llandefalle Hill before returning to the isolated church at **Llandefalle**, a surprisingly grand perpendicular building dedicated to Maelog with a good screen and memorials by the Brute family of stonemasons from Llanbedr Ystrad Yw. For contrast, continue a mile or so north-east of the church, where a simple Independent chapel was built in 1803 beside **Brechfa Pool**. At **Llanfilo**, beyond the Dulas, the parish church has a delightful interior with original pews and more Brute memorials. Its treasure, however, is the well-restored early sixteenth-century rood screen, almost a match for that at Patrishow, with intricately plaited leaves and pomegranates. The castle (Cadw) at **Bronllys**, to the south-east of the present settlement, dates from the beginning of the Norman subjection of Brycheiniog in the early 1090s. Its later, round keep built by Walter de Clifford, survives. The largest building in Bronllys is the well-proportioned former tuberculosis sanatorium, built during the First World War, on the grounds of a house that Howell Harris had built at Pont-y-wal.

Talgarth, a tricky road junction, has another hospital and a large church, dedicated to Gwendoline, one of Brychan's daughters, who is reputedly buried here. The house beside the church, Neuadd Felen, was the home of Jane Williams, Ysgafell (1806–1885), an unjustly neglected poet and social historian, and author of the fantastical *The Paper People*, published in 1856 with illustrations by Lady Llanover. The church is celebrated for its association with Howell Harris, the indefatigable organiser of Welsh Calvinistic Methodism. It was during a sermon preached by the minister the Revd. Pryce Davies on Palm Sunday 1735 that Harris was converted with momentous consequences for

Wales. Like John Wesley three years later, Harris felt his heart strangely warmed, and like his English contemporary, felt compelled to preach the Gospel beyond the confines of consecrated ground. A sermon by Harris in this churchyard in 1736 had a similar effect on the young William Williams, Pantycelyn, whose uncle was minister with the Independents at nearby Tredustan. The new enthusiasm was to shape the destiny of Wales for the next two centuries. Inside the church there are interesting monuments, including one to Howell Harris, another to his elder brothers Joseph and Thomas, and another to William Vaughan, the latter of interest because it is the work of Aaron Brute.

Harris's character was frankly unattractive: he was at once quarrelsome and priggish, snobbish and pig-headed, hyperactive and a social climber. We can follow him southwest of the town, to Trefeca, where he withdrew from public life in 1752, after an acrimonious dispute with his brothers in Christ. Here he established a kind of kibbutz based on the Moravian ideas that were such an important influence on the Methodist Revival. The community was housed in a building often described as Strawberry Hill Gothic, that may well have been designed by the indefatigable Harris himself. It was the source of contemporary astonishment. One room had an all-seeing divine eye as a ceiling decoration, another incorporated a spy-hole for Harris's personal use, to check that members of the community were indeed, as John Wesley was to find them, 'all diligent, all constantly employed, all fearing God and working righteousness'. Members, drawn from both sexes, lived a communal life, strictly methodistical, working a 280-hectare farm and worshipping three times a day. At its height, 'The Family' numbered 120. For John Wesley the place was a 'little paradise', and Lady Huntingdon, George Whitefield, Benjamin La Trobe and other distinguished visitors concurred. A keen agricultural improver, Harris joined the first

Welsh county agricultural society in 1755; it met at the Golden Lion in Brecon. Ever keen to fend off criticism that Methodism was in some way subversive, he demonstrated his loyalty by forming a Trefeca Militia. The youngest son, he had been doubly rejected by his social superiors, first in love, then as a candidate for holy orders. By the end of his life Howell Harris had made himself, by act of will, the squire and parson of his own earthly estate. From 1842 to 1906 Trefeca was a theological seminary for the Calvinistic Methodists and today Coleg Trefeca continues to function as a non-denominational retreat centre incorporating a fascinating museum. Nearby, Trefeca Fawr, once owned by the Rebecca Prosser after whom the village is named, also passed into the Harrisian circle. It has the most remarkable seventeenth-century plaster ceiling in the county.

Further up the Llynfi valley is **Llangors** (Llyn Syfaddan), the second largest natural lake in Wales and one well-known to archaeologists for its crannog, a rare Welsh example of a prehistoric – probably iron age – defended settlement, more commonly found in Ireland. Crannogs are built on artificial islands and use the lake as a natural moat. There are associated local legends of a drowned city in the 'bottomless' lake. Gerald of Wales, who knew the place well, regarded it as a place of wonder: its waters turning green to foretell invasions or becoming streaked with blood to presage other disasters. Even its waterfowl, he noted, were clairvoyant.

South of the lake, at **Llangasty Talyllyn**, is a fascinating monument to the Tractarian Movement, in the form of a group of buildings – house, church and school. Their patron was Robert Raikes, a relative of the more famous Robert Raikes from Gloucester who is known as 'the father of the English Sunday school'. This equally earnest Yorkshireman acquired the nearby Treberfedd estate in 1848 and set about introducing High Church practices into this part of rural Wales. The restored church displays remarkably intact Oxford Movement features, for example, the stoup in the porch. The architect, for both the restoration of Treberfedd and the church as well for the new school, was John Loughborough Pearson, whose masterpiece was to be Truro cathedral.

From Talgarth, the A479 heads south through The Forest to Crickhowell. **Castell Dinas**, near Pengenffordd, at 450 metres, is the highest castle site in Wales. This strategic location was in near continuous use from prehistoric times to the early modern period; Owain Glyn Dŵr used it as his operational base in 1401. **Llanfihangel Cwm-du**, on the banks of the Rhian-goll, was restored in the early 1830s by its incumbent, Carnhuanawc. His deep antiquarian interests account for a number of interesting survivals in the church, including a pillar stone inscribed in Latin and Ogham, a royal arms in marble, a Gothic organ and a churchyard preaching cross. He had a cromlech and a menhir erected in the garden of his vicarage. His sandstone tombstone, large and weathered, stands to the north-east of the church.

Tretower Castle (Cadw) was built by descendants of the original Norman occupiers of the Usk valley; in 1401, it was held for the king by Sir James Berkeley against Owain Glyn Dŵr. **Tretower Court** (Cadw) is a remarkable survival of mediaeval domestic architecture: a fourteenth-century manor house from which all later accretions have been removed. It passed into the possession of the Vaughan family in the fifteenth century. Charles Vaughan was the uncle of Henry Vaughan, the Silurist. The Court has had its woodwork painstakingly restored but is, as yet, empty of period furniture. The attractive courtyard is used for summer drama productions.

Crickhowell is the anglicised form of Crug Hywel, the name still in use to describe the hillfort 450 metres high up on the slopes of Pen Cerrig-calch that dominates the town. Approaching the town from the west is Gwern-vale, now a hotel, where Sir George Everest (1790–1866) was born.

Appointed Surveyor-General of India in 1830, at the end of his life he reluctantly agreed for the world's highest mountain to be named after him. He is buried in the churchyard of St Edmund's church; its interior is spacious and plain but with good monuments. T.H. Wyatt made a surprisingly good job of the Italianate Town Hall (1833–1834). The thirteen-arched stone bridge over the Usk, the longest stone bridge in Wales, is remarkable for having twelve arches on one side and thirteen on the other! Large parts of the Norman castle were pulled down in the nineteenth century when the fabric became unsafe.

Across the bridge is **Llangatwg**. The church is dedicated to St Cadoc, one of Brychan's sons. It has a formidable tower and inside the church are the former village stocks and whipping post and one of the best collections of Brute monuments. Returning to Brecon following the south bank of the Usk is slower but more attractive. The road has the river to one side and the canal to the other for several kilometres, the slopes of **Mynydd Llangatwg** rising beyond the canal. Under this mountain, in 1960, students from the University of Wales found the most extensive cave system in the British Isles. Now the large resident bat population is joined at regular intervals by cavers making their descent from **Craig y Ciliau**, where the nature reserve has rare Alpine flora. The mountain road from Llangynidr to Beaufort is one of the highest in Britain, reaching 516 metres at Cefn Onnau. The views back north are wonderful and the landscape contains numerous bronze age cairns.

Llangynidr has another splendid stone bridge over the Usk. With six great arches, it is possibly the oldest bridge on the river dating back to around 1600. **Mynydd Llangynidr** is the site of the Chartist Cave, where Chartist meetings were held prior to the march on Newport in 1839; it makes the object of a good circular walk from Llangynidr using Dyffryn Crawnon and Cwm Cleisfer. After a sequence of canal locks, the riverside church of **Llanddetty** looks all tranquillity but the bullet hole in the church door hints at more turbulent times. For this was the church where the Puritan Colonel Jenkin Jones, born nearby in Tŷ Mawr, was the incumbent during the Interregnum. When news reached him in 1660 that Charles II was being invited to return to England unconditionally, he mounted his horse and fired his pistol at the door, exclaiming, 'Ah, thou whore of Babylon, thou'll have it all thy own way now!' It is not known what became of him subsequently. As if to rub salt into his wounds, the church continues to display prominently the royal arms of Charles II, as required by the Clarendon Code. The Colonel's house, Llanddetty Hall is further along the road after another lock. Ironically, it was later the home of Disraeli's wife, Mrs Lewis.

We should cross the river at **Talybont-on-Usk** to pay our respects to the poet Henry Vaughan (1620–1695), the Silurist, one of the great Metaphysical Poets. He was born in the farmhouse of Newton and is buried in the churchyard at Llansanffraid where his brother was the rector. His poetry is sublime:

> There is in God (some say)
> A deep, but dazzling darkness; As men here
> Say it is late and dusky, because they
> See not all clear;
> O for that night! where I in him
> Might live invisible and dim

Vaughan was a monarchist; certainly Welsh-speaking, he chose to write his poetry in what he regarded as the civilising language of English. The tragedy of Civil War can thus be encompassed by making the short river crossing from Jenkin Jones' Llanddetty to Henry Vaughan's Llansanffraid.

The **Black Mountains**, north of Crickhowell are one of the most deliciously unspoiled parts of Wales, preserving the timeless character of rural life in ways that are nowadays unexpected. Symptomatic of this rural charm is the work of the Brute family of **Llanbedr Ystrad Yw**, memorial sculptors to the churches and chapels hereabouts for several generations. Working in a rustic, primitivist style that has only recently received due recognition, Brute monuments are characterised by careful lettering and ruddy-cheeked cherubs. Often described as slate work, close inspection of the memorials shows them to be of painted sandstone. St Peter's church has a memorial to the infant son of the family patriarch, Thomas Brute (1698–1767). There are more Brute memorials on the outside wall of the church. Llanbedr sits on the west bank of the Grwyne Fechan as it rushes down from the Black Mountains to join the Grwyne Fawr just below the village.

By following the Grwyne Fawr, it is possible to reach one of the best-preserved and most delightfully situated mediaeval parish churches in Wales, at **Patrishow**. Isolation preserved this church from Thomas Cromwell's men and it is possible by lingering here to soak up the atmosphere of Welsh religion before the Reformation. The fifteenth-century rood loft and screen is deservedly famous, with its elaborate carving of the dragon, representing the Evil One, consuming the vine, representing Gospel Truth. There is a remarkable Doom figure painted on the west wall of the nave and an early mediaeval inscribed font. The holy well and carved Maltese cross at Ffynnon Ishow, beside the stream that cuts through Patrishow Hill below the church, augment the mediaeval atmosphere. St Isio was martyred here and his relics lie in Capel-y-bedd, a separate chapel abutted at the west end of the nave. The only hint of the Reformation comes in the form of the fine 1620 Welsh Bible. There are also monuments by three generations of the Brute family. Outside, the south-facing wall has seats incorporated into it facing a fine preaching cross. This is an extraordinary site to visit at any time of year; in early spring, when the churchyard bursts with primroses and daffodils, it is simply magical.

Hay-on-Wye is a phenomenon. A sleepy market town, until the arrival of Richard Booth in 1965, it now claims to be the second-hand book capital of the world and hosts a major international literary festival in May each year. The heart of this transformation was the old cinema that Booth filled indiscriminately with second-hand books after the last film had been screened. Bookworms began to arrive in increasing numbers and they attracted other specialist booksellers. Now, every other shop specialises in some aspect or other of the book trade: rare editions from private presses, antique maps and prints, children's books, books on gardening, even books in Slavonic languages. A high proportion of the remainder of the shops is given over to cafés, bistros or restaurants. Richard Booth, self-proclaimed King of Hay, lives in the castle in the middle of town where surplus books may be collected free of charge from his courtyard. Once he offered surplus stock for sale as fuel for wood-burning stoves. Bundles of books were given different thermal ratings according to their subject matter: erotica was the fastest burning, Welsh theology the slowest! As for the locals, they must buy their groceries in Hereford.

The Hay, as the locals call it (Y Gelli, in Welsh), is a border town, the point of entry for the Normans into Breconshire. As was their wont, they threw up a motte in a meander of the Wye and laid out an enclosure, known in Norman French as *La Haie*. When the railway came to Hay-on-Wye – another Savin engineering project, linking Hereford to Brecon – the station was located in England. This charming old market town has a fine townscape: of note are the Cheese and Butter Markets, the former rebuilt in 1840 to serve as the Town Hall, the latter taking the form of a Doric temple. The oldest surviving building is The Three Tuns on the corner of Bridge Street, a small sixteenth-century cruck hall.

South-east of the town, the road follows the Dulas before climbing the scarp of the Black Mountains to a point below Hay Bluff where it descends through Gospel Pass to join the Honddu in the Vale of Ewyas. Offa's Dyke runs along the ridge to the east separating the Vale of Ewyas from the Olchon valley in Herefordshire. According to the late Professor Phil Williams, Pen-y-Gadair Fawr is the highest point at that latitude (51.95°N) between Saskatoon and Novosibirsk, knowledge of which can only invigorate a walk along this section of Offa's Dyke. At **Capel-y-ffin**, Breconshire meets Monmouthshire. Capel-y-ffin means the border chapel, although whichever border is being specified here, and there are several to choose from – England and Wales, Llandaff and St Davids, The Hay and Ewyas – must pre-date the Tudor county boundary. This chapel of ease is a quaint little building; it reminded Kilvert of an owl. It has some good period interior fittings. In 1869, Father Ignatius (Revd. Joseph Lyne, 1837–1908) chose this place to found an Anglican Benedictine monastery. Under his direction elaborate building work commenced in an attempt to replicate nearby Llanthony Abbey, the ruins of which he had failed to purchase. Needless to say, the plans were over-ambitious. Building ceased in 1882 and in 1920 the vaults collapsed. A church and scaled-down cloister remain intact. The buildings later passed into the hands of Eric Gill (1882–1940) who established an artist colony here that attracted the likes of Laurie Cribb and David Jones (1895–1974). There are examples of Eric Gill's celebrated calligraphy on graves both in the chapel burial ground and in the monastery, as well as on the beams of another chapel Gill had organised in the main house.

There is something bizarre about the vocation of Father Ignatius, and it is not easy for this Calvinist to warm to his elaborate processions, all bells-and-smells, not to mention the apparitions of Our Lady in a rhubarb clump. On the other hand it is only fair to report that Kilvert, no Puseyite, found him genuine enough, even if the monks he gathered around him seemed a bunch of misfits. A man of unflinch-ing convictions, who earned his place in the pantheon of Welsh eccentrics, his grave lies close to the site of the high altar. Since the career of Eric Gill has also fallen under the shadow of scandal, perhaps we should clear our heads before departing the county by visiting the simple eighteenth-century Baptist chapel tucked away behind the chapel of ease. The cause here is a very early one, dating back to 1663 and members were baptised in the river Honddu in view of the chapel; there is a Brute gravestone in the burial ground. A path behind the chapel leads over the ridge to the Olchon valley in Herefordshire, cradle of the Welsh Baptist cause.

II
South Wales

5

Monmouthshire

THE INCLUSION OF MONMOUTHSHIRE in the Oxford Circuit, following the Act of Union when the remainder of Wales was placed under the jurisdiction of the Court of Great Sessions, gave rise to intermittent claims subsequently that the county was not properly part of Wales. References to 'Wales and Monmouthshire' were still being made in the 1960s but historic and contemporary realities have now combined to suppress such nonsense. Welsh was widely spoken in the county until the eighteenth century and survived in the country districts into the middle years of the nineteenth; although rapid decline set in with compulsory schooling in English, there are hopeful signs that the bilingual schools movement of the late twentieth century may arrest and reverse the trend.

From Hay Bluff, 677 metres above the Wye, a magnificent section of the Offa's Dyke Path follows the high ridge between the Olchon valley on the English side and the Vale of Ewyas as it descends from Breconshire into Monmouthshire on the Welsh side. To the west, kestrels, ravens and ring ouzels soar and glide over the treeless rocky ridges of Darren Llwyd and Tarren-yr-Esgob. The path continues with the Black Hill to the north and The Vision farm below, both incorporated into Bruce Chatwin's *On the Black Hill*, a moving evocation of rural life in this territory in the first half of the twentieth century. The film of the book opens with memorable aerial celebration of Welsh border country.

Below Black Darren (*tarren* being the Welsh for knoll), there are wonderful views of **Llanthony Priory** (Cadw), founded in 1103 by William de Lacey for the Austin Friars. It is the Honddu, as it runs through the Vale of Ewyas, which gives the priory its Welsh name, Llanddewi Nant Honddu. The priory ruins are some of the most beautifully evocative in the country, and walkers should allow time to make the detour. They can find both refreshment and accommodation at the Abbey Hotel, a hostelry that was originally built into the priory ruins as a shooting box by Colonel Mark Wood MP in 1803. The west tower, transept and enough of the nave walls and arcades of the priory survive to conjure up the spirit of a mediaeval monastery, especially in the evening when the setting sun intensifies the colour of the local red sandstone from which the priory was constructed. In 1808, Wood sold the property to the English writer Walter Savage Landor (1775–1864) who moved here from Bath to escape from his wife. Like Father Ignatius at Capel-y-ffin, he had ambitious plans to reconstruct the ruins and develop an ideal community in the Welsh hills but unlike him he was sadly deficient in saintly attributes. Disappointed in the failure of his schemes, he heaped racist abuse on the locals: '. . . if drunkenness, idleness, mischief and revenge are the principal characteristics of the savage state, what nation, I will not say in Europe, but in the world, is so utterly tattooed with them as the Welsh? . . . I shall never cease to wish that Julius Caesar had utterly exterminated the whole race of Britons. I am convinced that they are as irreclaimable as Gypsies or Malays.' Before long, he had departed the area for good, bound for Florence. The former infirmary forms the parish church of St David, which has good rustic wall tablets, including one by J. Brute. The barn at the entrance from the road used to be the abbey gatehouse.

Not far down the valley is the attractive church at **Cwmyoy**, its leaning tower the result of land slippage. It has a raised churchyard with the ruined stump of a preaching cross, and good memorials inside and out, including several

Brutes. The church has an idyllic setting, with a number of good properties around it. Not far below the churchyard gate is the remains of a cider mill, a reminder that this county traditionally shared the Herefordshire taste for cider. The Honddu swings north at **Llanfihangel Crucorney** to join the Monnow. Here, Llanfihangel Court, a Tudor manor house, opens to the public in the summer months. It is famous for its tree-lined avenues, especially the huge Spanish chestnuts. Raymond Williams (1921–1988), the Welsh critic and novelist, was born in **Pandy** where his father worked as a railway signalman. The village was the inspiration for his novel, *Border Country*. His *People of the Black Mountains* engages with the early history of this territory, from prehistoric times to the Battle of Agincourt. Pandy has two quirky chapels, Zoar for the Baptists and Hope for the Calvinistic Methodists. In the latter, John Davies (1843–1917), the antiquary, ministered for 47 years; he is buried in the chapel graveyard.

Monmouthshire takes its name from the Monnow (*Mynwy*, in Welsh), a river that has its source in England near the remains of Craswall Priory. It enters Wales at Glandŵr, then forms the national boundary as far as **Monmouth Cap**, a village that took its name from a public house named after the knitted headwear for which Monmouth was once famous. The B4347 follows the Monnow down to Monmouth, but before following it we should make a brief border incursion to visit **Kilpeck**, situated in the heart of what was once the Welsh enclave of Ergyng, later anglicised as Archenfield. Both names derive from the Roman fort of *Ariconium*. The twelfth-century church of St Mary and St David (Llanddewi Cilpeddig, in Welsh) is a renowned masterpiece of mediaeval ecclesiastical sculpture. Two Welsh warriors wearing Phrygian caps guard the entrance at the south door. For centuries after the fixing of the county boundaries in 1536, parts of Herefordshire remained Welsh in speech. In the Teme valley, the altar rail of St Mary's church at **Llanfair Waterdine**, fashioned from the church's rood screen, is inscribed in Welsh. Significantly, Queen Elizabeth appointed the Bishop of Hereford in addition to the Welsh Bishops to supervise the translation of the scriptures into Welsh. The coming together here of Celtic, Anglo-Saxon, Scandinavian and Romanesque traditions to produce an artistic masterpiece celebrates the peculiar richness of material and spiritual life that has characterised the Border tradition.

Together with Skenfrith and White Castle, **Grosmont** is one of the Three Castles that form the Trilateral, a defensive triad around Graig Syfyrddin, a partly wooded hill rising to 423 metres. The castle (Cadw) was built by William Fitz Osbern to control this fertile country and the routes that pass through it. Grosmont, as its name suggests, is a great mound on which the ruins of Hubert de Burgh's original tower still stand. The remarkable fifteenth-century chimney is a later addition. There is a deep moat, now dry, but surrounded by good stands of oak and ash. St Nicholas's church has been too big for its congregation for centuries. Seddon, in his imaginative restoration of 1869, restricted the area used for worship to the transept by means of a glazed screen that renders the Early English nave with its vaulted ceiling redundant. The latter houses a great chest known as the Grosmont Hutch and the effigy of a knight. A stained glass window in the chancel, depicting the Feeding of the Five Thousand, commemorates J.E. Rolls of The Hendre, who funded the restoration. Grosmont never recovered from being sacked by the forces of Owain Glyn Dŵr in 1405. The remains of a considerable civil and military settlement now lie under the fields.

The road cuts through wooded hills to Norton, whence it is but a short distance to the border settlement of **Skenfrith,** where the castle guards the strategic bridge over the Monnow. In Welsh the town is Ynysgynwraidd, the Isle of Cynwraidd, a sixth-century chieftain. Skenfrith Castle

(Cadw) has a rectangular bailey surrounded by a curtain-wall with rounded towers. Inside, there is a rounded keep perched on its motte. Hubert de Burgh had the castle constructed in the early thirteenth century. The church of St Bridget, the Irish domestication of the Virgin Mary who became the focus of a mediaeval cult in western Britain, here has her most easterly dedication in Wales. The saint is depicted on the modern lectern, with the acorns of her home church of Kildare, the church of the oaks in Irish, *Cill Dara*. Externally, the two-tiered pyramidal dovecote timber belfry serves a defensive purpose. Internally, the church is notable for the quality of its tombs and pews. Of the former, the elaborate tomb of the last governor of the Three Castles, John Morgan, Steward of the Duchy of Lancaster, who died in 1557, is justly celebrated, as is the elaborate Jacobean Morgan family pew. In the church, there are two representations of the pomegranate, an Early Christian symbol of eternal life: on the sanctuary carving of the Spanish royal coat-of-arms and on the church's treasure, the magnificent fifteenth-century embroidered cope. The village is spacious and peaceful, with nothing much to disturb the sound of water tumbling over the weir of the mill-leet. For the best view over it, climb Coedanghred Hill to the south.

White Castle (Cadw) has the most spectacular remains of the Trilateral. It is situated midway between Skenfrith and Abergavenny off the B4521. It has a deep moat that is filled with water. In spring the sides of the moat are all primroses and daffodils, and the resident ducks are at their most active. The plan of the defences is elaborate: the Inner Ward is reached through a gatehouse which in turn is guarded by a Hornwork, a crescent-shaped island on which defences once stood. The castle was re-fortified around 1270 by Edmund of Lancaster against Llywelyn ap Gruffudd. From the towers there are good views of the **Skirrid** (NT), the legendary mount of Ysgyryd Fawr, an outlier of old red sandstone from the Black Mountains situated on the northern outskirts of Abergavenny. Rising to 486 metres, the mount had a chapel dedicated to St Michael, of which traces survive, that was the object of pilgrimage before the Reformation; a car park is provided for latter-day pilgrims. The cleft in the side of the mount was reputed to have occurred simultaneously with the rending of the curtain in the Temple at the time of the Crucifixion. In March each year the Three Peaks Challenge takes place over the three peaks surrounding Abergavenny: Skirrid Fawr, Blorenge and Pen-y-fâl. After these exertions, refreshment might be sought at **Llanddewi Skirrid**, either at the Skirrid Inn, which claims to be the oldest tavern in Wales, or at the Walnut Tree, where Ann and Franco Taruschio created one of the finest restaurants in the country in an out-of-the-way country pub. St Teilo's church at **Llantilio Pertholey**, with its impressive Norman tower, has some of the best early Brute memorials and stained glass by John Petts.

Abergavenny occupies a strategic location on the Usk, commanding routeways from Hereford to the north, Raglan and Monmouth to the east, Brecon and Merthyr to the west and Newport to the south. The Romans had a fort here, *Gobannium*, and the Normans threw up a motte, the ruins of which can be seen beside the Angel Hotel. A nineteenth-century hunting-lodge, built on the site of the castle keep, now accommodates the Abergavenny Museum. A market town *par excellence*, its centre is the 1871 Town Hall in Cross Street with the prominent King's Head hotel next to it, of mediaeval origin. The Priory Church of St Mary was founded by the Benedictines in 1100 and flourished until it was destroyed by Owain Glyn Dŵr in 1403. Following the Reformation it became the parish church of the town. It has some intriguing treasures, including an extraordinary carved wooden Jesse, probably originally from the reredos, and in the Herbert Chapel some celebrated tombs of the owners of Raglan Castle, dating from the mid-fifteenth century. There were early dissenting congregations here in the mid-seventeenth century and, a century later, John Wesley found his audience here to be the best-dressed in Wales! For good views down onto the town, climb Pen-y-fâl, popularly known as the Sugar Loaf (NT), an outlier of the Black Mountains to the north-west of the town that rises to 598 metres.

West of Abergavenny, the **Brecon and Monmouth Canal** has been restored and reopened for recreational use. Built by William Crossley between 1809 and 1812 to transport coal, iron, lime and agricultural produce, pleasure boats can be hired to navigate the canal from the wharf at **Llanfoist**. The canal runs beside the great massif of Blorenge – a major venue for hang-gliding and paragliding competitions – to **Llanofer**, a name that immediately conjures up memories of a family that made a significant contribution to Welsh cultural life in the nineteenth century. The castellated gatehouse is all that remains of their home, Llanover Court, but there is a striking monument to Lord Llanover (1802–1867) in the churchyard of St Bartholomew's. As Benjamin Hall, he was Commissioner of Works in 1855 when the Gothic Revival Houses of Parliament were augmented by the clock that has since borne his name, Big Ben. In Wales, he was a prime mover for church reconstruction in the Llandaff diocese and an early advocate for the use of Welsh in church affairs. His wife, Augusta Waddington, Lady Llanover (1802–1896), was a folklorist. Her collection of costume drawings defined traditional Welsh costume and her name is commemorated in a folkdance, the Llanover Reel. She was also a temperance enthusiast, buying up public houses and turning them into coffee-houses. At her bequest, in 1898, a Welsh Church was built on the Llanover estate for the Calvinistic Methodists. Hanover Chapel (named after the Protestant dynasty and not a misnomer for Llanover) is an earlier and more attractive Independent chapel, founded by

Rees Davies in 1744. The Baptists have their attractively whitewashed eighteenth-century chapel in the eponymous Saron Lane. The canal continues south towards Pontypool via **Goetre**, where the Goytre Wharf Heritage Centre is a hive of activity. When the living of Goetre became vacant in 1860, the Marquess of Abergavenny, in whose power the appointment lay, opted for a non-Welsh speaker. The appointment was opposed by the bishop, with a court ruling in the bishop's favour following an acrimonious legal wrangle. The case is revealing of the transitional state of the language in this part of Monmouthshire a century and a half ago.

Returning to Monmouth from Abergavenny following the B4233, the church of St Teilo at **Llantilio Crossenny** appears to have been built on ancient earthworks. It was restored by Seddon and Prichard and contains some fine memorials, including a touching marble slab by Flaxman, showing Mary Ann Bosanquet on her deathbed in 1819 with her infant son, who died in his first year, sliding down sunbeams to greet her. Just to the north-west of the village is the rectangular moat of **Hen Gwrt** (Cadw), which was a residence for the Bishops of Llandaff in the Middle Ages and of the Herberts following the Reformation. The moat is magical in early summer with moorhens darting between the water lilies and with bulrushes, bur-reeds and water fig-worts to complete the picture. St Michael's church at **Llanfihangel Ystum Llywern** contains a brass plaque commemorating the county historian, Sir Joseph Bradney (1839–1933); he lived nearby at Talycoed Court.

The church of St Cadoc at **Llangattock vibon Avel** was substantially rebuilt by T.H. Wyatt as the Rolls family chapel. Inside the church, which retains its original Norman tower, are crumbling memorials to the Rolls family. Amongst the graves in the churchyard is that of Charles Stewart Rolls (1877–1910), the celebrated engineer and pioneer aviator. A rare seventeenth-century grave memorial in Welsh on a flat stone in the south porch reminds us that the language was once prevalent here: Llangattock School, on the Newcastle road, is a splendid example of Board School architecture. It opened in 1872 under auspices of Forster's 1870 Education Act, a piece of legislation that did much to accelerate the spread of the English language in Wales.

The Hendre, originally the shooting box of the Rolls family, had become their principal seat by 1830, thereafter dominating the life of the district for close on a century. In 1892 John Allan Rolls was elevated to the peerage as Baron Llangattock of the Hendre and put the finishing touches to a substantial country house that stood in 400 hectares of deer-park with a three-kilometre carriage drive laid out from Rockfield Lodge. The subsequent history of the family was a tragic one. Baron Llangattock's eldest son and heir, John Maclean Rolls died of bullet wounds inflicted at the Battle of the Somme. His younger brother, Charles Stewart Rolls, was the first British victim of an air crash when he died aged 33 in an aeronautics display over Bournemouth in 1910. Six years earlier he had entered into partnership with Mr Royce, opening an engine works, first at Crewe, then at Derby. The family never recovered from these blows and it fell to Lord Llangattock's only daughter, Lady Shelley-Rolls to divide up the estate. The deer-park is now a golf course for which The Hendre serves as the club-house. It would appear that sensitive restoration of the house is taking place, however, and it would be especially gratifying if this work were to be extended to include the gardens. There is a wonderful walled kitchen garden with pineapple house *in situ*.

Monmouth is reached by crossing the remarkable thirteenth-century Monnow Bridge, the only bridge in Wales to retain its defensive gate. West of the river, the small twelfth-century church of St Thomas-à-Becket in Overmonnow has its original Norman chancel arch. Prichard's restoration was in keeping with the church's

Norman origins. Monmouth is situated on a peninsula at the confluence of the Monnow and the Wye and has had a long history of flooding. Spacious Monnow Street, with its good red-brick town houses, formerly accommodated the mediaeval market. It leads to the town's mediaeval core, a constricted site at the narrowest point between meandering Monnow and Wye. The Norman castle nestles on the banks of the latter but only the Great Tower and Great Hall survive. Great Castle House (Cadw) was built in 1673 for the Marquess of Worcester, later to be elevated to Duke of Beaufort. It has an astonishing seventeenth-century interior with original plaster ceilings, paneling and chimneypiece. The building is still in military use by the Monmouthshire Royal Engineers who maintain a small museum.

St Mary's Church is close by in Priory Street, the latter named after the Breton Priory to which the church was originally entrusted. Geoffrey of Monmouth (1090–1155), author of the *History of the Kings of Britain*, a major Arthurian text that was a bestseller in its day, was probably a Breton member of the Marcher Lord of Monmouth's retinue. 'Geoffrey's Window', in Priory Street, is too recent to have had anything to do with him, although he did live in the priory. It was through the Breton connection that the Arthurian tales of the British entered the mainstream of European literature in what has been described as Wales' greatest contribution to European culture. The church was subject to major rebuilding work in the eighteenth and nineteenth centuries. Its churchyard contains an intriguing encrypted gravestone apparently devised by its subject to confuse the devil on the day of judgement. His four-word epitaph – *Here Lies John Renie* – is in the form of an acrostic of 285 characters. A housepainter by trade, John Renie, who died in 1832 aged 33, must also have been an accomplished mathematician.

The heart of the town is Agincourt Square, so named after the famous battle in which Henry V (1387–1422), who was born in Monmouth Castle, defeated the French against the odds with the aid of Welsh archers at Agincourt in 1415. Shakespeare has Fluellen remind the king that:

> 'the Welshmen did good service in a garden where leeks did grow, wearing the leeks in their Monmouth caps; which your majesty knows, to this hour is an honourable padge of their service; and I do believe your majesty takes no scorn to wear the leek upon Saint Tavy's day . . .'

The handsome Shire Hall, built in 1724, has a niche of Henry V set into its wall. In front is the prominent Goscombe John statue to Charles Stewart Rolls, proudly holding a model biplane. St James's Square has an 1837 Methodist Chapel, designed by George Vaughan Maddox, in Ionic style and Glendower Street has the magnificent 1844 Congregational chapel now attractively converted to offices. The assertive nineteenth-century mock-Gothic buildings of Monmouth School, founded by William Jones, a City of London haberdasher in 1614, cast their shadow over Wyebridge Street. The old bridge over the Wye at the end of the street, elegantly widened in 1879, leads us along the east bank of the Wye in the direction of Chepstow. For a good introduction to this historic town visit the Nelson Museum and Local History Centre, housed in the neo-classical former Market Hall in Priory Street; its collection of Nelson memorabilia was amassed by Georgina, Lady Llangattock.

The Kymin (NT), overlooking Monmouth on the east bank of the Wye, explains the Nelson connection. In the late eighteenth century, on summer Tuesdays, members of the local gentry would meet here to enjoy pleasant views and conversation, the latter made convivial by 'a cold collation, and a dessert of fruits, with wines and other liquors to a certain limitation'. In 1800, they erected a Naval Temple, to commemorate British victories. It was dedicated to the Duchess of Beaufort, daughter of Admiral

Boscawen. The small, square building is decorated with the medallions of the various commanders and the dates of their victories. Horatio Nelson (1758–1805) breakfasted here in 1802 with Sir William Hamilton and Emma en route to Pembrokeshire and was delighted with the temple describing it as 'the only monument of its kind erected to the English navy in the whole of the kingdom'.

From The Kymin it is possible to survey the Wye as it re-enters Wales from Herefordshire. The church of St Peter at **Dixton**, just to the north of Monmouth, has an exceptionally long nave; brass plates on the chancel arch record exceptional flood levels. **Wyastone Leys**, a house on the west bank of the Wye that derives its name from the prehistoric Wye Stone to be found in its grounds, was acquired in 1976 by Count Numa Labinsky (1925–1994), the son of a Russian émigré. He founded the specialist recording company *Nimbus* that subsequently built a state-of-the-art concert hall with an exceptional acoustic used both for making live recordings and for public concerts.

The main road to Chepstow follows the Wye south to the ruins of **Tintern Abbey** (Cadw) which, thanks to Wordsworth, continues to generate significant tourist revenue. His 1798 *Lines composed a few miles above Tintern Abbey* is a Romantic celebration of the most substantial abbey ruins in Wales. The abbey was founded in 1131 by Walter Fitz Richard, a Marcher Lord based in Chepstow. One of the earliest Cistercian houses in the British Isles, it was largely rebuilt in the course of the thirteenth century, when the abbey was under the patronage of Roger Bigod, the wealthy Earl of Norfolk, who had come into possession of Chepstow Castle. It is possible to trace the outline of a good deal of the monastic site but it is the extensive ruins of the abbey church that are the most evocative. Miraculously, the vaulted arcades of the nave and transept still stand with the windows retaining much of their original tracery; the glass has gone but the views out onto the wooded hillside more than compensate. For a good view of the abbey ruins from above, it is worth climbing up to another ruin, the derelict parish church of St Mary's Chapel Hill. Was this where Wordsworth stood and communed with 'these steep woods and lofty cliffs, and this green pastoral landscape'?

Narrow, winding lanes lead to **Wyndcliff**, from which vantage-point there are exceptional views into the Wye valley below and southwards over the Severn. A more direct route, up or down, is via the flight of 365 steps cut into the cliff by Osmond Wyatt in 1828 for the Duke of Beaufort. The steep cliffs of the Wye valley are well wooded with oak, spruce, wild yew and stands of beech and noted as one of the richest areas in the British Isles for white-beams. A large forest reserve has been created here that stretches northwards to Blackcliff. This area is a walker's paradise. The Wye Valley Walk, that covers 218 kilometres from Pumlumon to Chepstow, is here at its most spectacu-lar. The more challenging Offa's Dyke Path offers alterna-tive views from the opposite bank.

Chepstow Racecourse, the premier turf venue in Wales, was developed between the wars on a site formerly famed for its house and gardens. The house was Piercefield, an elegant pile built to the designs of John Soane and Joseph Bonomi from the profits of slave sugar by Valentine Morris (1727–1789), who was born in Antigua, the son of a plan-tation owner, and who returned to the West Indies to become Governor of St Vincent. His park, occupying an incised meander of the Wye, had all the accoutrements of the age: grotto, druid's temple and lover's leap, the latter a testing drop of over 50 metres. Clive of India, Joseph Banks and John Wesley were each favourably impressed as they passed by on their several projects. In 1802, the house was purchased by Nathaniel Wells, son of a Cardiff sugar plan-tation owner on St Kitts and one of his father's slaves. Educated in England, he inherited his father's estate and so became a slave owner himself. He rose to become Sheriff of the county and deputy lieutenant, exceptional for that era. Although derelict, the main façade of the house survives.

From here it is possible to return to Monmouth following the B4293 via the interesting village of **Trelleck**, a name deriving from the Welsh for three stones, *tri llech*. The three large bronze age megaliths, some two metres tall and rusty in colour, still stand to the south-west of the village. They are known locally as Harold's Stones; according to Gerald of Wales they commemorate Harold's victories over the Welsh. The megaliths are of geological interest being good examples of conglomerate, with alternative layers of sand, gravel and pebbles indicating a distant origin on the ocean floor. Tump Terret, a castle motte, lies hidden behind the houses. The fact that the Virtuous Well has been so well cared for is a reminder that this county had the highest proportion of recusancy in Wales. Dedicated to St Ann, the well was reputed to cure barrenness. It is a delightful surviving holy well, with liverwort, cresses and water speedwell adding to its charm. The church of St Nicholas has a preaching cross outside and contains a sundial that also used to stand outside following its erection in 1689 by Lady Magdalen Probert. On three sides there are representations of the village's principal monuments: stones, well and castle. Recent archaeological excavations suggest that Trelech may have been the largest urban centre in Wales in the thirteenth century.

Two of the finest castles in Wales are located in this south-east corner of the country, Chepstow and Raglan. This is not altogether surprising given their strategic importance in the March. Both were continuously occupied until the Civil War but whereas Cromwell's troops repaired the former, they destroyed the latter. Chepstow is one of the earliest Norman castles to be built in Wales, whereas Raglan is one of the latest. The sheer splendour of **Raglan Castle** (Cadw) astonishes as it is approached: this is as it was meant to be and the lack of any development around the castle perfectly preserves this mediaeval quality, a brilliant battleship in a grassy sea. The celebrated Yellow Tower of Gwent, the hexagonal Great Tower surrounded by its own moat with double drawbridge, was built by Sir William ap Thomas (1432–1445). His son, Sir William Herbert, elevated to Earl of Pembroke as a valued supporter of Edward IV during the Wars of the Roses, made rapid progress on the castle until he was beheaded in 1469. It had a fine Long Gallery and Hall with a hammerbeam roof. The castle stayed in the family through the Tudor period. As royalists in the Civil War, the Herberts endured a siege from which the castle never recovered. In 1683, the family was rewarded in the Restoration by the new title of Beaufort and began the construction of a new property at Badminton, in a location that finally severed their residual Welsh connection. Raglan is dwarfed by its castle and, since the A40 by-pass was built, has become sleepy and sedate. The church of St Cadoc, savagely restored by T.H. Wyatt in 1868, contains damaged fragments of Herbert effigies in its Beaufort Chapel. The first Lord Raglan (1788–1855) fought with Wellington in the Peninsular War before losing his sword arm at Waterloo. He was given command of British forces in the Crimea and gave the disastrous order for the Light Brigade to charge at Balaclava. His monument is the Raglan overcoat. Friends and admirers presented his son with Cefn Tilla Court, a seventeenth-century manor house south of **Llandenny** in 1858; it was then greatly enlarged by T.H. Wyatt. His grandson, the fourth Lord Raglan made a notable contribution to the history of his native county, collaborating with Sir Cyril Fox to produce the splendid, three-volume *Monmouthshire Houses*.

Chepstow, meaning market town in English, is very much a border town. Its impressive castle defends a strategic bend on the river and bridging point over the Wye. An old Welsh word for bend, *ystraigyl*, gave us the Marcher Lordship of Striguil, a territory combining parts of Monmouthshire and Gloucestershire, presided over by the Clare family from Chepstow for several generations. The primacy of the castle is conveyed in the current Welsh name for the town, *Cas-gwent*, Castle of Gwent. Good sections of the old town walls survive and it is satisfying to enter at the upper part of town through Town Gate. High Street then runs downhill, broadening into Beaufort Square, before separating into two narrower streets, Middle Street and St Mary's Street, that have good eighteenth- and nineteenth-century town houses. The former Assembly Rooms are in Beaufort Square. Bridge Street runs down to cross the Wye over the elegant iron bridge erected in 1816 by John Rastrick, on the advice of John Rennie. There is a classic textbook geological fold visible as the road turns sharply to the left beyond the bridge.

The view of **Chepstow Castle** (Cadw) from the iron bridge is dramatic. It stretches out to occupy its strategic position, with an exhilarating drop of limestone cliff beneath the Great Tower to the river below. If the Great Tower was indeed built by William Fitz Osbern – doubts have recently been cast on this supposition – then it would date from the 1060s. The great Norman military architect William Marshal came to Chepstow in 1189, following his marriage to Strongbow's daughter, one of the Clare family. The round towers and shooting-slits he introduced to Chepstow were novelties in the British Isles at the time. William Marshal's sons continued their father's work. At the end of the thirteenth century the castle passed into the hands of Roger Bigod, Earl of Norfolk, who added Marten's Tower, an immense round tower at the south-east corner of the site. In 1468, the castle was acquired by the Herberts who added the larger windows and fireplaces that were in vogue in the sixteenth century. The castle was besieged during the Civil War, falling twice to the Parliamentarians; damage was subsequently repaired and the castle was used as a garrison. One of the prisoners kept here was

Henry Marten, the regicide, one of the judges at the trial of Charles I.

His tomb can be seen inside the cavernous parish church of St Mary's Priory: it has an acrostic inscription that he composed himself. Originally a Benedictine priory, the church has suffered at the well-meaning hands of several Victorian restorers. There are some other interesting tombs, including those of Thomas Shipman and the 2nd Earl of Worcester. There is a good view of the river from The Back. The high wooded cliffs of Gloucestershire form the backdrop on the opposite bank and there are good views of both the iron road bridge and of Brunel's railway bridge. The tidal range is extraordinarily impressive here – some 12 metres a day at spring tides – and any boatman working these waters needs to know his tides and mudbanks. For more information on the town's seafaring history, the admirable Chepstow Museum, in the premises of a former hospital, has good collections. For old times' sake, it is interesting to go down to the slip-way at Beachley to see where the ferry used to depart on its crossing to the English shore.

The church of St Jerome at **Llangwm Uchaf**, on the attractive B4235 that winds its way from Chepstow to Usk, is a real gem. There are a cluster of good surviving rood screens in the vicinity of the Usk but that of Llangwm Uchaf, with its loft still in place, is the pride of them all; dating from the fifteenth century, it is one of the most ornate in Wales. Walter Cradoc (1610?–1659), the Puritan, is buried here; he was born close by at Tre-fela. This corner of the county has several attractive little churches: **Gwernesney** has screen fragments but no loft, whereas **Llangeview** has a loft but no screen. There is another surviving loft at **Mamhilad** and, at Persondy, a remarkable survival of seventeenth-century carpentry in the interior of the former parsonage. At **Betws Newydd**, four kilometres north of Usk, one of the most complete rood screens and lofts in Wales has survived. Its out-of-the-way location protected this church from the improving hands of both Tudor and Victorian reformers.

The quiet market town of Usk, named after the river that flows through the town, has a long history of settlement. The first substantial Roman fort built in Wales was situated here; known as *Burrium*, it was a base for securing control of the country. The ruins of the Norman castle, improved by William Marshal, dominate the town from above the church. Three sons of Usk merit our attention: St David Lewis (1616–1679), the last Catholic priest to die for his faith in Britain; Adam of Usk (c.1352–1430), the mediaeval chronicler; and Alfred Russel Wallace (1823–1913), whose biological investigations led him to the same conclusions about human evolution as Darwin was to put forward in his *The Origins of the Species.* The parish church, originally a Benedictine priory, has been much altered but a restored rood screen survives; on it is a brass plate with a *cywydd* epitaph to Adam of Usk. T.H. Wyatt, the church restorer and architect, designed the polished granite tomb for his brother in the north-west corner. St David Lewis is buried in the churchyard as is Philip Mason, 'who died 1772 aged 51 weighing 554 pounds'. Alfred Russel Wallace was born in Kensington Cottage, on the banks of the Usk, less than half a kilometre out of the town on the Caerleon Road. He surely merits a monument in the town of his birth.

It is possible to reach Newport and the M4 very speedily by joining the A449 at Raglan, but a more leisurely pace following the minor roads south will be more rewarding. The legionary whose grave-slab is now set in the wall of St Andrew's parish church at **Tredunnock** had been based at *Isca Silurum*, now known as **Caerleon**, a contraction of the Welsh for Camp of the Legions. Founded around AD75, it flourished in the second-century as the base of the Second Augustan Legion. Caerleon has an honoured place in the story of Christianity in the Britain being the place of martyrdom of Julius and Aaron in the third century, two of the three named Romano-British Christian martyrs. It also figures prominently in the *Matter of Britain*, as a place of Arthurian associations. According to *Y Mabinogi*, it was the most accessible place in his dominions, by sea and land. Certainly for the Romans, the memory of whose Christian civilisation this Welsh hero was defending against the pagan Saxon advance, Severnside had been a major area of activity and settlement in Britain. It was following a stay in the Hanbury Arms, on a rare excursion from England, that Tennyson (1809–1892) wrote *The Idylls of the King*. Arthur Machen (Arthur Jones, 1863–1947), the novelist – note his Christian name – was born in Caerleon; his *The Hill of Dreams* brings the Roman town to life. The attractive old town is now surrounded by suburban housing, for Caerleon has long been regarded as an up-market suburb of Newport, the port that eventually replaced it. The parish church, significantly perhaps, is on the site of the Roman Praetorium. There is an excellent Legionary Museum (NMGW), with good inscribed tablets. Nearby are the excavated remains of the Barracks and the celebrated Amphitheatre (Cadw), the most complete Roman remain in Wales: it could seat an entire legion, some six thousand people.

Newport cannot now be avoided. Ever the poor cousin of Cardiff, the surge of growth in the capital since the establishment of the National Assembly, served only to widen the stylistic gulf between these commercial rivals. Things may be set to change. The granting of city status in 2002 was followed a year later by the opening of a Velodrome and an architecturally interesting Theatre and Arts Centre is currently nearing completion. Elsewhere, the city is not totally devoid of interest and with the Ryder Cup due to take place at the Celtic Manor Resort on the outskirts of the city in 2010 Newport may yet become a tourist destination. Newport's emblem is its transporter bridge, built in 1906 and one of only two in Britain. It closed in

1985 but public pressure and a massive local fund-raising campaign saw it proudly restored to full working order a decade later as the world's largest surviving example of this ingenious method of transportation. Cars, bicycles and pedestrians can now cross the tidal reaches of the Usk at a height of 75 metres.

Newport grew rapidly in the nineteenth century on the export of iron from its docks, built at the confluence of Severn and Usk. At Newport, the Usk has the greatest tidal range of any British river, and the resultant mud-banks, decorated with abandoned supermarket trolleys, form a grim finale for a river of such early charm and promise. Yet mud has its uses: in 2002 the remains of a fifteenth-century ocean-going cargo ship were found well preserved in these anaerobic conditions. Another public campaign to ensure the preservation of this internationally important archaeological discovery appears to have been successful and may yet transform Newport into a desirable tourist destination.

In 1839 Newport was briefly the talk of Britain after John Frost, the town's former mayor organised a Chartist rising throughout the iron-working districts of Monmouthshire. The Newport Rising culminated in the death of 20 protestors under army fire at the town's Westgate Hotel. Frost and some of his companions were transported to Tasmania. The Westgate unfortunately closed its doors recently; it is situated at one end of a typically unimaginative British pedestrianised high street that leads into a frightful 1970s shopping centre. There, the town's Museum and Art Gallery has a real treasure, a fourth-century pewter bowl from Caerwent with a chi-rho monogram, the earliest Christian artefact found in Wales. In addition there is material relating to the Chartist Rising and a good programme of visiting exhibitions. Outside, the Automaton Clock, designed in 1992, provides welcome amusement.

The best view of the twelfth-century castle ruins (Cadw) is probably from the railway that bisects the town. Beyond the railway, the self-important 1930s Civic Centre has a fascinating series of murals by Hans Feibusch, illustrating the history of the county, that were completed in 1964. The parish church of St Woolos became a cathedral in 1921 to serve the new diocese of Monmouth. Gwynllyw, to use the founder's Welsh name, married Gwladys, one of Brychan's daughters. The church, on the ancient site of Gwynllyw's cell, has been harshly restored but has a good Norman nave and clerestory.

To either side of Newport, on the Severn shore, is a unique wetland landscape that has been under constant threat in recent years from proposed developments: a relief motorway for the M4 and, even more absurd, an airport for Newport. The **Wentloog Levels** to the west and the **Caldicot Levels** to the east consist of an area of drained marshland, the drainage cuttings known locally as reens. This is a unique habitat for such plants as reed sweet grass and pollarded willows that has been sympathetically farmed for generations. Sterling work by the Monmouthshire Naturalists Trust in preserving a section of this landscape near Magor urgently needs to be extended. Enjoy it while it lasts: the approaches to the Second Severn Crossing (1996), itself a surprisingly graceful structure, have already encroached to the east. Gwynllwg, of which Wentloog is an anglicisation, was the ancient territory over which Gwynllyw held sway. Two churches on the levels have historic flood markers for the great flood of 20 January 1606: **St Bride's Wentloog** and **Goldcliff**.

Tredegar Park, on the outskirts of Newport, is the finest late seventeenth-century house in Wales. Built between 1664 and 1674 by the Morgans of Tredegar, a family that waxed glorious on a combination of royalism, advantageous marriage and industrial exploitation to provide a succession of Members of Parliament and Lords Lieutenant for this and the neighbouring county of Brecon. Sold by the 5th Baron in 1954 to pay death duties, the property risked falling into dereliction, but has been admirably restored and opened to the public by Newport City Council. The exterior is quite magnificent and the interior, all paneled rooms, sumptuous plaster ceilings and fine portraits, does not disappoint. The adjacent walled gardens have been lovingly recreated and part of the immense stable block refurbished to house a tea-room. The Morgans had their mausoleum at St Basil's church, **Bassaleg**, a restored church on an ancient site.

Returning to Chepstow from Newport on the A48, the delightful, fortified towerhouse of **Penhow** dates from the early fourteenth century. Built by the St Maur family, who, as the Seymours, provided a wife for Henry VIII, the house is privately owned and, at the time of writing, is offered for sale. **Llanfaches** is famous for the 'gathered church' of William Wroth (1576–1641). Formerly the Rector of St Dyfrig's parish church here, he became a Puritan and resigned the living in 1638. In the following year, he convened the first dissenting meeting in Wales where the Tabernacle United Reformed Church now stands, the mother church of the Welsh Independents.

A visit to **Caerwent** should be linked with one to Caerleon. Caerwent was the Romano-British town of *Venta Silurum*, the market town of the Silures. Once Julius Frontinus had subdued the local Silures in AD74, the Romans followed their usual practice of bringing the Britons down from their hillforts, in this case the one at Llanmelin (Cadw), a kilometre to the north, and settling them in civil settlements. **Caerwent Roman Town** (Cadw) is a remarkable survival of such a tribal settlement, a civil counterpart to a legionary centre, such as that of Caerleon. The present village is surrounded with good sections of the original Roman wall. The foundations of Roman shops and houses can still be seen in Pound Lane. The handsome parish church of St Stephen and St Tathan, itself partly constructed using old Roman bricks, contains several Roman items including two inscribed stones.

Caldicot is now largely suburban but preserves its fine castle in over 20 hectares of parkland. Its twelfth-century circular keep and early modern refinements such as the gatehouse and upper hall were restored in the late nineteenth century by the antiquary Joseph Richard Cobb (1821–1897), the promoter of the Brecon and Merthyr Railway that was parodied as the 'Breakneck and Murder'. From **Portskewett**, legendary landing-place of the Irish St Tathan and, more recently, of the New Passage ferry, it is possible to survey more than a century of Severn crossing engineering: the 1966 and 1996 suspension bridges lie to the east and west respectively. At **Sudbrook**, the Severn Tunnel pumping station removes water from the Severn Tunnel at a prodigous rate as it has done continuously since the tunnel opened in 1886. For over a century after its opening, it was the longest under-sea tunnel in the world and it continues to serve the main line between west Wales and London.

6

The Valleys

THE HEADS OF THE VALLEYS road that cuts through high moorland from Gilwern to Dowlais Top was constructed in the post-war years to facilitate the economic regeneration of a depressed region. It is a road into a distinctive territory, 'The Valleys', those uniquely Welsh industrial communities that cascade down from this high moorland towards the Severn Sea, and which have such deep cultural resonance for Welsh people. In the nineteenth century, this region was the world's major producer of coal and iron and the sudden contrast between urban and rural landscapes has always been a shock to the sensibilities. But we must never forget the human links that bound these contrasting landscapes together. It is not uncommon for the English media to use 'The Valleys' (invariably inhabited by 'boyos') as a derogatory synonym for the whole of Wales. In fact, although there are many valleys in Wales, when the Welsh refer to 'The Valleys' the reference is specifically to these unique communities of iron and coal, particularly those of Monmouthshire and Glamorgan, the subject of this chapter.

The Valleys produce a stock of clichéd responses and as with all clichés they contain a grain of truth: rugby football and male voice choirs, chapels and miners' institutes, terraced housing and pit-head winding gear, pubs and Bracchis, the latter Valleys dialect for cafés from the name of an Italian family from Bardi in the Appenines. The clichés are nourished by nostalgia for the distinctive community values that arose when coal was king. The troubadour of Valleys nostalgia in the late twentieth century was Max

Boyce who lamented that the pit-head baths were a super-market now. At the nostalgic end of the literary spectrum, Alexander Cordell (1914–1997), an English surveyor who settled in Monmouthshire in 1936, wrote two trilogies: highly popular, romanticised accounts of industrial life in the Valleys that enabled him to end his days as a tax exile on the Isle of Man. At a time when an unprecedented influx of English settlers into Wales has transformed the nature of community life throughout the country, the Valleys have maintained a predominantly Welsh cultural identity albeit one that is now expressed predominantly in English. We shall explore the valleys downstream, from east to west.

Llwyd

In the year 2000, **Blaenafon**, at the head of the Afon Llwyd, was declared a Unesco World Heritage Site in recognition of the remarkably complete survival of a nineteenth-century industrial landscape that is preserved hereabouts. The successful bid for World Heritage status completes a cycle that began with a surge of population into the area, much of it from rural and Welsh-speaking Wales, and saw iron production peak in the Edwardian years. That was followed within a generation by unemployment and a haemorrhage of population through emigration in the 1920s and 1930s. There were attempts at job creation through the relocation of light industry into the area in the 1950s and 1960s, little of it sustainable, culminating in the present attempt to salvage some pride and employment through the heritage business. There is a Cordell Museum, for example, in Lion Street.

Iron production began here in 1789, using local ore and charcoal. The founders of the works, Thomas Hill and Samuel Hopkins, also built the neo-Gothic church of St Peter, with its iron font and galleries. Dominating the town is Tŷ Mawr, the former home of Samuel Hopkins.

Higher still are the remains of the Blaenafon Ironworks (cadw), the best-preserved eighteenth-century ironworks in Europe. A tramroad connected the works to a branch of the Monmouthshire Canal at Crumlin. In 1877, two cousins Percy Gilchrist and Sydney Gilchrist Thomas developed a technique that enabled the local phosphoric ore to be smelted in Bessemer converters. Within a decade their process had been adopted internationally, Andrew Carnegie paying $250,000 for the right to use it in the United States. The American steel maker remarked: 'These two young men, Thomas and Gilchrist of Blaenafon, did more for Britain's greatness than all the Kings and Queens put together.' It was at Blaenafon, during his 1936 tour of the depressed South Wales Coalfield, that King Edward VIII made his famous observation: 'Something must be done.' At the end of that year, over half the work force in this district joined the king in unemployment.

In addition to the ironworks, it is possible to descend underground at Big Pit (NMGW), a colliery that ceased production in 1980 and to visit a new surface gallery that provides an excellent introduction to the history of the coalfield. There are plans to reopen the Pontypool and Blaenafon Railway, which closed at the same time as Big Pit. The Workmen's Hall, opened in 1894, has reopened as a cinema. Forge Row in **Cwmavon**, further down the valley, a terrace of twelve early nineteenth-century dwellings built for skilled workers at the Varteg Forge, has been commendably restored. The ironworks at **Abersychan** was opened in 1826; its High Street has several chapels but the Anglican church occupies an isolated site on the hilltop. The politician and biographer, Roy Jenkins (1920–2003), was born here, the son of the local Labour MP Arthur Jenkins. A successful Labour Chancellor of the Exchequer he courted controversy by quitting the Labour Party in 1981 to found the Social Democrats. With the demise of the latter, he was translated via the European Commision to the heart of the English establishment as Chancellor of Oxford University, by which time he had acquired a very plummy English accent. Harold Wilson once suggested that Roy Jenkins was indolent. Nye Bevan provided an ironic case for the defence: 'How can a boy who comes from Abersychan end up with an accent like that and be called l-l-lazy?'

Pontypool has been an industrial town since the sixteenth century. Richard Hanbury began smelting iron here and was followed by John Hanbury who pioneered the tinplate industry. It is claimed that emigrants from Pontypool constructed the first forge in America in 1652. The subsequent development of the japanning trade – the town has a Japan Street – established Pontypool's eighteenth-century reputation. The Monmouthshire Canal, built between 1794 and 1799 by Thomas Dadford, connected Pontypool with Newport. The opening of coal mines in the nineteenth century greatly increased the population of the town and their closure in the late twentieth century caused considerable distress. The former home of the Hanburys can be seen at Pontypool Park, now a secondary school; there is an elaborate set of wrought-iron gates at the main entrance to the park in Rockhill Road and the 1831 stable block houses an interesting museum. The Shell Grotto was imaginatively restored in 1991 as a performance venue.

Cwmbrân is that Welsh rarebit, a planned new town. The Tower, built in 1949, was the first example of high-rise architecture in Wales. As the good people of Warsaw used to say of Stalin's House of Culture, the best views of the town are from inside the building. Lack of imagination was also evident when the planners decided to concrete over the old Monmouthshire Canal, thereby frustrating plans to reopen it for navigation. **Llantarnam** has the architecturally-complex church of St Michael and All Angels with an adjacent inn, The Green House. The latter has its sign, dated 1719, in Welsh: *Y Tŷ Gwyrdd.* Llantarnam Abbey, originally a twelfth-century Cistercian daughter house of

Strata Florida, became a house for the local gentry following the Dissolution. In 1835, T.H. Wyatt was commissioned to make improvements; he incorporated fragments from Strata Florida Abbey. The abbey subsequently passed into the hands of the Cory's, the Cardiff shipping magnates, before returning to monastic use when the Sisters of St Joseph took possession of the property in 1954. It is possible to follow the mediaeval pilgrimage route that links St Michael's church with the shrine of the Virgin Mary at Penrhys in the Rhondda. The Cwmbrân by-pass brutally bisects the parkland of Llantarnam Abbey. Enough said: a minor road from Pontnewydd to Upper Cwmbran leads up to the well-named Mountain Air Inn at 200 metres, beyond which there are splendid views back towards Pontypool or on down the valley towards Newport.

Ebbw Fawr and Ebbw Fach

Brynmawr, at the head of the Ebbw Fach, vies with Blaenau Ffestiniog for being the highest town in Wales. In both cases, it was the opportunity for employment in the extractive industries that led to settlement in these otherwise inhospitable places. St Mary's church was built in 1895 to replace the earlier one that had blown down. A claim to architectural interest, Ove Arup's Dunlop Semtex factory, completed in 1953, disappeared when it was demolished in 2001 to make way for retail development. The adjoining iron town of **Nantyglo** was the source of fame and fortune for the Bailey brothers, Joseph and Crawshay. As the name of the younger brother suggests, they were related to the Crawshays of Cyfarthfa. By 1827, the Baileys were operating seven blast furnaces here, linked by tramroad to the Monmouthshire Canal at Llanfoist. Nantyglo was home to the Scotch Cattle, an early form of industrial protest that owed much to the old days of the moral economy. Groups of men, their faces blackened, enforced class solidarity over such issues as wage reductions. The name of Crawshay Bailey (1789–1872) lives on in the Valleys and beyond in the traditional singing of innumerable extempore and often ribald verses sung to the tune *Y Mochyn Du* and with the refrain 'Did you ever see (repeated three times) such a funny thing before?' The following examples, from the pen of Kyffin Williams, may serve to whet the appetite:

> Crawshay Bailey's sister Alice
> Was the cook at Lambeth Palace
> But she burnt the Bishop's haddock
> So was sent home to Llangadog

> Crawshay Bailey craved for knowledge
> So he went to Cardiff College
> He didn't do much thinkin'
> But an awful lot of drinkin'

A journey down the Ebbw might begin at **Beaufort**, a town originally known as Cendl from the eighteenth-century proprietor of the ironworks, Edward Kendall. In 1833, the ironworks was acquired by the Baileys. The ironworks at **Ebbw Vale** was founded in 1789 by Jeremiah Homfray of Penydarren and is thus contemporary with that at Blaenafon. Two centuries later, the British Steel plant here was the most advanced of its kind in the country but the collapse of the industry in the 1980s led to Ebbw Vale being chosen as the site of the 1991 Welsh Garden Festival. Twenty-five hectares of the site have now been consolidated as a park, but the associated retail and housing developments lack character. A welcome decision to reestablish the rail link with Newport and Cardiff offers promise for the future.

The town has made a significant contribution to British politics through the careers of its parliamentary representatives, Aneurin Bevan and Michael Foot. Aneurin Bevan (1897–1960), an ex-miner, was idolised as the architect of

the National Health Service but disappointed many of his
followers on the left by arguing for the retention of British
nuclear weapons. His striking memorial, above the town
in the direction of Tredegar, the town where he was born,
was erected in 1972. It comprises four monoliths: one
in the centre surrounded by the other three representing
the Ebbw, Sirhowy and Rhymney valleys. His protégé and
biographer, the distinguished Labour intellectual Michael
Foot, represented the constituency after Bevan's untimely
death, including a brief period from 1980 to 1983 as leader
of the Labour Party. An impassioned nuclear disarmament
campaigner, he nevertheless rallied the Labour Party
behind Mrs Thatcher's Falklands War. The miners' institute
at **Oakdale**, a model village begun in 1907 by the Tredegar
Iron and Coal Company for employees at their new Oakdale
Colliery, was the largest and most complex building to be
dismantled and re-erected at the Museum of Welsh Life when
it was moved there in 1995.

Sirhowy

A descent of the **Sirhowy** begins at the settlement of that
name where an ironworks was operating as early as 1778.
Two great ironworks grew up in the valley below at
Tredegar, the later one belonging to Samuel Homfray of
Penydarren, who married the daughter of Sir Charles
Morgan (formerly Gould) of Tredegar, the grandfather of
the first Lord Tredegar. Aneurin Bevan, a man of diamet-
rically opposite political persuasions, was born in Charles
Street a generation later. The isolated mediaeval ridgetop
church of **Bedwellte**, dedicated to St Sannan, gave its name
to the constituency of Neil Kinnock, who was also born in
Tredegar and succeeded his mentor Michael Foot as leader
of the Labour Party. The scourge of Plaid Cymru and principal architect of their defeat in the 1979 referendum, he
ironically lost the 1992 General Election because Middle

England could not bring itself to trust a "Valleys' boyo." As a European Commissioner, he presided over the federal structure he once so bitterly opposed.

Rhymney

Historically, the ridge between the Sirhowy and the Rhymney valleys formed the county border between Monmouthshire and Glamorganshire. Just off the Heads of the Valleys road sits **Bute Town**, an interesting example of an early model village from the very beginning of the nineteenth century, preserved unaltered when the iron industry moved downstream. The village was named after the Scottish peer, the 2nd Marquess of Bute (1793–1848), whose grandfather had acquired the vast Glamorganshire estates of the Windsors through marriage. The estates were rich in iron ore and underground coal seams so that the Marquess became as wealthy in his day as Saudi oil princes are in ours and for the same reason: he controlled a significant part of the world's primary source of energy. He will figure prominently as we travel though this part of Wales.

The 2nd Marquess built three iron furnaces in **Rhymney** to ancient Egyptian designs, based on the ruins of Dendera, fitting symbolism for a latter-day Pharaoh: he had bought out Crawshay Bailey in the 1820s. Andrew Buchan of the Rhymney Iron Company paid for St David's Church, erected in 1839–43, but most of the ironworkers frequented the town's chapels, of which Penuel Welsh Baptist chapel in Coronation Terrace is the most architecturally interesting. Rhymney has had some famous sons. Thomas Jones (1870–1955), cabinet secretary to four Prime Ministers and a man passionately committed to educational and social reform, was born in High Street. His *Rhymney Memories* are an essential complement to his *Whitehall Diaries*, providing an affectionate glimpse at life in this valley in the boom years at the end of the nineteenth century. Boom was followed by bust, and to feel the effects of economic depression on the valley we should turn to the poetry of Idris Davies (1905–1953) who was also born in the town. A miner turned poet, his work celebrated this valley community in the hard times of inter-war unemployment, notably in his long but accessible dramatic poems *Gwalia Deserta* (1938) and *The Angry Summer* (1943). The former closes with the following verses:

> In the places of my boyhood
> The pit-wheels turn no more,
> Nor any furnace lightens
> The midnight as of yore.
>
> The slopes of slag and cinder
> Are sulking in the rain,
> And in the derelict valleys
> The hope of youth is slain.
>
> And yet I love to wander
> The early ways I went
> And watch from doors and bridges
> The hills and skies of Gwent.
>
> Though blighted be the valleys
> Where man meets man with pain
> The things my boyhood cherished
> Stand firm, and shall remain.

In **New Tredegar**, the winding-house from Elliot Colliery that closed in 1967 has been preserved. The valley sides down to **Bargoed** are lined with terraced housing built for the former miners. The engaging Anglo-Welsh poet John Tripp (1927–1986) was born here, his verse providing an ironically perceptive but compassionate commentary on late twentieth-century south Wales.

A kilometre north of Nelson, the fine Tudor manor house of **Llancaiach Fawr** has been imaginatively restored by the local authority and provides a welcome counterpoint to the industrial heritage that surrounds it. The house belonged to Colonel Edward Prichard who changed sides during the Civil War to become a prominent Parliamentarian. Not only do the staff wear period costume but they also engage the visitors in conversation using Elizabethan English; it would add authenticity if we could also hear some of Bishop Morgan's Welsh. The gardens are also being restored to their seventeenth-century splendour.

A minor road north from Ystrad Mynach follows the old Roman road from Cardiff to Brecon along the ridge to a height of some 450 metres near Carn y Bugail. At **Gelligaer**, the remains of a Roman fort are clearly visible besides the rectory. The best Roman bathhouse in Wales, after that at Caerleon, was excavated here in the first decades of the twentieth century. The heavily restored church is dedicated to St Cadog, many of whose churches were located along the Welsh network of Roman roads. The church has an interesting immersion font, designed to stem the flow of worshippers to the Baptists. Penallta Colliery continued production here until 1991.

From Ystrad Mynach, the Rhymney flows through Llanbradach down to **Caerffili**. Caerffili Castle (Cadw) is an extraordinary example of the art of castle building. The second largest castle in area after Windsor in the British Isles, and one of the largest in Europe, it is magnificently situated at the heart of the town. It replaced an earlier Norman motte built to the north-west of the present castle on the site of a Roman fort, the latter situated beside the Cardiff to Brecon Roman road. Like Beaumaris and Harlech, the present castle, started by Gilbert de Clare in 1268, was of the concentric design. The castle was built to counter the influence of Llywelyn ap Gruffudd following his recognition by the Crown as Prince of Wales the previous year. Just six years earlier, in 1262, De Clare had gained control of the Welsh lordship of Senghennydd. While construction was underway, in 1270, Llywelyn sacked the castle, but De Clare resumed work and this extraordinary architectural treasure was completed in just four summers. Following the success of the Edwardian conquest in 1282, the castle lost its strategic value and thereafter saw very little active service. It was besieged in local risings in 1316 and 1321 and was vandalised by the royalists during the Civil War to prevent the Parliamentarians from making use of it. A delightful memento of these royalist depredations is that Caerffili acquired a leaning tower, 25 metres high and 3 metres out of perpendicular. The waterworks were drained and housing encroached on the site. Successive Marquesses of Bute began the task of restoration, clearing the encroachments and refurbishing the moats, work admirably continued by Cadw and by a local authority that, in these post-industrial times, has woken up to the tourist potential of having one of Europe's finest mediaeval castles at its centre. Some eight hectares of lake defend the castle on three sides; on the fourth side some 300 metres of curtain-wall rise behind a wide moat. There are excellent interpretative displays inside the castle and re-enactments of mediaeval siege weapons take place during the summer months. A monument beside the castle moat commemorates David Williams (1738–1816), the deist and political pamphleteer who played a prominent part in both the American and French revolutions before retiring to write a voluminous history of the neighbouring county of Monmouthshire.

The Aber valley runs north of Caerffili through **Abertridwr**, where the Miners Institute, next to the cleared site of the Windsor colliery, is now a bingo hall. Siôn Cent, the fifteenth-century Welsh poet, is thought to have been born here. **Senghennydd** was the scene of Britain's worst mining disaster in 1913 when 439 men lost their lives in a horrific gas explosion at the Universal colliery. A memorial has been erected on the site of the colliery, which never resumed production, and the community centre has a small but interesting exhibition on both the 1913 and an earlier disaster in 1901. The graves of the miners can be seen in the public cemetery at **Penyrheol** back in the direction of Caerffili. To the west of Abertridwr a minor road leads up to St Ilan's church at **Eglwysilan** church, a solitary mediaeval upland church with only a public house for company. Behind the pulpit, there is a memorial by Goscombe John to William Edwards (1719–1789), spiritual and temporal bridge builder; of the latter his most celebrated was the single stone arch at Pontypridd. He combined his job as an engineer with the ministry of nearby **Groes-wen** Independent chapel, built as the first Methodist meeting house in Wales but registered in 1745 as an Independent chapel under the terms of the Toleration Act following a congregational defection. The chapel and its interesting burial ground is in urgent need of restoration. The Independent cause at **Watford** (originally Bodffordd), where another David Williams (1709–1784) was minister in the mid-eighteenth century, is the mother church of Independency in this part of the country. Following the historic Methodist synod held here in 1743, Whitefield's Calvinism prevailed over Wesley's Arminianism.

The lower Rhymney has two notable properties. **Ruperra Castle** is a seventeenth-century fortified manor house built by Sir William Morgan, steward to the Earl of Pembroke. Further downstream is **Cefn Mabli**, once one of the great houses of Glamorgan. Home to the Kemeys family, it took its name from Mabilia, daughter of the Earl of Gloucester. The house served as a hospital between 1923 and 1980 but suffered a serious fire in 1994 and has now been redeveloped as private apartments. A failure in the male line, characteristic of several Welsh gentry families in the long eighteenth century, saw the Kemeys family trying to maintain its lineage as the Kemeys-Tyntes but by 1923 they had vanished. The inscriptions on their tombs, in the south transept of St Michael's church at **Michaelston-y-Fedw** make poignant reading.

Taf

The Heads of the Valleys road runs through Dowlais Top before descending into the Taf valley at **Merthyr Tydfil**. By 1831, iron production had propelled Merthyr Tydfil to head the census as the largest centre of population in Wales. Four English ironmasters controlled the lives of a frontier community of workers drawn from all parts of Wales, the other nations of the British Isles and beyond: Guest at Dowlais, Homfray at Penydarren, Hill at Plymouth and Crawshay at Cyfarthfa. They leased land that contained abundant quantities of coal, iron ore, limestone and running water, the perfect combination of ingredients for iron manufacture. In the reform crisis of 1831, the town experienced an outbreak of sustained rioting which Dowlais historian Gwyn Alf Williams insisted on upgrading to The Merthyr Rising. For a time Merthyr was synonymous with sin to the Nonconformists of rural Wales: in the eyes of Dafydd Rolant from Bala, 'Samaria was the Merthyr Tydfil of the land of Canaan.' Subsequently, the town's radical tradition merged with Nonconformity to produce a distinctive politics. Henry Richard, the Apostle of Peace, was returned as the town's MP in 1868. Keir Hardie, the first Labour MP elected to Parliament, followed in 1900, with the slogan 'The Red Dragon and the Red Flag'. They were followed in turn by such idiosyncratic Labour members as S.O. Davies and Ted Rowlands and in 1976 Plaid Cymru took control of the council under the leadership of Emrys Roberts. Architecturally, the town suffered brutal redevelopment in the 1970s, losing much of its heritage and character, with the notorious housing estate of Gurnos brutally exposed to the elements. Notable Anglo-Welsh writers from the town have portrayed this vibrant community, including Jack Jones (1884–1970) and Glyn Jones (1905–1995).

The association of the Guest family with the ironworks at **Dowlais** began in 1767 when John Guest from Broseley in Shropshire was appointed works manager. In 1782, he bought into the partnership that had founded the works in 1759. Through the efforts of his grandson, Josiah John Guest, the Dowlais Iron Company became the leading centre of iron production in the world. When Merthyr secured the right to its own parliamentary representation in 1832, Josiah John Guest became the town's Liberal MP. His wealth made him an attractive catch and in 1833 he married Lady Charlotte Bertie, daughter of the Earl of Lindsey, who, as Lady Charlotte Guest, was to publish her 'translation' of *Y Mabinogi* in 1849. This was the first complete rendition into English of that rich treasury of early Welsh myth, legend and romance. Little tangible evidence of all this activity now remains. An impressive but derelict nineteenth-century blast-engine house still stands as do the Dowlais stables, saved from demolition following a successful national campaign and now adapted to domestic use. The Guest Memorial Reading Room and Library, opened in 1863, has been similarly converted.

Francis Homfray, from Stourton in Staffordshire, established the ironworks at **Penydarren** in 1784. The first time a steam engine had drawn a load on rails was in 1804 on the railway designed by the Cornish engineer Richard Trevithick (1771–1833) to transport iron from Penydarren to the Glamorgan Canal at Quaker's Yard for onward transportation to Cardiff. The Trevithick Memorial commemorates this achievement. The Plymouth Ironworks at Abercanaid was named after the landowner from whom the site was leased. The Triangle, built between 1839 and 1844 as model houses for Plymouth workers was shamefully demolished in 1974. At **Georgetown** the birthplace of Joseph Parry (1841–1903), first Professor of Music in the University of Wales, can be visited in Chapel Row, a surviving terrace of early ironworker's housing built in 1825. Similar terraced housing at **Rhyd-y-car** has been relocated to the Museum of Welsh Life where an imaginative chronological sequence of domestic interiors has been created spanning two centuries.

The floor of the valley below was once entirely occupied by the **Cyfarthfa** ironworks, the great rival to Dowlais. Here the rival captain of industry was the Yorkshireman Richard Crawshay, who had bought the ironworks from Anthony Bacon, a Londoner, in 1786. The Crawshays were able to look down on their works from their citadel of Cyfarthfa Castle which today accommodates the town's school and an excellent museum and art gallery. Completed in 1825, even the lake at the front had the practical purpose of supplying water for the works. Now, the extensive grounds make an attractive municipal park and a pedestrian link gives access to the six recently restored Cyfarthfa Furnaces. The church is dedicated to Tydfil, another daughter of Brychan, reputedly martyred by the Saxons. At the height of industrialisation, the presiding genius of the Cyfarthfa ironworks was Robert Thompson Crawshay (1817–1879). His Ynysfach Engine House, dating from 1850, houses a museum of the iron industry. He had a new church constructed at **Faenor** in 1867: his tomb in the churchyard is inscribed: 'God Forgive me'.

The Taff Vale Railway linking Merthyr to Cardiff opened in 1841, the first modern all-locomotive haulage railway in Wales. In 1900, the line achieved national celebrity when the House of Lords ruled that its workers were financially responsible for the losses suffered by their employers during a period of strike action. According to G.D.H. Cole, 'The Taff Vale Railway case created the Labour Party.' Using the improved A470 trunk road, it is now possible to reach Cardiff from Merthyr in little more than half an hour. In October 1966 Pantglas primary school at **Aberfan** was engulfed in coal slurry from the mountain above the village, killing 111 children in a catastrophe that had been waiting to happen. There is a memorial garden in Moy Road in addition to the chilling rows of white graves on the hillside.

Castell Coch (Cadw) is a totally unexpected sight viewed from the M4 or the Tongwynlais interchange. A German *schloss* rather than a Welsh castle, it is as much the product of the 3rd Marquess of Bute's fantasy as Neuschwanstein is of mad King Ludwig's. Both had plenty of money to realise their projects. The 3rd Marquess of Bute commissioned the architect William Burges (1827–1881) to reconstruct the hillside ruin of a former Norman castle built by Gilbert de Clare to guard the entrance to the valley. Restoration work was carried out from the 1870s to the 1890s: the Burges interiors are wonderful, with a banqueting room, guest bedrooms and the Marquess's own bedroom with a restored copy of his Viollet-le-Duc bed. Recent restoration work has enabled the original Kitchen Tower to be opened to the public so that the massive walls of the original mediaeval castle can be inspected. In its heyday Castell Coch even had a reputable vineyard. How far we have travelled on our short journey down the Taf!

Cynon

It is still difficult to accept the fact that The Tower Colliery at **Hirwaun** is the last working deep pit in Wales. The story of its survival after the miners' strike of 1984 is an epic one, fittingly made the subject a contemporary opera by Alun Hoddinot. Tyrone O'Sullivan, the local miner's leader achieved heroic status in the Valleys by successfully organising a workers' buy-out of the colliery in 1992. Hirwaun has a proud industrial pedigree. This was the first place in Wales to smelt iron ore using coke instead of charcoal, in 1757, at an ironworks opened by John Maybery from Worcestershire. The Crawshay empire acquired this ironworks in 1819. Four of the original blast furnaces remain standing north of the Cynon.

Aberdare, originally an iron town, greatly expanded with the sinking of coal pits in the valley in the middle of the nineteenth century; by 1869 production of steam coal was running at two million tonnes per annum. In Victoria Square there is a fine statue by Goscombe John of Griffith Rhys Jones (1834–1897). Known in Wales as Caradog, he conducted the famous South Wales Choral Union, *Y Côr Mawr*, to numerous victories at eisteddfodau and, famously, at the Crystal Palace. The informative Cynon Valley Museum is housed in a former tramshed in Depot Road, Y Gadlys, close to more surviving blast furnaces. It contains a fascinating collection of portraits of nineteenth-century ironworkers by W.J. Chapman. Nearby, the chapelry of St John the Baptist stands on a stack of coal that was never mined in order to protect the foundations of this much-loved mediaeval building.

Rhondda

The two Rhondda valleys, Rhondda Fawr and Rhondda Fach, must be the most famous of Welsh valleys. In 1807, Benjamin Heath Malkin famously observed 'such scenes of untouched nature as the imagination would find it difficult to surpass'. As late as 1848, a traveller could describe the Rhondda in bucolic terms: 'the people of this solitudinous and happy valley are a pastoral race, almost entirely dependent on flowers and mountain plants – a sabbath stillness reigns'. By the 1860s, intensive mining of steam coal had transformed a pastoral landscape into an industrial one, with men like Walter Coffin, George Insole, Thomas Powell and David Davies making their fortunes from 'black gold'. Boom has been followed by bust, chapels and Workmen's Institutes have closed and become derelict. The Rhondda Heritage Museum on the site of the former Lewis Merthyr Colliery at **Trehafod** tries its best to convey a flavour of this tradition for the passing tourist trade. For the time being, the guides are ex-miners with real experiences to share: but who will replace them and what tales will they then tell?

The Rhondda remains a bastion of left-wing politics. Founded in 1898, the South Wales Miners Federation, known in the Valleys simply as 'The Fed', wrote the abolition of capitalism into its rulebook from 1917 onwards. In 1910, Churchill had secured lasting unpopularity in Wales by ordering troops into the Rhondda valley to put down striking miners following riots at **Tonypandy**. George Thomas (1909–1997), a popular Speaker of the newly televised House of Commons, accepted a peerage as Lord Tonypandy. A former Secretary of State for Wales, he had been a bitter opponent of plans for devolution. As impresario of the 1969 Caernarfon Investiture of the Prince of Wales, he had sought to stem the growing tide of nationalist sentiment in Wales in the 1970s. The Rhondda nonconformist tradition, in which George Thomas was raised, is in decline here as everywhere else in Wales. Ebeneser chapel, for example, with its impressive interior, is struggling for survival. Lewis Jones (1897–1939), political activist first and foremost but author of two strikingly atmospheric Rhondda novels, *Cwmardy* and *We Live*, was born in the village of **Clydach Vale**.

Trealaw is where George M.Ll. Davies (1880–1949), the Welsh internationalist and conscientious objector, spent many years helping the unemployed from his base at the Maes-yr-haf Quaker community. **Treorchy**, to the northwest, grew up around the Abergorki colliery. It is still famous for its male voice choir; the Park and Dare Workman's Hall in Station Road, their home venue, is the heart of the community. Cadwgan in **Pentre**, the home of Gwyn and Kate Griffiths, was the venue for meetings of *Cylch Cadwgan*, a group of Welsh-language writers who met during the Second World War and whose discussions stimulated the production of innovative Welsh writing. Poet and novelist Rhydwen Williams (1916–1997), a prominent member of the group, was born in the village. Above **Llwynypia** on Mynydd-y-Gelli is a well-preserved embanked stone circle, popularly called the 'Rhondda Stonehenge'.

In 1856, **Porth**, where the Rhondda Fach joins the Rhondda Fawr, was the scene of the worst pit disaster to date in Britain with over 100 fatalities. Disaster struck again at the same pit in Cymer in 1877, with a dramatic rescue that inspired Joseph Parry to compose his typically melodramatic Miners' Anthem incorporating the hymn that the trapped miners sang as they awaited deliverance. It proved enormously popular at singing festivals. Porth is also the birthplace of British pop, not the music but the soft drink. Here, Thomas and Evans began production of *Corona* at the beginning of the twentieth century. The novelist Gwyn Thomas (1913–1981), born in Cymer, is the enduring voice of Rhondda solidarity. He portrayed his people with brilliant affection from his home base in Meadow Prospect. From Llwynypia, a minor road crosses over into the Rhondda Fach past the brutally exposed hilltop housing estate at **Penrhys**. Gwyn Thomas had a comradely understanding for these 'voters who like to live in high places' that frequently eluded the London politicians. The estate has engulfed the mediaeval pilgrimage chapel at Penrhys, originally built by the Greyfriars. The new ecumenical church of Llanfair Penrhys opened in 1992. **Maerdy**, at the head of the valley, with its Workmen's Institute dwarfing the tiny church, was known as 'Little Moscow' for its strong Communist leanings, but communism with its roots in Nonconformity. Arthur Horner (1894–1969) and Noah Ablett (1883–1935) were both products of chapel Sunday School as was Mrs Annie Powell, elected Britain's first communist Mayor in 1979.

A minor road ascends a ridge through the St Gwynno Forest to **Llanwynno** where the ancient parish church preserves the memory of Griffith Morgan (1700–1737). As Guto Nyth Brân, he is celebrated in Welsh folk memory as a legendary runner. His grave records his epic race against an Englishman in which he covered the twenty kilometres from Newport to Bedwas in fifty-three minutes, only to be

given a congratulatory slap on the back by a female supporter that caused him to collapse and die.

Pontypridd is the gateway to the Rhondda, where that
valley meets the Taf. Its historic market has been a traditional focal point for several valley communities. William
Edwards' masterpiece, the single-arched stone bridge over
the Taf, was constructed in 1756 and is now preserved in all
its glory for pedestrians. The bridge was his fourth attempt
at achieving this 40-metre span and succeeded through
the device of inserting three large holes in the structure
to lessen its load. The original Welsh name of the town
pre-dates the bridge, of course: *Pont-y-tŷ-pridd*, the bridge
by the earthen house. After Edwards built his bridge the
town was briefly known as Newbridge. The Victorian
Railway station has been renovated. Ynysangharad Park,
with its rocking stone, has a memorial by Goscombe John
to Evan James (1809–1878) and his son James James
(1832–1902), composers of the Welsh national anthem. It
was at Ynysangharad in 1818 that Samuel Brown, a former
naval officer and contemporary of Nelson's navy, joined
forces with his cousin Samuel Lenox to open a chain works
that supplied British ship and bridge engineers with a
replacement for rope. Anchors and chains for the *Lusitania*,
Queen Mary, *Renown* and *Hood* were made at Brown Lenox.
Sardis Independent Chapel, built in 1852, gives its name to
the adjacent rugby ground, Tabernacl Chapel in Bridge
Street now houses the excellent Pontypridd Historical
and Cultural Centre and the former Wesleyan chapel in
Gelli-wastad Road, built in 1894, is now an Arts Centre.

Ely

Although the Ely rises in the coalfield, this river is mainly
associated with the very different landscape of the Vale of
Glamorgan. The hilltop settlement of **Llantrisant**, partially
moated by the Clun and Ely rivers, makes a dramatic contrast

to the mining communities. Understandably, the Normans built a castle on this commanding site: all that remains of it is the ivy-clad Tower of Ravens at the town's highest point. Adjacent to it is the church, with its sixteenth-century tower and fine stained glass windows by Burne-Jones and Morris commemorating the ancestors of John Prichard who carried out the restoration of the church in 1873. The three eponymous saints are Illtud, Gwynno and Tyfodwg. Beside the church is the Guildhall, built in 1773 by Lord Mountstuart. A former mediaeval borough, Llantrisant has a county town feel to it and delightfully blends the pleasures of townscape with splendid views over the rural Vale of Glamorgan to the south. Regrettably its hillsides are being engulfed by extensive housing development that began when the Royal Mint relocated to Llantrisant from London in 1968. One local wit, overstating the case, summed up the result by appending some choice words to the town's welcome sign, so that it read: 'Llantrisant – the Hole with the Mint'.

To the west of the town is **Caerlan**, the hill on which Dr William Price (1800–1893) attempted to cremate his son Iesu Grist Price (Jesus Christ Price) in 1884, to the outrage of the townsfolk who intervened and prevented the occurrence. His son had died in infancy aged five months. Price attempted the cremation again two months later, was arrested, prosecuted but acquitted. When Dr Price died in 1893 he was cremated legally at the same place before a large crowd, the first public cremation in Britain. Sartorially eccentric – he sported a white cloak, red waistcoat, and green trousers offset by a fox-skin hat – Price was also a vegetarian and an advocate of free love. A man ahead of his time in so many ways!

Ogwr, Garw and Llynfi

Gilfach Goch, claustrophobically surrounded by Mynydd Maesteg in the confines of the Ogwr Fach, was the setting for Richard Llewellyn's 1939 blockbuster *How Green Was My Valley*, a work that laid the foundations of Valleys cliché on which Alexander Cordell subsequently built. Richard Llewellyn (1906–1983) had worked for a few months as a collier in Gilfach Goch in prepartion for his first novel. A massive reclamation scheme, partly financed from the proceeds of the Hollywood adaptation of the novel, in which many of the Welsh characters have Irish accents, has obliterated any traces of colliery workings. The title of the final work in Llewellyn's Valleys trilogy, *Green, Green My Valley Now* refers to this transformation.

The Garw, to the west, has a string of typical Valleys mining settlements: Blaengarw, Pontycymer and **Llangeinor**, where Richard Price (1723–1791), the philosopher and political pamphleteer who championed both the American and French Revolutions, was born at Tŷ'n Ton. The district centred on Maesteg and Llangynwyd, between Llynfi and Afan, used to be known as Tir Iarll, the Earl's Land, after Robert, Earl of Gloucester and his successors, the agents of the Norman conquest of this part of Glamorgan. A long poetic tradition in the area was represented at the end of the twentieth century by Brinley Richards (1904–1981), in Welsh, and Vernon Watkins (1906–1967), in English. Cadrawd (T.C. Evans, 1846–1918), blacksmith and folklorist, was also born here: his collection of bygones was donated to the Museum of Welsh Life. Once an iron town, **Maesteg** grew as the centre of the colliery district in the Llynfi valley. It has six listed chapels, including three – Bethania, Tabor, and Zoar – built by the same architect, W. Beddoe Rees, one of the finest chapel architects of the early twentieth century. The Edwardian artist, Christopher Williams (1873–1934), painter of the *Awakening of Wales* as well as numerous portraits of Welsh public figures, was born in Commercial Street, one of several in the town to have benefited from recent urban regeneration. **Llangynwyd** was home to Wil Hopcyn, who achieved immortality for reputedly composing the famous

Welsh folk-song, *Bugeilio'r Gwenith Gwyn* (Watching the Wheat). The churchyard has the grave of Samuel Jones (1628–1697), a former minister of the parish church, who was ejected from the living for refusing to conform to the Act of Uniformity in 1662. He founded a Nonconformist academy of note at Brynllywarch in the parish that trained a generation of men for the Nonconformist ministry. Of course, the grave of Wil Hopcyn is also in the churchyard but his true love, Ann, the maid of Cefn Ydfa, is buried inside as befitted her social status, the crucial difference between them, on which this story of unrequited love hinges.

Afan, Nedd, Dulais and Tawe

The Afan, Nedd and Tawe valleys run north-east to south-west into Swansea Bay. **Pont-rhyd-y-fen** first acquired celebrity by virtue of the majestic stone aqueduct built in 1827 by John Reynolds to supply water for his blast furnaces and copper works, then subsequently through the career of Richard Burton (1925–1984) who was born into a mining family here as Richard Jenkins. Such was his popularity that the plaque marking his birthplace below the viaduct had to be replaced continually.

Margam Abbey was founded in 1147 by the Cistercians, on the site of a former Celtic monastery. One of the great Welsh Cistercian houses, it passed into lay hands at the Reformation. The beneficiaries were the Mansel family, which as a result of marriage settlements assumed the name Talbot. Between 1830 and 1835, Christopher Rice Mansel Talbot, long-serving Liberal MP for Glamorgan, had Margam Castle constructed. The architect was Thomas Hopper, and Margam Castle was considered his masterpiece; partly ruined as a result of a fire in 1977, it has been consolidated and partially restored as the centrepiece of Margam Country Park. What remains of the mediaeval building is near the vast Orangery, designed by Antony Keck in 1787 for

Thomas Mansel Talbot. Theodore Talbot, only son of C.R.M. Talbot, was responsible for refurbishing the abbey church in the Tractarian manner with seven brass sanctuary lamps and other fittings. He suffered an identity crisis in 1869, briefly forsaking the life of a squire to do good works in the London slums before reverting to type and dying whilst riding to hounds at the tragically early age of 37, thereby precipitating one of the periodic crises of succession that beset this family. His marble effigy under a gothic canopy is in the north aisle of the church. In the south aisle, there are a splendid group of Mansel tombs from the sixteenth and seventeenth centuries. The stained glass is by Burne-Jones. A former school-room houses the Margam Stones Museum (Cadw), a remarkable collection of sculptured stones from the Early Christian period, including the Wheel Cross of Cynfelyn, together with the Maen Bodfog brought from Mynydd Margam. Above the Abbey stand the ruins of the fifteenth-century Capel Mair while Margam Park contains a herd of fallow deer and of the local Glamorgan cattle, a rare breed here saved from extinction. There is a maze, planted in 1982 and an innovative outdoor sculpture exhibition.

Port Talbot takes its name from the Talbots of Margam. C.R.M. Talbot was responsible for the Acts of Parliament of 1834 and 1836 that improved the harbour at Aberafan, thereby facilitating the export of coal and iron from the valley. Aberafan has now been absorbed into Port Talbot, a town solely dependent on the employment provided by the gigantic steelworks built here after the Second World War. Production has been considerably cut back in recent years, causing high unemployment in the town but considerably cleaner air. **Aberafan**'s chief claim to fame is that Dic Penderyn (1807–1831) is buried in St Mary's churchyard. Born Richard Lewis, in a cottage called Penderyn in nearby Pyle, Dic Penderyn secured lasting fame as the martyr of the Merthyr Rising. His last words on the gallows in Cardiff Gaol, *O Arglwydd, dyma gamwedd!* (O Lord, what an injustice!), have echoed in the Welsh folk memory ever since.

The Dulais joins the Nedd at Aberdulais, where, for over three hundred years, the spectacular waterfall at **Aberdulais Falls** (NT) has provided power for local industry. The waterwheel is the largest in Europe used to generate electricity and the Turbine House accommodates an attractive information centre. **Seven Sisters**, further down the valley, was given its English name for the daughters of the mine owner, David Bevan. He had wanted to name the first mine in the valley after his favourite daughter, Isabella, but his son insisted that no preference be shown. **Creunant** had the deepest anthracite mine in the world, now the Cefn Coed Colliery Museum.

The Romans established a major base at **Neath** in AD120, which they called *Nidum*. The remains of the fort, uncovered in 1949, are on the western bank of the river and it is still possible to trace the old Roman road of Sarn Helen north-east over the hills to Brecon. A Norman motte was thrown up to defend this strategic river crossing as elsewhere along the coast of the Severn Sea; the impressive fourteenth-century gatehouse survives. Neath Abbey (Cadw) was founded in 1129 by Richard de Granville, becoming a Cistercian house in 1149. The abbey has a good collection of decorated mediaeval floor tiles. Following the Dissolution, Richard Williams acquired the site and built himself an imposing mansion. Gilbert de Clare had granted the town its charter in 1280 but it was the coming of industry at the end of the seventeenth century that was to transform the life of the valley. Sir Humphrey Mackworth (1657–1727) recognised the value of the town's coastal location together with its plentiful supplies of timber, charcoal, and fast-flowing streams to power the bellows and hammers of metal-smelting furnaces. He imported Cardiganshire lead and silver and Cornish copper to feed his new furnaces. He is also remembered as one of the founders of the S.P.C.K. (Society for the Promotion of Christian Knowledge) that established schools for the children of his workers, both in Neath and at Esgair Mwyn in Cardiganshire. Sir Humphrey married Mary Evans, the heiress of Gnoll, a house demolished in 1957; its delightful and extensive landscaped gardens remain as an extraordinary civic asset. In the eighteenth century Cornish Quakers established the Abbey ironworks: the ruins of two of their furnaces can still be seen behind the abbey along with their meeting house, said to date from 1799, set into the walled forecourt north of the castle gatehouse. In the nineteenth century these ironworks were run by Joseph Tregelles Price (1784–1854), another Quaker and founder of the Peace Society, who refused to make cannons or shot and went to London to intercede with Lord Melbourne for Dic Penderyn. The parish church, dedicated to St Thomas-à-Becket, has a fine monument to Sir Robert Mackworth (1764–1794), tucked away behind the organ that he had donated.

Leland had described Neath Abbey as 'the fairest Abbey in all Wales'. By the time George Borrow passed by, he found 'immense stacks of chimneys, surrounded by diabolical-looking buildings, in the neighbourhood of which were huge heaps of cinders and black rubbish'. Prosperity had arrived: 'So strange a scene', noted Borrow, 'I had never beheld in nature.' The exuberant 1847 Mechanics Institute that now houses a local history museum was designed by Alfred Russel Wallace, who worked as a surveyor in Neath with his brother from 1841 to 1848. When the railway arrived from Cardiff in 1850, it further stimulated growth; the Victorian station expresses the confidence of the times. Neath has been relieved of through traffic by the construction of ingenious road bridges over the estuary at Llansawel, or **Briton Ferry**, as it became known in English. The dock, one of Brunel's last projects, developed as out-port for the Neath Canal.

The lower reaches of the Tawe were a notorious example of industrial despoilation that the Lower Swansea Valley Reclamation Project has sought to address. Moving up the valley, the impressive Victorian churches of St John the Baptist at **Clydach** and of St Peter at **Pontardawe** were bult by the local tin and ironmasters. By contast, a fine old Unitarian chapel is hidden away on Mynydd Gellionnen. Pontardawe also has a memorial to the poet David James Jones (Gwenallt, 1899–1968) and his companions. Gwenallt was born in the nearby village of Alltwen. **Ystalyfera** has plenty to interest enthusiasts of industrial archaeology, including early examples of a tramroad and canal aqueduct.

7

Cardiff and the Vale of Glamorgan

Cardiff

WITH THE ESTABLISHMENT of a Welsh Assembly in 1998, Cardiff came into its own as the supreme Welsh metropolis and has taken to promoting itself, with the usual quotient of veracity that slogan-mongers find acceptable, as 'Europe's youngest capital city'. It had been rehearsing this role for some time. By the last quarter of the twentieth century, Cardiff had replaced London as a magnet for the ambitious youth of the country. The Welsh capital is home to a plethora of national institutions, three of which – Welsh National Opera, the National Dance Company, and *Urdd Gobaith Cymru* (the national youth movement) – are housed in the Millennium Centre in Cardiff Bay where a new home for the National Assembly, designed by Richard Rogers, is also under construction. In short, a Cardiff address has become both necessary and fashionable and the city has developed a civic pride often lacking in the larger conurbations of a still over-centralised United Kingdom.

The story of its rise to metropolitan status can be traced in its built heritage. A good place to start is in the centre of the city at **Cardiff Castle**. Originally a Roman fort built in the third century to protect the Severn Sea approaches, it was one of the most elaborate such structures in the country. The 3rd and 4th Marquesses of Bute had its walls restored (too high for historical accuracy, but high enough for aristocratic privacy) so that it now gives a striking impression of its earliest incarnation. Within its walls is the

Norman keep constructed in the 1130s for Robert, Earl of Gloucester. William the Conqueror had passed through Cardiff on his way to St Davids in 1081, and raised the motte. The 3rd Marquess of Bute asked William Burges to refurbish the castle in 1868. In the course of the following decade the astonishing Chaucer Room, Arab Room, Library, Chapel, Banqueting Hall and the Winter and Summer Smoking Rooms were completed on the inside and the delightful Animal Wall and Clock Tower added to the exterior.

Cardiff Castle thus tells the story of its city. Of Roman foundation, lightly touched by the Normans, the town, if such it was, slumbered through the Middle Ages until the arrival from Merthyr Tydfil of the Glamorgan Canal in 1794 and the Taff Vale Railway in 1840. The linking of the Taf estuary with the mineral deposits of its hinterland allowed Cardiff to enjoy meteoric growth based on the single export commodity of coal. By the end of the nineteenth century, Cardiff was the world's largest coal-exporting port. The Cardiff we see today is thus characterised by the architecture of the late nineteenth century, some of it of great distinction.

The few remnants of the mediaeval period can be covered quickly. The castle itself has fifteenth-century domestic buildings behind the Beauchamp Tower, now used for those excruciating mediaeval banquets that tourist groups find so diverting. **St John's Church**, by contrast, is the pride of the city; its gloriously elaborate tower of 1473 still raises the spirits when viewed from the end of Church Street. The high altar reredos is the work of Goscombe John.

A tour of the city centre north of the railway, memorably described by Rhodri Morgan, currently the country's First Minister, as 'Cardiff's Mason-Dixon Line', cannot but start beside Cardiff Central Station at the **Millennium Stadium**, completed for the Rugby World Cup in 1999. Bold and confident in design, it has put Cardiff on the map as a major international sporting venue. **St Mary Street** leads back north to the castle. It has the usual chain stores of any British town, although the department store of Howells retains the name of its founder James Howell. In the men's department it has a plaque commemorating the Puritan Rawlins White (1485?–1555), the Cardiff fisherman burnt at the stake in the reign of Queen Mary. From St Mary Street, a series of **Arcades** run through to The Hayes where David Morgan's department store survived into the twenty-first century still run by its founding family. The Arcades are one of the delights of the city and owe their existence to the survival of burgages in Cardiff's mediaeval period of stagnation. Beside Howells is the impressive wrought iron **Central Market**, completed in 1891. It has a plaque marking the site of the execution of Dic Penderyn in 1831. The former **Cardiff Free Library**, which failed to survive into the new millennium as a museum of contemporary art, is a stylish building of great civic potential, dating from 1896; by contrast, the new City Library, part of the redevelopment of the city centre completed in 1982, is grimly functional. **The Hayes** has its famously cheerful island snack bar, a taste of old Cardiff not yet sanitised or commercialised out of existence, presided over by the statue of John Batchelor, 'Friend of Freedom', who was elected mayor of Cardiff in 1853 to oppose the Bute interest. Opposite, **St David's Hall**, home to the National Orchestra of Wales, is a surprisingly pleasant concert hall situated inside Cardiff's premier shopping mall, the **St David's Centre**. The latter, completed in 1982, seeks to retain, not entirely without success, the spirit of the nineteenth-century arcades, although the linking of our ascetic national patron saint with this shrine to consumerism is shockingly inappropriate. At the heart of the St David's Centre is a statue depicting the ample frame of a man who may be said to have acquired heroic if not saintly status in his native country: Gareth Edwards, the genius of the national rugby team in the 1970s.

The pedestrianisation of **Queen Street** has to be applauded although the resultant throng of shoppers is invariably depressing; my antidote is to stand facing the life-like statue of Aneurin Bevan and imagine him leading a perpetual march on the castle. **Park Place** has more to offer: the Edwardian New Theatre and Park House, built in the 1870s by Burges for the Marquess of Bute's engineer, John McConochie. **Windsor Place** is an elegant side street, with the stylish City United Reformed Church at its heart. To the east, **West Grove** has Cardiff's Mansion House, built as a private house for James Howell, the draper, and acquired by the city fathers in 1913. The previous home of James Howell in The Walk was also acquired by the city council, first for judges' lodgings and subsequently for use as a hospital from 1918 to 1977. Sir John Lynn Thomas, a surgeon at the hospital, built the half-size replica of the St Lythan's neolithic burial chamber in the small front garden of the house. An elegant *porte-cochère* has survived all these changes.

Edwardian Wales was a time of national self-confidence and its supreme monument is Cardiff's Civic Centre at **Cathays Park** which has drawn comparison with Washington D.C. for its visionary triumphalism. From the town centre, a pedestrian underpass crosses from the Boulevard de Nantes, where an attractive new public space has been created that has mercifully preserved the delightful drinking fountain given to the town by its mayor, William Alexander, in 1860 and originally situated in St Mary Street. National institutions, such as the National Museum, were conjured into existence during the period of national revival at the beginning of the twentieth century. The headquarters of the **National Museums and Galleries of Wales** (NMGW) offers a rich diet under a single roof. It is not only the National Art Gallery but also a diverse museum collection spanning prehistory, natural history, geology and arts and crafts. The bequest of their impressionist and post-impressionist paintings, including Renoir's *Blue Lady*, by the unmarried granddaughters of David 'The Ocean' Davies, Gwendoline and Margaret, form the core of a distinguished art collection.

Adjacent to the NMGW are the **Cardiff Law Courts** and the **City Hall** (1906). The sculpture sequence of Welsh heroes (no heroines, regrettably) inside the building and the proud dragon perched on the roof embody the confident cultural renaissance of Edwardian Wales. It was firmly expected that the new Welsh Assembly would inherit the latter building but it was not to be. Political squabbling sent the Welsh Assembly to the derisory accommodation of Crickhowell House in Cardiff Bay, likened by a visiting London journalist to an airport transit lounge and guaranteed to promote public indifference. W.D. Caröe's ornate **University College of South Wales** (now Cardiff University) was opened in 1883. The delightfully miniature **Registry** of the proudly federal University of Wales sits between the Law Courts and the former offices of **Glamorgan County Council**, the latter adorned with self-important sculpture. The foundations of the former Technical Institute (now the **Bute Building** of Cardiff University) were laid in 1913, the first work of the architect Percy Thomas, today the largest Welsh architectural practice. On the corner of Edward VII Avenue and College Road is the **Temple of Peace**, which surprises as a remarkable example of inter-war modernism, again by Percy Thomas. Built for Lord Davies of Llandinam, it houses the Welsh Centre for International Affairs, a charitable organisation that does excellent work promoting peace and international understanding under the auspices of the David Davies Trust. At the heart of the civic centre is the **Welsh National War Memorial**, completed in 1928, a model of its kind in grace and dignity set in a peaceful park. The former **Welsh Office** building (1938), with its moated and monitored 1970s extension, should be preserved for posterity, if only because it so concretely makes the case for a democratically-elected Welsh Assembly. When the plans for the civic centre were laid out this inspiring architectural ensemble was to have been continued northward to end with a flourish with a Welsh Parliament. World War and Depression put paid to that and the land to the north of the site was used for a ruralist housing development named Queen Anne Square, and Cardiff University's Music Department which has a Barbara Hepworth sculpture outside. The mock-Elizabethan Aberdare Hall for female students of the University opened in 1895.

South of the railway, Tiger Bay is now known as **Butetown**. A triple assault was made on this multi-racial, multi-lingual and multi-ethnic community by the *Luftwaffe* (in the 1940s), Cardiff's city fathers (in the 1960s) and the Cardiff Bay Development Corporation (in the 1990s), the latter two mistaking a vibrant community that was a beacon of hope for an intractable problem. The **Cardiff Bay** project is one of the largest of its kind in Europe but to date it is far from being the most visionary. Whereas the comparable community of Bilbao acted boldly to attract Frank Gehry's Guggenheim to kick-start quality urban renewal there, Cardiff had cold feet in 1991 and rejected Zaha Hadid's inspired design for a world class opera house which would undoubtedly have had the same effect here. Its replacement, the **Millennium Centre** that opened in 2004, is boldly unfashionable. It was quickly nicknamed The Armadillo, and first reports suggest a sensational accoustic. Close by, new retail developments, such as Mermaid Quay, are predictably soulless and the luxurious St David's Hotel and Spa looks inappropriately like a nun. Central to the planning concept of Cardiff Bay has been the completion in 2001 of a vast barrage that dams up the fragrant waters of the Taf. Some argue that this will lead at best to the creation of a noxious pond and at worst to severe flooding problems as levels of ground water inevitably rise. A few attractive buildings from the original dockland community survive: the **Norwegian Church**, re-erected at the waterfront in 1992; the **Pierhead Building** built in 1897 as the headquarters of the Cardiff Railway Company; and the once-frantic **Coal Exchange**, designated as the home of the Welsh Assembly that was still-born in 1979.

Cardiff is blessed with good parks. The line of green running north to south alongside the Roath Brook provides several such spaces, including a boating lake at **Roath Park**, with its Scott Memorial commemorating the ill-fated *Terra Nova* that set off from Cardiff in 1910. The church of St Margaret's of Antioch, at the junction of Albany and Waterloo Roads, is a distinguished example of John Prichard's polychrome; he also constructed the adjacent Bute Mausoleum. An even more impressive swathe of green runs beside the Taf from the castle in the city centre to **Llandaf**, the ancient ecclesiastical centre of south-east Wales. The supposed possession of the relics of Saints Teilo and Dyfrig made the cathedral a place of pilgrimage. Llandaf Cathedral has had an architectural history as chequered as the careers of its incumbents. By the nineteenth century the mediaeval structure had fallen into ruin; John Prichard's Victorian restoration suffered severe damage from a German landmine in 1941. An innovative rebuilding was undertaken in the post-war years that included the siting of Jacob Epstein's *Majestas* to span the nave. The cathedral is sited protectively in a hollow and is surrounded by a charming ensemble of buildings, ecclesiastical and secular, which fleetingly give the impression of Trollopian tranquillity. The adjacent village has Goscombe John's fine war memorial and St Michael's Anglican Theological College. The college incorporates the former home of John Prichard who lies buried in the Cathedral.

To the west of Cardiff, the delightful village of **St Fagans** is home to one of the principal visitor attractions of Wales, the **Museum of Welsh Life**. The museum opened in 1948 as the National Folk Museum, with Iorwerth Peate as curator, following the gift of St Fagans castle and its park to the National Museum the previous year. The castle, country retreat of the Windsors, local aristocrats grown rich on coal, has been restored to its Elizabethan splendour and the park filled with examples of vernacular architecture, at first from rural Wales, latterly also from the industrialised districts, all threatened in their original locations. Craftsmen follow their trades, a new block displays historical costume and artefacts, and a library is available to researchers. The museum requires a full day to appreciate and a café and restaurant – not to mention the delicious homemade bread from the bakery (relocated, like the tollgate, from Aberystwyth) – provide ample refreshment. Commercial pressures are all too apparent but these have to date failed to detract from the integrity and vision of its founding curator whose ashes were scattered behind the Unitarian chapel relocated from Pen-rhiw.

Vale of Glamorgan

To the Welsh, Glamorgan was traditionally divided into two contrasting parts, *Blaenau Morgannwg* and *Bro Morgannwg*. The first part, Upland Glamorgan, comprises the industrialised Valleys already described. *Y Fro*, confusingly translated into English as the Vale of Glamorgan, is not a valley as such but rather a distinctive and, for Wales, extensive area of fertile lowland that gave rise to prettily thatched nucleated villages and enclosed farms on the English model. 'Delicious Vale! By nature dress'd in Beauty's rich array', was how the Vale's most famous son, Iolo Morganwg (Edward Williams, 1747–1826) described the place. His collections of *tribannau*, the traditional rhyming couplets of Vale of Glamorgan ploughmen, provide evidence of the rich Welsh culture of the Vale of Glamorgan now sadly in retreat before an anglicising gentrification. The Vale is bisected from east to west by the

A48 that follows a historic route from Gloucester to Carmarthen. The road was known evocatively as the Portway, a usage that is conveniently revived here. The Portway has now been superceded by the M4 to the north; for the purposes of this section, the Vale is taken to lie south of the M4 between Cardiff and Bridgend, west of Penarth and east of Porthcawl.

In the Vale all roads lead to **Cowbridge**, its central market town, where the ancient grammar school has aped the English public schools for over 300 years. Founded by John Stradling of St Donat's Castle, the now derelict mock Tudor buildings were designed by John Prichard and financed by Jesus College, Oxford, which was the school's patron. There is a plan to turn them into flats. Beside the school is the church of Holy Cross which has Victorian stained glass in the chancel commemorating two Victorian headmasters of the school, the Reverends J.F.C. Morrison and Thomas Williams. Several other headmasters have their memorials here. Also buried here is Benjamin Heath Malkin (1769–1842), author of one of the best of the Welsh tours. The south gate, close by, marks the mediaeval entrance to the town through a good surviving section of the town walls. Cowbridge is a linear town, its High Street once carrying the traffic from Cardiff to west Wales, hence the handsome Georgian coaching inn, The Bear. A plaque on the wall of number 14 marks the site of Iolo Morganwg's bookshop. A Unitarian and political radical, he was a fierce opponent of slavery refusing to stock slave-grown sugar; a sign in his shop window advertised the sale of 'East Indian sweets uncontaminated with human gore'. A brilliant, if flawed, child of the antiquarian revival, Iolo Morganwg was a stonemason and a poet, a collector and fabricator of Welsh literary manuscripts and the principal architect of the National Eisteddfod in its modern form.

Just south of Cowbridge lies **Llanblethian**, the original settlement, where Robert St Quentin, about whom we know next to nothing, is said to have founded St Quentin's Castle (Cadw) in the twelfth century. West of the town, the isolated church of St Brynach at **Llanfrynach** escaped nineteenth-century restoration and is delightfully evocative of the mediaeval Welsh church, with traces of the original wall paintings still visible. It is well worth walking along the banks of the Thaw from Howe Mill Farm to the mediaeval manor house of **Old Beaupre Castle** (Cadw), seat of the Basset family from the fourteenth to the eighteenth century. The house was built around a courtyard in the sixteenth century and is notable for its splendid 'tower of the orders', three stories of Doric, Ionic and Corinthian columns that decorate the Porch. There are stunning tombs to the Basset and Mansel families inside St Illtud's church at **Llantrithyd** that stands next to the crumbling ruined walls of the once great sixteenth-century mansion of Llantrithyd Place.

Back on the west bank of the Thaw, a pilgrimage should be made to **Flemingston** where Iolo Morganwg lies buried in an unmarked grave in the churchyard. There is a florid memorial to him inside the church. Flemingston Court is a fine example of a small sixteenth-century manor house. Further down stream is **St Athan**, famous for its Second World War aerodrome and still the scene of military activity. Close to the airstrip, the tiny Eglwys Brewys has a charming interior with sixteenth-century wall paintings and the royal arms of that constitutional quadruped, William and Mary. Its name may derive from the Norman family *de Breos*. The mediaeval church of St Tathan is dedicated to an Irish saint who was instructed in a dream to travel to Wales. Inside there is a wall memorial by Iolo Morganwg and elaborate tombs of the De Berkerolles family whose ruined mediaeval manor lies romantically on the wooded hillside above the river.

Llancarfan is reputed to be the site of a sixth-century Celtic monastic foundation, one of three such in the Vale.

Its church is dedicated to St Cadoc, the Carfan in the place-name coming from the name of the stream that runs through this attractive village. The late thirteenth-century church probably occupies the site of the former monastic site. It is spacious with a double nave and a fine early sixteenth-century window in the chancel. The delicate reredos and screen fragments are remarkable survivals from the fourteenth century. Two fine old farmhouses, Garnllwyd and Llanvithyn, a kilometre to the north of the village, are associated with the monastery in local tradition. Norman in origin, **Fonmon Castle,** two kilometres to the south-east, has been continuously inhabited for over eight hundred years. It was remodeled for Robert Jones (1738–1793) and retains its splendid eighteenth-century gallery hung with family portraits and a full-length portrait of Oliver Cromwell by Robert Walker. Robert Jones II (1706–1742) was a contemporary of Charles Wesley at Oxford and Wesleyan Methodism developed in the Vale under his patronage. He is buried with his famous Puritan ancestor, Colonel Philip Jones (1618–1674), at St Mary's church in **Penmark**.

Barry has been aptly described as the result of one man's quarrel. The man was David Davies, Llandinam, the self-made industrial tycoon and his quarrel was with his aristocratic rival, the Marquess of Bute. Both men were coal owners and needed to export that product. The Marquess of Bute, the principal landowner of Cardiff, developed and controlled the docks there and imposed a prohibitive tariff on David Davies's Rhondda coal. As a railway engineer enriched by coal profits, Davies's solution was to construct his own railway to his own alternative port at Barry, a village of some 500 souls in 1881 that had become a town with 13,272 inhabitants a decade later. By 1913, at the height of coal production, Barry exported over eleven million tonnes of coal. The town's first dock was completed in 1889. A statue of David Davies stands in front of the grandiose Custom House (1898). The composer Grace Williams (1906–1977) was born in the town, as was Gwynfor Evans, arguably the most influential figure in twentieth-century Welsh political history. His father Dan Evans owned the department store that still trades in the main thoroughfare, Holton Road.

Barry Island, which developed along with the docks as a holiday resort for the mining communities of the Valleys, was immortalised in Idris Davies's poem *Maggie Fach*. By the 1970s, no longer the preferred destination for Sunday School outings and its former clientele having taken to sunning themselves on the Costa del Sol, only *aficionados* of fairground glitz and steam locomotive enthusiasts came to visit. When diesel replaced steam on British Railways, the steam locomotives were retired to Barry Island where they evocatively filled the former coal marshalling yards. Butlin's holiday camp has closed but the fun fair, famous throughout the Valleys, survives.

Cosmeston, a deserted thirteenth-century village, was excavated by the Gwent-Glamorgan Archaeological Trust in 1981. The site is sympathetically presented to the public, with mediaeval buildings reconstructed on their original foundations, in the context of a country park. St Lawrence's church on the cliff at **Lavernock Point** is of mediaeval origin but largely rebuilt in the nineteenth century. A plaque on the churchyard wall marks the spot where the first wireless telegraphy across water took place in 1897, when G. Marconi and G.S. Kemp sent a message from Lavernock Point to a mast on Flat Holm. The cliffs are of considerable geological interest, with horizontal triassic rocks lying on top of steeply dipping carboniferous limestone. The coast is rich in fossils, particularly ammonites. It is possible to walk out to **Sully Island** at low tide. **Flat Holm** is a small, low-lying island, some four kilometres offshore, with an important lighthouse controlling shipping in the Severn Sea. The most southerly point in Wales, and forming part of one of the Cardiff parishes, it may have housed the hermitage of St Cadog in the sixth century; in 1972 it was declared a Site of Special Scientific Interest for its seabird colonies and flora. Together with **Steep Holm**, which lies off the English shore, its name is of Viking origin.

Penarth has been drawn increasingly into the orbit of Cardiff by the redevelopment of Cardiff Bay but retains a certain aloof detachment from the hustle and bustle of the Welsh capital. Docks were built here, opening in 1865, to ease pressure at Cardiff. Under the patronage of the Windsor family, a select residential district and seaside resort was laid out that retains much of its period charm. The former attracted retired sea captains, businessmen, ministers of religion, such as Elfed, and men of letters, such as Saunders Lewis. The Esplanade has a pier with a Moorish style pavilion. The public gardens running down to the promenade are recognisably Victorian and St Augustine's church, opening in 1865, was one of William Butterfield's finest works, with a remarkable polychrome interior. Situated on Penarth Head, the church is a prominent feature of the Cardiff Bay skyline and a traditional navigational aid for shipping. Fittingly, it has the tomb of that quintessentially Victorian composer Joseph Parry in its churchyard. The town has a Windsor Road, Windsor Terrace, and a Windsor Arcade similar to those in Cardiff. The Turner House Art Gallery (NMGW) houses regular visiting exhibitions. The second of the Vale's triad of Celtic monastic sites is at **Llandough**, associated with St Dochdwy, although there is not a hint of the simplicity and grace of the early Celtic church in S.C. Fripp's Victorian lavatory-brick interior. The churchyard, however, contains the Irbic cross, one of the finest Celtic crosses in the country.

On the Portway out of Cardiff from Culverhouse Cross, the village of **St Nicholas** preserves several thatched cottages and is the point of entry for Dyffryn House. The approach lane to the house and gardens passes the celebrated

Tinkinswood neolithic chambered tomb (Cadw) where some fifty bodies were found during the 1914 excavation by John Ward. Its low, huge capstone weighs just over 40 tonnes. Tinkinswood is one of a cluster of cromlechs in this vicinity. **Dyffryn House** is in the vulgar French Second Empire style, built in 1893–4 with no expense spared for John Cory (1828–1910), the vastly wealthy ship and coal owner, passing into the hands of Sir Cennydd Traherne and then the local authority which is now trying to dispose of it. The interior incorporated a number of fine chimneypieces obtained from other properties, the exact provenance of which regrettably remains a mystery. The house is still visited for its gardens, the brainchild of John Cory's son who employed Thomas Mawson, the celebrated Edwardian landscape gardener at Dyffryn. The result is the best Edwardian garden in the country: some 36 hectares are laid out formally with the Pompeian Garden, physick garden, cloister garden and an elegant glasshouse vying for popularity. Seddon and Prichard restored the saddleback church of St Bleiddian at **St Lythans** in the 1860s. It has a large Norman font and a curious arcaded entrance to the mausoleum of the Button family, owners of Dyffryn House before John Cory. Sir Thomas Button was knighted by James I following his expedition in search of the north-west passage in 1612–1613 in the course of which he explored Hudson's Bay. A neolithic chambered tomb (Cadw) lies a kilometre to the south-west of the village.

Returning eastward, north of the Portway, the road to **St George-super-Ely** passes Coedarhydyglyn, an exquisite regency villa built in 1820 for the Revd. John Montgomery Traherne (1788–1860). A distinguished Glamorgan antiquary and the local squire, he arranged the 1838 restoration of the mediaeval church in the village. At **St Brides-super-Ely**, his wife Charlotte Traherne, sister of C.R.M. Talbot of Margam Abbey, insisted upon incorporating a Norman arch from Margam into the south porch during its restoration.

A niche at the east window, transferred here from the demolished chapel of St Mary at nearby Sant-y-Nyll, was filled in 1969 with a seventeenth-century Venetian Madonna.

Coychurch, on the eastern approaches to Bridgend, has a church so grandly proportioned that it became known as the 'Cathedral of the Vale'. Dedicated to St Crallo, it dates from the thirteenth century. The south transept was destroyed when the tower collapsed in 1877; John Prichard was responsible for the restoration. The overall impression, inside and out, is austere yet authoritative. Iolo Morganwg's mother, Ann Matthews, is buried in the churchyard as is Thomas Richards (1710–1790), the Welsh lexicographer, who published his dictionary when curate of the parish. **Coity**, otherwise a dreary suburb of Bridgend, has both an interesting castle and parish church. Coity Castle (Cadw) was started by the Turberville family in the twelfth century. A high round tower was erected in the thirteenth century and an outer ward added in the fourteenth. These enabled the castle to withstand a siege by Owain Glyn Dŵr. The tall chimney dates from Tudor times when the castle passed into the hands of the Sydney family who occupied it until the eighteenth century. St Mary's church is largely fourteenth century, with effigies of the Turbervilles and other intriguing memorials, including one on the east wall to Joan William who died in a thunder storm in 1710 aged 84.

The Ogwr – now sometimes anglicised as Ogmore – flows under an old stone bridge that gives the name to **Bridgend**, Pen-y-bont-ar-Ogwr in Welsh. A new bridge has been constructed adjacent to it to meet the demands of modern traffic. Above it is Newcastle (Cadw), built in the late twelfth century to guard this strategic bridging point; it has a fine portal. The whereabouts of the old castle are a mystery. The town is a suitably bland home for Ford Motors, relocated here at the beginning of the 1980s and now a major source of employment at its large plant to the east of the town. The town centre has been redeveloped to meet the needs of consumers and has little of architectural interest.

Llantwit Major, the third of the Celtic monastic sites to be found in the Vale and one of the ecclesiastical glories of Wales, is a most unfortunate rendition into English of the original Welsh. Llanilltud Fawr means the Great Church of St Illtud, the Celtic saint who founded his great monastic school here in the sixth century. It was one of the great centres of Celtic Christianity. E.G. Bowen followed the seventh-century *Life of St Samson of Dol* in suggesting that Illtud combined elements from three separate cultural traditions, the ascetic Christian tradition of Gaul, the classical learning of Rome and the mysteries of the druids. 'Now this Illtud', the *Life* informs us, 'was the most learned of all the Britons: in his knowledge of the Scriptures, both Old and New Testaments; in every branch of philosophy and rhetoric, grammar and arithmetic; and he was most sagacious and gifted with the power of foretelling future events.' The subsequent Norman church was attached to Tewkesbury Abbey until the Reformation and then transferred to the care of Gloucester Cathedral. The remains of the Celtic monastic school, an inspiration to generations of Welsh people before the national university was established in 1872, are believed to lie above the church to the north. The unexpectedly large proportions of the church surprised John Wesley when he preached here in 1777: 'I suppose it has been abundantly the most beautiful, as well as the most spacious, parish church in Wales.' For two churches are here combined: a western and an eastern, to either side of the central tower. Looking west from the tower along the nave of the western or parochial church the eye is led through the tower arches and the choir arch into the sanctuary beyond. This part of the building now serves as a museum in which a remarkable collection of ninth- and tenth-century Celtic crosses have been gathered together, including the Houelt and Samson stones and the Illtud cross-shaft. The eastern or monastic church has a fourteenth-century reredos and murals of St Christopher and Mary Magdalene. Its treasure is the richly carved Jesse Niche, a thirteenth-century carving of the Tree of Jesse, no longer in its original location.

A more recent episode in the long Christian history of the village concerns the chapel of Bethesda'r Fro, built in 1806 for the Independent ministry of Thomas William (1761–1844) after he had left the Calvinistic Methodists at Aberthin, siding with Peter Williams (1723–1796) in the Sabellian dispute. Born in the Vale at Trerhedyn, he is remembered as one of the great Welsh hymn-writers and is buried in the chapel's burial ground. One of William's associates in founding this cause, John Williams (1728–1806) was also a gifted hymnist. The chapel was restored by the Royal Air Force in 1969. The village, increasingly suburbanised, still has good buildings worth seeking out: the thirteenth-century gatehouse of the monastic grange, the late sixteenth-century Old Swan and Old White Hart inns, and a *columbarium*. **Trebefered** is a curiosity: the nucleus of a 1930s Welsh Land Settlement Project intended to resettle unemployed miners from the Valleys. To the west, the street village of **Broughton** is where George M.Ll. Davies held his summer camps for unemployed Rhondda miners in the old Malthouse.

This stretch of coastline with the infamous Tusker Rock lying just off the coast at Ogmore-on-Sea has long been hazardous to shipping. Treacherous currents combined menacingly with a sudden constriction of the Severn Sea at **Nash Point** to provide regular employment for generations of wreckers. Help came in 1832, following a petition from over 400 Newport ship-owners after the wreck of the steam packet *Frolic* the previous year, when Joseph Nelson, the prolific lighthouse engineer, constructed the first lighthouse on the cliff. The second lighthouse is still in use, indeed it was one of the last manned lighthouses in the British Isles until automated in 1998. Single-storey keepers' houses, now available as holiday accommodation, and an impressive foghorn complete the ensemble. A bracing coast walk can be made due east to **St Donats** where, since 1962, Atlantic College has occupied the much-altered castle. The original castle building dates back to the fourteenth century and was the seat of the Stradling family until it failed in the male line in 1738. In 1925 the castle was acquired by that archetypal media tycoon, Randolph 'The Chief' Hearst for his mistress Marion Davies. The telegram he sent to his London agent read: 'Want buy castle in England'. Marion Davies soon tired of Wales, finding California more congenial, and Hearst switched his attention to San Simeon, but not before he had used his surfeit of dollars to raid Europe for works of art which he installed willy-nilly at St Donats. The ceiling of Wiltshires's Bradenstoke Priory here, a fifteenth-century screen from a Devonshire church and an antique French fireplace there, and so on *ad nauseam*. Atlantic College has an exclusive twin sister in New Mexico named in honour of another American tycoon, Armand Hammer. Deriving its educational philosophy from Kurt Hahn, the eccentric founding headmaster of Gordonstoun, pride of place in the curriculum of Atlantic College is given to 'outward bound' pursuits and sea-rescue activities. Interviewed with Hahn in the late sixties, a bemused Leo Abse, then Labour MP for Pontypool, inquired whether Hahn's character-building enterprise would not be better achieved by seconding Atlantic College students to his constituency: 'There, sometimes in grim conditions, miners face daily hazards and are only too often involved in rescue operations.' Atlantic College sits on the cliff edge of Wales, in more ways than one.

The parish church to the west of the castle houses the splendid tombs of the Stradling family. In 1991, the late sixteenth-century paintings of the Stradlings, executed on wood, were sensationally stolen from the church but have since been recovered; they now hang safely in the National Museum in Cardiff. Expect to have to ask for the key to gain admittance. There is a fine mediaeval cross, remarkably complete, in the churchyard.

Ogmore Castle (Cadw) has guarded the estuarine crossing of the Ogwr for a millennium. The twelfth-century keep survives, together with its original chimneypiece, looking down on St Teilo's Steps, although the original stepping stones of that name were a little further upstream on an ancient route over the Ewenni to Merthyr Mawr beyond the Ogwr. Sea-buckthorn is prolific hereabouts, its orange berries attracting thrushes and fieldfares; so are prehistoric implements – numerous flint arrowheads and scrapers have been found locally. But before crossing the estuary, be sure to visit one of the ecclesiastical treasures of Glamorgan, the magnificently fortified **Ewenni Priory** (Cadw). Originally a Benedictine foundation, it has been sensitively restored by Cadw to reveal more of its wonderful collection of mediaeval wall paintings. There is a fourteenth-century screen and interesting effigies in the south transept, including those of the abbey's founder, Maurice de Londres, and of the Carne family who acquired the priory following the Dissolution. Soar chapel close by, now a private house, was associated with the histrionic Calvinistic Methodist preacher Matthews Ewenni (Edward Matthews, 1813–1892), a former collier who delighted large congregations with his droll but dramatic delivery in local dialect. Ewenni pottery was famous in the eighteenth century with as many as fifteen kilns operating in this locality producing a distinctive ware with a yellow glaze. Traditional Ewenni designs can be obtained at the pottery which was re-erected in the Museum of Welsh Life in 1988.

On the west bank of the Ogwr, the idyllically thatched estate village of **Merthyr Mawr** has the Tractarian church of St Teilo, designed by Pugin's pupil and biographer,

Benjamin Ferrey. The extensive dunes of Merthyr Mawr Warren extend as far as **Newton Nottage**, on the outskirts of Porthcawl, where the church of St John the Baptist has an unusual fifteenth-century stone pulpit decorated with a flagellation scene. A kilometre to the west is Nottage Court, a rare survival in these parts of a Jacobean house that has retained much of its original interior decoration. Here lived the novelist R.D. Blackmore (1825–1900), author not only of *Lorna Doone*, but also of *The Maid of Sker*, a fine portrait of eighteenth-century Welsh society set in Sker House, a couple of kilometres to the west. Sker House, in danger of collapse in 1977, has been magnificently restored thanks to the Architectural Heritage Fund. Originally a grange of Neath Abbey, it passed into the hands of the Turberville family in the sixteenth century.

Porthcawl became a desirable holiday destination for working people from the Valleys. The annual Miners' Eisteddfod was held at The Grand Pavilion on The Esplanade from its inception in 1948 to 2002, a showcase for the cultural tradition of the Welsh labour movement. In October 1957, Paul Robeson, who had demonstrated consistent solidarity with Welsh miners in the depression years, sang to the eisteddfod via radio link, his passport having been confiscated by the McCarthyites in his home country, the U.S.A.

8

Swansea and Gower

Swansea

IN ENGLISH, **Swansea** has a Viking name, *Sven's Ey* (Sven's Island) that hints at the town's ninth-century origins; its Welsh name places it geographically at the mouth of its river, Abertawe. It was C.S. Lewis who noted that towns invariably show their worst faces to the railway, an observation that could have been made when entering Swansea from east or west. A pernicious combination of the most environmentally destructive heavy industries of the Industrial Revolution, the *Luftwaffe* and hasty post-war development produced Dylan Thomas's

> 'ugly, lovely town,
> crawling, sprawling
> slummed, unplanned
> jerry-villa'd and smug-suburbed'

Swansea is celebrated for the warmth of its people – affectionately known as Swansea Jacks – and its cultural vitality rather than for architectural splendour.

Swansea was not overtaken in size of population by Cardiff until the late nineteenth century, prior to which it could boast a kind of primacy. In 1804, it produced the first Welsh newspaper, *The Cambrian*, and, in 1814, the first Welsh-language weekly, *Seren Gomer*. It is claimed that the Mumbles Railway, opened in 1807, was the first passenger-carrying railway in the world. Of the captains of industry, the Dillwyns who operated the Cambrian Pottery produced the much-prized Swansea ware, examples of which can be seen at the Glyn Vivian Art Gallery and The Royal Institution of South Wales. Like other early copper kings, the Vivians came to Wales from Cornwall, opening the Hafod Works that began the environmental devastation that the Lower Swansea Valley Reclamation Scheme was created to rectify. Having begun to manufacture sulphuric acid from the copper smoke at Hafod, the Vivians sensibly made their home at Singleton Park where they constructed a Victorian Gothic Abbey open to fresh sea breezes. The Abbey is now the administration building of the local university, incorporated into the University of Wales in 1920. From Cardiff, the easiest entry into Swansea by road is to follow the west bank of the Nedd estuary from Briton Ferry along the coast to arrive directly at the new Marina which, with adjacent superstores and hotel, seems to encompass the town's contemporary architectural horizons. Wind Street and Mansel Street, by contrast, give tantalising glimpses of a more elegant past. Commercial activity in the docks has greatly declined, although there is a ferry service to Ireland, and an exciting new National Waterfront Museum (NMGW) is due to open here in 2005, dedicated to telling the story of the maritime and industrial heritage of Wales.

Culturally, Swansea has always had much to offer. The Grand Theatre was opened by Adelina Patti in 1897 and went on to survive the blitz and post-war neglect to be imaginatively redeveloped by the city council in the 1980s, preserving its charming Edwardian interior whilst gaining a new fly tower, dressing rooms and foyer. It is now home to the Wales Theatre Company and the only classical ballet company resident in Wales, *Ballet Russe*. The lively Taliesin Arts Centre at Singleton Park, run by the university, is open to the public as is the adjacent Egypt Centre that, since 1971, has housed the Wellcome Collection of Egyptian artefacts. The Guildhall, an example of homespun modernism, contains the Brangwyn Hall, named after the huge murals painted by Sir Frank Brangwyn in the late 1920s to adorn the Royal Gallery in the House of Lords but rejected for that location as too gaudy. The hall has a wonderful acoustic and is a regular venue for orchestral concerts. For many, Swansea has become synonymous with Dylan Thomas and the city council has not spurned the tourist revenues that the poet's fame brings in its wake. A Dylan Thomas Centre in Somerset Place provides an informative exhibition on the poet's life and the poet's birthplace in Cwmdonkin Drive in the Uplands district of the town has been leased by the council for occasional literary events. Close by is Cwmdonkin Park, where the cherubic young Dylan used to work on his early poems. An annual Dylan Thomas Festival is held in the autumn.

From the east, the city is approached through **Morriston**, famous for its hospital and its male voice choir, the Morriston Orpheus. The latter originated in Y Tabernacl, described as the 'Cathedral of Welsh Nonconformity', that was built by a local boy, John Humphreys, in 1870 to seat 1,800 worshippers. Morriston takes its name from Sir John Morris whose father came from Shropshire to establish copper works, brass-wire mills and collieries in the district. A model village, that survives only as the grid pattern of what is now a suburb of Swansea, was constructed between 1790 and 1796. Copper and zinc were smelted at **Llansamlet** until the 1960s, highly polluting industries that had replaced coal mining in this section of the valley by the end of the nineteenth century. **Landore** also had a similar tradition of metalworking that gave it a hellish reputation:

> It came to pass in days of yore
> The Devil chanced upon Landore
> Quoth he, 'By all this fume and stink
> I can't be far from home I think.'

It was here in 1868 that William Siemens opened a works using his newly discovered 'open-hearth' method of steel production that produced steel of superior quality to that produced in Bessemer converters.

Gower

Before the Act of Union, the Lordship of Gower was distinct from the lordship of Glamorgan and Swansea was its capital. The Gower peninsula to the west of Swansea is the town's delight: it would be difficult to imagine a greater contrast to the urban blight of parts of Swansea than this designated Area of Outstanding Natural Beauty with its rich heritage of archaeology, history and natural history. The Gower peninsula has a geological divide that is also a cultural divide. The fertile limestone country to the south and west came under Norse and Norman influence whereas the more acid soils to the north and east remained thoroughly Welsh. A band of unproductive millstone grit, used for common land, marks the boundary between these two zones. Dramatic limestone cliff scenery and sand dunes to the south-west contrasts with mud flats and salt marshes to the north-east.

Oystermouth, towards the southern tip of Swansea Bay, is the result both of a vain attempt by the English to pronounce Ystumllwynarth and of the widespread reputation of the local shellfish in the nineteenth century. It has the ruins of a Norman castle that passed in and out of Welsh and English hands until the fourteenth century. The parish church of All Saints has an out-of-scale extension built at the end of the nineteenth century to accommodate holidaymakers. The municipal cemetery has the grave of Morfydd Owen (1891–1918), the talented musician from Trefforest who died tragically after eighteen troubled months of marriage to Ernest Jones, assistant to, and biographer of, Sigmund Freud. Also buried in the churchyard is the Revd. Thomas Bowdler (1754–1825), immortalised as the editor of an expurgated family version of the works of Shakespeare.

To the south of Oystermouth is the **Mumbles**, with its pier, lifeboat station, lighthouse and recent fame as the birthplace of Catherine Zeta Jones. Moving west from Mumbles through Limeslade and Bracelet Bays towards **Langland Bay**, the coast becomes wilder and more rugged. Beyond **Caswell Bay** and the white pebble beach at **Pwll Du** are the archaeologically famous Minchin Hole and Bacon Hole caves, where the bones of prehistoric animals have been found. They are accessible only at low tide. **Threecliff Bay** has fascinating sand dunes that have invaded this little cove to partially bury two mediaeval churches and threaten Pennard Castle. The dunes and marshes of **Oxwich Bay**, one of Gower's finest, protect **Penrice Castle** from the sea. The ruins of this thirteenth-century castle are situated in the grounds of an eighteenth-century house built for Thomas Mansel Talbot of Margam. **Oxwich** has the delightful battlemented church of St Illtud, surrounded with sycamores and containing an attractive fourteenth-century tomb to the Delamare family and Oxwich Castle (Cadw), a Tudor fortified manor house occupying a commanding site overlooking the bay, was built by Sir Rice Mansel (1487–1557) to replace Penrice Castle. The small late Victorian church at **Nicholaston** was completed in 1894 by G.E. Halliday; thoroughly Tractarian in spirit, it has alabaster statues of Keble, Liddon and Pusey on its hanging pulpit. Further inland, and back in time, the village of Ilston was the location of the mother church of the Welsh Baptists, founded by John Miles in 1649. The ruins of his first chapel survive in **Cwm Ilston**, marked by a memorial that was unveiled by Lloyd George in 1928.

From the viewpoint above **Penmaen** (NT), paths lead north to the neolithic burial chambers of Pen-y-crug on the coast and the Giant's Grave at Parc le Breos (Cadw). The Le Breos family dominated Gower life for centuries, the estate being sold in the 1950s. The 'Red Road' west along the ridge of Cefn Bryn leads to a cluster of prehistoric cairns and burial chambers, including the greatest of Gower cromlechs, Arthur's Stone, with its enormous capstone. From Oxwich Bay, a coastal path follows magnificent limestone cliffs, eroded into fantastical shapes, westward to Worm's Head. These cliffs are rich in rare plants including horseshoe vetch, goldilocks aster, small rest-harrow, spring cinquefoil, hoary rockrose, hutchinsia and wild cabbage. In 1823, the oldest human remains yet found in Wales were discovered in **Paviland Cave** and promptly dubbed the 'Red Lady' because what has since been shown to be the skeleton of a palaeolithic man were stained with red ochre. **Worm's Head** itself is accessible for a few hours at low tide; it has a seabird colony of guillemots, razorbills, kittiwakes, shags and fulmars.

The great sweep of **Rhosili Bay** is a perfect place for sunsets, as the waves break over some three kilometres of unbroken sand, ending in **Burry Holms**, an island only at high tide with the remains of a mediaeval chapel. **Rhosili Down** (NT) which rises behind the bay to its highest point, the Beacon, at 193 metres, has two neolithic burial chambers, known as Sweyne's Howes. The church at **Rhosili** has a memorial to Petty Officer Edgar 'Taff' Evans (1876–1912) who was born in the village but perished at the foot of Beadmore Glacier when returning with Captain Scott from the South Pole. To the east of Burry Holms are the magnificent sand dunes of Llangennith Burrows and Broughton Burrows, with **Whiteford Burrows** (NT) beyond. This is a traditional place for the harvesting of seaweed for the Welsh delicacy of laverbread, delicious rolled in oats and fried with bacon. The parish church at **Llangennith** is built on the site of St Cennydd's sixth-century monastery; the stone with interlaced carving set into the west wall of the nave is reputedly his tomb. **Weobley Castle** (Cadw) is an attractive fortified manor house dating from the late thirteenth century occupying a commanding position overlooking the extensive salt marshes. The castle was in the continuous possession of the De la Bere family until it fell to Owain Glyn Dŵr.

The north shore of the Gower peninsula is a remarkable landscape of salt marsh with the mud and sand flats of the Loughor estuary beyond. The church at **Llanrhidian**, dedicated to saints Rhidian and Illtud, retains its massive defensive tower but otherwise suffered a severe Victorian restoration. In the porch is a curious inscribed stone, known as the Leper Stone, with stylised carvings of human and animal figures. At **Penclawdd**, around the corner from Crofty, the traditional harvesting of cockles has been mechanised so it is no longer possible to see the bands of cockle-women with their rakes and sieves loading their harvest into donkey paniers. Back-breaking work, for sure, too easily romanticised in retrospect, but part of an old Gower, the passing of which has understandably been regretted by surviving members of this distinctive community.

The ruins of **Loughor Castle** (Cadw) stand on a Norman motte that occupies a site archaeologists have revealed to contain a Roman fort. The strategic importance of the location, guarding the estuary, is obvious. **Pontarddulais**, a former tinplate township, is on the county border with Carmarthenshire. To visit the mediaeval church of **Llandeilo Talybont** it is necessary to go to the Museum of Welsh Life. Rescued from dereliction, it is being re-erected in the grounds of the musem, the first mediaeval church in Britain to be moved in this way. Its colourful wall paintings, discovered in the process of relocation, are being restored to their mediaeval glory.

III
South-west Wales

9

Carmarthenshire

THE M4 CROSSES the Loughor into Carmarthenshire just a few kilometres before it ends at Pont Abraham but the A48 trunk road that continues on to Carmarthen is of such a high standard that commuting between Carmarthen and Cardiff is no longer unheard of. Both the north and south coasts of Wales are shrinking, for the same reason. Fast these roads may be but interesting they are not. We shall have to slow down and explore the by-ways if we are to discover the county. The ending of the motorway is a salutary reminder to slow our pace as we enter the more rural south-west of the country.

The transition is gradual, however. **Ammanford**, on the west bank of the Aman where it joins the Loughor, was the anthracite capital for the Aman and Gwendraeth valleys. Anthracite was first mined in this area in the eighteenth century with the first deep mine being sunk at Brynlloi in **Glanaman** in 1757. When the railway arrived from Llanelli in the middle of the nineteenth century, production soared and continued until the end of the 1980s. The Aman valley has been a stronghold of Welsh culture. James Griffiths (1890–1975), appointed by Harold Wilson as the first Secretary of State for Wales in 1964, was born in **Betws** on the east bank of the river. His brother, D.R. Griffiths (Amanwy, 1882–1953), a poet, was the subject of the film *David* made to represent Wales in the 1951 Festival of Britain. **Brynaman** provided both the chaired and crowned bard at the 1972 National Eisteddfod and **Gwaun-cae-gurwen** nurtured a twentieth-century hero of Welsh rugby,

Gareth Edwards, who uniquely represented his country for fifty-three consecutive matches.

The anthracite deposits spread south along the Gwendraeth valley. Social stress consequent upon the rapid industrialisation of this district was a contributory cause of the 1904 Revival that had its epicentre in **Penygroes**, where the charismatic preaching of the young Evan Roberts (1878–1951) ignited the last great religious revival in Welsh history. The Apostolic Temple in the village is the heart of the Apostolic Church, a denomination founded by the collier pastor Dan Williams in the years following the revival that now has a worldwide membership. **Cefneithin** has a celebrated rugby club, founded in 1922, that nurtured two giants of twentieth-century Welsh rugby, Barry John and Carwyn James (1930–1983). Their new rugby field, inaugurated in 1976, was named after Carwyn. To the south, a string of former coal-mining villages, still largely Welsh-speaking, owe their existence to an outcrop of anthracite, some of which could be mined easily by open-cast methods. The drift mine at **Cynheidre**, which opened in 1956, closed in 1989. In the 1920s, Tom Nefyn began to preach a socialist gospel from the pulpit of the Calvinist Methodist chapel in **Tumble** with the result that he was drummed out of his denomination for heresy in 1928, another symptom of stressful times. Quietism prevailed over the social gospel, but it seems that neither end of the theological spectrum appeals to today's generation: both Llain-y-Delyn and Ebeneser Calvinistic Methodist chapels closed in the 1990s.

Llyn Llech Owain, four kilometres to the north-east, takes its name from an Arthurian tale. Owain, an Arthurian knight, is responsible for the size of the lake and for its boggy hinterland, since, contrary to strict instructions, he neglected to put the stone cover (*llech*) back on a well after he and his steed had refreshed themselves. Today the well and surrounding peat bog have been designated a Site of

Special Scientific Interest. There are good paths providing opportunities to view unusual woodland birds, birds of prey and wildfowl together with rare flora; rare Marsh Fritillary butterflies can also be seen in the summer months.

In 2000, the **National Botanical Garden of Wales** opened in the grounds of Middleton Hall at Llanarthne. It contains the largest single-span greenhouse in the world, an iconic structure designed by Sir Norman Foster, dedicated to the display of rare Mediterranean flora. Middleton Hall was built in the seventeenth century by the High Sheriff of Carmarthenshire, Henry Middleton. In the mid-eighteenth century the estate was sold in discharge of debts and acquired by William Paxton a wealthy banker who had made his fortune as a 'nabob' in India. Paxton built a new house and developed the parkland and it is this late property that is now being restored as the setting for the new Botanic Garden. Notable features being brought back to life include a rare example of a double walled garden. **Paxton Tower** (NT), two kilometres to the north-east, was built for William Paxton to commemorate Lord Nelson. It affords fine views over the Vale of Tywi.

Carmarthen has been the unchallenged capital of its region for centuries. With the main roads from Cardiganshire and Pembrokeshire converging on the town, it was a natural choice for the headquarters of Dyfed County Council when that unitary authority was created from the three counties in 1974. In Roman times it was Moridunum, a major civil and military centre, served by sea and linked by road to Caernarfon in the north and Caerleon in the east. A Roman amphitheatre has been excavated in Priory Street. In post-Roman times, the town continued as a Romano-British centre, around which stories about Merlin crystalised, for Caerfyrddin means Merlin's Encampment in Welsh. In Norman times a Franciscan friary and Augustinian priory were established in the town. In the latter, the Black Book of Carmarthen, generally regarded as the oldest manuscript in the Welsh language, was compiled some time in the twelfth or thirteenth centuries. It is now held in the National Library of Wales. Few traces of either foundation can be discerned today; Priory Street and Friars Park preserve their memory. The parish church of St Peter contains a monumental brass to Sir Richard Steele (1671–1729), 'first chief promoter of the periodical press of England' and the fine sixteenth-century tomb of Sir Rhys ap Thomas. There are also a number of interesting wall memorials, including one to the unfortunate Robert Ferrar, Bishop of St Davids, who was tried for leniency towards popery in the reign of Edward VI only to be burnt at the stake in Carmarthen in the reign of Queen Mary for his adherence to Protestantism. The former Art School, opposite St Peter's church, now houses a good art gallery, Oriel Myrddin.

Carmarthenshire was the largest in area of the historic Welsh counties and Carmarthen is the county town that has retained that function for longer than any other in Wales, an unbroken record since Edward I created the shire in 1284. Prior to the industrial revolution it was the largest town in Wales. Its county hall, built in 1938 and known locally as The Bastille – since it both resembles the building destroyed in the French Revolution and occupies the site of Nash's town gaol – is a striking feature of the skyline above the Tywi as the town is approached from the south-east. Regrettably, coracle fishing on the river did not survive the twentieth century, but the town has not been inundated in fulfillment of ancient prophecy: for, of an oak tree in Priory Street, Merlin is said to have foretold:

> When this oak shall tumble down
> So will fall Carmarthen town.

In 1978, the petrified stump of this oak was removed with some trepidation, from the junction of Priory Street and

Old Oak Lane, in a road-widening scheme. The only consequence seems to have been unprecedented growth and prosperity for the town, although it may still be premature to discount Merlin's prophecy. The stump of Merlin's oak can now be inspected at St Peter's Church House in Nott Square, the latter named after General Nott, a hero of the Afghan Wars, whose statue was designed by Edward Davis. The pleasing Guildhall, dating from 1770, witnessed scenes of ecstatic celebration when Gwynfor Evans became the first Plaid Cymru MP in 1967, a turning point in modern Welsh history. The imposing gatehouse of the original Norman castle survives just off Nott Square. The market, equally ancient, but rebuilt in utilitarian style in the 1970s, enlivens the town centre on Wednesdays and Saturdays.

Carmarthen has played a distinguished part in the history of Welsh education. In 1847 its old-established Presbyterian College, located on The Parade, obtained a royal warrant to award University of London degrees to its students making it the first institution of higher education in Wales to offer university degree courses. Like other Nonconformist academies, it had an advanced curriculum: the college's scientific apparatus is now on display at Cardiff University's Humanities Library. The college, which closed in 1963, nurtured generations of Nonconformist ministers. By way of contrast, the town's bilingual secondary school, which opened at the former Queen Elizabeth Grammar School in 1978, has nurtured the popular Indie band, *Gorky's Zygotic Mynci*, a group at the heart of the Cool Cymry phenomenon of the 1990s in which several sons of the manse participated. To the west of the town are two famous, if contrasting institutions, Trinity College and St David's Hospital. Trinity College, opened as an Anglican teacher training institution in 1848, largely through the efforts of Connop Thirlwall, Bishop of St Davids. St David's Hospital, 'The House of the Mad' of Caradoc Evans' stories, has shaken off its fearful reputation. Nearby, Picton Square has an appropriately imposing and clumsy monument to Sir Thomas Picton (1758–1815), who followed up his successes in the Peninsular War by fighting to the death alongside the 'Iron Duke' at Waterloo.

It was Bishop Barlow (c.1499–1568) who made **Abergwili** the administrative centre of the vast St Davids diocese, ensuring that the episcopal relocation was permanent by having the roof of the Bishop's Palace in St Davids pulled down. The replacement Bishop's Palace at Abergwili – rebuilt in 1906 after a fire – has housed an excellent county museum since 1978 when the diocesan administration again moved to new premises. It contains a sixth-century Ogham memorial stone inscribed to Voteporix the Protector and an interesting chapel on the first floor. A new gallery devoted to the agricultural history of the county opened in 2004. It was at Abergwili that William Salesbury (c.1520–1584?) translated the Book of Common Prayer into Welsh under the patronage of Bishop Richard Davies (1501?–1581), himself translator of parts of the New Testament. There is a memorial to Richard Davies inside the church of St David's at Abergwili, the wide nave of which is said to derive from the reluctance of Bishop Thirlwall to visit his cathedral to perform ordinations. To the south of the town, the churchyard at **Llandyfaelog** has a bicentennial monument to Peter Williams, the publisher of *Beibl Peter Williams*, who is buried in the churchyard. A convert to Calvinistic Methodism, he was expelled from that denomination at a *Sasiwn* – an Association meeting or conference – held at Llandeilo in 1791, accused of doctrinal weakness on the subject of the Trinity.

At **Cydweli** a splendid concentric Norman castle (Cadw), built on a steep ridge overlooking the Gwendraeth, affords fine views over the town. Dating from the twelfth century, its remarkable survival is due in large part to its having avoided involvement in the Civil War. The Great Gatehouse, protecting the entrance to the castle, consists of

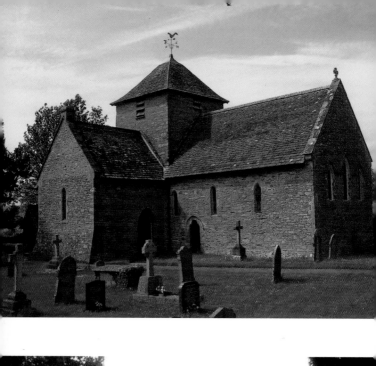

five levels and took over a century to complete. The stone castle dates from the thirteenth century, and succeeded an earlier structure that had changed hands between the Normans and the Welsh for close on two centuries. Famous owners of the castle included Lord Rhys, John of Gaunt and the Earl Cawdor. The southern gatehouse, between the castle and the bridge, is all that survives of the town walls. The fourteenth-century steepled church of St Mary has an alabaster figure of the Virgin above the altar that dates from the church's foundation. During the industrial revolution, the town pioneered the manufacture of tinplate.

Llanelli was also famous for its tinplate industry, rugby football and choral singing, encapsulated in the tireless singing of the town's unofficial anthem, *Sospan Fach*, that inspired the magnificent Scarlets to a famous victory against the All Blacks at Strade Park in 1972. Even the rugby posts have saucepans on them. The huge post-war steel-works at Trostre remains at the forefront of European tinplate production and Llanelli remains the largest town in the county. The town has a proud Nonconformist tradition. David Rees (1801–1869), for thirty years the editor of *Y Diwygiwr*, and one of nineteenth-century Nonconformity's doughtiest protagonists, ministered for the Independents at Capel Als and Jubilee Young (1887–1962) later ministered to the Baptists at Zion. The English cause at Park was established by David Rees in 1839. Llanelly House, on the corner of Bridge and Vaughan Streets, has been described as the finest Georgian town house in Wales; completed in 1714, it is undergoing welcome restoration. The former railway that linked the Gwendraeth coalfield with the docks at Llanelli is now an attractive leisure trail passing the Upper and Lower Liedi reservoirs. Further evidence of the greening of a former industrial landscape can be found at Penclacwydd, a kilometre to the east of the town, where The Wildfowl and Wetlands Trust has its only

Welsh centre. Some 200 hectares at the edge of Burry Inlet, one of the country's premier sites for wildfowl and waders, is now protected. Of particular interest is the population of Little Egrets, whose numbers have increased dramatically in recent years.

Following the Tywi upstream from Carmarthen and Abergwili, the native Welsh castle of **Dryslwyn** (Cadw), perched on a rocky knoll, enabled Rhys ap Gruffudd to withstand successive seiges by Marcher barons. Pellitory and Good King Henry grow in abundance amongst the ruined masonry. At **Aberglasney**, the 'Garden Lost in Time' has justifiably become a popular tourist destination. Praised in verse by Lewys Glyn Cothi as early as the fifteenth century, the property and its gardens passed into the hands of Bishop Rudd of St Davids in 1600. Subsequent owners further developed the gardens, including Robert Dyer and his son John, the pastoral poet and painter. John Dyer (1699–1757) died tragically young but left us *Grongar Hill*, named after the local iron age hill fort, singing the praises of the Vale of Tywi:

> When will the landscape tire the view!
> The fountain's fall, the river's flow,
> The woody valleys, warm and low;
> The windy summit, wild and high,
> Roughly rushing on the sky!
> The pleasant seat, the ruined tower, the naked rock,
>   the shady bower:
> The town and village, dome and farm,
> Each give each a double charm,
> As pearls upon an Aethiop's arm

Aberglasney subsequently passed into the hands of the Philipps family, who had made their money in India. The house and gardens were abandoned in the twentieth century until they were acquired by the Aberglasney Restoration Trust in 1995. A unique Jacobean garden has been uncovered and one of the most exciting garden restoration projects in the country inaugurated. Bishop Rudd and his wife are buried in a splendid bedstead tomb in the parish church of **Llangathen**.

Llandeilo is an attractive small market town nestled on the north bank of the river with good Georgian town houses. The town was originally an important religious centre, established by the community of St Teilo in the early Middle Ages. The Gospel Book of St Teilo, carried off to Mercia as booty, is still held at Lichfield Cathedral. The two fine Early Christian inscribed stones that can now be seen inside the parish church were excavated in the second half of the nineteenth century when the church was under restoration. They had apparently once been deliberately toppled and buried in a successful attempt to degrade the site at the end of the twelfth century. There is a remnant of an abbey wall in the town and some good surviving chapels, including Tabernacle for the Independents and Soar for the Baptists. Quay Street serves to remind us of a now forgotten aspect of the town's past.

To the west of the town are the extensive grounds of **Dinefwr** (NT), a site of great historical importance to this part of Wales. A recent archaeological survey has revealed that two Roman forts co-existed on this site. Rhodri Mawr (d.877) had Dinefwr as his base during a remarkable reign that saw the Vikings repulsed and his authority accepted over the greater part of the country. Following his death, Wales fractured and Dinefwr became the centre for Deheubarth. The subsequent Norman keep (Cadw) was rebuilt by Sir Rhys ap Thomas at the beginning of the Tudor period. In the seventeenth century, a new house was built less than a kilometre to the north that was again replaced in 1856 by R.K. Penson's forbidding Victorian pile, now known as Newton House. Requisitioned as a military hospital in the Second World War, the ground floor and basement of the property are now open to the public. These properties have occupied an impressive site, naturally moated by the meanders of the Tywi. Two stands of beech, prominently planted by

'Capability' Brown, are conspicuous in the landscape where the famous herd of white Dinefwr cattle grazes in the park.

The south bank of the river, magnificently spanned in 1848 with the longest stone arch of any bridge in Wales, can be explored west of Ffairfach. **Gelli Aur**, known in English as Golden Grove when it was the seat of the Vaughan and Cawdor families, is now a country park. The original sixteenth-century mansion of the Vaughans no longer exists; the present neo-Tudor house and matching estate village were completed for the Cawdor family in 1832. The estate, long the rival of Dinefwr, was famed for its deer. Richard Vaughan, earl of Carbery (1600–1686) commanded the royalist forces in Wales during the Civil War but the payment of a substantial fine enabled him to survive into the Restoration. Indeed he was responsible for protecting another royalist, the English theologian Jeremy Taylor (1613–1667), author of *Holy Living* and *Holy Dying*, the latter containing a moving tribute to Frances, saintly wife of Richard Vaughan. Her portrait, together with those of other members of this prominent local family, hangs in the library of Gelli Aur. Another member of this family, William Vaughan (1575–1641) was the founder of the ill-fated Welsh settlement in Newfoundland, Cambriol. Since 1952, Gelli Aur has done sterling work as an agricultural college. Its grounds are now a country park with nature trails that reveal a rich diversity of bird life and flora. Its deer park has been restored and a small herd of fallow deer established; a Victorian arboretum has Giant Redwoods and Monterey Pines as well as rhododendrons and azaleas. The hilltop church of Llangynnor contains a memorial to the essayist Sir Richard Steele (1672–1729) and a fine commandment board. David Charles (1762–1834), Calvinistic Methodist minister, hymn-writer and younger brother of Thomas Charles (1755–1814) is buried in the churchyard as is Sir Lewis Morris (1833–1907), barrister and poet. There are good views from the churchyard over the Tywi down onto the former Bishop's Palace at Abergwili.

South-east of Llandeilo are the ruins of one of the most dramatically situated of Welsh castles, **Carreg Cennen** (Cadw) sitting majestically on its limestone crag. It can be approached along the lanes that pass through Trap and there is parking on the north side. Its origins go back to the arrival of the Normans in Deheubarth at the beginning of the twelfth century and may have been built defensively by Lord Rhys. In mid-century the grip of the Plantagenets was broken by an alliance of the princes of Gwynedd, Powys and Rhys ap Gruffudd of Deheubarth, with the result that Carreg Cennen came into the possession of the latter only to have its ownership disputed in an inheritance wrangle following his death. The castle then passed alternately from Welsh to English hands, including those of such illustrious owners as Llywelyn Fawr, Edward I and Owain Glyn Dŵr. During the Wars of the Roses, Edward IV ordered the demolition of the castle and for the past five hundred years this romantic ruin has been subject to sporadic restoration, beginning with Tudor loyalist Sir Rhys ap Thomas and continuing to the present stewardship of Cadw. The castle, built to enhance a near perfect natural location, is a wonderful example of the most ingenious period of Norman military architecture. A dovecote constructed in the limestone cave beneath the south-east tower is an added attraction.

Trains on the Heart of Wales Line pass into the Vale of Tywi via Llandybïe, a pleasant village that was a centre of limestone quarrying for generations. The main road has two clapboard houses built in 1897 by the Davies family when it returned to the town after working in the United States as carpenters. The 1944 National Eisteddfod was held here at the end of the Second World War, its opening concert, sponsored by the British Council, assembling choirs from all over the world. The concert was such a success that it was decided to organise the International Eisteddfod in Llangollen in 1947 that has since become a successful annual event.

By following the lanes to the north-east of Carreg Cennen, it is possible to move back even further in time. If considered a single hillfort rather than a combination of two, then **Carn Goch** is the largest of its kind in Wales and certainly one of the most impressive. Huge ramparts of rubble accentuate the natural defences of the ridge. Inside the fort is a great pile of stones that may be the remains of a bronze age burial chamber. **Bethlehem** has a Post Office that does a roaring trade at Christmastide when mail has been known to arrive in sacks from embassies in London to have the stamps on their Christmas cards appropiately franked. The chapel, from which the village derives its name, is prominent on the hillside.

The Sawdde can be followed on foot to its source, the deep waters of **Llyn-y-Fan Fach** in a glacial *cwm* on the Black Mountain. A folk tale records the tragic life of a shepherd boy who met, courted and wed a beautiful Lady of the Lake, another of those enchanted maidens that connect us with the Celtic pre-Christian beliefs that venerated water sources. He was condemned to lose her were he to strike her thrice and this, under severe provocation, he fatefully did but not before he had fathered three remarkable sons who grew up to become the Physicians of Myddfai, a village that lies to the north. **Myddfai** was famous throughout Wales in the Middle Ages for these physicians, a tradition still alive in the nineteenth century. The thirteenth-century church of St Michael has a hatchment to the Gwynne family and, appropriately, a prominent memorial to a nineteenth-century surgeon in the porch. John Thomas (1730–1804), hymn-writer and author of *Rhad Ras neu Lyfr Profiad*, the first autobiography in the Welsh language, was born at Col. As a young man he was a manservant to Griffith Jones, Llanddowror, who arranged for him to receive an education at Trefecca.

Llangadog, beautifully situated between Brân and Sawdde, has a fine old parish church dedicated to St Cadog and the remains of a Norman motte, Castell Meurig. It was captured using 'catapults and slings' by Maelgwn ap Rhys in 1203 after which it seems to have become disused. Llangadog is also the village where Gwynfor Evans established the market garden that enabled him to devote his life to the political transformation of his country. His former home, Talar-wen, is a precocious example of Welsh organic architecture, built for him by his brother-in-law Dewi Prys Thomas in 1956, a wedding present from his father. Devotees of Frank Lloyd Wright should stop to admire it.

Llandovery (Llanymddyfri, in Welsh) has been a market and droving centre, clustered around its Market Square, serving the hill country around it for centuries. The financial needs of the drovers led them to create some of the first provincial banks in Britain issuing their own paper money. One such, *Banc yr Eidon Du* (The Black Ox Bank), was founded in the town in 1799 by Dafydd Jones, a drover. The ruins of an early Norman castle survive on a rocky hillock above the Afon Brân at the southern edge of the town. Here, a memorial sculpture was unveiled in 2001 to an ally of Owain Glyn Dŵr, Llywelyn ap Gruffudd Fychan. He was executed in Market Square six hundred years earlier; a plaque marks the spot near the useful Llandovery Heritage Centre. The parish church of Llanfair-ar-y-bryn, above the town to the north, is a large building on the site of a Roman fort, with a sturdy thirteenth-century tower. The cultural importance of Llandovery is revealed in its churchyard, where a pink granite obelisk commemorates William Williams, Pantycelyn (1717–1791), who was both baptised and buried here. Not only the supreme hymnist of Welsh Calvinistic Methodism, but also one of the greatest poets in the Welsh tradition, Pantycelyn has been known affectionately to generations of Welsh speakers as *Y Pêr Ganiedydd* (The Sweet Songster). His *opus* in large measure accounts for the enthusiasm of the Welsh for hymn-singing. Williams Pantycelyn famously described Wales before the Methodist Revival of the 1730s as languishing in a 'dark, fatal sleep, without a presbyter or clergyman or bishop astir, enveloped in thick darkness', a judgement that inaugurated a Calvinistic Methodist historiography that went unchallenged for generations. The conscientious Anglican Vicar Rhys Prichard (Yr Hen Ficer, 1579–1644) was born in the town and became its vicar. His much-loved and oft-quoted collection of moral rhymes *Canwyll y Cymry* (The Welshmen's Candle) is a salutary corrective to this version of history. Pantycelyn was himself brought up to attend services with the Independents at Cefnarthen and attended the Nonconformist academy at Llwynllwyd, serving as a curate in the Anglican Church until the day he died. A stained glass window by Kempe inside the parish church commemorates both Pantycelyn and Vicar Prichard; the William Williams Memorial Chapel is, ironically, the home of the English Methodists in the town.

Llandovery College was founded as the Welsh Collegiate Institution in 1848 in response to the Report of the Education Commissioners published in the previous year. It intended to give pride of place to the Welsh language in its curriculum, a worthy purpose that faded as the jingoism of Empire that had infected the country was mirrored in the school curriculum. More recently, the school has fostered its reputation as the most Welsh of the handful of public schools in the country. Carwyn James taught here and the school has produced a long line of Welsh rugby internationals. The original buildings are Victorian Gothic in style. **Pantycelyn**, the farm where William Williams lived following his marriage, is just two kilometres east of the town beside the Independent chapel of Pentre Tŷ Gwyn. His was the supreme achievement of a county famed for its hymn-writers; seen in a wider context, Pantycelyn is one of Europe's great Romantic poets. His descendants still live in the farmhouse.

North of Llandovery, the upper reaches of the Tywi were dammed in 1972 to form **Llyn Brianne**, flooding a delightful valley to provide water for Swansea. Blanket conifer afforestation completes the scene. New roads, built to service the reservoir, enable cars to reach Soar-y-Mynydd, the most isolated chapel in Wales. **Capel Ystrad Ffin**, a kilometre below the dam, once belonged to Strata Florida. A neglected chapel of ease at the county border it made a convenient meeting place for the early Welsh Methodists; the present structure is Georgian and retains many of its original interior fittings. **Ogof Twm Siôn Cati**, high above the Tywi, can be reached by following the Dinas Nature Trail (RSPB). The cave is named after a lovable rogue, the illegitimate son of Sion ap Dafydd ap Madog ap Hywel Moetheu of Fountain Gate near Tregaron and Catherine Jones, a descendant of Sir John Wynn of Gwydir. Twm courted and won the heiress of Ystrad Ffin, abandoned robbery and was appointed county sheriff. Below **Rhandirmwyn**, with its abandoned lead mines, lies **Cil-y-cwm** where the attractive mediaeval church of St Michael has interesting wall paintings. Capel-y-Groes, an Independent chapel built in 1859, represents a much earlier cause. Morgan Rhys (1716–1779), another celebrated hymnwriter from this county, was born in the nearby cottage of Efail Fach and was an early Methodist preacher. Between the two villages, in the farmhouse of Dugoedydd, the first *Sasiwn* of the Welsh Calvinistic Methodists was held in 1742. **Pont Dolauhirion** spans the Tywi less than a kilometre north of Llandovery, a graceful single arch that represents the work of William Edwards at his best.

The Cothi is one of the most delightful rivers in the county, its banks still preserving stands of sessile oak that form a perfect habitat for native fauna and flora. It has lent its name to Lewys Glyn Cothi (1420–1489), one of the greatest Welsh poets of the fifteenth century, to a notable Unitarian, Tomos Glyn Cothi and to a popular contemporary singer, Siân Cothi. **Cwrt-y-Cadno** was once celebrated throughout Wales for its *dynion hysbys*, rustic soothsayers of a kind common enough in the Welsh countryside before the combined effects of formal education and Nonconformist disapproval drove them to extinction. John Harries (d.1839) and his son Henry attracted a constant stream of both visitors and hostile editorials in the religious press. A small Calvinistic Methodist chapel glares at their home, Pantycoy.

Dolaucothi (NT) has Britain's only known Roman gold mine open to the public. Archaeological excavations have revealed a great deal about Roman mining techniques and this site, lying on the main Sarn Helen roadway, provides eloquent testimony as to the purposes of the Roman occupation of the hill country of western Britain. It is still possible to trace the rock-cut aqueduct that brought water to the mines from the Cothi. Mining has resumed intermittently since Roman times, most recently in the 1930s when soaring gold prices appeared to offer the chance of a favourable return on investment.

To the east, **Cynwyl Gaeo** has a church with a massive square tower dedicated to five Celtic saints: Ceitho, Celynnin, Gwyn, Gwynno and Gwynoro, quintuplets of a proud sixth-century father, Gynnyr Farfdrwch ap Gwron ap Cunedda. An Early Christian inscribed stone is embedded in the north wall of the tower and the graves of John and Henry Harries are in the churchyard, with Henry described as a Surgeon. Dafydd Jones (1711–1777), a drover from the village, translated the hymns of Isaac Watts into Welsh and published the first collection of hymns for his denomination, the Independents, in 1753. He had been converted by a Methodist preacher, Thomas Morgan, at Troedrhiwdalar, when returning home from a drove and went on to become a faithful member of the Independent congregation at **Crug-y-bar**. His career illustrates the 'Methodisation' of Old Dissent. Formerly a congregation of *sentars sych* (dry dissenters), the Crug-y-bar Independents rapidly gained a reputation for their emotional services, presided over by Nansi Jones (Nani Crug-y-bar). John and Morgan Dafydd, village cobblers also touched by the Methodist Revival, composed hymns that are still sung today, the tune Crug-y-bar being particularly popular at funerals. **Pumsaint**, where the Twrch joins the Cothi at the place of the five saints – the same quintuplets to whom the churches at Cynwyl Gaeo and Llanpumsaint are dedicated – was traditionally the market centre for this country and before that was a Roman station associated with the works at Dolaucothi. A Roman bathhouse and two forts were excavated here in 1972.

Talley Abbey (Cadw), situated mid-way along the undulating B4302 from Llandeilo to Crug-y-bar, was founded by Rhys ap Gruffudd for the Premonstratensian Order, an order founded in the early twelfth century that followed the Rule of St Augustine and shared Cistercian ideals. Established around the year 1180, it is the only house of White Canons to have been founded in Wales. The monastery was well endowed; the ancient *clas* church at Llandeilo, for example, was appropriated to it. It has a delightful situation at the southern end of a lake; Talyllychau, the Welsh name from which Talley is derived, incorporating the earlier Celtic word for lake, familiar to visitors to Scotland and Ireland, *loch* or *lough*. The lake would undoubtedly have been well stocked with perch for the monks' fast days. The abbey seems to have a hard time of it. It suffered from the jealousy of the Cistercian abbot of Whitland, and after the Conquest Edward I ordered the replacement of the Welsh monks 'by others of the English tongue who are able and willing to observe the religious life'. The original ambitious building plans were not completed and the damage sustained during the Glyn Dŵr Rising was never made good. By the time of the Reformation, the abbey had only eight canons. The eastern and northern walls of the tower remain and the outline of the nave, transept and presbytery remain. The parish church, built in 1772 but since altered externally, has preserved its pleasingly simple Georgian interior.

On the Llanybydder road north of Talley, the Cothi is immediately bridged at **Edwinsford**, the seat of Sir Rice Williams, one of a handful of landlords prepared to be lenient to local dissenters at the time of the Clarendon Code. He lies buried with his ancestors in Talley Abbey. It is appropriate, therefore, that **Llansawel** is dominated by Shiloh, an early Calvinistic Methodist chapel, and that in the hills to the north, at **Esgerdawe**, one of the county's oldest dissenting congregations should have established itself. The writer and nationalist D.J. Williams (1885–1970) was born here in Pen-rhiw. He celebrated his upbringing in the countryside around Esgerdawe and **Rhydycymerau**, the neighbouring village to which he moved at the age of six. Aber-nant, the farmhouse of his childhood and the heart of his acclaimed autobiography, *Hen Dŷ Ffarm*, lies just outside the village to the west on the Talley road. A prominent member of Plaid Cymru, and one of the 'Penyberth Three' he advocated what he called *cenedlaetholdeb y filltir sgwar*, locally-rooted nationalism. To the west of Rhydycymerau is a claustrophobic blanket of conifer plantations:

> *Coed lle bu cymdogaeth*
> *Fforest lle bu ffermydd*
> *Bratiaith Saeson y De lle bu barddoni a diwinydda*

> (Trees in place of community
> Forestry in place of farms
> English slang from the South instead of poetry
>   and theology)

The poet is Gwenallt, a close relative of D.J. The farms of his ancestors, his childhood haunts – Llywele, Esgeir Ceir, Tir-bach and Cilwennau Ucha – lie under the forestry, a metaphor for the destruction of a fine but fragile culture by a Philistine modernism.

It was in **Brechfa**, in 1796, that Thomas Evans (Tomos Glyn Cothi, 1764–1833) presided over the first openly

Unitarian place of worship in Wales. A weaver by trade, his enthusiasm for rational Christianity led to his being nick-named 'Priestley bach' in the locality. He served time in Carmarthen Gaol during the Napoleonic Wars for singing his own Welsh translation of the *Marseillaise* in public. The Mormons subsequently established themselves in the area, with a meeting house at Capel Silian. Dan Jones, a converted Calvinistic Methodist who had worked with Prophet Joseph Smith in America, led a major migration from these hills to Utah, the Mormon Zion. The church of St Teilo, delightfullly located beside the Afon Pîb at the extremity of the parish boundary has the grave of a local Mormon elder, Evan Morgan. The arrival of the Forestry Commission after the Second World War, with its own housing and an English section in the school, was the beginning of an increasingly rapid Anglicisation of this district. The surrounding hills contain numerous bronze age burial cairns, often known as *crugiau* locally.

Llanfynydd, nestled in Cwm Sannan, was the setting for the 1953 film, *The Valley of Song*, an early cinematic representation of Wales as a musical nation. The double-naved church of St Egwad has a massive battlemented tower and dates back to the thirteenth century. Restoration work in 1861 revealed evidence of a major fire in the sixteenth century, after which there was a significant amount of rebuilding. In the churchyard is the grave of the hymn-writer Morgan Rhys who spent the last years of his life here. **Capel Isaac**, two kilometres to the east above the Afon Dulas, is one of the earliest centres of Nonconformity in the county, the cause having been established by Stephen Hughes, the seventeenth-century 'Carmarthenshire Apostle'. The plain nineteenth-century chapel is a fitting monument to his integrity.

Llanybydder was long famous for its monthly horse sales and fortnightly sheep mart. BSE and foot and mouth took their toll but livestock remain central to the town's economy. **Llanfihangel-ar-arth** was the location of a nineteenth-century *cause célèbre* when voyeuristic tourists and journalists flocked to the village using the recently opened railway to witness the phenomenon of Sara Jacob, the fasting girl. She had apparently survived on faith alone for several months at the family farm of Llethrneuadd-uchaf when visitors began to pay to take a peep at her. The story did not end happily, the death of the emaciated girl in 1869 being variously ascribed to religious mania, bulimia or parental exploitation. The thirteen-year-old lies buried in the churchyard; her parents were brought to trial and committed to Carmarthen Gaol. Ironically, English evacuees in the Second World War pronounced the village Laughing Angel of Death.

Pencader expanded as a railway junction for the branch line to Llandysul and Newcastle Emlyn off the Manchester and Milford Railway line. For a taste of the days of steam, visit the Gwili Steam Railway that runs seasonal trains at Bronwydd. Formed in 1975, this company aims to reopen some ten kilometres of the line from Abergwili Junction to Llanpumsaint. Pencader was an early centre of Independency, with clandestine meetings taking place in Cwmhwplyn under the Penal Code before a chapel was opened in the village. The old chapel has been imaginatively restored as a community centre; its replacement, Y Tabernacl, is still active. According to Gerald of Wales, when Henry II was receiving the homage of Rhys ap Gruffudd in 1163, where a small castle mound can still be identified, he was given the following counsel by the Old Man of Pencader:

> 'This nation may now, as in future times, be oppressed, and greatly weakened and destroyed by your and other powers; but it can never be wholly subdued by the wrath of man, unless the wrath of God shall concur, nor do I think that any other nation than this of Wales, or any other tongue,

whatever may come to pass hereafter, shall in the day of severe searching before the Supreme Judge, answer for this corner of the earth.'

Like the castle mound, the slate inscription recording these prophetic words is overdue for refurbishment.

West of the A485, which runs down to Carmarthen from Alltwalis to arrive at the big modern hospital at Glangwili, is the village of **Llanpumsaint**, not to be confused with Pumsaint on the banks of the Cothi some twenty kilometres to the north-east. Among the village's famous sons are Brutus, the editor of *Yr Haul*, and William Williams (1788–1865), who as MP for Coventry secured the appointment of the 1847 education commission. To the west, **Cynwyl Elfed** commands the road junction for Llandysul and Newcastle Emlyn to the north and Carmarthen to the south. It is a pretty village with a fine chapel. Howell Elvet Lewis (1860–1953), a former Archdruid, took his bardic name, Elfed, from the parish in which he was born. He was both a poet and major twentieth-century writer of devotional hymns for the denomination he served as a minister, the Independents. A small museum has been established at his childhood home, Y Gangell.

The parishes of **Penboyr** and **Llangeler** to the north saw the development of a mechanised textile industry at the end of the nineteenth century. The coming of the railway enabled the area to supply industrial south Wales with shirts for colliers, furnace-men and tinplate workers. During the First World War, the industry enjoyed a boom from army uniform contracts. There is a fascinating Museum of the Welsh Woollen Industry (NMGW) at **Drefach Felindre** in the former Cambrian Mill, one of some forty such mills once clustered around this village, the remains of which can still be sought out. The Unitarian chapel at Penrhiw was re-erected at St Fagans in 1957. We are fortunate in having two superlative accounts of life in

Llangeler a century and more ago written by two of its sons. In English, the elegiac memoirs of Daniel Parry-Jones (1891–1981) – *A Welsh Country Upbringing, Welsh Country Characters, My Own Folk* and *A Welsh Country Parson* – written to counter the depiction of rural life found in the pages of Caradoc Evans – provide an invaluable record of now vanished agricultural practices in this corner of Carmarthenshire in the early years of the twentieth century. In Welsh, *Hanes Plwyfi Llangeler a Phenboyr* by D.E. Jones, based on an essay submitted for a competition at the local eisteddfod in 1897, is a remarkable piece of local historical research in which the author succeeded in establishing that Dol Goch, the home of Dafydd ap Gwilym's uncle, was in the parish of Llangeler, beside the Afon Bargod.

Newcastle Emlyn takes its name from its thirteenth-century Norman castle, moated by a meander in the river and designated new to distinguish it from either the older motte at Adpar or the castle at Cilgerran. It was substantially rebuilt in the fifteenth century before being blasted apart by Cromwell's men during the Civil War. Danish scurvy-grass grows on the ruined walls, surprisingly distant from its usual coastal habitat. **Adpar**, on the Cardiganshire side of the Teifi, was one of the rotten boroughs eliminated following the reform of Parliament in 1832. A plaque in the village marks the site of the first permanent printing press in Wales, established here in 1718 by Isaac Carter.

It is not hard to see why **Cenarth** has become a tourist honey-pot. The falls on the river are picturesque and easily accessible: dramatic after heavy rain and spectacular in September when Atlantic salmon leap upstream. Its distinctive stone-arched bridge was built by David Edwards in 1787. The ancient art of coracle fishing survives precariously here; the National Coracle Centre, located in the grounds of a restored watermill that once served a local monastic community, providing explanation. Although the church of St Llawddog, on a hill above the village, is a Victorian replacement for the original mediaeval church, it has an intriguing Early Christian inscribed stone in its churchyard.

South of Carmarthen, on the west bank of the Tywi estuary, lies the attractive former fishing village of **Llansteffan** with its Norman castle (Cadw) built high above the village on the site of an iron age promontory fort to guard the entrance to the Tywi. From the castle ruins there are magnificent views across the shifting sands of the tidal estuary to Ferryside and out across Cefn Sidan to Worm's Head on the western tip of Gower. The parish church, with its thirteenth-century tower, has good wall monuments and, beyond the castle, there is a holy well dedicated to St Antony where pins were thrown and wishes made. There is good vernacular architecture and a particularly fine property, Y Plas, which was the home of Sir John Williams, Queen Victoria's personal physician who helped found the National Library in Aberystwyth. **Llan-y-bri** has a curiosity in the ruined church around which the village is clustered. A former chapel of ease, it came into the possession of the Independents in the eighteenth century, inaugurating a period of continuous dissenting worship in a building previously dedicated to the Blessed Virgin that lasted for over two centuries. There is a new church to the south of the village and a new chapel, Capel Newydd, to the north-east. The ruined church of **Llandeilo Abercywyn** sits isolated on marshland beside the Cywyn. It is a romantic ruin in a splendid location that was the venue for Thomas Charles' first sermon. The adjacent farmhouse is called Pilgrims' Rest, suggesting a point of departure for mediaeval pilgrims to St Davids. The new church, built in Victorian times, contains the Norman font in which Thomas Charles was christened; he was born nearby at Longmoor, a farm since demolished.

The A40 trunk road heads west from Carmarthen to St Clears. **St Clears** has a classically proportioned Town Hall, built in 1848, opposite which a long path leads to the mediaeval parish church. Originally part of a Cluniac priory, it has a striking Norman chancel arch and interesting wall memorials. A motte and bailey on the riverbank also speaks to the former importance of this place in the Middle Ages. To the north-west, **Llanboidy** (originally, Llan-beudy) has been put on the map by the Jones family who have produced cheese here since 1985. The resurgence of traditional cheese-making in south-west Wales has enabled a cheese trail to be devised for interested visitors to follow. Neither Pant-y-caws, to the north, nor Nant-y-caws, back on the main road east of Carmarthen, have any connection with cheese, however, the *caws* in these place-names deriving from the English word 'causeway'. For a delightful Baptist chapel, dating from 1701, cross to the east of the A478, to seek out **Rhydwilym**, tucked away on the Carmarthenshire bank of the Eastern Cleddau. All Baptist activity in the county derives from the 'gathered church' first established here by William Jones in the seventeenth century.

The first attack on a tollgate by the Daughters of Rebecca, on 13 May 1839, was at **Efailwen**, a gate operated by the Whitland Turnpike Trust. A commemorative stone marks the spot. Tollgates were outward symbols of external authority at which a society under stress vented its anger. Local men, disguised in women's clothing, acted out a traditional form of protest in front of the turnpike gates, taking their name from a verse from *Genesis*: 'And they blessed Rebecca and said to her: *May your offspring possess the gates of their enemies*.' Following several years of disturbances throughout south-west Wales, a Royal Commission was appointed to investigate and the ensuing 1844 Turnpike Trust Act represented a substantial victory for Rebecca. Local pride in Rebecca is irrepressible: following the oil crisis of 1973, the name *Beca* was adopted for a local chain of petrol stations and there have been a number of celebratory community theatre projects, most recently at Efailwen in 2003.

It was at **Whitland** in the first half of the tenth century that Hywel Dda (d.950), the grandson of Rhodri Mawr and an admirer of Alfred of Wessex, produced his remarkable codification of the Welsh laws. By the end of his reign, Hywel Dda held sway over much of the territory of modern Wales. Dafydd Jenkins, our contemporary authority on this fascinating document, has demonstrated its remarkably progressive nature, for example with respect to women's rights and those of illegitimate children. The Hywel Dda Memorial, established on the site of the former cattle market in St Mary's Street, consists of six small gardens illustrating different aspects of his legal code and an interpretative centre. The site of the Council where the new legal code was promulgated is not known for certain but the scant ruins of the Cistercian abbey of Alba Domus, that gave Whitland its name, may occupy the same site. In the days of the Milk Marketing Board, Whitland had one of the largest and most modern creameries in Europe but the combined effects of the Common Agricultural Policy and privatisation resulted in its dramatic closure in 1994, leaving a legacy of betrayal in the community.

South-west from St Clears, the Tenby road passes through **Llanddowror**, ever linked in the Welsh memory with the career of its vicar, Griffith Jones (1683–1761). The effects of the typhus epidemic of 1727–31 impressed upon him the Protestant imperative of personal salvation through the reading of scripture. Thanks to funds provided by Madam Bridget Bevan (1698–1779), the wife of the local MP, and the protection of Sir John Philipps of Picton Castle whose sister he married, he became the indefatigable organiser of a national system of 'circulating schools'. These schools used the language of the people, predominantly Welsh at that time, with the result that Wales, in the last quarter of the eighteenth century, was one of the most highly literate countries in Europe. Madam Bevan, who continued this educational work after the death of Griffith Jones, lies buried beside him and his wife in the chancel of Llanddowror church. Llanddowror enters the twenty-first century with neither school, shop nor public house. **Eglwys Gymun** has a gem of a parish church, occupying an elevated, circular site of great antiquity. An Early Christian inscribed stone, in Ogham and Latin, has been casually incorporated into the churchyard path. Its original dedication to the Celtic St Cumyn was altered in the fourteenth century by the local lord of the manor, Sir Guy de Bryan, officially to St Margaret, Queen of Scotland, but possibly to honour Sir Guy's saintly niece, Margaret Marlos, who ran a small religious community nearby at Llandawke. Inside the church, there is a wonderfully early chancel arch, a fine fourteenth-century stone-vaulted roof, mediaeval frescoes on the north wall of the nave, a charming bilingual commandment board and a benefaction board. The excellent twentieth-century stained glass by F.C. Eden warrants a visit in itself. An effigy of Margaret Marlos can be seen inside the church at **Llandawke.**

It was on the firm and extensive sands of **Pendine** in the 1920s that Sir Malcolm Campbell and J. Godfrey Parry Thomas vied with each other in breaking the world land speed record. In 1927, tragedy struck and Parry Thomas died in a failed attempt to break the new record he had set just a few months earlier driving *Babs*. The last land speed record broken in Europe was achieved by Campbell in *Bluebird* at Pendine later in the year, but the *Babs* disaster had sounded the death-knell for Pendine as a venue for land speed record attempts which were thenceforth transferred to the United States. *Babs*, buried in the sands by Parry Thomas's friends in his memory, was excavated in 1969. Needless to say, the sands have since attracted a swarm of caravans.

Finally, to **Laugharne** made famous as the place where Dylan Thomas lived, wrote and lies buried. We may feel we know it already from *Under Milk Wood*, although critics debate how much of Cardiganshire's New Quay went into this heart-warming portrait of a day in the life of a Welsh fishing village. The ancient borough has a splendid situation overlooking 'the heron priested shore' of the Taf estuary. The Boathouse, where Dylan lived tempestuously with his wife Caitlin, is open to the public and contains in its grounds the recently restored wooden cabin, where he mused and worked. He is buried in St Martin's churchyard above the town beneath a simple white cross with gold Gothic lettering. His local, Brown's Hotel, still provides refreshments. There are good Georgian buildings and a clock-towered town hall. The Norman castle (Cadw), was extensively rebuilt by Sir John Perrot (1530–1592), the Elizabethan statesman popularly believed to have been an illegitimate son of Henry VIII. Beside the castle, there is a fine garden. Dylan's Diner is a brash reminder of the immense reputation Dylan enjoyed in the United States, one that was his undoing. He died in New York, the worse for drink, in 1953, a year short of forty. His mother came from **Llangain**, the neighbouring parish upstream towards Carmarthen, where he spent those blissful summers at *Fern Hill*, the farm of his aunt, Ann Jones:

> Now as I was young and easy under the apple
>   boughs
> About the lilting house and happy as the grass was
>   green,
> The night above the dingle starry,
> Time let me hail and climb
> Golden in the heydays of his eyes,
> And honoured among wagons I was prince of the
>   apple towns
> And once below a time I lordly had the trees and
>   leaves
> Trail with daisies and barley
> Down the rivers of the windfall light.

10

Pembrokeshire

FOR A BRIEF INTERLUDE, from 1974 to 1996, Pembrokeshire merged with Cardiganshire and Carmarthenshire to form a new entity that was given the ancient name of Dyfed. Resistance to Dyfed was strongest in Pembrokeshire, particularly so in the south of the county where most letterheads continued to use the name of the historic county. Politicians flout these local loyalties at their peril, for Wales is nothing if not a community of communities and one of the most distinctive communities in the country is 'Little England beyond Wales'. It lies to the south of the Landsker, a historic frontier that forms a cultural divide between the predominantly Welsh population to the north and an amalgam of Viking, Norman and Flemish elements to the south, the latter speaking their own distinctive dialect of English. Once the Normans had gained control of Milford Haven, one of the best natural harbours in the British Isles, they built a chain of defensive castles along the Landsker: Amroth, Narberth, Llawhaden, Wiston, Camrose and Roch, the latter just inland from the northern end of St Bride's Bay.

Pembrokeshire is united, however, by a strong maritime tradition and associated Irish influence. Thanks to the tidal waters of the Cleddau, nowhere in the county is more than ten kilometres from salt water and the distinctive, reflected light of the county has exerted a strong attraction on painters. Graham Sutherland (1903–1980) is perhaps the most famous of these; a major collection of his work that used to be exhibited at Picton Castle is currently looking for alternative accommodation. By contrast, Augustus John

(1894–1899) and his sister Gwen John (1876–1936), who were born in Tenby, rarely returned to Wales after leaving to study art together at the Slade in London. Whether they should be considered Welsh artists or not, therefore, has been the subject of heated debate. With a mild and bracing climate, the county is noted both for its early potatoes and daffodils and for its easterly-leaning hedgerows and mortared roofs. But for those who become acquainted with this part of the country there is another dimension beyond the five senses, for this is a land renowned for magic and fantasy, *Gwlad hud a lledrith*.

Following the Landsker from east to west, **Amroth** has a nineteenth-century house on the site of its vanished castle. Situated on the county border with Carmarthenshire, this straggling village, once a mining settlement, marks the starting point for the **Pembrokeshire Coastal Path**, one of the great long distance paths of Europe and the first to be opened in Wales when it was inaugurated in 1970. It follows the spectacular coast of the county, with its breeding colonies of Atlantic seabirds, for some 300 kilometres to St Dogmaels in the north. The path forms the outer boundary of the **Pembrokeshire Coast National Park**, designated in 1952 and embracing just over one third of the county. The coast here is subject to erosion, and Amroth is particularly vulnerable when spring tides coincide with south-easterly gales, conditions that also reveal sections of submerged prehistoric forest. The village church is situated safely inland; beyond it, there is a fine collection of rhododendrons and azaleas at Colby Woodland Garden (NT). **Narberth** – originally Castell yr Arberth – is the first place mentioned in *Y Mabinogi*. Pwyll, Prince of Dyfed, had his royal hunting lodge here and it was when riding out from it that he first saw the fair Rhiannon riding on her white charger. The castle ruins stand forlorn on the south side of this attractive market town, once famous for its hatters, clockmakers and shoemakers. There are some well-restored buildings, such as the Queens Hall in High Street, with its second floor art gallery, and the former Town Hall, now the Landsker Visitor Centre.

Llawhaden Castle (Cadw) was erected close to the highest point of navigation on the Cleddau by the Norman bishops of St Davids, seeking to defend their lands from the predations of the Welsh. The original castle, probably built by Bishop Bernard, was razed to the ground by Lord Rhys in 1193. A replacement thirteenth-century castle was adapted as a fortified episcopal palace in the following century when the Bishops recovered the site. The splendid moat is crossed to enter the castle through an impressive towered gatehouse. Beyond the central courtyard are the Great Hall and Bishop's Camera with adjoining kitchen and bakehouse. The chapel ruins of the thirteenth-century hospice survive at the western end of the village; the parish church of St Aidan sits beside the river below to the east. It has twin towers, the second built when the church was realigned following a change in the course of the river in the fourteenth century.

It is difficult to imagine that **Wiston**, now a tiny hamlet, was once a chartered borough. Its castle (Cadw) survives as the stump of its ruined keep on a prominent motte. To the north, **Spittal**, as its name implies, was once the site of a hospice, doubtless for pilgrims to St Davids. It has a simple bell-cote church. This nucleated village, sitting on the Landsker, still has strip fields around it dating from Norman times. **Roch Castle**, privately owned and let as a holiday cottage, is perched on an igneous crag. It was built by Adam de la Roche to defy a prophecy that he would die following a venomous snakebite, but a poisonous viper was subsequently carried into the castle in a bundle of firewood and the prophecy was fulfilled. Lucy Walter, mistress of Charles II and mother of the Duke of Monmouth, was born here. The church is modern, save for its porch but occupies an ancient, circular churchyard. The Landsker follows the valley to the sea south of Newgale.

The Landsker also marks a geological boundary, with the more recent sedimentary rocks lying to the south: sandstone, limestone and anthracite, the latter giving rise to a coal industry in the county that reached its peak of production at the end of the eighteenth century. An exploration to the south of the Landsker and east of the Cleddau might start on the coast at **Saundersfoot**, where an anthracite seam, exposed on the cliff-face, saw the port develop a coastal trade in coal from its deep harbour, now a haven for yachts. The disused Stepaside Ironworks is a fascinating industrial archaeology site. Opened in 1849 it made use of local limestone, anthracite and iron ore to export pig iron from Saundersfoot. Limekilns, beam engines, casting sheds and railway sidings evoke this industrial past. For contrast, the attractive parish church is situated at St Issels in the valley to the north-west of the village.

Tenby, lying south of the Landsker and developing as a seaside resort from the eighteenth century, feels thoroughly English. Its Welsh name, Dinbych-y-Pysgod, Little-fort-of-the-Fish, serves both to differentiate it from the other Denbigh in the north-east of the country and to remind us that the town once boasted a considerable fishing fleet. St Julian's, a small fisherman's chapel beside the harbour, is another reminder of that maritime tradition. Sir William Paxton of Middleton Hall improved the town's resort facilities, sponsoring a Public Bathhouse, that survives at Laston House below the castle, and a theatre that closed in 1824. The ruins of the Norman castle occupy a commanding position on the headland; it changed hands frequently between Welsh and English and, following a siege of town and castle, fell to Parliamentary forces in 1648. The town walls, also thirteenth-century, are much better preserved, although they have been punctured to accommodate the needs of the infernal combustion engine. St Catherine's Fort was built in the mid-nineteenth century in connection with the development of Milford

Haven. There are some interesting town houses, including the Tudor Merchant's House (NT) on Quay Hill where the remains of early frescoes survive on the interior walls. St Mary's parish church, with its tall steeple, testifies to the prosperity of the town in the fifteenth century when the original thirteenth-century church was largely rebuilt. It has stained glass by Kempe, wonderful bosses on the chancel roof, an elaborate Jacobean tomb to the ap Rees family and a memorial to Robert Recorde (c.1510–1558), the foremost mathematician of the sixteenth century. Born in the town, he introduced the equals sign to Mathematics; it is gratifying to know that a Welshman devised the symbol for equality. Some of his books are on display in the town museum on Castle Hill.

The town can get crowded at the height of the summer season but a convenient escape route is to hand with the ferry service to **Caldey**, Norse for Cold Island. Despite its name, the island enjoys a pleasant microclimate that enables its community of Trappist Cistercian monks to grow vegetables, herbs and flowers and make celebrated honeys and scents. The monks came from Chimay in Belgium in 1928 but they do not brew the wonderfully strong beer that has made their motherhouse so famous, perhaps because of the fate of their first abbot commemorated in the island's Welsh name, Ynys Bŷr: Pyro, the sixth-century monk, fell into a pond under the influence of drink and drowned. He was succeeded by Samson, a friend of St David, the water drinker. Samson later founded the monastery at Dol in Brittany where he is buried. An Ogham stone from this period is preserved in the priory church of St Illtud, built for the Benedictines in the twelfth century. The smaller parish church of St David's is in the village. **St Margaret's Island**, off the north-western tip of Caldey, is a bird reserve with the largest British colony of cormorants, some 300 breeding pairs. Both islands have produced a rich prehistoric archaeological record.

Penally, overlooking Caldey from its headland a couple of kilometres south of Tenby, was also a Celtic monastic site in origin; St Teilo was reputedly born here. Now dedicated to Saints Teilo and Nicholas, its church contains two high crosses with Northumbrian and Irish motifs removed from the churchyard to the south transept. Some of the best views of Caldey can be obtained by walking along the top of the limestone cliffs at **Lydstep Point** (NT). **St Florence,** inland to the north, has good examples of vernacular architecture, including what are locally called Flemish chimneys, tall round farmhouse chimneys that seem to date from the fifteenth century.

Gerald of Wales (c.1146–1223) famously described **Manorbier** as 'the pleasantest spot in Wales' and it still succeeds in conjuring up the Middle Ages. Gerald was born in the original castle. His Welsh mother, Angharad, was the daughter of Lord Rhys and the fair Nest, the Helen of Wales. His father, William de Barri, had succeeded his father Odo as lord of the manor. The family was to be involved in the Norman conquest of Ireland and has survived as a distinguished family in that country. The fine castle that now survives dates from the thirteenth century. In 1188, Gerald accompanied Archbishop Baldwin on a tour of Wales to preach the Third Crusade, a journey recorded in his *Itinerary,* one of the most remarkable documents to survive from the mediaeval period. His later ambitions for St Davids to become the seat of a separate Welsh arch-bishopric, with himself as Archbishop, were thwarted at the turn of the century. In consequence, we have inherited the incomparable source material that he then had the leisure to write and edit. The De Barri family must also have organised the building of St James' church, a curiously misaligned building which contains fragments of mediaeval painting that survived its Victorian restoration.

Lamphey Palace (Cadw) was in use by the Welsh bishops before the arrival of the Normans who quickly succumbed to its charms, their descendants staying in residence until the Reformation. A Bishop's camera was added to the early thirteenth-century hall later in the century. Following the Reformation, Lamphey Palace became the home of the Devereux family. Robert Devereux, 2nd Earl of Essex and the favourite of Queen Elizabeth in her old age, spent part of his youth here. An attractive gatehouse also survives. The parish church is dedicated to St Tyfai, from which the village takes its original Welsh name, Llandyfai. The ecclesiastical sites of Lamphey and Penally are linked by an ancient road known as The Ridgeway.

For a remarkable evocation of the age of the Celtic saints follow the lanes south to **St Govan's Head**, where St Govan's cell is wedged deep in a narrow gully between the cliffs. The identity of St Govan is something of a mystery: suggestions include Gawain of the Round Table or, more probably, St Gobham, Abbot of Dairinis in County Wexford. There are two holy wells at the site: a tiny one within the chapel and a larger one below the chapel near the shore, the latter retaining its stone hood. The cliffs here have magnificent displays of spring flowers: cowslips, early purple orchids and squills.

Bosherston has a mediaeval stone cross in its churchyard and is a good base from which to explore the Bosherston Pools (NT), created from the land-locked water of a tidal inlet by the Earls Cawdor between 1790 and 1840. The arms of the inlet were successively dammed beneath ornamental bridges built to span the pools in a number of places. An iron age promontory hill fort occupies the ridge between two arms of the inlet. Renowned for their water lilies, the pools were incorporated into a 'grand project' for landscaped gardens at Stackpole Court, the Cawdor property demolished in 1962. The nearby strand at Barafundle is delectable. The church of St James and St Elidyr at **Stackpole Elidor** (or Cheriton), at the head of the inlet, has an interesting collection of monuments to successive owners of the Stackpole estate dating back to the fourteenth century. **St Petrox**, the popular Cornish saint, has one of his three Welsh dedications some two kilometres to the west. As with many other South Pembokeshire churches, its high tower would have been used as a landmark and beacon for mariners.

Further to the west, the attractive church of **Castlemartin**, with its battlemented tower, has a curious ruin next to it known as The Old Rectory. Some of the first official bilingual signs to appear in Wales were to be found in the area south of Castlemartin, following the Second World War. They were not in Welsh and English, however, but in German and English: for the Castlemartin Artillery Range, created in 1938, was used during the cold war as a practice ground for *panzer* tanks. The German army withdrew in 1996 but red flags are still run up and the incongruous noise of weapons fire continues to disturb the peace of the national park. **Flimston** chapel survived deep inside the range. Of mediaeval origin, it was restored in the twentieth century and uses glacial boulders for gravestones. This is one of the most remarkable stretches of coastline in the British Isles with its dramatically eroded limestone cliffs with their natural arches, stacks and blow-holes. The Green Bridge of Wales is exceptionally finely proportioned and the twin Elegug Stacks are home to colonies of Atlantic seabirds: guillemots (*heligog*, in Welsh), razorbills and kittiwakes. **Angle**, overlooking Angle Bay, has a collection of interesting buildings: the Georgian Globe Hotel, the battery of a nineteenth-century fort and a fishermen's chapel raised above a crypt in 1447 and containing a stained glass window of Christ walking on Gennesaret. Opposite the church on the other side of the creek is a mediaeval Towerhouse consisting of three rooms, one above the other, built over a vaulted basement; nearby are a dovecot and limekiln. The Furzenip Peninsula has a seaweed-drying hut, a reminder of an industry that flourished in the first half of the twentieth century.

Pembroke is one of the finest of the many Norman castles in Wales, established in 1093 by Arnulph of Montgomery. The present castle is largely the work of William Marshal and his sons and benefits from its position on a limestone crag. The keep is one of the mightiest in Europe. There is a good gatehouse and the unusual Wogan cave, a natural feature that was used to create an entrance directly to the river. Today, the cave houses a colony of lesser horseshoe bats. The town walls are probably contemporary with William Marshal's work on the castle and can still be traced. The first of the Tudors, Henry VII, was born in the castle in January 1457 and landed in Milford Haven in 1485 to claim the English throne. The castle was never lost to the Welsh, but fell with the town in 1648 following the bombardment inflicted by Cromwell's forces during a long siege in the Civil War. The town's wide Main Street has good Georgian buildings. St Mary's parish church dates from the thirteenth century but was severely restored by the Victorians; it contains monuments from the seventeenth century onwards.

Pemboke Dock was established to replace Milford Haven as a naval dockyard in 1814 and continued to operate as such until 1926. Its imposing wall and gateway survive, as do two Martello towers, one of which accommodates an information centre, and the naval chapel. The town has never fully recovered from the closure of the dockyard, although a ferry service to Ireland has helped keep the port alive. Raymond Garlick, an English teacher in the town in the 1950s, established *Dock Leaves*, the journal that became the *Anglo-Welsh Review*, a seminal forum for Anglo-Welsh literature including his own poetry.

To the east of Pembroke, **Carew** has a fascinating collection of buildings. **Carew Castle** is the result of three separate phases of development that provides a perfect illustration of the transition from mediaeval fortification to Elizabethan manor house. The first phase, of which little remains, was a thirteenth-century motte and bailey built by Gerald of Windsor, the husband of Nest and Constable of Pembroke Castle. A subsequent stone structure, seized by King John on his way to Ireland in 1212, was improved upon by Sir Rhys ap Thomas. In 1507, he had the Order of the Garter bestowed on him here as a token of royal appreciation for his part in the successful march to Bosworth at a royal tournament staged here. Later developments are associated with Sir John Perrot, Lord Deputy of Ireland and reputed illegitimate son of Henry VIII who was granted the castle by Queen Elizabeth I in 1558. There are tombs and effigies of the owners of the castle in the parish church of St Mary's in **Carew Cheriton** and the tiles on the sanctuary floor may also be from the castle. The church was restored by Sir Gilbert Scott in 1855. **Carew Cross** (Cadw) is one of the finest Early Christian high crosses in the country. Some four metres high with a fusion of Celtic and Scandinavian design, it commemorates a great grandson of Hywel Dda who died in battle in 1035. Finally, **Carew Mill** is the only intact tidal mill remaining in the country. Twice a day, the mill-pond filled on the flood tide and drained to power the mill on the ebb tide.

On the north bank of the Eastern Cleddau is the attractive ruin of St John's church beside **Slebech Hall**, a mansion largely rebuilt in the 1770s. The effigies of a sixteenth-century knight and his lady were removed from this church to its dull nineteenth-century replacement that can be seen beside the A40. The adjacent, enigmatic ruins of The Sister's House may have been a hospice associated with the church, a monastic grange or a private mansion, their name deriving from a cistern or pool. **Blackpool Mill**, built as a corn mill in 1813, has recently been restored. It stands adjacent to a fine round-arched bridge at the highest navigable point of the eastern Cleddau, whence it is thought the Preseli bluestones were loaded onto rafts for onward shipment along the Severn Sea to the River Avon prior to the building of Stonehenge. The Cleddau is crossed by the A40 using the ancient bridging point of Canaston Bridge. Adjoining the Slebech estate to the west is that of **Picton Castle**, ancestral seat of the Philipps family, strategically sited at the confluence of the Eastern and Western Cleddau. Dating from the thirteenth century, it was modernised in the eighteenth. Sir John Philipps (1666–1737) was a major force in educational and religious reform, a leading light in the S.P.C.K. and principal patron of Griffith Jones, whose living at Llanddowror was in his gift.

Haverfordwest developed at the lowest bridging point on the Western Cleddau, just below the upper tidal limit of the river. Although all the roads of Pembrokeshire converge here, recent road improvements in the lower town have eased congestion. Quay Street, with its *Bristol Trader* inn, reminds us that, before the coming of the railway in 1853, the town was a busy port. The spring tides can bring over a metre of water to the quayside, some 25 kilometres inland. Restored as county town in 1996, Haverfordwest sits proud on its hill; its attractive Shire Hall is in High Street. Vikings, Normans and Flemings have made use of the haven in turn, the thirteenth-century Norman castle, in which the useful town museum is housed, being situated towards the upper part of town while the ruins of Haverfordwest Priory (Cadw) can be enjoyed downstream. As might be expected in a town where sedan chairs were still in use as recently as 1888, it has several handsome town houses, once used seasonally by the local gentry in a provincial centre dubbed 'little Bath'. Contemporary developments include the new County Hall on the banks of the Western Cleddau and a predictable riverside retail development.

There are several good churches, St Mary's, at the top of the town, especially so. It has a magnificent fifteenth-century oak roof, carved bench-ends and Early English arcading in the nave and chancel. The church also contains one of the few sepulchral brasses in Wales to have survived the Civil War, an effigy of a pilgrim, and monuments to the Philipps family of Picton Castle. The mediaeval church of

St Martin, mother church of the town, has an attractive small spire, whereas the prominent tower of St Thomas-à-Becket's church serves as a local landmark. The former Welseyan chapel, next to St Martin's, has been turned into retail premises but Albany United Reformed chapel in Hill Street continues to flourish. A foundation date of 1638 is claimed for this cause which would make it the mother church of Nonconformity in the county. The last Moravian church in Wales, built on St Thomas's Green in 1733, was demolished in 1961.

South of Haverfordwest, the main road leads directly to **Milford Haven.** Although the name of the haven derives from the Norse word *fjord*, the haven is not a fjord as now understood by geomorphologists but rather a ria, that is a sea-drowned valley but not a glaciated one. The deep sea fishing fleet is no more and the rapid development of the haven as an oil tanker terminal by the big oil companies in the sixties has also gone into decline, the original Esso refinery that opened in 1960 not surviving into the twenty-first century. The oil refineries brought the largest oil-fired power station in Europe to Pembroke in 1973. Fortunately, plans to burn Venezuelan orimulsion at the power station were withdrawn in 1996, the year in which 72,000 tons of oil spilled out of the *Sea Empress* off the Pembrokeshire coast, one of the largest and most environmentally damaging oil spills in European history. The power station is now largely demolished but the price of a healthy environment, even within a national park, remains eternal vigilance.

In the eighteenth century the land on which the township of Milford Haven was developed formed part of the manors of Pill and Hubberston, an estate inherited by Sir William Hamilton from his first wife Catherine Barlow. In 1790 he obtained the Milford Haven Harbour Act to 'make and provide Quays, Docks, piers . . . and to establish a Market, with proper Roads and Avenues'. The outbreak of the French Revolutionary Wars boosted the town's prospects. The newly constructed docks were greatly admired by Horatio Nelson when he first visited the town in 1802; indeed, he thought the harbour the best he had seen in the world. The attractive Hamilton Terrace, rising elegantly above the harbour, serves to remind us of an important Nelsonian connection, Sir William Hamilton's second wife, Emma. Thirty-five years younger than her husband, she was much taken with the dashing naval officer. At the height of his fame, after Aboukir Bay, Nelson returned to the town in triumph, although it is doubtful that he laid the foundation stone of the parish church of St Katherine, as is sometimes claimed. The church acquired such Nelson memorabilia as the truck of the mainmast of *L'Orient*, captured at Aboukir Bay; it has subsequently been removed to the Royal United Services Institute in Whitehall and replaced by a replica. Hamilton had appointed his nephew, Charles Greville, to be his agent in the Milford Haven project. Greville had invited a party of Nantucket Quakers, some seven families, to settle in the town in 1792 in order to develop a whaling fleet, whale oil then coming into use for street lighting. Their Quaker meeting house in Priory Street, where Waldo Williams (1904–1971) chose to worship, was completed in 1811. In 1814, the navy decided not to renew its contract with Milford Haven, following a breakdown in negotiations with the Greville family, and transferred its base to Paterchurch, now Pembroke Dock. *Sic transit gloria mundi.*

Neyland came into existence with the arrival of the South Wales Railway in 1856, and the small settlement at the terminus was given the name of New Milford when the Irish packet transferred there. Isambard Kingdom Brunel planned to upgrade the harbour as a transatlantic terminus for his *Great Eastern*, by far the largest ocean-going passenger vessel ever constructed when it was launched in 1858. But the Royal Navy raised objections and New Milford's dreams of transatlantic fame and fortune were transferred to the ill-fated Manchester and Milford Railway Scheme. In 1906, the town was renamed Neyland and three years later the Irish mail service was switched to the new port facility at Fishguard. The new bridge across the haven, opened in 1975, marked the end of the ferry service from Neyland to Hobbs Point.

South-west from Haverfordwest, the former fishing port of **Dale** has found a new lease of life as a yachting centre. Henry Tudor landed here from Brittany in 1485 to make his successful claim to the throne. **St Anne's Head**, to the south, is a great place for ocean watchers, the combination of Atlantic rollers and local tidal races can be dramatic. Along the Pembrokeshire Coastal Path between St Anne's Head and Martins Haven there are tantalising views out over the islands of Skokholm, Grassholm and Skomer. These islands, with their Norse names, are of international importance for their colonies of Atlantic seabirds: guillemots, razorbills, kittiwakes, fulmars and puffins. Grey seals loll on the rocks. In the dark of night, Manx shearwaters come ashore, often landing close to the burrow in which they were born, having spent a year or more far away in the south Atlantic. There are colonies of storm petrels, named after St Peter because they appear to walk on the surface of the sea. Among the numerous early and late summer migrants are sand-martins, pied flycatchers, redstarts, blackcaps and yellow wagtails. In the early summer their cliffs are adorned with lesser celandines, bluebells, thrift, sea campion and red campion amongst many others.

It was Ronald Lockley (1903–2000), who lived on **Skokholm** for twelve years from 1928, who made the island famous in his *Dream Island*, an account of his life there as a farmer-cum-naturalist. It is possible to stay on Skokholm for weekly periods in the former Lockley farmhouse, sharing in communal household tasks and savouring life without electricity or television, although mobile phones doubtless ring here too nowadays. **Grassholm**, known as *Gwales* in *Y Mabinogi*, is the second largest gannetry in the northern hemisphere and shimmers like a glistening iceberg in the westerly sun. It is not possible to land on Grassholm but boat trips around the island are organised in the summer season. **Skomer** has a fascinating archaeological record to add to its natural history attractions, with prehistoric field boundaries undisturbed by later ploughing. The island, which boasts an endemic land mammal, the Skomer vole, discovered in 1897, can be visited for a day excursion from Martins Haven and a limited amount of self-catering overnight accommodation is also available, the latter necessary for those wishing to see the Manx shearwaters. There are good footpaths around the island, converging on The Farm, last occupied by Reuben Codd in 1950. Grassholm and Skomer are detached parts of the parish of **Marloes**, which has a sturdy little cruciform church and curious town clock, erected in 1896 as a memorial to the local landowner, the fourth Baron Kensington.

There are fine beaches along the great sweep of St Bride's Bay to the north. The cult of St Bridget is associated with Ireland and the church dedication in the westerly cove of **St Bride's Haven** testifies to the strong links between Wales and Ireland in the Age of the Saints. **Newgale** has a massive storm-beach but it is the sands that attract the summer crowds. After storms, the remains of a submerged forest are occasionally revealed. **Solfach** (anglicised as Solva), back in Welsh Wales, is dramatically situated where a deep gorge, carved out by glacial meltwater, enters the sea. The contemporary Welsh folk singer, Meic Stevens, who was born here, has written a popular ballad in praise of his birthplace. A village with a long maritime tradition, Solfach now devotes itself to tourism, with a woollen mill, an art gallery in a former chapel and an old pharmacy converted to a restaurant. Attractive eighteenth-century limekilns survive at the harbour that once had its own fleet of sailing ketches and schooners, it now accommodates pleasure craft. Nearby **Brawdy** has a restored mediaeval church containing three Early Christian inscribed stones, two with Ogham inscriptions. The sinister cold war U.S. listening base is mercifully defunct, transformed into a business park.

Since 1995, when the Queen presented Letters Patent granting city status to **St Davids**, it can justly claim to be Britain's smallest city, whatever the significance of that might be. It is barely larger than a village but has the tea-rooms, restaurants, book shops and gift stores no place of pilgrimage can be without, including an eye-catching twenty-first century Information Centre at the eastern appoach to the city. Until the last quarter of the twentieth century, St Davids was predominantly Welsh-speaking and at the 2002 National Eisteddfod held in the town, the Archdruid, James Nicholas, delivered an impassioned plea to stem the anglicisation of his home town. In the days of Dewi Sant – as the Welsh call their patron saint – St Davids would have represented a central interchange in the western seaways, not the remote location perceived by our land-based culture. David was an ascetic and a preacher who defended orthodoxy against the Pelagian heresy; his reputation thus transcended the Reformation to appeal to both church and chapel traditions in Wales. Gwenallt imagined him as 'God's Gypsy'. The protective earthwork of **Ffos-y-mynach**, which traverses the peninsula from Nine Wells in the south to Carn Penberi in the north, probably marked the boundary of a sanctuary within which felons might be safe from prosecution and beyond which the monks of St Davids were not permitted to go. A footpath now follows its length and it may also have originally served as a trackway. There is evidence of prehistoric settlement at **Clegyr Boia**, a site occupied in neolithic and iron age times and in the Early Christian period by a chieftain called Boia who first opposed but then supported David's monastery. By the Middle Ages, pilgrims were making their way to St David's shrine along established pilgrim ways; two pilgrimages to St Davids were said to be equivalent to one to Rome.

Hidden shyly in Glyn Rhosyn, out of sight of raiders from the sea, is one of the country's greatest glories: **St Davids Cathedral**. It is extraordinarily beautiful, inside and out. Locally quarried, violet-grey sandstone patterned by lichens that flourish in the clean coastal air, enables the cathedral both to enhance its site and to blend into the landscape. Access from the bishop's borough into the Cathedral Close is through the original Gatehouse and down an attractive flight of thirty-nine steps. The present building dates from the twelfth century with sensitive restoration and rebuilding by Sir Gilbert Scott in the nineteenth. The powerful spiritual atmosphere evoked by the site must in part derive from an unbroken tradition of Christian worship since the sixth century. Inside the cathedral, the proportions are comfortable, the light mellow and the acoustic warm; it is not surprising that several well-attended music festivals are held here each year. An ensemble of features from different architectural periods combines to create something greater than its component parts, fine though these are: the twelfth-century arcades, fourteenth-century choir screen, sixteenth-century Irish oak ceiling and twentieth-century organ case, for example. The choir has a bishop's throne dating from the fifteenth century, irreverent carvings on the misericords and, uniquely, a royal stall – for the sovereign of England is a member of the cathedral chapter. Edmund Tudor, the father of Henry VII, is buried here and the relics of the saint himself, rediscovered during Scott's restoration and the object of many a pilgrimage, are preserved in an oak casket in the sanctuary. Modern forensic investigation has yet to conclusively identify the bones. Beyond the cathedral are the evocative remains of the fourteenth-century **Bishop's Palace** (Cadw), grouped around a spacious courtyard. By the eighteenth century it was a ruin, having been abandoned for Abergwili by post-Restoration bishops.

St Non's Chapel (Cadw) and holy well, the latter a curative well for eye complaints, form an attractive site on the coast to the south of the town; Non was the mother of David and a visit to this site would have formed part of a pilgrimage to St Davids. The nearby Chapel of Our Lady and St Non is a successful pastiche of an early Celtic chapel, built in 1934 by a Carmarthen solicitor, Cecil Hubert Morgan Griffiths, whose wife was a Roman Catholic. The stained glass depiction of St Non is of the William Morris School. The creek at **Porth-clais** nearby was the scene of a dramatic landing in 1081 when Gruffudd ap Cynan arrived in ships provided by his Irish ally king Dermot to join forces with Rhys ap Tewdwr to claim the throne of Gwynedd at Mynydd Garn. West of St Davids the little cove of **Porth Stinian** is visited for its ruined chapel of St Justinian, restored by Bishop Vaughan in the sixteenth century, and for its lifeboat station. Porth Stinian is also the point of departure for **Ramsey Island**, three long kilometres across Ramsey Sound, through which the tidal race can reach ten knots. The island is a RSPB reserve, with spectacular colonies of Atlantic seabirds and, along its western shore, the largest colony of grey seals in Wales. The present warden is working purposefully to rid the island of rats so that the island might once again become home to a breeding colony of Manx shearwaters. To the west of the island are a series of outlying rocks charmingly charted as the **Bishops and Clerks**.

North of **Porth-mawr**, the fine beach known in English as Whitesand Bay is a popular spot for sea-bathing. There are good walks to be had around **St David's Head**. A good place to start would be at the site of St Patrick's Chapel, marked by a plaque commemorating its excavation in 1924. It is one of several sites in Wales that claim to be the point of departure for Patrick's mission to Ireland. There is a neolithic burial chamber at Coetan Arthur and Carn Llidi, rising to 181 metres, has an iron age field system on its slopes. **Abereiddi** (NT) was originally a slate quarry that was later opened to the sea to make a small harbour. Geologists come here to find graptolites, delicate fossils that can be found in the stones on the beach. **Porthgain** is a natural harbour, tiny but the only haven along this inhospitable stretch of coast. The towering hoppers in which locally quarried stone was stored prior to shipment from the harbour still dominate the village. These are now scheduled monuments and the whole site jointly managed by the national park and the village community. The Sloop Inn has photographs of the port in commercial use up to the 1930s.

The village green at **Trefin**, which once boasted an episcopal palace, consists of slabs of glaciated shales. The disused corn mill at Aber-draw to the west of the village was the subject of a much-loved poem by William Crwys Williams (Crwys, 1875–1968); the contemporary singer, Cerys Matthews, whose family comes from the area, has named her firstborn after it. **Mathri**, once famous for its fair, is a delightful place that radiates antiquity. Professor Fleure noted a preponderance of dark-haired broad-headed Iberian types in this locality. It sits on top of a hill, surrounding the ancient circular churchyard of the Church of the Holy Martyrs. It has been suggested that the martyrs were the six brothers whom St Teilo rescued from drowning. The present church dates from 1869 but there are three Early Christian inscribed stones inside the church, one inscribed in Ogham. A further three such stones can be seen inside the church of **St Nicholas**, that gives its name to another picturesque village where one of the last surviving woollen mills in the county flourishes at Tregwynt. The church has a 'squinch' in the south transept, a feature that may enclose the original cell of its eremetical founder. Back on the coastal path at **Pwllderi**, beneath the iron age hill fort of Garn-fawr, is a monument to one of the most enigmatic figures in the public life of twentieth-century

Wales, Dewi Emrys, whose most famous poem, written in Pembrokeshire dialect, celebrates this delightful spot:

> *A thina'r meddilie sy'n dwad ichi*
> *Pan foch chi'n ishte uwchben Pwllderi*
>
> (Such are the thoughts that come to you
> When you sit above Pwllderi)

In May and June, the coastal path is adorned with the delicate blues of sheep's bit and spring squill, the pink of thrift and the brilliant whites of ox-eye daisies and sea campion, while the air is laden with the coconut scent of blazing gorse.

The powerful lighthouse on **Strumble Head**, together with its sister light on Bardsey, marks the western limits of the Welsh coast and aids navigation in Cardigan Bay. Built in 1908, it now also controls transatlantic aviation. Ireland is close, visible on a clear day from the Preseli mountains: Irish mobile phone networks, radio and even TV stations are sometimes better received in these parts than national services. It was the proximity of Catholic Ireland that worried the British authorities during the French Revolutionary Wars. The Wolfe Tone Rising in Ireland confirmed their fears as did a French invasion at **Carreg Wastad**, five kilometres east of Strumble Head in 1797. Under the command of the Irish-American Colonel Tate, the three-ship expedition proved to be a fiasco, the ill-disciplined invasion force pillaging local farms and soon showing signs of being the worse for drink. The French were quickly rounded up by the Earl Cawdor and the Castlemartin Yeomanry. A centennial memorial stone marks the site of the landing, and the Royal Oak in Fishguard preserves the table on which the Treaty of Surrender was signed. St Gwyndaf's church in **Llanwnda**, which overlooks the site of the invasion, has an associated holy well and five Early Christian inscribed stones set into its exterior walls. Its chalice went missing in the disturbances of 1797.

A remarkable work of embroidery, the Invasion Tapestry, completed by local women in 1997 along the lines of the Bayeux Tapestry for the bicentennial commemoration of the invasion, was put on display in the upper town of **Fishguard**. It is currently stored awaiting a permanent exhibition space. The Royal Oak and the grave of Jemima Nicholas in the churchyard of St Mary's Church return us to the 1797 invasion. Jemima received a pension to her dying day for having captured a dozen Frenchman by brandishing her pitchfork at them, or so the government propaganda machine of the day had it. It goes without saying that **Lower Fishguard**, used as the set for the film version of *Under Milk Wood*, has a picturesque harbour. Richard Fenton (1747–1821), the topographical author, lived here at Plas Glynmel. Lower Fishguard has preserved its period charm because a new port was developed at **Goodwick** in 1906, in a bid to capture a share of the lucrative transatlantic passenger trade. A new breakwater was built and the Great Western Railway extended to the town from Clarbeston Road. In 1909, the arrival of the *Mauretania* in the harbour was celebrated with a school holiday but passengers and their luggage had to come ashore by tender. Within a few years the new harbour was found to be silting up. The grand Fishguard Bay Hotel survives to evoke these grandiose dreams and to preside over the daily Irish ferry service to Rosslare that has been the only significant commercial activity in the port for nearly a century. The hotel doubles as the Fishguard Festival Club in the last week of July each year for a successful annual music festival that makes good use of the excellent acoustic in St Peter's church, built two years after the completion of the harbour that it overlooks by Bruce-Vaughan of Cardiff.

Cwm Gwaun is one of the most important meltwater channels from the last ice age to be found in the British Isles. It is also one of the last haunts of the otter and its steep valley sides preserve native woodland, including sessile oak, beech, alder, rowan, ash and willow. The remoteness of the valley accounts for the fact that New Year's Day is still celebrated here on 12 January, according to the Julian calendar. The new-fangled Gregorian calendar introduced in 1752 has not yet been fully accepted here. **Llanllawer** has a holy well affording an excellent view down the Trecŵn gorge. St Brynach's church at **Pontfaen** has two Early Christian inscribed stones standing in its circular churchyard. The church contains good memorials to the Arden family who lived in the adjacent Pontfaen House. The mountain road over to Newport passes Bedd Morris, a bronze age standing stone, then opens out to give spectacular views over Cardigan Bay.

The Royal Naval Armaments Depot with its warren of underground storage tunnels at **Trecŵn** closed in 1998 and this intriguing site passed into the hands of a property developer but has since changed hands; its future is uncertain. To the west at Llanstinan, the isolated church of St Justinian, a companion of St David, serves the village of **Scleddau**, a settlement that has drifted westward over centuries. Its ancient field system can still be traced in the vicinity of the church. A pair of rough-hewn bluestones in the churchyard records two local suicides in the nineteenth century; the rafters of the church accommodate a colony of long-eared bats. The A40 from Fishguard to Haverfordwest joins the railway to run with the Eastern Cleddau through the Treffgarne Gorge at **Wolf's Castle**, the passage through these Precambrian volcanic rocks guarded by a motte and bailey. The rocky outcrops here consist of igneous rocks, fantastically weathered; above the gorge, there are prehistoric hut circles and defensive earthworks. Even the primary school at **Puncheston**, to the east, is set within the defences of an iron age hillfort. The pacifist Waldo Williams, one of the most original Welsh poets of the twentieth century, was headmaster here and there is a memorial to another local poet, Evan Rees (Dyfed, 1850–1923) on the village square. **Little Newcastle** was the birthplace of *y morwr tal â'r chwerthiniad iach* ('the tall sailor with the hearty laugh'), namely Bartholomew Roberts (1682–1722) known as Barti Ddu in Welsh and Black Bart in English. He was second mate on *The Princess* when captured by his compatriot, the pirate Hywel Dafydd. Following the death of his captor he turned pirate himself winning notoriety in the Caribbean. Black Bart secured his place in maritime history as the first to fly the skull and cross-bones; he has a memorial stone on the village green.

Fishguard Bay is protected from the north-east by **Dinas Head** with Newport Bay lying beyond it to the east. There are high cliffs along the coast but to landward a wide valley separates what is aptly known as Dinas Island from the mainland. There are two good bays to either side, **Pwllgwaelod** to the west has an attractive inn and **Cwm-yr-Eglwys** has the remains of St Brynach's church, destroyed by a gale in 1859. **Newport** is no longer an active port but remains a chartered borough, the Court Leet and Court Baron meet at regular intervals throughout the year and they still beat the bounds here. Newport retains the dignity of a place with a distinguished past. It was once the heart of the barony of Cemaes, the lords of Cemaes occupying Newport Castle, built to replace an earlier one at Nevern. The gatehouse of the castle has been incorporated into a private residence. There is a Georgian Baptist chapel, with an outdoor baptistry, in Lôn-y-Felin and an Independent chapel, Ebeneser, built in 1845, in Heol Fair Isaf. The parish church has a buttressed mediaeval tower and cheerful weathercock; beside it is the church chapel, built in 1799, an interesting architectural survival of early cooperation between the church authorities and the Methodists. **Y Parrog**, on the coast, once busy with coastal trade, now sleeps through the winter to come alive when the summer visitors return. The remains of substantial limekilns can be found on both banks of the estuary.

For a good view down onto Newport, follow the lane up and around **Carn Ingli**, a hilltop rising to 347 metres that is steeped in prehistory. There are extensive remains of an iron age hillfort with associated hut circles set amidst frost-shattered rocks. Carn Ingli means Hill of Angels and was reputedly where St Brynach had his cell and was ministered to by a heavenly host. Outside St Brynach's church at **Nevern** stands one of the finest high crosses in the country. Dating from the eleventh century, a cuckoo was reputed to sing from it on 7 April each year to mark the date of Brynach's death. This is the jewel of an impressive collection of Early Christian monuments at Nevern: east of the porch, the Vitalianus Stone is bilingual in Latin and Ogham and outside the east wall of the Glasdir Chapel is a Consecration Cross. Inside the church are the Maglocunus Stone – also inscribed in Latin and Ogham – and the Cross Stone. Ancient yews fill the churchyard; one of them is said to bleed. Beneath them wild garlic grows in profusion. To the west of the village, on a path beside the Afon Nyfer, a pilgrims' cross has been cut in the rock with a kneeling recess and smaller incised cross, probably a wayside shrine for pilgrims to St Davids.

A cluster of neolithic burial chambers can be seen beside the main road, two kilometres west of Newport, including Carreg Coetan Arthur (Cadw). The cromlech at **Pentre Ifan** (Cadw), another neolithic burial chamber, has become the visiting card for Pembrokeshire; the huge capstone resting on its three high pillars in its spectacular setting never fails to impress. It has to be remembered, however, that the cromlech was originally covered with stones, a burial cairn that was part of a wider sacred landscape of megalithic monuments. Moving on to the iron age, the site of a hill fort at **Castell Henllys** has been imaginatively developed as an interpretative centre. There are authentic recreations of village huts, and strips planted with early crops such as bere wheat and woad, the latter a herb giving a blue dye that is usefully antiseptic when applied to the body, hence its use by Celtic warriors. In the summer season it is often possible to see excavations in progress and to talk with the archaeologists and excellent educational work is undertaken with local school children throughout the year.

St Dogmaels, on the western bank of the Teifi estuary, suffered a disastrous landslip of material from glacial lake deposits in 1994. The village is visited for its Abbey (Cadw), built on the site of a former *clas* in 1115. A daughter house of the French Abbey of Tiron, it was founded at the invitation of the Norman Lord of Cemaes. By about 1250 a surprisingly extensive group of ecclesiastical buildings had been built on the site. The parish church of St Thomas contains a sixth-century Early Christian monument inscribed in Ogham and Latin: when the new church was under construction in 1848, the stone was used to decipher Ogham script. Adjacent to the abbey is an exceptionally well-restored watermill, with mill-pond and ducks; its tea-room serves fresh baking using the mill's stone-ground flour. Further upstream, **Cilgerran** has a dramatically situated Norman castle (Cadw), established in the twelfth century but completed in innovatory fashion by William Marshal in the early thirteenth, a harbinger of the Edwardian conquest castles of later in the century. The Teifi below is beautiful in both directions: kingfishers, dippers and grey wagtails abound and occasionally an otter makes an appearance. This was the last river in Wales to have beavers, though they didn't survive the Middle Ages. Otters, on the other hand, can be viewed from the riverside trails of the Welsh Wildlife Centre at the Teifi Marshes Nature Reserve that opened in 1995. In the little church at **Manordeifi**, a coracle was used to protect the prayer books from frequent inundations. It also retains its box pews, two of which incorporate fireplaces. It is a delightfully unscathed example of a mediaeval parish church, dating back to the thirteenth century. From **Aber-cuch**, where a Victorian kitchen garden can be visited at the Clynfyw Countryside Centre, the Afon Cuch runs south, forming the boundary between Pembrokeshire and Carmarthenshire. Cwm Cuch is dramatically wooded, with associations that go back to *Y Mabinogi*.

To the west rises **Mynydd Preseli**, a sacred landscape in prehistoric times that is still able to impart a sense of the numinous to the twenty-first century. Waldo Williams, who celebrated it in *Preseli*, has a memorial on Foel Drigarn to the west of Mynachlogddu:

> *Mur fy mebyd, Foel Drigarn, Carn Gyfrwy,*
> *Tal Mynydd*
> *Wrth fy ngefn ymhob annibyniaeth barn*

> (Wall of my youth, Foel Drigarn,
> Carn Gyfrwy, Tal Mynydd
> Supporting me in every independent judgement)

Crymych has established itself as the market centre for Preseli, dominated by its bilingual secondary school, a monument to 1950s central planning. By contrast, the Christian Retreat Centre at **Ffald-y-brenin**, completed in 1998, adapts sensitively to its landscape in the best tradition of organic architecture. A forlorn attempt was made to develop **Rosebush**, a kilometre south-east of New Inn, as a spa at the end of the nineteenth century. A small hotel of corrugated iron construction was established to which visitors were encouraged to travel on the railway line that had been built to service the local slate quarries. Two artificial lakes were excavated and furnished with an oriental bridge and a pagoda but for some reason these amenities proved insufficiently attractive. By contrast, **Llysyfrân**, to the west, is a rare example of a Welsh reservoir opened without attendant protest. Together with the associated Rosebush Reservoir to the north, it provides water supply for the county. At the foot of the dam at Llysyfrân is a memorial to William Penfro Rowlands (1861–1937), composer of the popular hymntune *Blaenwern*, who was born close by at Dan-y-coed. **Maenclochog** has a rich variety of building styles clustered around its village green. The Victorian church of St Mary occupies a raised churchyard and there are two chapels, Horeb for the Baptists and Tabernacl for the Independents. East of the village is Temple Druid, a good Georgian house designed by John Nash. Twm Carnabwth (Thomas Rees, 1806–1876), a leader of the Rebecca Riots is named from his farm in the village.

The eighty-two bluestones that now form part of the celebrated prehistoric monument of Stonehenge may have come from these hills. There has been much speculation as to how they were transported to Salisbury Plain, but human agency rather than ice sheets is now generally given the credit. The best way to appreciate this unique landscape is to walk a section of the Bronze Age trackway that follows a ridge, at about 300 metres, to the west of Crymych to the highest point on the B4329, east of Cerriglladron. This section of the trackway starts below the iron age hillfort of Foeldrigarn, where 27 hut circles were discovered in 1899, and continues past Carnmenyn, source of the white-spotted dolerite from which the Stonehenge bluestones were quarried, possibly so greatly valued because they resemble the night sky. The highest point of Mynydd Preseli lies a little to the south of the trackway at Foelcwmcerwyn (537m.). From here it is possible to see Ireland on a clear day together with unrivalled views over southern Pembrokeshire and Cardigan Bay. Anyone with an interest in archaeology should allow plenty of time for the walk, for the area abounds in standing stones, stone circles and cromlechs. Noteworthy archaeological sites in this vicinity include the neolithic chamber tomb of Bedd-yr-Afanc near Brynberian and the bronze age stone circle at Gors Fawr, south-west of Mynachlogddu, one of the most complete in Wales. Moving to a more contemporary rock scene, the existence of a church dedicated to St Elvis in Preseli – the National Trust own the site to the east of Solfach – was the origin of a persistent story that the king of rock-and-roll was really Welsh, *Elfis Preseli*.

IV
North-west Wales

11

Merionethshire

THE HISTORIC TERRITORY OF GWYNEDD, comprising the north-western quadrant of Wales, was divided by Edward I into the three shires of Merioneth, Caernarfon and Anglesey. Gwynedd was resurrected as a political entity in the local government reforms of 1974 only to have Anglesey surgically removed by yet more 'reforms' in 1996. *Cadernid Gwynedd*, the Strength of Gwynedd, is how the Welsh characterise this territory, a mountain fastness that holds the living memory of independence. *Eryri*, known in English as Snowdonia, may mean 'Abode of Eagles' but has an almost mystical force in Welsh that commands respect. *Yr Wyddfa*, the Welsh for the mountain of Snowdon itself, means 'Burial Place', probably of some legendary giant. Physically, culturally and spiritually, Gwynedd has been for the Welsh a symbol of their continued existence as a people. Its territory inspires intense loyalty, of a kind evidenced in the career of Ioan Bowen Rees (1929–1999) who combined a distinguished career as Chief Executive of Gwynedd County Council with inspirational writing about the landscape of his native Snowdonia.

After Machynlleth, eastbound trains on the Cambrian Coast Line no longer stop in the Dyfi valley but rush onwards, through the Talerddig cutting, to Caersŵs. There was a time, however, when trains stopped at Glantwymyn, at a junction that, following railway company practice, was given the English name of Cemmes Road. From here a short-lived branch line, built by the quarry owner Sir Edmund Buckley, followed the Dyfi, through heavenly

Aberangell, where the Hendreddu Quarry produced slate slabs for urinals, and into the hills of Merioneth at Mallwyd, bound for Dinas Mawddwy. The former Peniarth Arms at **Mallwyd** has been renamed the Brigands Inn after the infamous 'red bandits' of the area, *Y Gwylliaid Cochion Mawddwy*. Supposedly of Irish origin, they may have taken their name from the colour of their hair as much as for the blood on their hands. Mallwyd is more respectably linked with the name of Dr John Davies (1567–1644), one of the greatest Welsh scholars of the Renaissance, who served as rector here for some two score years. He is credited with the fine 1620 revision of the Welsh Bible, as well as the compilation of grammars and catechisms. His seventeenth-century church has a boarded tower with faded Latin inscriptions on the outside.

At **Dinas Mawddwy**, the Cerist joins the Dyfi from the west and the main road follows this tributary over the mountain pass of Bwlch Oerddrws in the direction of Dolgellau. Scarred hillsides are reminders of the extractive industries: slate, lead, copper and even gold have been mined over the centuries where sheep now safely graze. An old tramway, the traces of which are still clearly visible, ran down the mountainside from one of these quarries to Minllyn, where the branch line from Cemmes Road terminated. The village has two handsome chapels, Ebenezer (1867) for the Independents and the disused Wesleyan Chapel (1868) on one side of the street and the companionable Red Lion Inn on the other. Just beyond the village on the main road a short valley runs down from **Maesglas** to join the Cerist. Hugh Jones (1749–1825), author of *O! Tyn y gorchudd* (Oh! Lift the veil), regarded by O.M. Edwards as the finest hymn in the Welsh language, was born in this valley. A sublimely meditative study on this valley community, taking this hymn for its title, won the prose medal for Angharad Price at the 2002 National Eisteddfod at St Davids.

Another Dyfi tributary, the Cywarch, can be followed to its headlands for the start of an exciting hill walk ascending the Arans. It is now hard to imagine that **Cwm Cywarch** was home to a thriving community of lead miners in the mid-nineteenth century, with a vigorous chapel culture producing the likes of Robert Evans, Perthyfelin, named *Eos Mawddwy* (Nightingale of Mawddwy) in 1855 in recognition of his musical accomplishments. A circular ascent of the Arans follows the river below Creigiau Camddwr and over the boggy expanse of Waun Camddwr, a haunt of herons, to the summit of Aran Mawddwy (907m.). From here, it is possible to enjoy sweeping views of the peaks of Snowdonia, with glimpses of the sea beyond and of Llyn Tegid in the valley below. The ridge can be followed northward to Aran Benllyn (884m.) before returning over Drŵs Bach to Drysgol where a memorial has been constructed to a member of an RAF mountain rescue team struck by lightning here in 1960. The return to Cwm Cywarch follows a gentle path through Hengwm.

Further upstream, St Tydecho's church overlooks the west bank of the Dyfi at **Llanymawddwy**. An unremarkable country church on the outside, it has a delightful interior. Thomas Charles served as a curate here for three months before moving to Bala in 1784. Bethesda, the minuscule Calvinistic Methodist chapel, was built adjacent to the church in 1884 in centennial tribute. On Christmas Day, two centuries ago, a *Plygain* party consisting of three women who had sung their carols in church at Llanymawddwy set off over the mountian for Mallwyd only to perish in a snowstorm. Three cairns, Carneddi'r Gwragedd, mark the spot where their bodies were found on Mynydd Pengelli. These hills abound with the names *hafod* and *lluest* that indicate the summer dwellings of shepherds living by transhumance; *Y Ffridd* indicates the open hilltop pasture grazed by their flocks in the summer months.

From Llanymawddwy it is possible to follow in the saintly footsteps of Deiniol who crossed these mountains on his way from Tywyn to Bangor back in the sixth century. In 1989, retracing the steps of his predecessor, the Bishop of Bangor placed a new cross where a mediaeval cross traditionally comforted pilgrims at the fork in the road for Llyn Efyrnwy at **Bwlch-y-groes** (546m.). From here, the road descends into Cwm Cynllwyd and on to Llanuwchllyn, where the Twrch joins the River Dee. Bearing right, the road skirts the south-eastern edge of Llyn Tegid to **Llangywer**, where the tiny church of St Gŵyr sits on the delta formed where the Afon Glyn enters Llyn Tegid. Euros Bowen (1904–1988), a major twentieth-century Welsh poet, was rector here for many years. The church preserves a horse bier, once common in the mountainous districts of the country. Slung between two horses, the bier facilitated the transfer of a coffin to the churchyard.

As the road continues towards Bala, the scale of the lake is clearly evident. At 7 km by 1 km in area and some 45 metres deep at its centre, **Llyn Tegid** is the largest natural freshwater lake in Wales, the name of which in Welsh is aptly suggestive of natural beauty. It is celebrated by fishermen not only for its perch, trout and pike but also for the mysterious *gwyniad*, the latter a deep-water fish that has been described as a freshwater whiting. Found nowhere else in Britain, the *gwyniad* has to be netted as it spurns the angler's line and hook. Bird-watchers will appreciate the lake's herons and water-fowl and it is an excellent spot for all those who love to mess about in small boats.

Y Bala (it requires the definite article in Welsh) is an attractive town rich in cultural interest. As befits a town that has made a disproportionate contribution to Welsh cultural life, it pioneered the use of Welsh in its signage at a time when there was much apathy, even opposition, to the use of the language in the commercial sphere. We must begin with Thomas Charles, a towering presence in the town as indeed he was for the whole of Wales for a century and a half after his death. There is a statue of him in front of the spired Calvinistic Methodist Capel Tegid and a plaque on the wall of Barclays Bank to mark where he used to live. Born in Carmarthenshire, he settled in the town in 1783 after marrying Sally Jones, daughter of a prominent shopkeeper in the town. The following year Thomas Charles joined the Calvinistic Methodists, going on to become the undisputed leader of their second generation after they had broken from the established church to form a separate denomination. His literary endeavours sprang from his devotion to the cause of popular religious education. He was a founder of the British and Foreign Bible Society, author of a remarkable Bible Dictionary and founder of the Welsh Sunday School system, distinct from its English counterpart in having classes for adults as well as children. The Calvinistic Methodists established Bala College in 1839 under Principal Lewis Edwards (1809–1887), the distinguished theologian and essayist who had married a granddaughter of Thomas Charles. His statue is at the front of the dignified Gothic building on the Ffestiniog Road. His son, Thomas Charles Edwards (1837–1900) became the first principal of the University College of Wales, Aberystwyth, before succeeding his father as Principal of Bala College and turning it into an exclusively theological seminary. It ceased to function as a seminary in 1963 and its precious library was shamefully dispersed; it now serves as a denominational Youth Centre. As both a religious and educational centre for a century and a half, Bala played an influential part in the life of the nation. Its printing presses produced books and journals that were distributed throughout the country, a task made easier with the arrival of the Ruabon to Barmouth railway in the town in 1868. A connection with Ffestiniog soon followed; Plase Chapel, now a heritage centre, was built by the Great Western Railway to meet the spiritual needs of their railway navvies.

Although the trains were withdrawn in 1965, a narrow gauge railway has been built for the tourist trade on the former track-bed between Bala and Llanuwchllyn.

Stryd Fawr, the tree-lined main thoroughfare of the town, is a wide market street of character, dominated by Goscombe John's melodramatic statue of Thomas Edwards Ellis (1859–1899), the much-loved Liberal MP for the county who died tragically young. He had been a resolute campaigner for a Welsh legislative assembly, a National Library and the cause of Welsh education generally. On the other side of the street, a plaque marks the house in which the blind Victorian preacher John Puleston Jones (1862–1925) was raised. The system of Welsh Braille that he devised is still in use. Tucked away in Heol-y-Domen is the Congregational Chapel (1816), a reminder that there was more to Bala than Methodism. Michael D. Jones (1822–1898) ministered here. His father had been the founding Principal of the Independents College that was opened opposite the chapel in 1842. Michael D. Jones is regarded as one of the founding fathers of Welsh cultural nationalism. His desire to save the distinctive language and culture of his country was to lead him to the distant shores of South America where, in 1865, he founded the Welsh colony in the Chubut valley of Patagonia. Descendants of that enterprise are still there today, living their lives bilingually in Welsh and Spanish. Returning to Wales from Patagonia, Michael D. Jones succeeded his father as Principal of the Independents College only to decamp to Bangor in 1892 following an arcane constitutional dispute about the college's governance that raged in the 1880s. Close by, a plaque marks the birthplace of Jack Evans (1889–1971), a Welsh international footballer, football being the preferred game of north Wales.

A kilometre northeast of Bala, the church of St Deiniol at **Llanfor**, an otherwise dull Victorian restoration by E.B. Ferrey, the son of Benjamin Ferrey, has a sixth-century

followed anticlockwise – affords dramatic views of the Mawddach and of Cadair Idris without any strenuous ascent. There is a convenient car park at the start of the walk. Good examples abound in the vicinity of what has come to be known as the Nannau style: rough stone cottages, farms and an arch to commemorate George III, work beginning on the latter the day he died in 1820. His tenants did not find his Gothic accommodations as comfortable as he thought them picturesque. **Llanfachreth** has many examples, including its candlelit church with its octagonal spire. It has a theatrical memorial to Anne Nanney (1692–1729), daughter and heiress of Hugh Nanney. A bilingual inscription in fulsome praise of Mad King George, composed in the year of the king's demise by Sir Robert, has been placed against the church tower to face the elaborate tomb of this loyal Nannau memorialist.

On the opposite bank of the Wnion, the village of **Brithdir** has Henry Wilson's Tractarian church of 1898. Sympathetically built of local materials and surrounded by rhododendrons, the church contains an unusual beaten copper altar and pulpit. The Clywedog rushes to join the Wnion to the west of the village and the well-built **Torrent Walk**, devised by the same engineer who constructed the Cob at Porthmadog, enables visitors to appreciate the falls. The path has a wonderful profusion of mosses and ferns and, in late spring, a heady bouquet of wild garlic. The path ends at a former fulling-mill.

Cymer Abbey (Cadw) was built where the Mawddach meets the Wnion, *cymer* being the Welsh for confluence. This Cistercian house was founded from Cwm-hir in 1199 by Maredudd ap Cynan, a grandson of Owain Gwynedd. The foundation never prospered but the remains are extensive and attractive. As usual the Cistercians chose an exquisitely peaceful location; it defies belief that planning permission was given to site a caravan park beside such a site in the heart of the Snowdonia National Park. A substantial farmhouse, incorporating some of the monastic masonry, dates back to the Dissolution. A fine silver gilt chalice and paten from the abbey, hidden from Cromwell's men at the Reformation, were discovered by two gold prospectors in 1890 and are now on view at the National Museum in Cardiff. St Illtud has his only dedication in north Wales at **Llanelltyd**, where the attractive early thirteenth-century church contains a curious mediaeval stone supposedly bearing the footprint of a pilgrim named Cinwrig. Above the remains of the abbey, to the south, is **Hengwrt**. The contemporary house dates from 1892 but the site is an ancient one. Robert Vaughan (1592–1667) of Hengwrt assembled an extraordinary personal collection of Celtic manuscripts. Together with the library from Nannau, his Hengwrt collection passed to W.W.E. Wynne of Peniarth in the Dysynni valley, thence, in 1909, thanks to Sir John Williams, to the National Library of Wales where this most important single collection of Celtic manuscripts is preserved as a national treasure.

Dolgellau was the county town of Merioneth from 1536 to 1974; the old Shire Hall, just across Y Bont Fawr that spans the Wnion, was built in 1825. The town's architectural unity of dark local stone, quarried in large blocks, with grey slate roofs perfectly fits its geographical setting, with a brooding Cadair Idris as dramatic backdrop to the town. Its predominantly Georgian buildings in a huddle of narrow streets are entirely human in scale; this is a town to be explored at leisure and on foot. Eldon Square, very much the town centre, is named after the early nineteenth-century English Lord High Chancellor who represented the local Nannau family at law. Y Tanws, near Pont-yr-Aran, was the last working fellmonger in the town, employing some 40 people as recently as 1975. Throughout the eighteenth century, Dolgellau was the main centre of the woollen industry in Merioneth and several fulling mills were situated along the Wnion that runs along the eastern flank of the town. There are typical nineteenth-century

Nonconformist chapels, for the Baptists, Congregationalists and Calvinistic Methodists respectively, in the vicinity of Cadair Road. The eighteenth-century parish church of St Mary stands on an ancient site. It has unique wooden pillars, made of Mawddwy oak, and a fine effigy of a knight, Meurig ab Ynyr Fychan from Nannau. The church has been much restored, by the Victorians in 1854 and, more recently, in 1992, when it acquired a Gallery Room and suburban-style fitted carpet. The old cemetery which adjoins Marian Mawr contains a striking obelisk commemorating Dafydd Ionawr, local poet and town gaoler, who died in 1827.

The country between Bala and Dolgellau was once a Quaker stronghold. Many local Quakers crossed the Atlantic with William Penn in the seventeenth century in the hope of obtaining their religious and linguistic freedom. Their hopes were fulfilled in respect of the former but dashed in the case of latter, for William Penn moved quickly to undermine the autonomy of the Welsh Tract. Today the Welsh heritage of Pennsylvania abounds in names from this district: Bryn Mawr, the home of the Quaker Rowland Ellis (1650–1731), on the slopes of Cadair Idris, for example, or Bala-Cynwyd township outside Philadelphia. The Pennsylvania Main Line has a string of Welsh place-names with Quaker associations as its stations: Haverford, Radnor, and so on, not to mention Merion (sic) itself. Marion Eames has written two historical novels exploring this territory, *Y Stafell Ddirgell* and *Y Rhandir Mwyn*, translated into English as *The Secret Room* and *Fair Wilderness* respectively.

From Bala, the A4212 follows the Tryweryn valley between the Arenigs, Arenig Fawr (854m.) to the south and Arenig Fach (689m.) to the north. **Fron-goch**, now notable only for Thomas Penson's quietly respectable Victorian church, has seen headier days. From 1882 to 1914 Richard John Lloyd Price of Rhiwlas ran his short-lived Welsh

Whiskey distillery here until the government requisitioned the building to house prisoners of war. One thousand eight hundred Irish rebels, including Michael Collins, were interned here following the 1916 Easter Rising; their sacrifice is commemorated in a trilingual roadside monument. Just the place to nurture a ballad-singer: Bob Roberts (1870–1951), farmed here at Cwm-tir-mynach and there is a memorial to him beside his cottage at Bwthyn Tai'r Felin.

At **Llyn Celyn**, as too often in Wales, where once a valley community made a living contribution to the landscape, the still waters of an out-of-scale reservoir, in this case one built for Liverpool Corporation, now dominate the scene. The building of this reservoir was a *cause célèbre*. Although every MP in Wales, regardless of party, opposed plans for the reservoir, a callous decision to drown this Welsh-speaking community was taken in 1957 by a majority of members of the U.K. parliament. The community had won a special place in Welsh hearts when the entire village school entered and won the group recitation competition at the National Eisteddfod. For a growing number of Welsh people the decision to drown Tryweryn confirmed their colonial status and boosted the fortunes of Plaid Cymru that, under the leadership of Gwynfor Evans, had led the defence of this community. Throughout Wales, the slogan *Cofiwch Tryweryn!* 'Remember Tryweryn!' was to inspire a generation. A memorial chapel has been built with stones from a former village farmhouse; the graveyard beside it contains headstones relocated from the Calvinistic Methodist chapel in the village, Capel Celyn. A national campaign is raising funds for a powerful memorial to Tryweryn, designed by John Meirion Morris.

For hill-walkers, an ascent of **Arenig Fawr** is well worthwhile. There is a small parking place on the Llyn Celyn side of the minor road at the base of a path that leads up the mountain via Llyn Arenig Fawr. On the summit is a memorial to the crew of a U.S. Flying Fortress that misjudged the height of the mountain in 1943. From it, there are particularly fine evening views to the south-west over to the Arans and north towards lake-studded **Migneint**. At the sumit of this high moorland, home to snipe, peewits and golden plovers, is a holy well that also marks the county boundary. Restored in 1846, it is inscribed: '*Yf, a bydd Ddiolchgar*' (Drink and be Thankful). It is an injunction that can be applied without reservation to the scenery for a gloriously wide radius.

Blaenau Ffestiniog is unique: an urban culture, based entirely on the nineteenth-century slate industry, surrounded by the Snowdonia National Park. At an altitude of 300 metres, it attracts high rainfall. I once opened the door of the local Woolworths to take shelter from the deluge only to see a wet sheep dart out. On a bad day, the combined effect of grey skies, mountains of slate waste and slate vernacular architecture can produce a grey Welsh equivalent of Antarctic white-out. Slate is now a subdivision of the heritage industry and such places as Llechwedd Slate Caverns and Gloddfa Ganol do a competent job of explaining the physical nature of a unique industry even if the rich cultural life associated with the quarries proves more elusive. The immense scale of the former workings that surround the town cannot fail to impress. In a town that was a stronghold of Nonconformity, Jerusalem Independent chapel, once famed for its eisteddfod, remains but the Calvinistic Methodist chapel of Gwylfa is now a garage and Bethesda and Bethania have been demolished. The former Anglican church at Manod is now the centre of the Wales Orthodox Mission.

Maentwrog lies some six kilometres down the Vale of Ffestiniog. It derives its name from Twrog's Stone, a glacial erratic, traditionally associated with the companion of St Beuno, that can be seen outside the west end of the church. The church was sensitively restored by John Douglas in 1896. Edmwnd Prys (1544–1623), author of the popular metrical version of the Psalms in Welsh, was rector here from 1572 until his death. Over the river stands **Tan-y-Bwlch**, the former home of the Oakeley family of slate quarry owners. Their attractive house and grounds are now in regular use by the Snowdonia National Park as a field study centre.

Garreg functioned as the estate village for Plas Brondanw, the ancestral home of the architect Clough Williams-Ellis. The house of his childhood was destroyed by fire in 1951 but quickly restored; the imaginative gardens continue to delight, and provide excellent views of Cnicht (690m.), instantly recognisable as the Matterhorn of Wales. To the north, the former slate-quarrying community in the **Croesor** valley was home to Bob Owen (1885–1962), an antiquary and bibliophile whose slate memorial seat adjoins the solid nineteenth-century chapel. He lived next to the chapel at Ael-y-Bryn. Needless to say, this is good hill-walking country. Heading west, a former tramway incline can be used to approach Cnicht. To the east, a path links Moelwyn Mawr (770m.) and Moelwyn Bach (711m.) across Bwlch Stwlan.

Portmeirion is invariably described as an Italianate village, lapped by the Gulf Stream, set in the heart of Snowdonia. It is Clough Williams-Ellis's most famous creation and an endearingly enduring monument to his sensibility. We are dealing with fantasy here, not the grainy reality that was left just a dozen kilometres behind in Blaenau Ffestiniog, but the place rarely fails to work its magic. A sliding-scale toll system discourages overcrowding as the visitors wander through what is essentially a stage-set of assembled parts, albeit partially occupied on a weekly rental basis, beneath the campanile and on down to the private beach. The food and service in the Portmeirion Hotel and in neighbouring Castell Deudraeth are exemplary, the former served on Portmeirion ware, designed by Sir Clough's daughter Susan Williams-Ellis and on sale in the gift shop. Her daughter, Angharad Menna has carried on the tradition; although manufactured in Stoke-on-Trent, Portmeirion ware sells here in quantity. The place has, appropriately, been in demand as a film set, notably for 'The Prisoner', and Noel Coward wrote 'Blithe Spirit' here in a single week while staying in the Watch House. Not entirely inappropriately, this gesture of defiance against modernism is today run as a very successful business by Sir Clough's grandson, the postmodernist Welsh novelist, Robin Llywelyn.

The main road to Harlech takes the coastal route over Morfa Harlech. At a bend in the road beyond the railway line, a narrow track leads to **Llanfihangel-y-traethau**. Although St Michael's church was rebuilt in 1871, two inscribed stones attest to the antiquity of the site. In the graveyard lies Mari Evans 'y Fantell Wen' (1735–1789), an impostor known to her contemporaries as 'Whitemantle'. She claimed to be betrothed to Christ and a crowd of followers attended her wedding service in Ffestiniog and the subsequent wedding feast in the local tavern. She became the focus of a white-robed sect that collapsed following her death; since she had claimed immortality, her body went unburied for much longer than usual but eventually a funeral had to be held. **Y Lasynys Fawr** was the home of Ellis Wynne (1671–1734), author of *Gweledigaethau y Bardd Cwsc* (Visions of the Sleeping Bard), a much admired classic of Welsh devotional literature.

The approach to **Harlech** from the north on the upper road is a dramatic one. The architect of Harlech Castle (Cadw), Master James of St George, made superb use of an unsurpassed natural setting to create, within the space of seven years, an architectural masterpiece that has endured for over seven centuries. The castle was one of eleven built at the command of Edward I of England in the final quarter of the thirteenth century to extinguish Welsh independence. With Llywelyn ap Gruffudd fallen at Cilmeri in

1282, Edward moved quickly to secure his victory by surrounding Llywelyn's power base of Gwynedd with some of the greatest military fortifications yet seen in Europe. Twenty stone masons were despatched to Harlech in 1286 to build a castle on a crag, at that time lapped by the sea; by 1294, it successfully withstood siege by Madog ap Llywelyn – for the Welsh were not pusillanimous. In 1404, Owain Glyn Dŵr recaptured Harlech Castle for the Welsh but the English repossessed it within five years. During the Wars of the Roses, Harlech was held by Dafydd ab Ifan for the Lancastrians, a moment of glory that gave birth to the martial air, *Men of Harlech*. During the Civil War, it was the last of the King's castles to surrender, its fall signalling the end of that conflict.

Harlech also has a prominent place in the second branch of *Y Mabinogi* concerning Branwen, daughter of Llŷr. Bendigeidfran, the gigantic king of the Island of the Mighty, as Britain then styled itself, was holding court in Harlech when he saw Matholwch, King of Ireland, approaching on the western sea. Matholwch was seeking the hand in marriage of Bendigeidfran's sister, Branwen, the fairest maiden in the western world. During the marriage feast, however, her nihilistic half-brother Efnisien mutilated Matholwch's horses. By way of compensation, Bendigeidfran offered Matholwch the Cauldron of Rebirth but reports of the treachery he had suffered so outraged Matholwch's kinsfolk when he returned to Ireland with his bride that he was obliged to confine her to domestic service. Her dramatic escape and return to Wales conclude the tale, in the course of which her heroic brother Bendigeidfran, having waded across the sea beside his fleet, lays across the Shannon forming a human bridge to enable his warriors to effect a crossing. The latter incident gave rise to a Welsh aphorism, *'A fo ben bid bont'* (He who would lead must be a bridge) that serves as the motto of **Coleg Harlech**, the residential adult education college that opened, at the instigation of Thomas Jones, in 1927. The college has given a welcome second chance to generations of deserving students and has also served as a conduit for Welsh Patagonians to enter the national university. The college is housed in a sombre Edwardian pile, formerly known as Wern Fawr, which had been built for George Davison, a Kodak executive. Its south wing was destroyed by fire in 1968 and a visually inappropriate new wing was constructed, housing a useful community arts centre, *Theatr Ardudwy*.

Above the town, the clearly visible remains of a late iron age village, known as **Muriau'r Gwyddelod**, are a comparatively recent intrusion into a sacred landscape of late neolithic and early bronze age cairns, standing stones and burial chambers. St Peter's church, **Llanbedr**, where Ellis Wynne lies buried beneath the altar, contains a bronze age stone inscribed with the spiral motif often associated with eternal life. Two tall standing stones beside the Artro may mark the beginning of a bronze age trackway that leads through an extraordinary landscape studded with small lakes and dominated by Rhinog Fach (711m.) and Rhinog Fawr (720m.) with Diffwys (750m.) in the direction of Bala. Known to climbers and geologists as the **Harlech Dome**, these rugged hills can also be appreciated by following the Artro up to Cwm Bychan, then crossing through Bwlch Tyddiad by the Roman Steps. The latter were probably constructed by the ancestors of Henry Lloyd (1720–1783), a prominent Jacobite who served in the Prussian, Austrian and Russian armies and wrote influential texts on military strategy; they farmed in Cwm Bychan. This unique landscape is brilliantly described in Thomas Pennant's *Tours of Wales*.

Back nearer the village, on the Nantcol road, is **Salem** Baptist chapel, the interior of which was transformed by Sydney Curnow Vosper (1866–1942) into a national icon. The lady who modelled for his picture, Siân Owen, was reputed to be vain, hence the devil visible in the folds of her shawl. Vosper's original is in the Lever Gallery at Port Sunlight; it once figured prominently in an advertising campaign for soap. Its spiritual lather was worked up in countless Nonconformist homes where a reproduction hung on the wall. Nantcol has its own rugged beauty and impressive waterfalls to contrast with the charms of Cwm Artro. At the head of the valley is **Maes-y-garnedd**, birthplace of John Jones (1597–1660), the regicide. Having signed the king's death-warrant and then married Oliver Cromwell's sister, it is not surprising that this cultivated man faced execution at the Restoration.

Three kilometres south of Harlech, where the Artro meets the sea in its dune-enclosed lagoon, the church of St Tanwg at **Llandanwg** has been virtually engulfed by dunes, now kept sufficiently under control to enable occasional lamp-lit services to be held. The church contains an Early Christian inscribed stone but its fifteenth-century font was relocated to a new church of the same dedication built in Harlech in 1841 by Thomas Jones. The coastal dune system south of the river at **Mochras** contains a rich variety of seashells: it attracted Victorian collectors and acquired the name Shell Island. Siôn Phylip (1543–1620), from a local bardic family, farmed here; his Protestant verses are characterised by displays of Elizabethan learning. He was drowned returning home by ship from Anglesey and is buried beneath the east window at Llandanwg. Stretching out westward into Cardigan Bay in a straight line for some twenty kilometres, runs **Sarn Badrig**, on which many ships have foundered. Romantically rendered as St Patrick's Causeway, its name may derive from the Welsh for shipwreck, *badrhwyg*. In Welsh legend, it forms one of the embankments of Cantre'r Gwaelod, the flooded cantref of Cardigan Bay.

Dyffryn Ardudwy has an impressive neolithic burial chamber (Cadw), excavated in 1960. What now looks like two separate chambers was once a single monument. A kilometre to the south, the chapel added to St Dwywe's church at **Llanddwywe** contains good seventeenth- and eighteenth-century monuments. Some of these are of the Vaughans of Cors-y-Gedol, an ancient Merioneth family, whose late-sixteenth century house stands at the end of a long drive opposite. John Jones, Maes-y-garnedd, is buried in the churchyard. An old drover's road follows the Ysgethin, crossing it at the much-photographed **Pont Scethin**, before heading south-east for the Mawddach at Bontddu. Miners also picked their way through these hills in search of lead, silver and gold. It has become fashionable to have wedding rings made from the gold still sporadically mined at Clogau near **Bont-ddu**.

The road from Barmouth to Bont-ddu affords glorious views over the Mawddach in the direction of Cadair Idris. **Caerdeon** is associated with the greatest Victorian naturalist of them all. The Darwin family had their summer home here and Charles spent several happy summers walking these hills in the company of his brother and later of fellow students from Cambridge. Aged 60, he returned to Plas Caerdeon with his family for recuperation. The house is now an outdoor education centre for Liverpool Hope University. The idiosyncratic church of St Philip was built following a local ecclesiastical dispute. The Rector of Llanaber's refusal to provide services in English was challenged by an incomer, the Revd. W.E. Jelf. The dispute was settled by the passing of the English Services in Wales Act (1863), by which such English services could be provided if ten or more parishioners requested them. This modified the language policy of the Elizabethan Settlement by which services in predominantly Welsh districts were to be held in Welsh.

The **Mawddach** estuary is a stunning landscape best appreciated on The Panorama Walk (from Barmouth) or the New Precipice Walk (from Llanelltyd). The footbridge beside the **Barmouth railway viaduct** enables walkers to see the estuary at close quarters, with oystercatchers pecking at the sand below at low tide. When the viaduct was constructed for the Cambrian Railway, arrangements had to be made to swing the bridge open for passing vessels. The viaduct faced a crisis in 1980 with the discovery that teredo worms had made the timber footings of the viaduct unsafe but, to some local surprise, the costs of repair work were borne by British Rail and the viaduct reopened within a year. It is entirely fitting that the first property acquired by the National Trust, **Dinas Oleu**, should overlook the estuary. Donated by Mrs G.T. Talbot in 1895, she also bequeathed adjacent land to John Ruskin, another Victorian visitor to the area, for an intriguing social experiment known as the Guild of St George, the object of which was 'the education of the English peasantry'. Cottage-style accommodation was constructed for carefully selected tenants who were to be monitored and improved.

It is only fair to say that **Barmouth** is no longer the genteel resort of a century ago when fine villas, such as the romantic Plas Mynach, were taken for the season by the likes of Mrs Perrins, of Worcester sauce fame and fortune. Today the beach is flanked by a funfair and an amusement park. The town derives its English name from Y Bermo, the Welsh contraction of Aber Mawddach. On the quayside, a block of carrara marble, raised from the 1709 wreck of a Genoese galleon, has been used to produce an imaginative millennium sculpture. Every midsummer's day since 1977, Barmouth is the point of departure for the original Three Peaks Race, with yachts and their crews competing to sail to and climb up the highest peaks of Wales, England and Scotland. The church of St David by the harbour was originally the fishermen's church; the commodious church of St John the Evangelist, with its Westminster chimes, was completed in 1898, having been paid for by Mrs Perrins. The mother church of Barmouth is at **Llanaber**, some three kilometres up the coast; built by a grandson of Owain Gwynedd, it is a gem of thirteenth-century church architecture. Inside, there are two inscribed stones, recovered from the beach and a painting by John Parker (1798–1860) showing the original structure before restoration work in 1858. To appreciate the strength and beauty of the building, stand beneath the chancel arch and look along the nave on a sunny afternoon.

From Dolgellau, the Ruabon to Barmouth railway ran along the water's edge to join the Cambrian Railway at Barmouth Junction. Closed by Dr Beeching, the track has been turned into a trail for walkers and cyclists and the station, no longer a junction, is now known as **Morfa Mawddach**. The first stop out of Dolgellau was at **Penmaenpool** where the station buildings are now part of a hotel, the former signal box houses an RSPB information centre and a rattling wooden toll bridge, constructed in 1879, spans the Mawddach. The Penmaenpool Reedbed, one of the largest stands of common reeds in Wales, is the breeding ground of otters and wetland birds. The next station was in the little quarrying village of **Arthog** where an RSPB bird-watching trail on the edge of Cors Arthog provides a good opportunity to look for reed bunting and listen to the piping of the curlew.

South from Morfa Mawddach, the Cambrian Coast Line squeezes along the narrow coastal strip from Y Friog to Tywyn. The village of Y Friog was transformed into the beach resort of **Fairbourne**, making use of the sands of Rô Wen. The railway used to construct the place was retained to give pleasure rides to visitors and is now one of the 'Great Little Trains' of Wales. Further down the coast, the old church of St Celynin at **Llangelynin** contains a double horse bier, wall texts, benches and family pews. In the churchyard is the grave of Abram Wood, the patriarch of *Teulu Abram Wood*, as the Welsh gypsies were known. He had migrated to Wales in the early eighteenth century and died in 1799. A score of his descendants were skilled folk harpists.

Rounding the headland at Tonfannau, the Dysynni estuary is also enclosed by a sand-spit, Morfa Gwyllt; the resulting lagoon, **Broad Water**, is a gathering point for cormorants. The sea once covered what is now the flood plain of the Afon Dysynni, lapping at the foot of **Craig yr Aderyn**, Bird Rock. This fact must account for its historic inland cormorant colony which in turn accounts for the profusion of red campion found here in the summer, flourishing on the nitrate-rich droppings. On the north bank of the river St Egryn's church at **Llanegryn**, otherwise over-restored by E.B. Ferrey in 1878, has one of the best surviving rood screens and lofts in Wales. Dating from the sixteenth century, the western parapet of the rood loft has canopies that once contained images; the eastern parapet has intricate carving. The sockets for the roods are still visible. Outside Ebeneser Independent chapel, there is a memorial to the Puritan, Hugh Owen, (1637–1699), Bronyclydwr, 'apostle of Merioneth' to his denomination, the Independents. He is buried in the churchyard. Ferrey was commissioned by the Wynne's of nearby **Peniarth**; it was William Watkin Edward Wynne (1801–1880), the antiquary, who inherited, catalogued and added to the Hengwrt collection of manuscripts now housed in the National Library of Wales.

Further up the valley is **Castell-y-Bere** (Cadw), romantically attached to a narrow spur of rock that rises up from the valley floor. A native Welsh castle, it was rescued in the 1950s from beneath dense undergrowth by Cadw's predecessors. The castle was built by Llywelyn Fawr in 1221 and was the last Welsh castle to fall to Edward I on 25 April 1283. Close by is the village of **Llanfihangel-y-Pennant** where, in 1884, Mary Jones (1784–1866) was born in the humble cottage of Ty'n-y-ddol beside the Afon Cader, half a kilometre beyond the plain little church where she was baptised. Having learned to read in a circulating school, she walked over the mountains to Bala to purchase a Bible from Thomas Charles. So moved was he by her determination, that the British and Foreign Bible Society was formed in 1804; today, it publishes Bibles in some 875 different languages. The story of Mary Jones and her Bible is recounted in an exhibition in the church vestry and a monument in her memory was erected in the ruins of Ty'n-y-ddol in 1907. She lies buried in the Calvinistic Methodist chapel at **Bryncrug**. The Pony Path to the summit of Cadair Idris starts in the village: it is the easiest but longest of the paths up the mountain.

The Dysynni can be pursued upstream through what geologists term an elbow of river-capture, to its source near Tal-y-llyn. **Abergynolwyn** is the terminus of the Tal-y-llyn Railway. It runs along the valley where, in prehistoric times, the Dysynni ran its course. This narrow gauge railway, now a tourist attraction, was originally a mineral line, built in 1866 to carry slates from McConnel's quarries in the Gwernol valley down to Tywyn Wharf. In 1950 it became the first of the former mineral lines in Wales to be turned into a 'Great Little Train' for the tourist trade by the world's first railway preservation society. Within a few years the truly hideous village store had been erected; close by, two rows of workers' terraced housing evoke a proud industrial past. The peaceful church of St Mary at Tal-y-llyn contains a wonderful wooden ceiling above the chancel painted with Tudor roses. Llyn Mwyngil, placid between Cadair Idris and Moel Rugog, is nowhere more than four metres deep. Fishing boats can be hired from the lakeside hotel.

As at Barmouth and Blaenau Festiniog, the boundary of the Snowdonia National Park skirts around **Tywyn**, as though it were a Catholic enclave in gerrymandered Ulster. The reason is neither social, political or religious, however, but aesthetic. Yet, in spite of the accretion of retirement bungalows, Tywyn has a significant history as one of the holy places of Wales. On the site of the parish church, St Cadfan, the Breton saint to whom it is dedicated, had his *clas*. The church contains the Nitanum stone, the earliest surviving Welsh inscription. It has been dated to around the eighth century and there are several interpretations as to its meaning. The church has been much altered on an ancient site but the massive double-aisled nave from the twelfth century invariably impresses. There are also two fourteenth-century effigies, of a knight and a priest, that remind us of Cadfan's traditional association with warriors. Opposite the hotel, the former Assembly Rooms are now a cinema.

Even Rasselas would be charmed in **Happy Valley**, as Cwm Dyffryn-gwyn was translated for the first generation of tourists. A delightfully scenic minor road runs inland from Tywyn to Capel Maethlon. Now a private dwelling, it retains its burial ground containing a monument to the young headmaster of Aberdyfi School who drowned in the estuary in 1867. **Llyn Barfog** is the object of a popular summer walk when its yellow water lilies are in bloom. The lake has been given Arthurian associations: the Bearded One was either one of the Knights of the Round Table, or Arthur's foster father. Arthur's horse left a hoof-print, marked at Carn March Arthur, when it leapt over the Dyfi – at a most unlikely angle – to save Arthur from his enemies. Beside the lake a quaint slate sign points to a place where one may practise an echo. The main road from Tywyn rounds the headland at **Aberdyfi**, a place famous in melody for its legendary bells that can he heard ringing beneath the waters of Cardigan Bay, another distant memory of Cantre'r Gwaelod. Its southern aspect gives the place a cheerful feel, with brightly coloured houses on the sea front and a bustle of activity at the little harbour. An evening walk along the vast sandy beach, or behind the town over Yr Horon, offers exhilarating views over the Dyfi estuary.

Owain Glyn Dŵr chose **Pennal**, along with Harlech, Dolgellau and Machynlleth, as a fitting place to summon one of his parliaments. In 1406, he wrote his famous letter to his ally, Charles VI of France from Pennal, an event celebrated in a stirring painting by Aneurin Jones exhibited in the little church of St Peter ad Vincula, the only such dedication in Wales. The church, formerly dedicated to St Tanwg and St Erthrias, now proudly styles itself Owain Glyn Dŵr's 'chapel royal'. It is also worth visiting for its Edwardian stained glass memorial windows. Pennal was also important to the Romans who had a wharf here. The farm of Cefn-gaer is built on the remains of the Roman fort. Today Pennal is a peaceful place, the eighteenth-century house Plas Talgarth now transformed into a leisure resort. A couple of kilometres east of the village is Dol-gelynen, the ancestral home of Lleucu Llwyd, object of one of the finest love poems in the Welsh language, written in the fourteenth century by Llywelyn Goch ap Meurig Hen. A couple of kilometres more and it is possible to cross the Dyfi, into Montgomeryshire at Machynlleth.

To return to Dolgellau the main road continues up the Dulas valley with the steep slopes of Tarren-y-Gesail to the west, to the former slate quarrying village of **Corris**. Where real craftsmen once worked in the slate caverns under Mynydd Braich-goch, tourists now take a mysterious boat ride into King Arthur's Labyrinth. The scale of the underground workings is more impressive than the gaudy Arthurian models that have been elaborately set up there. Corris still has its Institute, but most of the chapels and village shops have closed. The former mineral line, built in 1859 to carry slate down to Derwenlas, is one of the younger 'Great Little Trains', reopening for passenger traffic in 2002 after a break of seventy-two years. The place is still atmospheric and **Aberllefenni**, further up the valley, even more so, not least because the slate quarry here is still productive, albeit only employing a handful of men. Opposite the dressing floor of the quarry is a delightful row of quar-rymen's cottages. The tiny old schoolhouse still has its bell *in situ* and the disused quarries on the hillside rising to the north are wonderful reminders of the age of slate.

After Corris, the main road drops down to Minffordd at the foot of **Cadair Idris**, then climbs up Bwlch Llyn Bach towards Cross Foxes. Minfordd is a good point of departure for the ascent of Cadair Idris, for generations one of the classic hill-walks of Wales. Richard Wilson set up his easel here in 1773 to paint Cwm Cau: his painting, now in the Tate Gallery in London, suggests that the artist supposed Cadair Idris to be an extinct volcano, confusing a glacial *cirque* for a *caldera*. Charles Darwin had a better grasp of the geology, but also appreciated the mountain for its beauty: 'Old Cader is a grand fellow and shows himself off superbly with ever changing light. Do come and see him.' As a naturalist, he appreciated the sight of pied flycatchers and wheatears darting among the rocks, ravens and merlins soaring overhead and such plants as the common sundew, bog asphodel and parsley fern. For those unable to make it on foot to Pen-y-gadair (893m.), the view from Bwlch Llyn Bach in the direction of Tal-y-Llyn is sublime.

The A470 (T) uses the route of the former railway to by-pass Dolgellau and head up the Mawddach in the direction of Ffestiniog. With the Precipice Walk high above to the east, the road continues north to **Ganllwyd**, point of depar-ture for a tour of three beautiful but contrasting waterfalls. Nearest the village is Rhaeadr Ddu (NT), then, by follow-ing the Mawddach upstream, Rhaeadr Mawddach and Pistyll Cain, the latter the most impressive of the trio being higher and narrower. **Trawsfynydd** – Y Traws, to the locals – uniquely blends ancient and modern in tragic fashion. Set in a sacred bronze age landscape, the village is a bastion of Welsh language and culture. It is famed for its sheep-dog trials, an activity that has its origins in these hills.

Modernity made its first tragic intrusion in 1917 when, during the ceremony of the chairing of the bard at the National Eisteddfod, held that year in Birkenhead, it was discovered that the poet who had submitted the winning entry had died in the mud of Flanders. The chair was draped in black. His *nom-de-plume* for the competion had been *fleur-de-lys*; born in 1887, his real name was Ellis Humphrey Evans. Today he is known throughout Wales as Hedd Wyn, Blessed Peace. In the grounds of Capel y Fro, in the centre of the village, there is a statue to this gifted local shepherd and his chair, the Black Chair of Birkenhead, is still an heirloom in his farmhouse, Yr Ysgwrn, beside the Afon Prysor. A film about his life released in 1992 was the first Welsh language film to be nominated for an Oscar. A second intrusion followed half a century later with the opening of Trawsfynydd Nuclear Power Station, a sinister concrete pile, shockingly situated in the middle of a National Park. Within a generation the false hopes promulgated by the nuclear industry had evaporated. With tragic irony, it was Snowdonia that bore the brunt in the U.K. of the radioactive fall-out from the Chernobyl disaster in 1986. The power station was decommissioned in 1993 but it is unclear – not least to the nuclear boffins themselves – what can now be done with the site.

East of the village is **Tomen-y-mur**, the site of a Norman motte, thrown up by William Rufus in 1095, that uses the remains of a Roman fort as its bailey. It is possible to identify many other features of what must have been a substantial military complex by walking the adjoining fields: a parade ground, bathhouse, tribunal and amphitheatre have been excavated. The site is marked on most maps as a fort, a fact that presumably accounts for the German bomb dropped on it during the Second World War. As Mur Castell, this site figures in *Y Mabinogi*. Lleu Llaw Gyffes was holding court here when he was murdered by his wife's lover, Gronw, before being transformed into an eagle. Blodeuwedd, the beautiful but unfaithful wife, conjured from flowers, fled the scene with her maidens. They were all so frightened that they walked backwards, the maidens tumbling into a lake and drowning. Blodeuwedd survived, only to be transformed into an owl.

12

Caernarfonshire

Eifionydd

THE POET ROBERT WILLIAMS PARRY described Eifionydd as a land between sea and mountains, '*y fro rhwng môr a mynydd*'. The mountain fastness of Arfon protects it from the north, with remote Llŷn stretching westward beyond the Afon Erch. Both Porthmadog, its market centre, and Tremadoc, the prior settlement, derive their names from the same colourful individual, William Alexander Maddocks (1773–1828), who was largely responsible for the present appearance of these places. A leading advocate of parliamentary reform, he abandoned a political career (as MP for Boston, in Lincolnshire) to bring prosperity to this part of Wales only to die in Paris, like a true Romantic, in parlous financial circumstances.

Tremadoc feels different from the usual organic Welsh settlement precisely because it was planned by a single mind. It was in the first decade of the nineteenth century that William Maddocks built his model town here on land he had recently reclaimed. His intention was that his town would prosper by virtue of its position on a proposed new route, for postal services and military personnel, linking London to Dublin. Unfortunately for Maddocks, but fortuitously for this part of Snowdonia, the route that Telford finally developed lay many miles to the east. What remains of Maddocks' dream is most attractive: a well-proportioned Square with an arcaded market hall and his own home, Tanyrallt, which started a fashion for such Regency properties in this corner of Wales. It was in Tanyrallt that Shelley's 'attempted murder' took place. Other men of English letters associated with the town are T.E. Lawrence (1888–1935), better known as Lawrence of Arabia, who was born here at Snowdon Lodge, opposite Capel Peniel, and Bertrand Russell (1872–1970), the distinguished Welsh philosopher, who spent the last years of his life here. St Mary's, currently under restoration, was one of the first Gothic revival churches in Wales; Capel Peniel, a short distance away, also benefited from Maddocks's patronage, the latter an unusual example of gentry patronage of Welsh Nonconformity, reflecting Maddocks's progressive views on religious toleration. From the latter tradition sprang the likes of William Jones (Crudyrawel, 1896–1961), a local librarian who composed the popular poem, *Y Llanc Ifanc o Lŷn*.

Maddocks' great project was the construction of the **Cob**, or embankment, across Traeth Mawr; it was completed in 1811 only to be breached by a gale the following year. The damage was repaired but the financial costs of the project had been so high as to prevent Maddocks advancing with the associated land reclamation scheme. His marriage in 1817 to a rich young widow, Eliza Gwynne, enabled him to launch a fresh project, the construction of a harbour at **Porthmadog** and the construction of a linking railway to the slate quarries of Blaenau Ffestiniog. His death in 1828 meant that he did not see either of these projects come to fruition. The Port Madoc Harbour Act was passed in 1824, with the Ffestiniog Railway opening in 1836, one of the earliest railway companies in the world. For the rest of the nineteenth century the harbour was the focus of Eifionydd's economic prosperity. By 1863, steam engines had replaced horses on the busy narrow gauge railway and locally built 'topsail' schooners of the Western Ocean Yachting Company – owned by local syndicates of grocers, ministers of religion and others of the 'middling sort' – were supplying the world with Welsh slate. The returning ships brought *guano* and the ballast from which Ballast

Island, by the mouth of the harbour, was formed. A Maritime Museum, housed in an old slate shed on Oakeley Wharf, is full of information about these wonderful vessels, as are the walls of *Y Llong*, the harbourside tavern.

The **Ffestiniog Railway**, with its terminus on the quayside, is now the most sophisticated of the 'Great Little Trains' of Wales. The original railway closed abruptly in 1946 but by 1955 a group of amateur enthusiasts had revived it. It is now professionally, but no less enthusiastically, operated as the Ffestiniog Railway Trust. On some summer evenings, there is fine dining aboard, a *rendez-vous* with dessert being made at the halfway point. The journey from Porthmadog up to Blaenau Ffestiniog is well worth making for the scenery alone: accompanied by gourmet food and fine wines it is a memorable experience.

From Porthmadog to Beddgelert, the road follows the course of the Glaslyn, a tumbling stream that has its source on the slopes of Snowdon. There are good views of Cnicht and the Moelwyns before the view disappears as the valley constricts at **Aberglaslyn Pass**, one of the classic Welsh 'beauty spots'. Before the construction of the Cob at Porthmadog the river was tidal and navigable up to this point. It is still prized for its fishing, although dense nineteenth-century conifer planting and invasive rhododendrons now make the valley feel gloomier than it should. The famous stone bridge, seventeenth century in origin, was widened at the end of the eighteenth. The valley was used for the final stage of the ill-fated **Welsh Highland Railway**, which linked Caernarfon with Porthmadog via Rhyd-ddu and Beddgelert between 1881 and 1940. Although this scenic railway is now being revived for the tourist trade, it is worth recalling that Ruskin vigorously opposed the 'desecration' of the valley when the railway was being constructed in 1898.

Beddgelert is a handsome village that has historically acted as a gateway between Meirion and Arfon. In 1802,

David Prichard opened the Royal Goat Hotel and proceeded to develop Gelert's Grave for his own commercial purposes. It flourishes still, a monument to the gullibility of the tourist. A local tale told of a faithful hound heroically killing an intruding wolf after having been set to guard his master's infant son while his master went hunting. The reward for the faithful pooch was to be killed in turn by his returning master who mistook the bloody scene for betrayal. The tale was made more dramatic by having the master named as Prince Llywelyn and building a grave for Gelert, the name given to the hound, now also to be seen on delivery vans supplying a locally produced dog food. It is nevertheless worth following the signs (To Gelert's Grave and Toilet) to appreciate the Alpine setting of the village. Architectural highlights include seventeenth century Bwthyn Llywelyn and nineteenth century Craflwyn Hall, both owned by the National Trust, the latter refurbished as an Environmental Centre. St Mary's church once formed part of an Augustinian Priory, itself built on the site of a sixth-century Celtic monastery. It has some good mediaeval features, including a thirteenth-century east window that contains late Victorian glass commemorating James Wyatt, the agent of Richard Pennant. The curious font was inscribed in the nineteenth century using the Nennius and Bardic scripts respectively. Beddgelert is a popular starting point for an exhilarating ascent of Moel Hebog (782m.) and Moel Lefn (638m.), a climb rewarded with broad vistas out to Bardsey in the west and over Cardigan Bay to the south. An easier descent (or ascent) can be made via Cwm Llefrith from Cwm Pennant or via Cwmystradllyn.

Cricieth, along the coast west of Porthmadog, is a Victorian resort grafted onto a Norman borough, the resultant townscape possessing great charm and character. It was Llywelyn Fawr who built the original castle (Cadw) here in 1230, recognising the strategic opportunities of a splendid site on a rocky peninsula commanding superb views over Tremadog Bay. Edward I took the castle over at the conquest and established an English borough beside it, but the castle fell into Welsh hands again in the course of the Glyn Dŵr Rising, suffering so much damage that it was never used again. St Catherine's church has a double nave; it dates from the fourteenth century but was heavily restored in 1870. A disused sundial of 1734 on the church-yard wall gives bearings and distances to ports the world over. The town's second phase of growth came when the arrival of the railway coincided with the fashion for seaside holidays in the mid-nineteenth century. The cottages in Wellington Terrace give a surviving glimpse of the town's appearance prior to these developments.

Llanystumdwy is renowned as the village in which David Lloyd George (1863–1945) spent his formative years, learning rhetoric from regular attendance at the local cobbler's workshop and the Campbellite Baptist chapel in the village. He had been born in Manchester but came to live here at the age of two following the death of his father. He lived with his uncle, Richard Lloyd, in a humble cottage, Highgate. His career was not without con-troversy: a pioneer of the Welfare State, he was loved by the ordinary people for the state benefits that he introduced to deal with 'the four spectres which haunt the poor, old age, accident, sickness and unemployment'. The rich in general, and the landowners in particular, who funded these bene-fits through taxation, were less enthusiastic. As Prime Minister during the Great War, his prosecution of consci-entious objectors was an affront to many within his own Nonconformist tradition. It must also seem incredible to today's world of tabloid journalism that he lived a separate life in London with a mistress and their daughter from his life of married respectability back home in Wales. The village boasts an informative Lloyd George Museum and his suitably dramatic memorial, designed by Clough Williams-Ellis, a massive granite boulder on the banks of the Dwyfor. Clough Williams-Ellis also designed Moriah, a new chapel for the Calvinistic Methodists that opened in 1936 replacing its predecessor that had been destroyed by fire. Tŷ Newydd, the retirement home of Lloyd George, is now a residential centre for creative writing in Welsh and English, run by the Welsh Academy.

Jan Morris, the celebrated author, acquired **Trefan**, on the banks of the Dwyfor, half a century ago. She has since moved into its converted outbuildings and given them the name Trefan Morys. One of her last books, *A Writer's House in Wales*, is a delightful description of her home and, as with all her writings, a brilliant evocation of the spirit of this particular place. Her son, the poet and singer Twm Morys, who lives in the adjacent lodge, was chaired bard at the National Eisteddfod in Meifod in 2003. Upstream, there is a neolithic burial chamber at **Rhos-lan**. Robert Jones, Rhos-lan (1745–1829), the Calvinistic Methodist exhorter and author of *Drych yr Amseroedd* was born at Suntur and R. Tudur Jones (1921–1998), the religious historian and theologian, at Tyddyn Gwyn.

From Llanystumdwy the coastal road to Pwllheli continues to **Afon Wen**, a former railway junction renowned for inducing melancholy in its waiting room. Dr Beeching cut the link between the Cambrian Coast Line and the main line from London to Holyhead making it impossible to travel by rail between north and south Wales without making a detour through England. The route taken by the old railway must now be followed by road. East of this road lies the remote and beautiful valley of **Cwm Pennant**. Eifion Wyn (Eliseus Williams, 1867–1926) concluded his poem on the valley with a heart-felt question to his Maker: 'Why did you make Cwm Pennant so beautiful and the life of a shepherd so short?'

How **Butlin's** came to build a holiday camp in the middle of a national park makes an instructive case study. In 1940, at the height of the Second World War, the Admiralty was urgently seeking training camps in safe areas. Butlin's had acquired this site, west of Afon Wen, for possible future development but ceded it to the Admiralty and the huts, refectory and so forth were quickly constructed, the usual requirement for planning permission waived for the war emergency. After the war, the property was returned to Butlin's who sought planning permission for a holiday camp. There was considerable local opposition but Clough Williams-Ellis, representing both the county council and the Council for the Protection of Rural Wales, idiosyncratically spoke in favour of the camp, on the grounds that concentrating this type of tourism in one self-contained site represented effective damage-limitation. The camp had its own railway station at Penychain and provided its own on-site entertainment. Since 1998 it has become Hafan-y-Mor Holiday Park.

From Afon Wen a lane leads north to **Penarth Fawr** (Cadw), a remarkable fifteenth-century hall house attractively altered in the seventeenth century. **Chwilog** has a memorial to Eifion Wyn in its public cemetery that was unveiled by Lloyd George. At **Llangybi**, St Cybi's Well (Cadw) was revived as a spa by the enterprising squire of Rhiwlas, William Price; this accounts for the motley but evocative appearance of the ruins.

Llŷn

The Afon Erch marks the boundary between Eifionydd and the northern of the two peninsulas of Wales that reach out towards Ireland. The name Llŷn incorporates the same element as is contained in Leinster; some say that the Irish were the clever Celts who could swim. For centuries Llŷn has been a bastion of the Welsh language and culture but the attraction of its south-facing strands and relatively cheap property has induced recent English settlement that poses a threat to the traditional character of the area. A millennium and a half after the first Anglo-Saxon settlements on the east coast of Britain, they are now established on our most westerly shores.

Pwllheli, the contemporary estuary of the Erch following centuries of extension of the sand-spit of Morfa Aber-erch, is the market centre for Llŷn and terminus of the Cambrian Coast Line, some six hours journey time from Cardiff, two hundred kilometres away. The line enters the town on reclaimed land to terminate at a typically stylish Great Western Railway station. The town falls into two halves. The old town has attractive shop-fronts in High Street and an open square, Y Maes, where the town's lively weekly market takes place. In Penlan Street, plaques mark the birthplaces of Cynan (Albert Evans Jones, 1895–1970), thrice-crowned bard of the National Eisteddfod, and of the modern Welsh philosopher J.R. Jones (1911–1970). Penlan Fawr Inn is the oldest building in a town noted for its past support for the temperance cause. Penlan Independent in Gaol Street is a stylish mid-nineteenth century chapel (the cause began in 1646) and there is an impressive Calvinistic Methodist chapel at Penmount. In the latter, the Revd. John Puleston Jones preached pacifism at the height of the Great War in opposition to the Revd. John Williams, Brynsiencyn.

The coming of the railway led to the development of seaside villas at Marian-y-De (South Beach) to meet the holiday needs of the north Wales quarrymen. The town is still famous for Pwllheli Rock, sold at fairs throughout Wales. Solomon Andrews from Cardiff developed the town, hence Cardiff Street in which the English chapel is situated. He developed a tram service from the town to Llanbedrog that operated until 1927. The town name derives from the Welsh for salt pool and the sheltered harbour has a proud maritime history from the days of sail.

Plaid Cymru traces its origins to the 1925 National Eisteddfod in Pwllheli. In 1936, three prominent members of Plaid Cenedlaethol Cymru (Welsh National Party), as it was then known, Saunders Lewis, a university lecturer, Lewis Valentine (1893–1986), a Baptist minister, and D.J. Williams, a schoolmaster, set fire to an RAF bombing school that had been established at **Penyberth** outside Pwllheli. They gave themselves up and were put on trial. Insisting on giving evidence in their own language in their own country when the trial opened in Caernarfon, the trial was transferred out of Wales to the Old Bailey in London where guilty verdicts were handed down and the Penyberth Three sent down to serve time in Wormwood Scrubs. On their release, they returned to heroes' welcomes in an awakened Wales.

The beach at **Llanbedrog** is owned by the National Trust. The village is divided by the main road: on the sheltered seaward side are the holiday and retirement homes of the incomers; to the landward, the windy streets where locals still live. The church is dedicated to Petrox, a sixth-century saint whose dedications span an arc from Brittany to this most northerly outpost, with their greatest concentration in Cornwall. It retains its mediaeval screen; the sixteenth-century chancel was added to a mediaeval nave. Tremvan Hall was built by Gwenogfryn Evans (1852–1930), the palaeographer; he spent a productive retirement here editing mediaeval Welsh manuscripts. He is buried close by in a rock-grave he had prepared for himself and his wife. Plas Glyn y Weddw, a Victorian Gothic mansion, now houses an art gallery.

A few kilometres inland, **Llangian** has a very early memorial in its churhyard, to a sixth-century doctor. It is inscribed in Latin on a granite pillar. Inside, the church has a fine fifteenth-century roof and interesting memorials to the Edwards family of **Nanhoron**, a delightful Regency house three kilometres to the north-west. For contrast, visit the isolated eighteenth-century dissenting meeting house of **Capel Newydd,** the earliest surviving Nonconformist meeting house in north Wales. Tucked away in a field off the main road from Llanbedrog to Botwnnog, it dates from

1769 and was carefully restored in 1958 to retain the original beaten earth floor, box pews, candelabra and hat pegs. Mrs Edwards of Nanhoron joined this congregation following the death of her husband, an unusual move for one of her class. The Horon, in its delightful wooded glade, can be followed north on a road constructed by Richard Lloyd Edwards of Nanhoron in memory of his son who had died in the Crimean War, hence the Inkerman Bridge. Rising to the north, at 371 metres, is the iron age hill fort of Garn Fadryn, whence you can see from sea to sea. On the other side of Garn Fadryn is **Madryn Castle**. Four centuries of antiques and curios were dispersed under the auctioneer's hammer when this estate was finally sold in 1910 and only the gatehouse remains to guard a caravan park where the sixteenth-century mansion once stood. The name lives on in South America, for Love Jones Parry was one of the founders of *Yr Wladfa*, the Welsh settlement in Patagonia. The first landfall of the *Mimosa* in 1865 was named Porth Madryn (Puerto Madryn) after his ancestral home.

The sheltered harbour at **Abersoch** has made this a popular resort for yachtsmen and holidaymakers and its whitewashed cottages have been engulfed in modern development. Beyond Penrhyn Mawr (NT) to the south-east are **Ynysoedd Tudwal** (St Tudwal's Islands); the southern island has a lighthouse and the northern one the remains of the sixth century saint's cell. A shipwreck on the islands on 18 October 1858 was the origin of the popular Welsh sea shanty, *Fflat Huw Puw*. Inland to the south-west, **Llanengan** has one of the finest churches in Llŷn, the product of extensive restoration in the sixteenth century. The original roof timbers and screens survive, in the case of the one over the south aisle, also retaining its rood loft. **Botwnnog** is renowned for its school, founded from a bequest from Bishop Henry Rowland (1551–1616).

Mynydd Cilan, the southeastern tip of the Llŷn peninsula, has cliff walks with fulmar colonies and glorious

views over to Bardsey. Beyond the six-kilometre strand of
Porth Neigwl, known in English as Hell's Mouth, is
Mynydd y Rhiw (NT). The seventeenth-century house of
Plas-yn-Rhiw (NT) has one of the most delightfully romantic gardens in the country. Acquired in 1930 by Mrs Keating
and her three daughters, they lovingly recreated the abandoned and overgrown garden in an informal cottage
garden style. There are breathtaking displays of snowdrops
and bluebells in the spring. The delectable mediaeval
church at **Llanfaelrhys**, with its original box pews, overlooks the sea. A path leads down to a seaside waterfall.

For centuries **Aberdaron** was the place where pilgrims
on the way to Bardsey gathered and sought refreshment.
Y Gegin Fawr, the communal kitchen that served the latter
purpose, still survives. The pilgrim church of St Hywyn was
built so close to the shingle beach that you yearn to cross
over to the 'Isle of Two Thousand Saints' with every breaking wave. That the church is so spacious is understandable,
although it would have taken a throng of pilgrims a long
time to file through the single, small, late Norman doorway. Too large for the village, a new church was constructed
by John Welch in 1841, but its design was generally
despised and it was soon abandoned. The old church was
repaired in 1860. The poet R.S. Thomas, a keen ornithologist, was rector here from 1967 to 1978. Richard Robert
Jones (Dic Aberdaron, 1780–1843), the eccentric polyglot,
is buried in the churchyard.

Bardsey Sound has a reputation for furious tidal surges,
encapsulated in the island's Welsh name, Ynys Enlli. The
fury of the Sound and the hump of Mynydd Enlli, hiding
any view of the island settlement, add to the mystique of
Bardsey. Such was the island's legendary reputation as the
preferred burial ground of the Celtic saints that the Isle of
Two Thousand Saints sometimes swells to twenty thousand, depending on the source. The island seems to have
remained a centre of Celtic monasticism until well after the

Synod of Whitby had officially marked a *rapprochement* between Celtic Christianity and the Church of Rome. The stump of the thirteenth-century church is all that remains of the abbey on the northern tip of the island. Some cross slabs and the remains of monastic huts survive. The island's English name is of Viking origin, Badr's Island, the Vikings being the scourge of Celtic Christian sites around the British and Irish coast. Boat trips out to the island are available from Aberdaron but they are very much time, tide and weather dependent. Few who have visited the island, however, fail to be touched by a sense of the sacred.

Bardsey is almost perfectly designed for an island community with its sheltered landing place (Y Cafn), open meadows and the protection of Mynydd Enlli (167m.). Continuous settlement of the island ended with evacuation in 1926 but the island has been farmed sporadically since by tenants of Lord Newborough, the latter responsible for various improvements to the cottages. Cristin, the largest farmhouse, was home to the island's 'king' in the nineteenth century. The last 'king', Love Pritchard, died in 1926, the year of the evacuation, and is buried at Aberdaron along with many victims of the Sound. The lighthouse dates from 1821, its powerful beam a problem for migrant birds. The bird observatory staff makes every effort to help birds recover from collisions. The writer and painter Brenda Chamberlain (1912–1971) stayed in Carreg from 1947 to 1961 describing the experience graphically in *Tide Race*. The island is now in the care of the Bardsey Island Trust.

The 'whistling sands' at **Porth Oer** squeek like dry snow as you run over them, round and uniform quartz grains producing a note of uniform pitch. St Gwynhoedl's church at **Llangwnnadl** is the last of the pilgrim churches before Aberdaron is reached along the mediaeval pilgrim's way from Clynnog, Pistyll and Nefyn. We should not be surprised by its spaciousness, therefore, with three broad aisles, the northern one added in 1520 to accommodate pilgrims. **Cefnamwlch**, on the slopes of its mountain, was home to the Griffith family, prominent members of the local gentry, for centuries. The house became a household name throughout Wales during the Methodist Revival when 'Madam' Sydney Griffith became the constant companion of Howell Harris and the 'Prophetess of Welsh Methodism'. The nature of their relationship has been the subject of much tortured analysis, starting with that of Harris's wife. Modern scholars dispute whether or not the relationship was carnal but the impact of the relationship on contemporaries resulted in a split in the ranks of Welsh Methodism. From the holiday village of **Morfa Nefyn** it is worth a detour to contemplate one of the might-have-beens of modern Wales at **Porth Dinllaen**. An attractive promontory, it now seasonally accommodates a publican, a coastguard, holidaymakers and seals, seeing little action for the remainder of the year save for the occasional launching of its lifeboat. Yet this might have been a busy port had William Maddocks realised his plan to build a port for the London to Dublin route here. It was a plan also favoured by the Great Western Railway, but in both cases Holyhead carried the day. All that remains of the scheme are the straight roads from Morfa Nefyn to Pwllheli and Cricieth, constructed by the Porth Dinllaen Turnpike Trust.

In 1284, **Nefyn** was the scene of an Arthurian tournament as Edward I celebrated his conquest of Wales with a round table banquet: the site, Cae Iorwerth, is to the east of the village at the foot of Mynydd Nefyn. Nefyn has a proud maritime history: the Lleyn Historical and Maritime Museum is housed in the former St Mary's church with its ship weathervane and watchtower. The quayside is attractive and a good starting point for coastal walks. Nefyn was declared a borough by Edward I and served as an important market centre for Llŷn before the arrival of the railway at Pwllheli put it into eclipse. Until 1885, it was one of the Caernarfon Boroughs that returned a Member of

Parliament. St Beuno's church at **Pistyll** is another pilgrim church, dating from the twelfth century and enlarged in the fifteenth. It has an attractive healing well. Rupert Davies (1916–1976), the actor fondly remembered for his portrayal of Maigret in the early days of British television, is buried in the churchyard. Tom Nefyn Williams (1895–1958), the Calvinistic Methodist minister expelled from his church in 1926 for his socialist beliefs, was born on a local farm, Bodeilias; there is a plaque to his memory on the wall of Capel Bethania.

Llithfaen, as its name suggests, grew up around its granite quarries. It is a convenient point of departure for a number of interesting excursions. Towards the sea, a minor road leads down to **Nant Gwrtheyrn**. This deep, shady valley, named after Vortigern who supposedly died here, was settled when the surrounding hills were being quarried for slate. When the slate quarries closed at the end of the 1950s, the village went into decline. Having lost its last inhabitant, it has staged a remarkable comeback and is now a residential study centre for learners of Welsh. The little pier from which the slate was exported survives. The three-pronged mountain above the village is known as **Yr Eifl**, The Fork (sometimes corrupted into English as The Rivals). The most northerly prong is crowned with a bronze age cairn, while the southern prong is the site of **Tre'r Ceiri**, one of the most notable of the many iron age hill forts in Wales, containing the extensive remains of stone-built hut circles. The central prong is the highest at 564 metres, from which point there are exceptionally beautiful and extensive views of the coastline, from sea to answering sea.

Arfon

Moving out of Llŷn into the mountainous country of Arfon, there are more pilgrimage churches. The mediaeval church of St Aelhaearn at **Llanaelhaearn** contains attractive box pews and a sixth-century Christian inscribed stone commemorating a man from Elmet, the British territory in the vicinity of modern Leeds. There is another such stone in its original position in the graveyard outside. **Clynnog-fawr**, as the name implies, was of historic importance, for here was the tomb and shrine of St Beuno, often described as the patron saint of north Wales. Lying on the pilgrimage route to Bardsey, the church was much frequented and generated considerable income, hence the great chest preserved in the nave. The interior is spacious and has an attractive oak roof; the chancel, with its large window, retains its Tudor stalls and misericords. Capel y Bedd, a sixteenth-century extension to the south-west of the church, marks the site of Beuno's original cell. Outside the chapel is an interesting twelfth-century sundial thought to be of Irish origin. Beside the road, in sight of the sea, is St Beuno's Well.

Glynllifon, former seat of the Newboroughs, is now a campus of Coleg Meiron-Dwyfor and its extensive grounds have been opened to the public. They contain some 30 hectares of walks, follies and rare woodland plants, a fort and an unfinished mausoleum for the Newboroughs. Henry Kennedy's Victorian restoration of St Twrog's church in the estate village of **Llandwrog** was financed by Lord Newborough and contains the family monuments in the south chapel. The tall church spire has been used as a navigational aid in the Menai Strait since its erection in 1860. For the best view of Caernarfon Castle follow the coast road along the eastern edge of Foryd Bay, where St Beuno dropped his book of sermons when crossing over to Anglesey at low tide. The book was found and returned by a curlew, and, in answer to the saint's prayer, God blessed all curlews by making their nests invisible. The road eventually arrives at the mouth of the Seiont with the castle in all its glory on the opposite bank, especially so at high tide.

Caernarfon has been the administrative centre for its region throughout recorded history. The Roman fort of **Segontium** (NMGW), one of the first excavations of Mortimer Wheeler in the 1920s, is open to the public, with a museum displaying other finds from a wider area, including a Temple to Mithras. Segontium is the home of one of the founding myths of the Welsh, that of Macsen Wledig, known in Latin as Magnus Maximus. Originally from Iberia, he rose to command the Roman forces in Britain. In AD383, when the Empire was disintegrating, he assumed the title 'The Great' at Segontium and crossed with British legionaries to Gaul to defeat the Emperor Gratian, contriving to become Emperor of the West and establishing his imperial court at Trier. Returning to Caernarfon, with a symbolic portion of Roman soil, he married the daughter of a prince of Gwynedd, the beautiful Elen, after whom the Roman roads linking Caernarfon with Carmarthen and Caerleon are named. After seven years in Britain, a usurper seized Rome, and Macsen in the company of Elen's brothers set off to Rome to reconquer it. At the end of the twentieth century, Dafydd Iwan could write a successful ballad based on this tale; it registers a crucial sense of the Welsh as a civilised and Christian people on the eve of the invasion of the island of Britain by the barbarian and pagan Angles and Saxons.

Caernarfon Castle (Cadw), constructed a millennium later, is one of the tourist icons of Wales. A few years ago, the Wales Tourist Board got into hot water at home by basing their annual promotion on Wales being 'A Land of Castles', still seen as symbols of colonial oppression in some quarters. The 1969 investiture of the Prince of Wales, the formal title of the heir to the throne since the Edwardian conquest, boosted the town's tourist profile but also fuelled controversy. The castle was clearly designed to cow the local population: it is an extraordinarily impressive piece of architecture, rightly, along with the other Edwardian castles of the Welsh conquest, on the Unesco World Heritage list. World travellers will note the similarity of the castle walls to those at Constantinople, Constantine's new capital in the east. Unlike the other Edwardian castles, that have plain stone walls designed to be whitewashed, Caernarfon was designed with layers of decorative tiles, polygonal towers and, on an Eagle Tower, triple turrets suggestive of legionary standards. It is all show, however. Begun in 1283 and incorporating an earlier Norman motte, the castle was never completed. Inside there is nothing of substance, an unintended but effective architectural metaphor for a bully's bluster.

Like most of the Edwardian castles in Wales, Caernarfon was strategically situated with its own port. Slate Quay was built close to the castle in the early nineteenth century but today the harbour has fishing boats and a new marina facility has been constructed at Victoria Dock where the Maritime Museum is situated. The adjacent town has preserved large sections of its town walls containing a grid pattern of streets full of architectural interest. The splendid Market Hall in Palace Street was built in 1832 and a timber-framed house in the same street (No. 6) has been commendably restored. The classical former County Hall in Castle Ditch now houses the law courts and the new, sympathetically designed offices for Gwynedd County Council occupy the former gaol in Shirehall Street. Beyond the walls, Castle Square has Goscombe John's statue of Lloyd George and Milo Griffith's of Hugh Owen. St Mary's church, with its rare Jesse window, incorporated the town wall as its north and west wall; known as the Garrison Chapel, it was built in the fourteenth century. The original parish church at Llanbeblig is next to the Roman fort at Segontium; Peblig (Publicius) was a son of Macsen Wledig.

To the south of the town is a unique swathe of landscape, where a network of lanes and smallholdings spreads over the slopes of Mynydd Mawr to look down on its much-quarried south-eastern flank in Dyffryn Nantlle. This landscape has entered a wider Welsh consciousness through the fiction of one of the giant's of twentieth-century Welsh literature, Kate Roberts (1891–1985). The book that was her personal favourite was set here, *Te yn y Grug* (Tea in the Heather) and the cottage in which the author was born, Cae'r Gors, can be visited in **Rhosgadfan**. In an area rich in literary association, mention should also be made of John Gwilym Jones (1904–1988), dramatist and man of letters, who lived in **Groeslon** and Owen Wynne Jones (Glasynys, 1828–1870), writer of ghost stories and fairy tales, who was born in Ty'n-y-ffrwd in **Rhostryfan**.

Brutal road improvements now enable motorists to rush east to Conwy in little more than half an hour. For the more leisurely traveller, however, there is much to see along the way. **Felinheli** was developed for the export of slate from the Dinorwic quarries in Llanberis, a tramway being constructed in the 1820s between these two places. Given the English name of Port Dinorwic, slate schooners have long since been replaced here by pleasure yachts. The owner of the quarries was Thomas Assheton Smith (1752–1828) whose family had lived in style overlooking the Menai Strait at Vaynol Park since being granted the estate by William III. **Y Faenol**, to give the place its Welsh name, is set in the middle of its walled estate village. The grounds of Vaynol Hall, an Elizabethan house with a chapel from the same period, are now the venue for an annual music festival organised by local bass-baritone Bryn Terfel.

Bangor has never recovered its urban coherence since Telford pushed his post road through the park of the Bishop's Palace. But, with both a cathedral and a university, not to mention BBC studios, it is the unchallenged cultural capital of north Wales. The cathedral, in the lower town, is counted as the second oldest in Britain, after Whithorn in Galloway. St Deiniol came here from Ninian's Strathclyde, becoming Bishop of Gwynedd in AD546.

Most of the present building dates from the thirteenth century but the mood is set by the nineteenth-century restoration of Sir Gilbert Scott and his son, John Oldrid Scott. Externally, the tower seems too small for the nave, whereas, internally, the choir seems too large in comparison. The 'Mostyn Christ', a fourteenth-century wooden calvary on permanent loan from Lord Mostyn is exquisite; it may previously have hung in Llanrwst and, before that, in Maenan Abbey. Eva's tomb and Bishop Anian's Pontifical, both from the fourteenth century, are also worth seeking out, in the museum corner of the north aisle and the library respectively. Any opportunity to hear the organ should be taken. The former Bishop's Palace, a sixteenth-century house, is now used as offices for Gwynedd County Council. The adjacent Bible Garden was designed by Tatham Whitehead in 1962 to contain every herb mentioned in the Bible. Bangor Museum and Art Gallery, housed in the former Canonry, has extensive local history collections, an art gallery and gift shop.

The University College of North Wales, as it was first known, occupies an impressive site in the upper town. It was opened in 1884, thanks to financial contributions from local slate quarrymen. A new building was designed by H.T. Hare in Jacobean style and opened in 1911; it is the work of an accomplished architect at the height of his powers. The Pritchard Jones Hall, used for public concerts, contains interesting Edwardian paintings. Less sympathetic buildings (most by Percy Thomas) now crowd the site. Theatr Gwynedd is a useful but unattractive edifice whereas the Victorian pier pleasingly combines utility with joviality. Restored in 1988, it retains its original kiosks along its length.

Bangor is flanked by the estates of nineteenth-century quarry owners. To the east of the town is **Penrhyn Castle** (NT), completed by Thomas Hopper in 1847 for the second Lord Penrhyn. Financed by the combined profits of

Welsh slate and the Atlantic slave trade and containing a slate bed made for the visit of Queen Victoria, it is not a place to be approached light-heartedly. It does contain an outstanding collection of paintings by Rembrandt, Gainsborough and Canaletto and is set in extensive parkland containing a Victorian walled garden. The stable block houses a doll collection and an industrial railway museum. **Llandegái** is the estate village for Penrhyn Castle, with neat pairs of gabled mock-Tudor cottages. Its church, outside the estate walls, contains some good monuments, including one to Archbishop John Williams (1582–1650). As a child he fell from a wall; in the words of Thomas Pennant, 'the fall was on so critical a part, as ever to secure him from all reproaches of unchastity'. He became Archbishop of York in 1640 and, after the arrest of Laud, was effectively head of the Anglican church. The best monument is to Richard Pennant, the first Lord Penrhyn; the organ was originally made for the castle chapel. In the graveyard is a slate pyramid commemorating Benjamin Wyatt (1744–1818), long-serving agent to Lord Penrhyn and architect of many of the estate buildings.

Between **Llanfairfechan**, where the architect Herbert Luck North (1871–1941) developed an attractive private estate, and **Penmaenmawr**, the old road and railway squeezed between the cliffs and the sea. The new expressway characteristically tunnels through the massive extinct volcano of Penmaen Mawr, by-passing the town that shelters behind it. The remarkable Victorian church of St Seiriol, one of Alfred Waterhouse's best, was built at the instigation of William Gladstone who used to frequent the town. There is a bust of the great Liberal Prime Minister facing Brynmor Terrace. Before the construction of a coastal road in 1772, through traffic had to make its way precariously over the mountains from Conwy via the Sychnant Pass popularising the stone circle at Moelfre with the Romantics, hence the name Druid's Circle. A neolithic axe-head factory operated nearby at Graig Lwyd; a map in the museum at Bangor shows an extensive trade in Graig Lwyd axe-heads throughout southern Britain.

Conwy is the finest remaining mediaeval walled town in the country. The walls, with their twenty-one towers and three double-towered gates, enclose the Edwardian borough and castle as a single architectural conception on a constricted site with natural defences. Until 1991 the town was plagued with severe traffic congestion but coastal traffic now passes under the town through Britain's first immersed tube tunnel, a remarkable engineering feat that has restored this gem of a mediaeval town to pedestrian enjoyment. There is much to see. Work on **Conwy Castle** (Cadw), directed by Master James of St George, was begun in 1283 and was substantially completed within four years. It is long and narrow, situated on a rocky outcrop naturally moated on three sides by the confluence of the Conwy and the Gyffin. Built by the greatest military architect of the day, Conwy castle must rank as one of his outstanding achievements: it possesses an elegance and unity of form that still astonishes the first-time visitor. The inner ward has four turreted towers and is designed for maximum security to protect the sovereign should the royal court be held in Conwy; the larger outer ward, with its four round towers housed the permanent garrison. The castle has only been captured twice: daringly, for Owain Glyn Dŵr on Good Friday 1401 and for the Parliamentarians in 1646. The richly vaulted Chapel Tower contains the chapel royal with its beautiful chancel. The towers can be climbed for a wonderful overview of the walled borough that was given its charter in 1284. Thanks to the restoration work of Cadw, it is now possible to walk many sections of the walls, with views over the attractive harbour. Access to the town is by road or rail. Telford's suspension road bridge was built in 1822 and was saved from demolition by the National Trust when its clumsy modern successor was built in 1958.

Robert Stephenson brought the railway into the town in 1849 using the innovatory tubular bridge design he was to use again to cross the Menai Strait.

The town is a pleasant place to explore. St Mary's church is in the middle of the town: it was still under construction for the Cistercian monks of Aberconway Abbey when Edward I had them removed to Maenan to make way for his castle borough. Aberconway Abbey was built under the patronage of Llywelyn ab Iorwerth whose statue stands in Lancaster Square. The church has a fine fifteenth-century rood screen and several good memorials. Sir Gilbert Scott undertook restoration in 1872. Aberconway House (NT), in Castle Street, is a remarkable example of a timbered stone-built merchant's dwelling; each room has been decorated to illustrate different periods of its history. Plas Mawr (Cadw) in High Street is the finest surviving Tudor town house in Wales, superbly restored by Cadw. Built in 1576 by Robert Wynne, it looks modest from the outside and the interior surprises by its grandeur. For over a century it housed the Royal Cambrian Academy – the senior art institution in Wales, founded by English expatriate artists in 1881 – until an elegant contemporary gallery was constructed for it behind Plas Mawr in Crown Lane in 1993. Two artists were born in the same year close to the town: Hugh Hughes (1790–1863) at Pwll-y-Gwichiaid and John Gibson (1790–1866) at Gyffin.

Gloddaeth, now a private boys' school, dating back to the sixteenth century, and Bodysgallen Hall, now a hotel, dating back to the seventeenth century, were both previously owned by members of the Mostyn family, the oldest land-owning family in Wales after the Crown. Patrons of Welsh culture in the early modern period, the Gloddaeth manuscripts now form a valuable holding of the National Library. It was E.M.L. Mostyn's decision to put the eastern coastal strip up for sale in 1846 that led to the creation of **Llandudno**, now one of the best preserved Victorian resorts in the country. Coats of arms and other estate memorabilia are displayed in the foyer of the Mostyn Estate Office in Mostyn Broadway. Plans were drawn up by Williams and Jones, two Welsh architects practising in Liverpool, and the resort was constructed within a decade, taking its name from Tudno, the Celtic saint who probably had his cell at Ogof Llech on the Great Orme. It is the uniformity of architectural style, rather than the merits of individual buildings, that satisfies. The principal street, needless to say, is Mostyn Street. It contains a number of well-preserved shop-fronts with their original cast-iron verandas and the splendid Beaux Art NatWest Bank. The Mostyn Art Gallery and the Post Office in Vaughan Street are outstanding examples of the town's Edwardian architecture. Gloddaeth Street houses the fascinating Llandudno Museum, home to the Chardon collection of *objets d'art*. The east shore – with its hotels, promenade and pier – forms an elegant curve, framed by the limestone headland of the Great Orme to the west and the Little Orme to the east. The most recent addition to the sea front is the charmless 1994 North Wales Theatre, a much-needed but sadly municipal facility. The west shore has the better distant views, of Conwy and Penmaenmawr with Anglesey beyond. Marine Drive (a toll road), linking the two, provides a rewarding circumnavigation of the Great Orme.

The iron pier and its pavilion, nestled beneath the Great Orme, were completed in 1883. Visitors from Liverpool disembarked from steamers here while others waited to embark for the Isle of Man. The town attracted and inspired some famous Victorian visitors. Matthew Arnold, author of *On the Study of Celtic Literature*, stayed at Trevone in St George's Crescent. He thought of Wales, romantically, as a place where 'the past still lives' but was convinced of the 'practical inconvenience of speaking the Welsh language' and criticised the amount of Welsh used in the 1864 National Eisteddfod held in the town. The

Queen of Romania, the author and folklorist Carmen Silva, preferred the Marine Hotel. Alice Liddell, the inspiration for *Alice in Wonderland*, holidayed with her parents in Llandudno staying first at what is today the St Tudno Hotel and then in the holiday home the family had built at Penmorfa. Opposite the latter, also now a hotel, is the charming statue of The White Rabbit unveiled by Lloyd George in 1933 and now housed in a vandal-proof cage. The Rabbit Hole in Trinity Square recreates the Alice in Wonderland experience for visitors.

The Great Orme can be climbed on foot, by funicular tram, or by ski lift. It is a place of great archaeological interest: in addition to the Llety'r Filiast neolithic burial chamber, Pen-y-Dinas iron age hill fort, and the remains of a mediaeval village – the Great Orme Long Huts, with its ridge-and-furrow field system still visible – a bronze age copper mine was discovered in 1987. It is the only such mine in Europe where the public can take a guided visit into untouched bronze age galleries. The extent of these copper workings, a key resource for bronze age culture, has led archaeologists to believe that the Great Orme was in the forefront of copper production not only in prehistoric Britain but in continental Europe also. The site on which the mediaeval church of St Tudno is built goes back to the days of the Celtic saints; two coffin lids affixed to the south wall pre-date the thirteenth century. Somewhere, in a cave that has probably collapsed by now, Robert Pugh operated a secret press to print Gruffydd Robert's recusant tract, *Drych Cristianogawl*, in 1586.

The Vale of Conwy has long formed a frontier: it marks the eastern boundary of Gwynedd and that between the historic counties of Caernarfon and Denbigh. It is an important routeway through which pass both roads and the happily reprieved Conwy Valley line to Blaenau Ffestiniog; completed in 1879, the latter is a delightful way to experience the valley. Historically the valley was densely

wooded and tracts of the original mixed deciduous woodland survive on its slopes, the rich soils of the valley bottom
making fine farmland. Settlement in the valley can be
traced back to prehistoric times. Following the B5106
south from Conwy is the most leisurely way of appreciat-
ing the Arfon side of the valley. Bishop Richard Davies, the
biblical translator, was the son of the parish priest of St
Benedict's church, **Gyffin**. Its ceiling, with its painted
panels of saints and apostles, must have been freshly
painted when he was born. The impressive iron age hill fort
of Pen-y-Gaer, complete with *chevaux-de-frise* defences,
dramatically overlooks the village to the south-west. The
foundations of a dozen huts can be seen inside.

The isolated church of **Llanrhychwyn**, reached by a
winding lane, is known locally as 'Llywelyn's Old Church';
it dates from the twelfth, but is predominantly fifteenth
and sixteenth century. It has a fine oak roof, a seventeenth-
century baroque pulpit and fragments of mediaeval
stained glass. Llywelyn Fawr, it is claimed, had a new
church built for his wife Siwan at **Trefriw**, where he had a
hunting lodge, but the present church is a Victorian
restoration of a fifteenth-century structure. The village
developed as a late nineteenth-century spa, recently
revived, that offered an iron spring for bathing and a sulphur spring for drinking. It was much frequented by
Nonconformist divines. A.G. Bradley observed wryly, 'It
may seem strange that men who lead temperate, well-
nourished, well-occupied, but not laborious lives, amid the
fresh breezes of the Welsh hills, should be so fond of filling
their insides from these nauseous fountains.'

The road continues up to Llyn Crafnant where the
botanically rich crags at the head of the lake are protected
as part of the Cwm Glas Nature Reserve. Beyond the
Crafnant lie the **Carneddau**, princely walking country,
with Carnedd Llywelyn (1062m.) the highest peak followed by Carnedd Dafydd (1044m.). Crossing the dam at

the end of Llyn Cowlyd and passing more botanically rich crags at Creigiau Gleision, it is possible to climb both peaks before descending dramatically into the glaciated valley below at Llyn Ogwen. Llyn Cowlyd was the deepest natural lake in Wales before its adaptation as a reservoir. The section from Y Foel Fras to Penyrole-wen, averaging some 900 metres above sea level, is the highest ten kilometres in Wales. Heading north-west a descent can be made at Bethesda after crossing the Ysgolion Duon and then following the Afon Llafar. The Welsh topographical names here would make a fascinating study. Llywelyn and Dafydd are named after Llywelyn Fawr and his son but other features have much older and more obscure legendary associations.

Gwydir Castle was home to the Wynn family, whose high-handed landlordism earned them a miserable reputation beyond the confines of the Vale of Conwy which Sir John Wynn's classic *History of the Gwydir Family* fails to dispel. A fine house was gutted by fire in 1912 and again in 1922 but it has been faithfully restored, complete with screaming peacocks. **Gwydir Uchaf Chapel** (Cadw) was built by Sir Richard Wynn in 1673. It preserves a remarkable painted ceiling with high church iconography and Latin texts. Gwydir Uchaf, on the hillside opposite, was built in 1604 by Sir John Wynn (1553–1627); it is now a youth hostel.

Betws-y-coed grew to prominence with the opening of Telford's road. In 1844, David Cox and a group of other notable Victorian ruralists established an artists' colony here. Today it is a popular tourist centre frequently pronounced as though the village were a mixed-sex educational establishment. Betws is, in fact, an early Welsh borrowing of the Saxon for 'bede house', house of prayer. Coed (pronounced 'coid') means wood, so the name of the village might be translated as the Oratory-in-the-Woods. The woods are presently supplied as conifers planted since

1921 by the Forestry Commission, one of the largest such plantations in Wales. There are several pretty walks, to places with contrived names like The Fairy Glen. The old church of St Michael, surrounded with magnificent yews, lies beyond the railway. It contains the effigy of Gruffudd ap Dafydd Goch, great-nephew of Llywelyn Fawr, who fought under the Black Prince. The church of St Mary on the main road was built in 1873 and incorporates an imitation Irish Round Tower. The Royal Oak is the most distinguished of the string of hostelries; inside it displays its original sign, painted by David Cox. After the old church, the best feature of Betws-y-Coed is its bridges. There are seventeenth-century stone bridges over the Llugwy at Pont-y-Pair and over the Lledr at Pont-ar-Ledr. The stone bridge over the Conwy at Pont-yr-Afanc dates from 1800; the wooden Miners' Bridge over the Llugwy leads to the former lead mines. Most impressive is the Waterloo Bridge, built in 1815, as its name implies, the date and the name of its engineer, Thomas Telford, being inscribed boldly on the arch. It is a cast-iron bridge carrying the London to Dublin road across the Conwy, its spandrels decorated with roses, shamrocks, thistles and leeks in celebration of the union. A smaller pedestrian suspension bridge, built in 1930, is also attractive. The railway, from which the best views are obtained, crosses the Afon Lledr by a castellated bridge and continues through a six-kilometre tunnel under Moel Dyrnogydd to Blaenau Ffestiniog. The arrival of the Conwy Valley line from Llandudno Junction in 1868 propelled Betws-y-Coed from rustic obscurity to commercial prosperity.

About two kilometres south of Betws, a minor road crosses the Lledr at Pont-ar-Ledr. This is not the simplest – there are steep sections and numerous gates – but one of the most attractive ways to approach the birthplace of Bishop William Morgan (1545?–1604) at **Tŷ Mawr** (NT) in the Gwthernant valley. In 1588, the year of the Armada,

Bishop Morgan completed his brilliant translation of the Bible from the original Hebrew and Greek into Welsh with an impact that is inestimable. Wales was secured for Protestantism and the Welsh language given a new lease of life. Tŷ Mawr is an attractive seventeenth-century house, so this is emphatically Bishop Morgan's birthplace rather than the house in which he was born. It houses a fascinating exhibition of Welsh Bibles and a growing collection of Bibles in other languages donated by a wide circle of visitors.

A better road leads on into the Machno valley, crossing the river over the five-arched bridge at **Penmachno**. The village is famous for its five Early Christian inscribed stones, one of which has a chi-rho monogram, preserved inside the otherwise sparse interior of St Tudclud's church, a mid-Victorian replacement for an earlier structure. Tradition has it that Iorwerth 'Snubnose', the father of Llywelyn Fawr, is buried here. Bethania chapel, a remarkable example of Nonconformist classicism, is at the heart of the village. Returning to Betws, beside the Afon Machno, **Ty'n-y-coed Uchaf** (NT), is a perfectly preserved smallholding of the 1830s with a farmhouse open to the public. A riverside walk through traditionally flowering meadows is a poignant reminder of a fast disappearing heritage.

For another good walk, rich in historical associations, follow the mediaeval pack-horse track west to **Dolwyddelan** back in the Lledr valley. Alternatively, motor back over Waterloo Bridge, to the same destination. If travelling by train, this would be a good place to break the journey. Built by the Welsh in the thirteenth century to defend this land-locked pass, Dolwyddelan Castle (Cadw) is by tradition the birthplace of Llywelyn Fawr. Its capture by Edward I in 1283 was a turning point in the War of Conquest. An exhibition inside the keep, heavily restored in the nineteenth century and perched on its rocky outcrop, tells the story of the other Welsh castles of the period. The church of St Gwyddelan dates from the sixteenth century. Its south chapel was added by Robert Wynne, the builder of Plas Mawr in Conwy. The church retains its original rood screen and possesses a rare Early Christian bronze hand-bell with Celtic designs that may date back to the ninth century. There is both a brass and a heraldic wall monument to Maredudd ab Ieuan who had the church built. Tan-y-castell, the birthplace of one of the giants of the Calvistic Methodist pulpit, John Jones, Tal-y-sarn (1796–1857), and his three brothers, has an enormous commemorative plaque on its wall and a monument in its grounds paying tribute to their gifts of eloquence, music, poetry and theology. In 1821, the famous preacher delivered his first sermon at Capel-y-Garnedd in Blaenau Dolwyddelan. His great-grandson, George M.Ll. Davies, was also born in these upper reaches of the Afon Lledr. His memorial, together with those to a clutch of local poets, scholars and ministers, is on the schoolroom of Moriah (1880), another Calvinistic Methodist chapel. From Dolwyddelan, the road climbs over Bwlch Gorddinan (Crimea Pass) into Merioneth.

From Betws-y-Coed, Telford's brilliantly engineered road leads to Bangor and on to Holyhead. Three kilometres west of Betws are the **Swallow Falls**, the beauty spot from which Betws-y-coed derived its popularity. The name is a mistranslation of the Welsh, *Rhaeadr Ewynnol*, which might be translated as Foaming Torrent; *gwennol* is Welsh for 'swallow'. Passing the site of a Roman fort, Caer Llugwy, to the south of the river, the post road comes to **Capel Curig**, a centre for mountain-climbers and hill-walkers alike. Curig might be the patron saint of hill-walkers: the preferred dedications to this sixth-century Celtic saint are all in hill country. His little church, dating from the thirteenth century, is down by the river. Between Curig's time and the discovery of Snowdon by the Victorians very little had changed here. Above the church is a former inn, built in 1801 by Richard Pennant (1737?–1838) to serve the road he had built through Nant Ffrancon a generation before Thomas Telford. Formerly known as the Royal Hotel, as Plas-y-Brenin it now serves as a mountaineering centre and is run by the Sports Council. A ribbon of hotels followed in Victorian times, of which the delightfully named *Cobden's Snowdonia* may serve as an example. The best ascent of **Moel Siabod** (872m.) is from Pont Cyfyng, where the hotels start. The steep ascent passes the glacial *cwm* occupied by Llyn-y-foel, followed by a scramble up crags where ring ouzels sing and mountain flora flourish. A less strenuous path follows the ridge to the summit and descends to Pen-y-Gwryd via Cefnycerrig (415m.), the latter a good viewing-point.

Whereas Pennant's road took the south side of the Llugwy and the west side of Nant Ffrancon, Telford engineered his road on the opposite banks; thus, walkers can now use Pennant's road in tranquillity. From the south bank, at Gwern-y-Gof Uchaf, a trail leads up **Tryfan** (917m.), one of the celebrated peaks of Snowdonia, with its breath-catching step from Adam to Eve. To the south lie the **Cludeiriau**, or the Glyders as they have become known to English hill-walkers. The path between Glyder Fach (994m.) and Glyder Fawr (999m.) looks down onto the Llanberis Pass. From Twll Du (known as The Devil's Kitchen by English tourists), a path descends to **Cwm Idwal**. Charles Darwin, more a budding geologist than a biologist when he came here with Sedgwick in 1831, later described how they had failed to appreciate this classical glaciated landscape for what it was: 'the plainly scored rocks, the perched boulders, the lateral and terminal morraines . . . phenomena . . . so conspicuous that . . . a house burnt down by fire did not tell its own story more plainly than this valley'. Cwm Idwal, the first Welsh national nature reserve when it was established in 1954, is home to rare arctic flora, including the tiny white Snowdon lily, *Lloydia*, named after the Edward Lhuyd who discovered it in the late seventeenth century. The Idwal

Slabs, surrounding this glacial *cwm*, have attracted climbers since 1895. The classic U-shaped valley of Nant Ffrancon lies below it to the north and the shallow ribbon-lake of Llyn Ogwen to the east.

Passing Y Garn (946m.) and Mynydd Perfedd (812m.) to the west, Nant Ffrancon opens out at **Bethesda**, one of many Welsh places that has acquired a Hebrew name after its chapel. The Independent chapel in question is still a prominent feature; built in 1820 and enlarged in 1840, it now contains the offices of the local housing association. Siloam and Jerusalem chapels were built in the 1870s with amphitheatre-like interiors. The congregations comprised quarrymen and their families whose labours have eaten into the northern edge of the Cludeiriau in what has been described as the biggest man-made hole in the world, some 400 metres deep. The slate quarries at Bethesda were developed by Richard Pennant from the profits of slave sugar. He married the heiress of half the Penrhyn estate in 1765, purchasing the remainder in 1785. He acquired a monopoly on writing-slates just as elementary education was taking off in the British Isles. By 1865, the village had grown to a town of some six thousand people. Labour friction erupted in 1900 with a lock-out lasting three years, memorably described in T. Rowland Hughes' novel, *Y Chwalfa*. The result was social catastrophe, the result of the callous obstinacy of a single plutocrat: the 2nd Baron Penrhyn (1836–1907), a title the family had acquired in 1866. Caradog Pritchard (1904–1980), author of the twentieth-century Welsh classic *Un Nos Ola Lleuad*, was born in the town. Unlike many more wistful autobiographical novels of childhood set in rural Wales, his account evokes a repressed society laden with endemic madness, perversity and violence.

From Capel Curig to Caernarfon, the main road skirts to the south of the Cludeiriau to **Pen-y-Gwryd**, a hostelry situated in the grounds of a Roman encampment where members of the 1953 Everest expedition left their initials carved on the ceiling. It then climbs steeply past **Pen-y-Pass** youth hostel, before descending into the Llanberis Pass. At the head of the valley, the pass is strewn with boulders, one of them reprieved from a road-widening scheme after vigorous protest. The northern side of the valley has attracted rock climbers since the mid-nineteenth century; they can often be seen negotiating the rock faces from their precarious footholds. At the head of Llyn Peris sits **Nant Peris**, the old village of Llanberis, with its old church of St Peris, severely restored by Henry Kennedy in 1848. Ffynnon Beris lies to the east: once a single lake, it was separated by the outwash from Afon Goch and Afon Arddu. The lakes are deep and contain char as well as trout. At the foot of the lake is **Dolbadarn Castle** (Cadw), another Welsh castle, this one probably also built by Llywelyn Fawr. Partially dismantled after the English conquest, the 10-metre high keep remains a dominant feature. To the west is the spectacular waterfall of Ceunant Mawr.

Llanberis owes its existence to the slate industry and, latterly, to the Snowdon tourist trade. The spacious late Victorian church of St Padarn was built for the latter, the numerous chapels in Llanberis and its surrounding villages for the former. Dinorwic Quarry was opened in 1809 by Thomas Assheton Smith. The railway to Port Dinorwic ceased commercial use in 1969 but a section beside the lake was revived in 1972 as one of the 'Great Little Trains' of Wales, affording dramatic views of Snowdon. Dinorwic means 'fort of the Ordovices', the name the Romans gave to the British inhabitants of north-west Wales; ironically, it is precisely because the older Cambrian rocks here lie above the more recent Ordovician rocks that the hillsides were suitable for slate-quarrying. Dinas Dinorwic at **Llanddeiniolen** is a late iron age hill fort with a rare Welsh example of glacis construction. The poet, scholar and critic W.J. Gruffydd (1881–1954) was brought up in the village and lies buried in the churchyard. From Llyn Peris, 100 metres above sea level, a series of 20-metre terraces extends up the mountain to a height of 700 metres, forming the world's largest slate quarry. In its heyday it employed 3,000 men and produced tens of thousands of roofing slates annually. Its story is told in the excellent **Welsh Slate Museum** (NMGW), which has occupied the former quarry workshops since their closure in 1969. Its Pelton Wheel was the largest waterwheel in Wales to power machinery.

In 1973, a controversial project to construct the **Dinorwic Pumped Storage Power Station** was given the go-ahead. Water from Marchlyn Mawr races through hydraulic tunnels to power underground turbines, installed in the largest man-made cavern in Europe deep within the mountain, before flowing out into Llyn Peris, the banks of which were raised by over three metres. Using off-peak electricity rates, the water is then pumped back up to Marchlyn Mawr. The water level of the lake rises and falls by some four metres when the plant is operating at maximum capacity supplying the national grid. Work at the lake brought to light the sixteenth-century clinker Peris Boat and a twelfth-century dugout canoe now on display at the visitor centre from which underground tours are available in the summer months.

The most famous of the 'Great Little Trains' of Wales is probably the **Snowdon Mountain Railway**, a rack railway constructed for Victorian tourists in 1896, in the teeth of local opposition to the desecration of mountain solitude. Thousands of visitors are transported daily to the summit each season and it can be disconcerting for hill-walkers to arrive at the summit and see children in pushchairs admiring the view over an ice-cream. The summit café is notoriously hideous. Thanks to the efforts of Anthony Hopkins, the National Trust aquired the mountain as part of the Hafod-y-Llan Estate in 1998 and there are now plans for more sympathetic development.

Snowdon transcends these considerations. Rising to 1085 metres, it is the highest mountain in the British Isles outside Scotland and one of the finest for the hill-walker. There are a number of well-established paths to the summit. The Llanberis Path, the easiest gradient but least interesting walk, follows the railway track. The Pyg Track (an unfortunate acronym from the original starting point, Pen-y-Gwryd) and the Miners' Track, utilising the former track to the copper mines, reach the summit by-passing over the southern slopes of Crib Goch and start, conveniently, in the generous car park of Pen-y-Pass. The Watkin Path is named after the railway tycoon Edward Watkin who had a summer home near its start in Nant Gwynant. A plaque at Gladstone Rock commemorates the opening of this path by the Liberal Prime Minster in 1892. The Rhyd-ddu Path departs from the village of that name and the Snowdon Ranger Path, probably the oldest path to the summit, from the youth hostel beside Llyn Cwellyn that was formerly the home of an early mountain guide. For experienced hill-walkers, the classic ascent of Snowdon is the Horseshoe Path, a circular route from Pen-y-Pass that involves negotiating the narrow ridge of Crib Goch. Llyn Llydaw and Llyn Ffynnon Las lie below to the south with Cwm Glas, a repository of rare Snowdonian flora, to the north. Any mountain walk should be undertaken with forethought, preparation and respect; the Horseshoe Path emphatically so.

From Pen-y-Gwryd, Snowdon can be circumnavigated by road by following **Nant Gwynant** to Beddgelert and then taking the Caernarfon road. This route offers wonderful views of Crib Goch and Yr Wyddfa. From Bethania, between the two beautiful lakes of Llyn Gwynant and Llyn Dinas, a back road leads over Blaen Nanmor into the Nanmor valley with compelling views of Cnicht. It leads down to the village of **Nanmor** that gave its name to one of the finest poets of mediaeval Wales, Dafydd Nanmor (fl.1450–1480) who lived somewhere near the present Cae Dafydd. He was banished from the district for writing verses to a married woman, Gwen o'r Ddol, who lived at Dolfriog. His pupil, Rhys Nanmor (fl.1485–1513), another distinguished poet, lived at Hafod Garegog, at the bottom of the valley, although only part of the original house now remains.

Llyn Dinas takes its name from **Dinas Emrys**, the legendary fortress that overlooks it. Difficulty of access and the vulnerability of the remains mean that all visitors should first contact the warden at the National Trust shop in Beddgelert. From there, an attractive path leads to the early mediaeval fort that archaeologists confirm as variously inhabited between the fifth and twelfth centuries. The site is associated with Gwrtheyrn (Vortigern), despised in Welsh legend for having invited the Saxon Hengist into these islands as a mercenary and having failed to get rid of him. As recounted in *Y Mabinogi*, Gwrtheyrn fled west to establish this fortress. Several versions of a tale, prophesying struggle between the white Saxon dragon and the red dragon of Wales to culminate in the triumph of the latter after many trials and tribulations, are located at Llyn Dinas and Dinas Emrys. The fort takes its name from a youth, Emrys (Ambrosius, in English) who interpreted the prophecies for Gwrtheyrn. To the surprise of sceptical archaeologists, excavations have confirmed the chronology of stories recounted by such notoriously unreliable chroniclers as Nennius, Gerald of Wales, and Geoffrey of Monmouth. Plas Gwynant, a fine property between the lakes, was, as it happens, the home of the great mediaevalist J.A. Froude, whose name is a by-word for reliability. The ruins of a chapel of ease associated with Madoc, the mythical Welsh discoverer of America, lie beyond Llyn Gwynant to the west.

From Beddgelert the main road cuts northward through Nant Colwyn to **Rhyd-ddu**, with Snowdon to the north-east and Moel Hebog to the south-west. A starting point for one of the Snowdon paths, Rhyd-ddu was the home of T.H. Parry-Williams (1887–1975), a towering presence in twentieth-century Welsh culture as poet, essayist and scholar. To read just one of his poems, *Hon*, would be a perfect point of entry for an understanding of the contemporary Welsh predicament.

> *Beth yw'r ots gennyf i am Gymru? Damwain a hap*
> *Yw fy mod yn ei libart yn byw. Nid yw hon ar fap*
> *Yn ddim byd ond cilcyn o ddaear mewn cilfach gefn,*
> *Ac yn dipyn o boendod i'r rhai sy'n credu mewn trefn.*

> What do I care for Wales? It's a mere accident
> That I happen to live within its boundaries. On a map
> It's just a bit of land in the back of beyond
> And something of a nuisance to those who believe in
> order.

The road continues past the Snowdon Ranger hostel on the banks of Llyn Cwellyn to Caernarfon via **Waunfawr**. This village has two famous sons. Dafydd Ddu Eryri (David Thomas, 1759–1822), poet and bardic teacher, was born at Pen-y-bont, and John Evans (1770–1799), the young Calvinistic Methodist minister who went to America in search of Welsh-speaking Indians, the supposed descendants of Madoc, was born in Gwredog Ucha. He never found them and died disillusioned in New Orleans but Thomas Jefferson subsequently passed his maps of the upper Missouri to Lewis and Clark, enabling them to win the west for the United States. Antur Waunfawr has a John Evans room open to the public.

To the west of Rhyd-ddu lies **Dyffryn Nantlle**, opened up for slate quarrying at the end of the eighteenth century and now evocative in its industrial decay. Here, the slate outcropped in the valley bottom and was quarried in deep pits that have now filled with water. The largest, the Dorothea, astonishing in its immensity, can be reached through **Tal-y-sarn**, a place also associated with the celebrated nineteenth-century Calvinistic Methodist preacher, John Jones. He first worked on Telford's road through Nant Ffrancon, then as a quarryman, becoming general manager of the Dorothea, before devoting himself full-time to preaching and composing hymns. **Penygroes** is a substantial former quarrying village that grew out of the older settlement of Llanllyfni as the slate industry developed. It has typical rows of terraced housing and, surprisingly, a new chapel, Capel y Groes, completed in 2003 on the site of a nineteenth-century Calvinistic Methodist chapel, Saron, demolished the previous year. In the west, Mynydd y Bwlch Mawr guards the approach to Llŷn. Returning eastward in the direction of Rhyd-ddu, **Drws-y-coed** is associated with the Griffith family. In the eighteenth century, they invited the Moravian missionary David Mathias into this part of north Wales, and in the twentieth century they provided Ireland with the patriot Arthur Griffith (1872–1922) who founded Sinn Féin in 1905. From a vantage-point, between Craig-y-Bera and Y Garn, there is a remarkable view of Snowdon, captured on canvas by Richard Wilson: but like Tryweryn's water, the painting is in Liverpool – at the Walker Art Gallery.

13

Anglesey

ANGLESEY PROUDLY PERSISTS with its claim to be Britain's largest island despite the 2003 European Community ruling that it is now too integrated with the mainland by its two bridges to qualify for the financial benefits of insular status. This reflects contemporary, but not historical reality. Less than a century ago, ferries plied their way over the frequently treacherous waters of the 25-kilometre Menai Strait to reach the island. According to Nelson: "If you can sail the Menai Straits, you can sail anywhere in the world." The island's English name is deceptive; it has nothing to do with the Anglo-Saxons. Rather, the name derives from Viking times: Ongull's Isle. In the ninth century, the Irish Sea was a Viking lake and the coast of Wales is strewn with Viking place-names. The Vikings had many different words for different types of island: 'sey' as in Ramsey, Bardsey, Swansea, and Anglesey, where there is good flat meadowland; 'holm', for smaller islands with more rugged terrain, as in Skokholm or Grassholm; or 'skerries', a string of tiny islands close to shore. In prehistoric times, Anglesey was a druidic fastness. According to the well-known description by Tacitus, the Romans under the command of Suetonius met stiff resistance when trying to prize the island, with its rich copper deposits, from British control in AD61. To the Welsh, Anglesey was the 'Mother of Wales', *Môn Mam Cymru*, a designation that goes back to the days when the island's wheat fed the people and princes of Gwynedd.

The first bridge over the Menai Strait was Telford's elegant iron suspension bridge, the world's first, built between 1818 and 1826. It was a marvel of construction that secured its designer a place in the pantheon of civil engineers. His friend Robert Southey penned some verse in Telford's honour on the occasion of the opening of his Caledonian Canal in 1822:

> Telford who o'er the vale of Cambrian Dee
> Aloft in air at giddy height upborne
> Carried his navigable road; and heavy hung
> High o'er Menai's Strait the bending bridge
> Structures of more ambitious enterprise
> Than minstrels in the age of old Romance
> To their own Merlin's magic lore ascribed.

The original wrought iron was replaced by steel in 1938. The bridge was built some 30 metres above the sea to enable sailing ships to pass beneath. The same was true for Robert Stephenson's tubular **Britannia Bridge**, which carried the railway across the strait in 1850. That bridge was severely damaged by fire in 1970; its subsequent repair incorporated a new road bridge built above the railway track. The original pairs of lions, by John Thomas, continue to guard the railway bridge: 'four fat lions without any hair, two over here and two over there'. An obelisk commemorates those who died in the execution of the original project. All three passages over the strait serve the same primary purpose: to facilitate the movement of people and goods between England and Ireland. Neither Telford's nor Stephenson's great engineering projects were devised to meet Welsh needs: their primary objective was strategic, to secure London's control over Dublin.

It is entirely appropriate, therefore, that a pair of military monuments should greet us after the crossing celebrating those victories over the French during the Napoleonic Wars that precipitated the Act of Union with Ireland. The commemorative column to the achievements of the Marquess of Anglesey, Wellington's second-in-command at Waterloo, can be climbed for a splendid panorama of the island. The tower was built in 1816, and the statue added in 1860.

The view from the top provides a perfect introduction to the geography of the island: there are no mountains, rather, a series of low hills of varying geology, lakes, marshes and dunes make for a landscape rich in variety and interest. A short walk down to the strait leads past Nelson's Column, designed and executed in 1873 by Admiral Paget, son of the first Marquess. The Angleseys had their seat three kilometres to the south-west at the magnificently situated **Plas Newydd**, rebuilt in the neo-Gothic style by James Wyatt in the first decade of the nineteenth century. The dining room has celebrated wall paintings by Rex Whistler from the 1930s and in the grounds are two of the neolithic burial chambers that exist in profusion on the island. There is a fine spring garden and Australasian arboretum, at their best in early summer and massed hydrangeas and autumn tints later in the year. 'Do you know the Angleseys?' the young Goronwy Rees was surprised to be asked when he arrived as a student in Oxford. 'I thought there was only one', he replied.

Just beyond the column to the Marquess, on Telford's road, is the village of Llanfairpwll. When the railway opened a station here its name was extended – by a local tailor with an eye on the tourist trade – and joined to that of the neighbouring village of Llantisiliogogogoch. The result was to secure for **Llanfairpwllgwyngyllgogery-chwyrndrobwllllantysiliogogogoch**, an enduring entry in the Guinness Book of Records. The station has probably earned more revenue from the sale of platform than travel tickets and a tourist honey-pot has been augmented with multiple 'craft' shops, each of which stocks the inevitable postcard. The village has other claims to fame, however. The distinguished Welsh scholar Sir John Morris-Jones (1864–1929) spent most of his life in Tŷ Coch and is buried in the churchyard here with a Celtic-revival cross as his memorial. Ironically, a major anglicising influence on Welsh communities, the Women's Institute, established its first branch here in 1915. As a counterbalance, an alternative women's organisation, conducting its business in Welsh, was founded in 1967, the optimistically named *Merched y Wawr*, Daughters of the Dawn.

Beaumaris, as the name suggests, is Anglo-Norman. The site was a *beau marais*, a fine salt marsh where, in 1295, Edward I commissioned Master James of St George to build the last of his splendid castles to intimidate the Welsh. Until Telford's and Stephenson's time Beaumaris was the largest town on the island. The castle (Cadw) is one of the most perfectly planned concentric castles in Europe. It never saw military action and its towers stand intact, reflected in a moat that also incorporates a private dock and mill. Writing from Conwy to his paymasters in London in 1296, Master James of St George observes: 'As to how things are in the land of Wales, we cannot be any too sure. But as you well know, Welshmen are Welshmen and you need to understand them properly; if, which God forbid, there is war with France and Scotland, we shall need to watch them all the more closely.' Together with Caernarfon, Beaumaris was designed to control the Menai Strait and prevent the export of grain to Gwynedd in any such eventuality. There are excellent buildings: many of the Anglesey gentry had town houses here. A seventeenth-century Court House with a hammer-beam roof opposite the castle reminds us of the town's former legislative functions as does the Gaol on Skinner Street, imaginatively restored by the Gwynedd Archive Service and containing a working treadmill. Beaumaris Courthouse, also recently restored, was built in 1614 and there is a Museum of Childhood Memories in Castle Street, based on the personal collection of Robert Brown. The fourteenth-century parish church contains its original misericords and two items of historic interest brought here from Llan-faes Friary, the alabaster altar tomb of William Bulkeley and the sarcophagus that once contained the body of Siwan, wife of Llywelyn Fawr and daughter of King John.

The Bulkeleys, Anglesey's leading gentry family lived at Baron Hill above the town, now an evocative ruin. The family is commemorated in the Bulkeley Memorial, a tall obelisk a kilometre to the north-west of the town in the direction of **Llanddona**, a village with some pretty white-washed cottages. The extensive woodland covering Mynydd Llwydiarth to the west supports a rare population of red squirrels. The parish church has a fifteenth-century deco-rated doorway reset in the south wall of the nave. St Catherine's church at **Llan-faes** is another nineteenth-century restoration. It contains a fine memorial to Sir Robert Williams of Fryars (1764–1830) and, outside, a mediaeval sandstone cross with a carved figure and Latin inscription and a prominent memorial to the Revd. John Williams, Brynsiencyn, who is buried in the graveyard. Scarcely a trace remains above ground of the former Franciscan Friary that once flourished here.

On the tip of the peninsula stands a remarkable group of mediaeval buildings, **Penmon Priory** (Cadw). The church is atmospheric inside and out. Its central tower with pyra-midical roof is perfectly proportioned. Inside, there are two mediaeval crosses: the fine eleventh-century Penmon Cross, showing the temptation of St Anthony, that has been placed in the chancel to protect it from the elements and an earlier cross, set amidst the interlaced arcading of the south transept. The Prior's House, still inhabited, adjoins this transept with the ruins of the thirteenth-century refectory close by. Across the lane, the early seventeenth-century dovecote, with its extraordinary honeycomb interior, was built by a member of the Bulkeley family. Penmon is associ-ated with St Seiriol, brother of the founder, St Cynlas. St Seiriol's Well, with what may be the foundations of his cell beside, and another Celtic cross a short distance to the west, complete the site. **Ynys Seiriol** (alternatively Priestholm or Puffin Island) lies just off the coast, the ruins of its twelfth-century church marking a Christian presence that dates back to the age of the Celtic saints. It is claimed that the sixth-century king, Maelgwn Gwynedd, great-grandson of Cunedda, is buried on the island. There are boat trips to the island from Beaumaris. Is that the clang of the bell-buoy out by Perch Rock, or a Celtic saint calling us to prayer?

The parish of **Penrhosllugwy** is the ancestral square mile of the four Morris Brothers – Lewis, Richard, William and John – who were brought up at Pentre Eirianell. Lewis Morris (1701–1765) was one of the most accomplished Welshmen of his day. He combined a working life as a surveyor and engineer with a deep interest in the literature and antiquities of his country and engaged in extensive correspondence on these subjects. Irascible by nature, he collected enemies in addition to manuscripts. Fortunately, many of his letters survive and are a treasured resource for students of Welsh history and letters. Richard Morris (1703–1779) founded the Cymmrodorion Society in 1751; William Morris (1705–1763) was the Customs Officer for the port of Holyhead; John Morris (1706–1740) shared his brothers' literary interests whilst following a naval career. Together, they are commemorated by a massive granite Celtic-revival cross, erected by the Cymmrodorion in 1910 on a prominent mound beside the main road just north of **Brynefail**.

Goronwy Owen (1723–1769, Goronwy Ddu o Fôn) was born at Brynteg in **Llanfair Mathafarn Eithaf**. He was a scholarly poet, more the former than the latter according to his contemporary, Edward Richard, Ystrad Meurig: '*Mwy o ddysg nag o athrylith*' (More pedant than poet), was his judgement. Together with the Morris Brothers, they constituted the core of an influential eighteenth-century School of Welsh Augustans. Although Owen had served briefly as a curate in the parish church here, he was to die in exile in America. His contribution to Welsh literature and scholarship has been honoured by a later generation of Welsh exiles who contributed to the memorial pulpit in the church, dedicated on the bicentenary of his death. The family of William 'Accomplished' Jones (1746–1794) also had its roots in this area. His father, William Jones the mathematician, was from Y Merddyn, the cottage next to Fferem, where Richard and William Morris were born. The son entered into the service of the East India Company and became an accomplished linguist. It was he who first realised that the Indo-European languages were related and shared a common ancestor in Sanskrit. He was once introduced to the king of France as a man who could speak all the world's languages but his own, for the circumstances of his life deprived him of the opportunity to speak the language of heaven.

Traeth Bychan was the scene of the 1939 *Thetis* disaster, when a pre-war submarine trial went badly wrong, causing the captain to beach his vessel with significant loss of life. The Anglesey coast is infamous for wrecks: off **Moelfre**, the *Royal Charter* ran aground in 1859 on its way home from Australia, an incident described by Dickens in the opening pages of his *Uncommercial Traveller*. Not surprisingly, Moelfre has a famous lifeboat station that has seen distinguished service. It can be visited at the imaginative Seawatch Centre in the village. Overlooking Moelfre is a remarkable prehistoric survival. **Din Lligwy** (Cadw) is an iron age hill fort that has used local limestone for its ramparts; these, together with hut circles also made of limestone, make this an exceptional survival. Archaeologists have found the remains of an iron-smelters workshop in the north-east corner of the site. The remains of a mediaeval chapel (Cadw), complete with crypt and a nearby neolithic burial chamber (Cadw) with a massive capstone are added attractions. Six kilometres inland to the west, **Mynydd Bodafon** (178m.) has bronze age hut circles, here known in Welsh – as is often the case – as Irishmen's Huts, *Cytiau'r Gwyddelod*. With its lake, quartzite rocks and heather, this is an attractive picnic spot.

In the nineteenth century messages were semaphored from **Mynydd Eilian** (177m.) to confirm that ships had rounded Holyhead for their Liverpool owners. Such messages took under ten minutes to transfer to Liverpool. A plaque on the wall of a cottage at Craig-y-Gwynt, one of the semaphore stations a kilometre north-west of Llanrhyddlad, commemorates this telegraph service. Below Mynydd Eilian on the coast road is **Llaneilian**, one of the most interesting churches on the island, with wonderfully surviving fittings from the fifteenth century, including both rood screen and loft. St Eilian's Sanctuary was rebuilt in the fourteenth century and is linked to the chancel by a passage. The painting of the saint at the west end of the church may be the origin of the belief that the saint had five fingers and a thumb. The saint's holy well was much frequented and the sturdy Cyff Eilian (Eilian's Chest) preserved in the church secured the revenue it generated.

Mynydd Parys was Europe's largest copper mine within a quarter of a century of the first vein being discovered in 1768 – or, rather, rediscovered: for the copper deposits of Mynydd Parys were known to the Romans. Exhausted within a generation, Copper Mountain lies derelict; its summit hollowed out into a vast crater. There are eerily beautiful industrial heritage trails on the mountain where some of the rock face has oxidized to add a bluish sheen to an otherwise bronze and pink moonscape. In the eighteenth century, the copper ore was exported to Neath for smelting from the port of **Amlwch**, which at that time accommodated up to thirty vessels at a time. Today this excellent natural harbour shelters Liverpool tugboats and pleasure craft. A plan by the Shell Oil Co in 1973 to develop the harbour for the use of oil tankers was mercifully abandoned. The graveyard of the parish church of St Eleth, the latter belatedly built by the mining company for its workers in 1800, contains the graves of captains, surgeons, smelters and coal merchants.

Seen from the north, the skyline of **Llangefni** is dominated by disused windmills. In his charming volume of autobiography, *Across the Straits*, Kyffin Williams, the landscape and portait painter who was born here, described his native county as 'a land of ochres and umbers'. The town took over the functions of county town from Beaumaris following the 1888 County Councils Act, functions it has recovered after the interlude of 1974–1996 during which time Anglesey was incorporated into Gwynedd. Two stars of the nineteenth-century Welsh Nonconformist firmament are associated with the town: John Elias and Christmas Evans. John Elias (1774–1841), an uncompromising High Calvinist, lived at Y Fron and has a splendid memorial chapel, Moreia, opened in 1898. Known as the Anglesey Pope, such was his influence that it was said that, at the time of his death in 1841, had a roof been put over the island it would have constituted the greatest Calvinistic Methodist chapel in Wales. His Baptist contemporary, the powerful preacher – or, as he preferred to say, 'fisher of men' – Christmas Evans (1776–1838) lived at Tŷ Capel, Cildwrn, on the outskirts of the town, ministering to the entire island for some 35 years. Capel Penuel was built in the heart of the town in 1897 as a memorial to the island's 'Baptist Bishop'. Llangefni was once a port, with the Cefni navigable from Malltraeth Bay, and benefited from its situation on the old road to Holyhead. Time has deprived it of both of these commercial advantages: a land reclamation scheme closed off access to the sea in 1818 and Telford's new road by-passed the town a few years later. **Malltraeth Marsh**, once a tidal estuary, is home to wind-blown reeds and meadowsweet.

Four kilometres east of Llangefni is **Penmynydd**, where a substantial farmhouse, the ancestral home of the Tudor dynasty, enjoys spectacular views to the south of the island with the mountains of Snowdonia as a backdrop. In the lonely church of St Gredifael is the impressive alabaster tomb of Henry VII's ancestors, Gronw Fychan ap Tudur ap Gronw and his wife. Over the years respectful pilgrims have broken off pieces of the alabaster convinced that if ground into a paste they would make a healing balm. Geologists will want to seek out the grave of A.C. Ramsay, appropriately consisting of a glacial erratic. To the south-west, **Llangristiolus** has a simple mediaeval church, overlooking Malltraeth Marsh, with a thirteenth-century chancel arch and a twelfth-century font. The grounds of Henblas have the best display of snowdrops that I know of anywhere in the country.

The coast between Amlwch and Holyhead is rugged, exposed and unspoiled, with large portions of its magnificent cliffs under the protection of the National Trust. **Dinas Gynfor** is an iron age promontory hill fort frequented by choughs. Offshore, **Ynys Patrig** (Middle Mouse), the most northerly fragment of Wales, has associations with St Patrick, who scholars insist was as British as St David was Irish. The island has a cave named after him containing a freshwater well. Local lore has the saint sailing from **Llanbadrig** on his mission to convert the Irish. The mediaeval church, one of only three dedications to St Patrick in Wales, was restored in the nineteenth century by Bertrand Russell's uncle, Lord Stanley of Alderley, a Muslim convert. The blue tiles in the sanctuary are of Islamic design and a pre-Christian standing stone, set against the west wall, has been decorated in the seventh or eighth century with carvings of a crossed fish and a palm tree similar to those found in churches in the eastern Mediterranean. **Cemaes** is the most northerly village in Wales. The late Bill Condry aptly described Cemaes Bay as 'Beauty and the Beast'. Beauty for the eastern shore in the care of the National Trust, with the view west as the Beast, the glowering hulk of the nuclear power station at **Yr Wylfa**, which has dominated the scene since 1971. Pylons carry power lines to the aluminium smelting works at Holyhead. Both of these employment-generating projects were supported by the local MP, Cledwyn Hughes

(1917–2001), a doughty promoter of Welsh interests within the Labour Party.

Moving quickly inland, there are several small churches well worth investigating. The curious conical tower on St Mechell's church at **Llanfechell** was supposedly placed on top of the bell-tower as a noise suppressant at the insistence of William Bulkeley (1691–1760), the diarist and squire of Brynddu who claimed that the noise of the bells soured his beer. The churchyard has an interesting collection of inscriptions. From it, it is possible to see three standing stones on the crest of the hill to the north. Five kilometres to the west, in splendid isolation beyond the main road, is the diminutive twelfth-century church at **Llanrhwydrys**. Reached by a causeway over the marsh, it has a curious doorway leading to a minstrels' gallery. Further south, three curious mediaeval faces greet you over the door at St Pabo's church in **Llanbabo**. Inside this simple church, there is a fine fourteenth-century memorial to Pabo, thought to be a north Briton who sought refuge on the island. Its ancient circular churchyard is one of the most attractive on the island. **Llantrisant**, to the south, was saved from ruination by the Friends of Friendless Churches in 1972. **Llanfigael**, four kilometres due west, has its complete set of early nineteenth-century fittings. Members of the congregation knew their place: there are box pews for the well-to-do, backless benches for their social inferiors and standing room for paupers.

Lakes and swamps are characteristic features of the Anglesey landscape. **Llyn Alaw**, a natural lake that has been extended to act as a reservoir, figures prominently in *Y Mabinogi*, for it was here that Branwen was laid to rest after she died of a broken heart. A bronze age tumulus on the banks of the Alaw, a couple of kilometres to the southwest of the lake, has been named Bedd Branwen (Branwen's Grave) from this tale. Three kilometres to the south-west lies **Llyn Llywenan**, a natural lake with numerous wildfowl darting amongst the reeds; the two Presaddfed Burial Chambers (Cadw) lie close to its southern shore and the impressive Tregwehelydd Standing Stone (Cadw) to the north. **Llyn Garreg-lwyd**, north of Llanfaethlu, is a reed swamp rather than a lake, but also rich in wildfowl. In 1978 the county council admirably restored an eighteenth-century windmill, Melin Llynnon, near **Llanddeusant**; its sails now turn again to produce stone-ground flour for sale to visitors. The high price of grain during the Napoleonic Wars encouraged investment in a series of new windmills of which this is a splendid example. It is wonderful to see, and hear, when in operation. It is the only working example left of an island tradition, although Melin Howell, a watermill on the Afon Alaw, has been similarly restored.

Holyhead, although pronounced 'holly', is indeed linked to the Age of the Saints. The Welsh name of the town, Caergybi (Cybi's Fort), provides us with both the identity of the saint and the location of his sanctuary. In AD555 Cybi built his monastic cell inside the remains of the Roman fortlet (Cadw) and a church bearing his name has occupied the site ever since. Sir Gilbert Scott restored the present fourteenth-century structure during 1877–9; it has stained glass by William Morris and Burne-Jones. The Stanley tomb is by Hamo Thorneycroft. The *raison d'être* of Holyhead today is the ferry service to Ireland, the busiest of the Welsh-Irish ferry links because the shortest. For centuries, Irish surnames have been familiar in the town and St Patrick's Day celebrated with as much enthusiasm as *Gŵyl Ddewi*. Telford's road consolidated the port's primacy when it was completed in 1823; the crossing to Holy Island was achieved by constructing an embankment, named after the man who helped finance it, Lord Stanley of Alderley, who had married the local heiress of Penrhos. The Stanley Embankment replaced the earlier crossing at Four Mile Bridge and the railway subsequently made use of it. The railway station, built in 1845, has looked pleased with itself ever since. A fine cast-iron clock commemorates the extension of the harbour in 1881, when Britain's longest breakwater was constructed; the earlier Admiralty Pier had been constructed by John Rennie in 1821. The old harbour has an elegant but understated Customs House and Harbour Office. The busy new container terminal reflects the power of the Celtic Tiger economy since Ireland acceded to the Treaty of Rome in 1973. Holyhead Maritime Museum, located at the old lifeboat house on Newry Beach, tells the whole story with displays of model ships and nautical photographs.

Holyhead Mountain on the northern tip of the island has spectacular cliffs and breath-taking views. The cliffs are home to Atlantic seabird colonies: puffins, guillemots, razorbills and fulmars. On the proverbial clear day, a climb to this, the highest point on Anglesey (220m.), will be rewarded with an extensive view over the island with the mountains of Snowdonia as a distant backdrop and, occasionally, the Wicklow Mountains in Ireland far out to the west. The folds in the rocks at South Stack, on which another lighthouse was built in 1809, provide insight into the geological history of the island and ideal nesting sites for seabirds. That Holy Island was a favoured place of settlement for prehistoric man is quickly evident from the remains of a neolithic burial chamber at Trefignath (Cadw), bronze age hut circles (Cadw) and an iron age promontory hillfort at Caer y Tŵr (Cadw). There are standing stones at Penrhos Feilw (Cadw) and Tŷ Mawr where excavations in 1987 demonstrated continuity of settlement from the mesolithic through to the iron age.

To many in Wales, it seemed an act of desecration to build a military air base overlooking Holy Island. That was in 1943, when wartime emergency powers could be invoked, and the base has enabled the rural communities of Wales to be tormented by the regular scream of low-flying jets ever since. In so far as anything good can be said to have come from this project, we might point to the richest iron age discovery ever made in Wales, the Llyn Cerrig

Bach hoard, discovered when the RAF was filling in a delightful little lake to construct their principal runway. The hoard, consisting of a collection of over one hundred items – swords, spears, shields, scabbards, currency bars, chariot wheels and slave-chains – is on display in the National Museum in Cardiff. The air base was built at **Llanfair-yn-Neubwll**, a name the RAF did not have patience for: their name for the base is Valley. For a holiday combining beach-lolling with plane-spotting, one of the caravan parks at the resort town of **Rhosneigr**, at the southern end of the airfield, would be a perfect choice.

We can escape the present by visiting the neolithic decorated passage grave of **Barclodiad-y-Gawres** (Cadw), situated on the headland south of Rhosneigr. The name means the 'Apronful of the Giantess', implying a legendary origin. The distinguished Welsh archaeologist Glyn Daniel demonstrated that this chambered tomb is related to those of the Boyne valley in Ireland. They share spiral artwork and are all so aligned as to allow sunlight to enter the passage grave at the time of the winter solstice. **Aberffraw** reminds us of nobler times, for here the Princes of Gwynedd had their seat of government. But it is a very feint memory: no architectural features of the royal court survive in this sleepy dune-enclosed village. St Beuno's church, originally twelfth century, has intriguing carvings on its doorway. **Llangadwaladr** church contains the most important gravestone in Anglesey, commemorating St Cadfan, 'wisest and most illustrious of all rulers', who died in the first quarter of the seventh century. The church has a twelfth-century nave, a fourteenth-century chancel and its original stained glass in the east window, depicting the crucifixion. In the winter it is lit with brass chandeliers. It would have been a logical place for princely worship. Cadwaladr, to whom the church is dedicated, was Cadfan's grandson. A kilometre up the coast is the island church of **Llangwyfan**. Mostly fourteenth century, it is only accessible at low tide. It clearly occupies an ancient site and it is good to see that occasional services are still held. Four kilometres north of Aberffraw, beside Llyn Padrig, is the mediaeval chapel of **St Mary Tal-y-llyn**. Rescued from dereliction in 1969, this twelfth-century structure contains its original eighteenth-century plank pews.

Edward I established **Newborough**, after the completion of Beaumaris, by resettling the Welsh here from Llan-faes. Their land was donated to the new burghers of Beaumaris and rivalry between the two communities persists to this day. Newborough was a chartered market town that came to specialise in matting, cord and nets made from the marram grass on the nearby dunes. St Peter's church is fourteenth-century in origin with carved grave slabs in the chancel. The nearby archaeological site of **Llys Rhosyr** is uncovering a pre-conquest royal court of the Welsh princes; an audio-visual show at the Prichard Jones Institute in the village provides background information. A long, straight road leads through Newborough Forest, a post-Second World War development by the Forestry Commission associated with dune control. It opens out to an immense expanse of sand before continuing on to **Ynys Llanddwyn**, the island sanctuary of Santes Dwynwen, a daughter of Brychan, who came here in the fifth century. She is the Welsh patron saint of lovers who have made her holy well a place of pilgrimage. Her feast-day has been revived and is celebrated throughout Wales on 25 January. The ruins of a later church still stand, along with a Celtic cross commemorating those buried on the island and a Latin cross in honour of the saint herself. Beyond Newborough Forest lies Newborough Warren. The Normans are reputed to have introduced rabbit farming into the British Isles, building warrens at places such as this. When the tide goes out, it is possible to understand why some have argued that this was the place where Suetonius succeeded in crossing the strait.

Llangeinwen has an attractive little church, mediaeval in origin but largely rebuilt. It contains several ninth- and eleventh-century grave slabs built into the north-west and south-west buttresses of the nave. **Llangaffo**, an uninspiring nineteenth-century church from the outside, contains a remarkable collection of early mediaeval Christian memorials. St Caffo was an associate of St Cybi and it is likely that he had a monastery on this site. The old church was demolished in 1844, as happened two years later at **Llanidan**, where John Welch designed a new Victorian church. The romantic yew-encircled ruin of its old church, with its surviving fifteenth-century arcade, should not be missed. The decision to partially demolish the fine old church was disputed, and the heat it generated can still be felt in the pages of *Archaeologia Cambrensis*.

A man who was convinced he knew the mind of the Almighty was the Revd. John Williams (1854–1921), Brynsiencyn, most notorious of the Great War clerical recruiters and a man never far from Lloyd George's side whenever the wartime Prime Minister made appearances in Wales. He was called to minister to the Calvinistic Methodists at **Brynsiencyn** in 1878. Another famous son of this corner of Anglesey is the educational reformer Hugh Owen (1804–1881), who was born in Y Foel, overlooking the Strait to the south. His persistent organising ability brought teacher-training colleges into existence in Bangor and Swansea, and helped nurture the infant University College of Wales in Aberystwyth, an institution that subsequently conferred an honorary doctorate on the Revd. John Williams. There are fine views over the strait to Caernarfon, the town Lloyd George represented as a Member of Parliament, and where both the former Prime Minister and Hugh Owen are commemorated by statues.

At **Bryn Celli Ddu** (Cadw), a short distance north of Llanddaniel Fab, there is a fascinating combined henge monument and neolithic burial chamber, one of the most celebrated in Wales. Other neolithic burial chambers in the care of Cadw in the southern part of the island include those of Tŷ Newydd, Din Drifol and Bodowyr. These are places to pause for reflection. This island has been continuously inhabited for millennia: a sacred landscape in the bronze age, some four thousand years ago, it has had a continuous tradition of Christian worship for the past one and a half thousand years. As a consequence, the island retains a numinous quality that contemporary commercial pressures have so far failed to dispel.

V
North-east Wales

14

Denbighshire and Flintshire

The political boundaries of north-east Wales are even more complicated than elsewhere in the country. Stability, as in the rest of Wales, was provided by the Tudor shires, introduced in 1543 and surviving until the reorganisation of local government in 1974. But here, even the Tudor shires were complicated. Flintshire, the smallest county in Wales, was divided into two, a larger part with the north Wales coast and the Dee estuary as its northern limit and a smaller detached part in border country to the east of Offa's Dyke, known as Maelor Saesneg. There was even a third enclave of Flintshire made up of the townships of Marford and Hoseley, near Gresford, surrounded by Denbighshire. As far as the old county of Denbighshire is concerned, the old territory of Powys Fadog in the east never really gelled with the culturally distinct territory of the Perfeddwlad to the west. Following 1974, the historic county town of Flintshire, Mold, was made county town of a new county named Clwyd, an amalgamation of the two historic counties. Its monument is Theatr Clwyd, one of the most dynamic centres for the arts in Wales. Since 1996, this territory has been quartered – if not hanged and drawn – with the larger part of the old Flintshire revived using its historic name, the creation of a truncated Denbighshire, a shadow of its former self, and two new unitary authorities, Wrexham, carved out of Denbighshire and added to the detached part of Flintshire, and Conwy, created from the old Denbighshire in the west.

Some four kilometres south of Conwy, on the A470 to Llanrwst at Tal-y-Cafn, are the gardens of **Bodnant** (NT), one of the most spectacular gardens in Europe, with entrancing views westward to Snowdonia. The gardens were started in 1875 by Henry Pochin, a rich chemical manufacturer and proprietor of china-clay mines, from Salford. His daughter married the first Lord Aberconway and the gardens have been finessed over four generations of the same family. Broadly speaking, the gardens divide into two, with formal arrangements around the house – a rather grim Victorian pile, closed to the public, in which the family still live – and a vast woodland garden set in a ravine cut by the Hiraethlyn, a tributary of the Conwy. The Pin Mill, a charming pavilion, overlooks a delightful lily pond. The rhododendron collection is one of the finest in Britain but the crowning delight is the laburnum tunnel, hung with thousands of yellow blossoms in June.

Beyond Tal-y-cafn, the Conwy follows a geological fault line that marks the frontier between the Ordovician rocks of Gwynedd and the Silurian rocks of Denbighshire. At **Maenan** there are traces of the foundations of a Cistercian abbey, moved inland from Conwy by Edward I when laying out the site for his walled town; for this reason, the tongue of land on which the abbey was built became part of the historic county of Caernarfonshire. A fine property a kilometre to the south-east, called Maenan, was constructed using the original abbey masonry following the Reformation; it has splendid sixteenth-century plasterwork.

Llanrwst is the market centre for the Conwy valley. It has an eye-catching three-arched bridge popularly ascribed, without firm evidence, to the hand of Inigo Jones (1573–1652). The period is correct: a Stuart coat-of-arms from 1636 is clearly visible on the parapet. The narrowness and steep gradient of the bridge combine to challenge the contemporary motorist crossing to or from Gwynedd. The church of St Grwst retains both its rood screen and loft, dating from around 1500, with intricately carved designs including trailing vines, pecking birds and pigs foraging on acorns. The Gwydir chapel was added by Sir Richard Wynn in 1633–4, in perpendicular style, as a private family chapel and is full of Wynn memorials. Pride of place, however, is given to a tomb, said to be that of Llywelyn Fawr, removed first in 1283 from Aberconway, the abbey he had founded, to Maenan, then transferred into the church at Llanrwst at the Dissolution. Its final move into the Gwydir chapel, in the seventeenth century, is commemorated on a brass plaque.

The best way to cross from the Vale of Conwy to the Vale of Clwyd is to take the A458 from Llanrwst. Above the river to the east, the village of **Llanddoged** clusters around its church, the latter an eclectic Victorian restoration retaining its box pews and an ancient font. The pulpit is illuminated with an unusual round skylight and we are reminded of Thomas Kyffin, whose memorial close by informs us that his mind was 'improved by an Acquaintance with several branches of polite Literature'. Back on the main road, the former church of **Llanddewi**, now converted to a dwelling, was built in this lonely spot in 1867 for H.R. Sandbach, a Liverpool West Indiaman. His house, a kilometre west of Llangernyw, bears the ironic name of **Hafodunos**, the term used for the lowliest of Welsh squatters' dwellings, built overnight, but here applied to one of the finest country-houses built by Sir Gilbert Scott. Regrettably, this neo-Gothic masterpiece was destroyed by fire in 2004. There are monuments to the Sandbach family in St Digain's church at **Llangernyw**. This village also has a fascinating museum of Welsh rural life at Y Cwm, the birthplace of Sir Henry Jones (1852–1922). One of a family of six who made their home in this tiny cottage, Henry Jones became Professor of Moral Philosophy at the University of Glasgow. **Gwytherin** in the Cledwen valley was once the resting-place of St Winefride, who had retired to the *clas* here from Holywell. Her body was subsequently removed to the Abbey of St Peter and St Paul in Shrewsbury. More interesting than the restored church is its setting in the midst of a bronze age megalithic alignment; on one of the stones is an inscription from the Early Christian period.

The Harp Inn at **Llanfair Talhaearn** in the delightful Elwy valley is where John Jones (Talhaiarn, 1810–1869) first saw the light of day and where he died, by his own hand. He had superintended the construction of the Crystal Palace in London before returning to Wales with the onset of arthritis. Disappointed in his attempts to win the Chair at the National Eisteddfod on more than one occasion, he laid the blame, as a churchman, at the feet of Nonconformist adjudicators. His public, however, preferred the words he wrote for popular songs to his strenuous efforts at *cynghanedd*. **Garthewin**, to the west of the village, housed the most famous and influential of the small theatres established in Wales in the twentieth century. Saunders Lewis was closely connected with the place and perfected his dramatic art there with the help of the Garthewin Players. The property had come into the Wynne family through marriage in the seventeenth century and in the following century they refashioned the house, attractively, in Georgian style. It was Robert Wynne, the inheritor of the property in 1933, three years after his conversion to Roman Catholicism, who built the little chapel in the grounds and commissioned T.S. Tait to convert the barn to a theatre. Wynne had joined Plaid Genedlaethol Cymru in the same period and was thus linked to Saunders Lewis through a heady trinity of art, politics and religion. One of Saunders Lewis's most successful plays, *Siwan*, was first performed here. Sadly the theatre is now closed to the public.

A monument by Goscombe John in **Llansannan**, five kilometres to the south on the banks of the Aled, showing a girl in Welsh costume, seated before an obelisk and holding a garland, commemorates five great writers all born in the vicinity: Tudur Aled (c.1465–c.1525) one of the greatest of the *Beirdd yr Uchelwyr* (Poets of the Gentry); William

Salesbury (c.1520–1584), translator of the New Testament into Welsh; Henry Rees (1798–1869) a leader of the Calvinistic Methodists, and his brother William (Gwilym Hiraethog; 1802–1883), a minister with the Independents, editor of *Yr Amserau* and radical journalist; and Edward Roberts (Iorwerth Glan Aled, 1819–1867), Baptist minister, writer and poet. The village church contains an eighteenth-century pulpit, originally from a church in Liverpool, and monuments to the Yorkes of Dyffryn Aled. South of the village, the Aled can be followed upstream to another two reservoirs, Aled Isaf and Llyn Aled. To the north-east, the Aled flows through a steep and delightfully wooded valley to its confluence with the Elwy.

North of the attractive B5382 east of Llansannan is **Berain**. Now a farm, it was built at the end of the seventeenth century for Katheryn of Berain (1535–1591), who was nicknamed Mam Cymru for her four marriages. Her third husband had asked for her hand in marriage on the way to her second husband's funeral and for this reason she declined a second marriage proposal made on the way back from the funeral, softening the latter blow by promising to marry this suitor should her third husband die before he did. And so it transpired. She lies in the attractive church at **Llanefydd**, reached by a labyrinth of lanes. Thomas Edwards (Twm o'r Nant, 1738–1810) was born at Penparchell Isaf in this parish but brought up at Nant Ganol, Henllan, hence the nickname by which he was always known. He is remembered for his robust interludes, which form a link in the tradition of drama in Welsh between the mediaeval and modern periods. The road from Henllan offers good views of Denbigh Castle.

The historic county town of **Denbigh** began as an Edwardian borough. It has plenty of character that can be well appreciated from the walls of its castle (Cadw), built on a steep hill overlooking the town. Dafydd ap Gruffudd, younger brother of Llywelyn ap Gruffudd had his stronghold here. In the year of Llywelyn's defeat, Edward granted the site to one of his chief commanders, Henry de Lacey, Earl of Lincoln, who began work on the present castle. Its finest feature is its impressive triangular Great Gatehouse, possibly designed by Master James of St George, with two hexagonal towers on the outside and an octagonal one inside. The statue in the niche of the outer gate may be of Edward I himself. Large parts of the town walls survive, including the fine Burgess Gate to the north of the castle. In 1563, control of the castle passed to Robert Dudley, Earl of Leicester, who began work on the church that now bears his name to the north-east of the castle. Originally intended to replace the cathedral at St Asaph, these grand designs were never accomplished. Leicester was a supporter of the extreme Protestant party, those beginning to be called Puritans, and the internal design of a preaching-house was probably intended. Nearby is another ruined church, St Hilary's, built at the beginning of the fourteenth century as a chapel to serve castle and town, and partly demolished in 1923. Like the remains of the Carmelite Friary that survive at the end of Abbey Road, it is in the care of Cadw. There are two heavily Italianate chapels in Swan Lane, for the Independents and the Calvinistic Methodists respectively.

The main street in the lower town is attractively arcaded and has an Arts and Crafts Town Hall, completed in 1916 and the Twm o'r Nant Theatre, occupying the former Memorial Hall. The Pierce Monument in Vale Street was built, in his lifetime, to honour Dr Evan Pierce in gratitude for his work during a cholera epidemic. The good doctor added the two fountains to commemorate the 1887 Jubilee, the whole composition an amalgam of Victorian kitsch and pomposity. Howell's School, built by Herbert Williams, is a sister institution to the school of the same name that he built in Llandaf. The original building, to which generally sympathetic additions have been made, was opened in 1860. There is a good footpath from the school, going under the walls and returning to the upper town. We should not leave without remembering the orphan John Rowlands who was born in a cottage in the castle precincts but spent his childhood in St Asaph's workhouse. The boy subsequently achieved fame as the explorer and writer, Henry Morton Stanley (1841–1904).

The parish church of the town, St Marcella's, lies nearly two kilometres east of the town in a surprisingly rural setting at **Llanfarchell** (Whitchurch). Dating from the fourteenth century, it is a double-naved, late Perpendicular building, characteristic of the Vale of Clwyd, with a striking hammer-beam roof. It contains an interesting group of memorials, including a monument to Humphrey Llwyd (c.1527–1568), antiquary and map-maker, a brass to Richard Myddelton (c.1508–1575), governor of Denbigh Castle and MP for the borough, and the painted alabaster table tomb of Sir John Salusbury of Lleweni, patriarch of Rûg and Bachymbyd. Twm o'r Nant is buried in the churchyard. Also at a distance from the town, a kilometre to the south-west, is the former **North Wales Mental Hospital**, an institution that opened in 1848 and which occupies the equivalent place in the cultural history of north-east Wales as does its counterpart in Carmarthen for the south-west. It figures in Kate Roberts' novella, *Tywyll Heno*, for the gifted writer moved to Denbigh in 1938 when she and her husband purchased Gwasg Thomas Gee, the celebrated Welsh publishing-house, in the town. Kate Roberts and Thomas Gee (1815–1898) are both buried in the town's municipal cemetery. Samuel Johnson stayed with the Myddeltons at **Gwaunynog**, a little to the east of the town – for just a few days in 1774 – but his reputation in England was sufficient to ensure the transformation of a riverside cottage in the grounds into a literary shrine, a sad contrast to the neglect of Saunders Lewis at Garthewin.

The road south to Rhuthun mercifully by-passes **Llanrhaeadr-yng-Nghinmeirch** where the characteristically double-naved church of St Dyfnog has some of the finest stained glass in Wales, including a wonderfully complete sixteenth-century Jesse. There is also a baroque monument to Maurice Jones (1672–1702) of nearby Llanrhaeadr Hall, the avenue of which has been bisected by the by-pass. St Dyfnog's Well survives in a wood behind the church. The road crosses the Clywedog at **Rhewl** where Robert Ambrose Jones (Emrys ap Iwan, 1851–1906), Calvinistic Methodist minister and cultural nationalist, is buried in the graveyard of his denomination's chapel.

Rhuthun is one of the most attractive of small Welsh towns. It is clustered on a ridge, with its castle at the southern end and the parish church to the north and with the Clwyd flowing below to the east. As at Denbigh, the castle site was originally occupied by Dafydd ap Gruffudd but was taken over following 1282 on behalf of Edward I by Reginald de Grey, the new Marcher Lord of Rhuthun. An unsuccessful attack on the castle marked the beginning of the Owain Glyn Dŵr Rising; it finally succumbed to the Parliamentarians during the Civil War. Only remnants of the mediaeval castle now remain, notably a gatehouse. A massive, castellated private residence was progressively elaborated on the site in the first half of the nineteenth century; surrounded by a beautiful park, it is now a hotel. Reginald de Grey's son, John, founded the church of St Peter as a collegiate church in 1310. It has elaborately decorated roofs to each of its naves, especially the northern one, and notable brasses to Edward Goodman. His son, Dr Gabriel Goodman, born in the town, rose to become Dean of Westminster and endowed the collegiate buildings as Christ's Hospital for a priest and twelve poor persons; as a consequence, the Rector is called the Warden. The parochial close, an attractive ensemble of buildings dating from the sixteenth century, consists of Christ's Hospital, The Old Cloisters, The Old Grammar School and Almshouses, the latter remodelled in the nineteenth century. The wrought iron churchyard gates with their elaborate scrollwork are by Robert Davies (1675–1748), a member of the celebrated family of smiths of Croes Foel, Esclusham. The town is full of architectural interest. St Peter's Square has the Castle Hotel and Castle Street has Nantclwyd House, a cruck hall dating from the fifteenth century. Plas Coch in Well Street was built from sandstone removed from the castle. Record Street has the attractive County Hall, completed in 1790 and the combined Town Hall and adjoining Market Hall, completed in 1865, in Market Street. The Old County Gaol in Clwyd Street now houses the county record office.

The upper Clwyd can be explored southwards by following the A494 in the direction of Corwen. Some seven kilometres south of the town the river flows through the grounds of **Nantclwyd Hall**, an astonishing place, where the Liverpool banking fortune of Sir Vivian Naylor-Leyland gave free rein to Sir Clough Williams-Ellis to indulge his fancies. These included a fibreglass temple, a clock tower, a ceremonial arch, gazebos, a dovecote and formal gardens around which statuary brought from Scarisbrick Hall in Lancashire, following a sale, has been distributed. The house is of seventeenth-century origins. **Llanelidan** church is characteristic of the Vale of Clwyd, with its double nave. It contains a Jacobean pulpit, a restored rood screen, Welsh commandment boards and monuments to the previous owners of Nantclwyd, one of whom is reputed to have gambled away his fortune playing at fives against the church wall.

To explore the north bank of the upper Clwyd, take the B5105 from Rhuthun in the direction of Cerrigydrudion. There are two surviving rood screens in this vicinity, at St Foddhyd's church in **Clocaenog** and St Mary's **Derwen**, the latter also retaining its loft. The road continues to **Llanfihangel Glyn Myfyr** where it crosses the Alwen on Thomas Penson's handsome early nineteenth-century stone bridge, with the same architect's Crown Inn to one side of the river and St Michael's church to the other. Tyddyn Tudur nearby was the home of the Jones family, a talented brood whose members included Owen Jones (Owain Myfyr, 1741–1814), a patron of Welsh letters who founded the Gwyneddigion Society in 1770 and whose collection of Welsh manuscripts were published as *The Myvyrian Archaeology of Wales*. His only son, of the same name, became a famous architect, decorator and illuminator.

To explore the eastern side of the Vale of Clwyd, take the road for Mold out of Rhuthun and then turn north at **Llanbedr Dyffryn Clwyd**. Even those not especially enamoured of Victorian churches are unlikely to be able to resist the charms of St Peter's, built in 1863 for John Jesse, whose Llanbedr Hall, to the north of the village, also delights in polychrome. Jesse inherited the house from Joseph Ablett, a Manchester businessman who fined his servants if they spoke Welsh. Adjacent to the house is the ruin of the old church, abandoned following the construction of St Peter's. Ablett is buried beside the north wall of the old church. The mediaeval church of St Saeran, situated between the rivers Clywedog and Clwyd at **Llanynys**, was built on the site of a sixth-century *clas* in the thirteenth century, then enlarged with a second nave in the local manner; a model of simplicity, its exterior walls were once whitewashed. The well-restored churchyard contains ancient yews; otherwise the church has only a public house and a brick-built vicarage for company. Interior delights include three chandeliers, two of wood from the eighteenth century and one of brass from the nineteenth, the latter originally from Rûg, and a fifteenth-century wall painting of St Christopher revealed in 1967. The seventeenth-century altar table is supported with lions bearing shields. An unusual fourteenth-century sepulchral cross, showing a bishop on one side and a crucifixion on the other, has been moved into the church from the churchyard. The wooden dog-tongs were used to expel dogs from divine service. St Cynhafael's church at **Llangynhafal**, on the slopes of Moel Famau, contains an unusual Pelican in her Piety. There is an interesting example of the Late Victorian restoration work of W.E. Nesfield in the church at **Llandyrnog**. Nesfield is known for his 'pies', decorative roundels taken from oriental porcelain, and these appear on the porch and on the fine sanctuary bench. Moving up-slope, but back in time, the charmingly unrestored church at **Llangwyfan** retains stocks in its churchyard.

A main road east to Mold from Bodfari follows the Afon Chwiler (anglicised as Wheeler) through the Clwydian range between the two imposing iron age hill forts of Moel-y-Gaer and Moel-y-Parc. From it, there is an opportunity to visit the intriguingly named village of **Sodom** that lies on the Offa's Dyke Path, a little to the north. To the east, the tranquillity of the village of **Caerwys** conceals a bustling past. It was founded as an Edwardian market town in 1290 but was eclipsed by rival boroughs with better communications. Then, in the sixteenth century, two great gatherings of poets and musicians were organised here to regulate the bardic crafts, which are sometimes seen as part of the ancestry of the modern eisteddfodic movement. St Michael's church contains an effigy reputed to be that of the wife of Dafydd ap Gruffudd. The countryside around is rich in bronze age tumuli. One of the finest gold torcs ever found in Britain was unearthed by a farmer in 1816 at **Ysceifiog**, three kilometres to the east, where the plain lancet church of St Mary contains a fourteenth-century effigy of a priest in the west porch. Another St Mary's, at **Nannerch**, conventionally restored by T.H. Wyatt in the mid-nineteenth century, contains a monumental sculpture by Grinling Gibbons commemorating Charlotte Mostyn and a magnificent nineteenth-century brass chandelier.

Cilcain, five kilometres to the south, is exactly as its name translates, 'a pleasant retreat'. Its double-naved church, dedicated to St Mary, has a magnificent mediaeval roof with shield-bearing angels, sixteenth-century stained glass in the east window and an eighteenth-century monument to the Mostyns of Mostyn Hall. The village is a good place from which to make an ascent of **Moel Famau**, the highest peak of the Clwydian range with uninterrupted views over the Vale of Clwyd below. At the summit (554m.) is the Jubilee Tower, built by Thomas Harrison in 1810 to commemorate the jubilee of the accession of George III. It is noteworthy as the first Egyptian-style monument to be built in Britain, less impressive since suffering storm damage in 1862 although tidied up a century later for European Conservation Year. It is also situated on the county boundary between Denbighshire and Flintshire and on the Offa's Dyke Path. This section of the path passes through an exceptionally rich archaeological landscape. There are two bronze age cairns close to the Jubilee Tower and a sequence of impressive iron age hillforts, running from Moel Fenlli in the south to Penycloddiau in the north, the latter one of the largest and highest hillforts in Wales. Were these refuges in times of crisis for the dwellers in the Vale or places of ceremony for them at significant points in the year's turning? Or, when the lowlands were uncleared forest, did a more favourable microclimate enable an iron age community to inhabit these heights? Today, these uplands provide a dramatic contrast with lush arable country in the Vale of Clwyd below, extensive heather moors now providing cover for grouse, stonechats and curlews, and flowering a magnificent purple in late summer.

The hillside village of **Tremeirchion** has the only mediaeval church dedication to Corpus Christi in Britain, containing a well-preserved fourteenth-century canopy tomb, thought to be that of Dafydd Ddu Hiraddug, Canon of St Asaph, a poet and scientist. When Dr Johnson visited the church he claimed that a wall text from St Paul contained a typographical error. Instead of *Y Gwŷr, cerwch eich gwragedd* (Husbands, love your wives), it read *Y Gwŷr, curwch eich gwragedd* (Husbands, beat your wives). **Brynbella**, completed in 1795, is an appropriately Italianate villa delightfully situated in wooded parkland. It was built for Gabriel Piozzi, an Italian music teacher after his advantageous marriage to his pupil, Hester, a member of the Salusbury family, who, as Mrs Thrale, was a friend of Dr Johnson. Mrs Thrale had lived at **Bach-y-Graig** before her second marriage and the construction of Brynbella unfortunately resulted in the abandonment of that unique property which, by 1817, had been demolished. Bach-y-Graig was one of the first houses in Wales to be built of bricks. It was built in Flemish style using materials imported from Flanders for Sir Richard Clough who was the agent in Antwerp of Sir Thomas Gresham, the founder of the Royal Exchange.

Again, we find ourselves in Beuno country. His holy well, Ffynnon Beuno, is beside the main road to the south of the village. Two kilometres to the north is **St Beuno's College**, a Jesuit foundation, completed in 1849, 'decent outside, skimpin within, like Lancing College done worse', according to its most famous student, Gerard Manley Hopkins (1844–1889). His poetry, mainly written while he was a student for the priesthood here from 1874 to 1877, was greatly influenced by his study of Welsh *cynghanedd* so that his poetry has been seen to prefigure that of Dylan Thomas in some ways. Another dominant influence on his poetry was the beauty of the Vale of Clwyd:

> . . . *woods, waters, meadows, combes and vales*
> *All the air things wear that build this world of Wales*

The collegiate buildings incorporate the church of the Holy Name and there is a small Rock Chapel a kilometre to the south-east, the latter built by another student at the college, Father Ignatius Scoles.

St Asaph (Llanelwy) is one of the five Welsh episcopal sees. The cathedral is situated on a bank between the Elwy and the Clwyd, a site in continuous Christian use since the mid-sixth century when Cyndeyrn (known as Kentigern in

England and Mungo in Scotland) established a monastic site here while in temporary exile from Glasgow. On his return to Scotland, he left his pupil, Asaph, as his successor. It is the smallest of the Welsh cathedrals, having the dimensions of a large parish church, and, it must be admitted, the least interesting. Grave and austere on the outside, with a slightly asymmetrical fifteenth-century bell-tower, the latter the result of repairs to eighteenth-century storm damage, the interior has retained its mediaeval canopied stalls and has some colourful Victorian stained glass windows. Sir Gilbert Scott completed a thorough restoration in 1868, installing his own reredos depicting the Way of the Cross. There is no cathedral precinct and the former Bishop's Palace has been converted into accommodation for the elderly. Outside the cathedral, a Memorial to the Translators was completed in 1892 having been commissioned for the tercentenary of the translation of the Bible into Welsh by Bishop William Morgan and his precursors and collaborators, Richard Davies, Richard Parry, William Salesbury, Thomas Huet, Gabriel Goodman, Edmwnd Prys and John Davies. Also outside, in the churchyard, is the grave of William Mathias (1934–1992), one of the greatest of twentieth-century Welsh composers.

The so-called 'Marble Church' at **Bodelwyddan** was completed in 1860 by John Gibson for Lady Willoughby de Broke, in memory of her late husband. Doubly conspicuous in glistening white local limestone and with its 60-metre spire, the lavishly fitted interior verges on the vulgar, with Lady Willoughby's two nieces carved in Carrara marble holding a shell as the font, for example. Lady Willoughby was one of the Williams family from **Bodelwyddan Castle** that employed Welch and Hansom to create the present turreted and battlemented appearance of the house in the second quarter of the nineteenth century. In the twentieth century the castle was home to Lowther College, a private boarding school for girls but since 1988 it has housed a branch of the National Portrait Gallery, with a permanent collection of Victorian portraits complemented with period furniture from the collection of the Victoria and Albert Museum. The castle is set in parkland with a formal garden designed by Mawson in 1910. To the north of the main road are two interesting properties dating from the sixteenth century, Faenol Bach and Faenol Fawr.

To the west of Bodelwyddan Park is the adjacent estate of **Kinmel Hall**, the product of a fortune derived from Anglesey copper by the Revd. Edward Hughes, following an advantageous marriage at the end of the eighteenth century. This first house was destroyed by fire, and a new property was completed by Thomas Hopper in 1843 for Hughes' son, who had been created Lord Dinorben in 1831. By 1874, this property was given a major transformation at the hands of W.E Nesfield, pioneer of the so-called Queen Anne style using warm red brick and stone and, as with his church at Llandyrnog, decorated with his characteristic 'pies'. Another example of his architecture in Queen Anne style is **Botryddan Hall**, east of Rhuddlan, set in a formal garden also of his design.

Returning to the east bank of the Clwyd, **Rhuddlan** is situated at what was for centuries the lowest bridging point on the river, and before that a place where the river could be forded. Little more than a large village now, its place in Welsh history is disproportionate to its present size. As early as AD796, the Welsh are said to have been defeated in battle here at the hands of Offa of Mercia, an event commemorated in the sombre tune of Morfa Rhuddlan. Subsequently, this strategic location was controlled in turns by the Welsh and the Normans, the latter throwing up a motte that survives as Twthill (Cadw). Rhuddlan was crucial to the success of the Edwardian conquest and a major castle (Cadw) was built to the north of Twthill to the design of Master James of St George, concentric with a moat on three sides. In the course of its construction, the

Clwyd was canalised up to this point from the sea. It was from Rhuddlan, in 1284, that Edward I proclaimed the Statute of Wales, also known as the Statute of Rhuddlan, which, amongst other things, created five of the historic Welsh counties of Flint, Caernarfon, Anglesey, Merioneth, Cardigan and Carmarthen and replaced the Welsh with the English legal system. The pattern of the Edwardian borough can be traced in the grid of streets, with High Street being crossed by Castle and Church Streets. An inscription in Parliament Street claims that Edward I held a parliament there. The double-naved parish church of St Mary also dates from the thirteenth century but was restored by Sir Gilbert Scott in the 1860s and contains many of his furnishings. It contains interesting monuments and sepulchral slabs from the thirteenth century and has a battlemented mausoleum appended in 1820 for William Davies Shipley of Botryddan, Dean of St Asaph.

The less attractive features of modernity are inescapable along the north Wales coast from Colwyn Bay to Connah's Quay, in the form of rushing traffic along the A55 express-way, caravan parks and unfashionable seaside resorts, the latter dubbed by cynics either the *costa geriatrica* or places where the rainfall of Snowdonia meets the radioactive tide from Sellafield. **Colwyn Bay** developed as a select resort for Lancashire tradesmen following the sale of the Pwllycrochan estate in 1865 and its construction must have boosted production at the Ruabon brickworks. The railway runs between the town and the beach, so that a rail journey is a good way of seeing both. The town's crematorium was journey's end for two notable twentieth-century peace campaigners, Bertrand Russell and Lewis Valentine. Beyond the Dulas, the theatrical neo-Gothic castellated mansion of Gwrych Castle has been reduced to a shell by vandals; it was completed in the 1820s by Lloyd Bamford Hesketh whose father had married the heiress of the Lloyds of Gwrych. St Michael's church, **Abergele**, has the biggest double-naved church in Wales built on the site of a Celtic *clas*. Parts of its original rood screen survive and a stained glass window, the colour of boiled sweets, was installed by Hesketh to commemorate the Lloyds of Gwyrch. The graveyard has a conspicuous memorial to the 33 victims of the 1868 railway disaster when runaway goods waggons collided with the *Irish Mail* from Chester near the town. Abergele again hit the headlines when two young men died attempting to sabotage the royal train bringing Prince Charles to Caernarfon for the Investiture ceremony. Hesketh was responsible for financing a remarkable parochial ensemble of church, school and vicarage at **Towyn**, now incongruously surrounded by bungalows and caravans.

To prepare for a visit to **Rhyl**, consider it Llandudno's *alter ego*: hard and brashly hedonistic in place of charm and reserved gentility. With enormous railway platforms and a promenade extending for over two kilometres, it was the earliest of the north Wales coastal resorts to be developed. Beginning in the 1820s and expanding rapidly with the coming of the railway in 1848, its stature as a Victorian resort was secured on canvas by David Cox in *Rhyl Sands* (Birmingham Art Gallery). The life and work of Robert Scourfield Mills (Owen Rhoscomyl, 1863–1919), the adventurer and author of boys' stories and patriotic history who is buried in the municipal cemetry, epitomises the high Victorian mood of Rhyl in its prime. The main attraction provided for the contemporary visitor is the Sun Centre, completed in 1980, replete with monorail, wave machine and tropical vegetation. Neighbouring **Prestatyn**, a younger and even less interesting resort than Rhyl, marks the northern end of Offa's Dyke. Holiday chalets, caravans, a golf course, numerous shops and cafés can be seen along the coast from the inland cliffs by which the Offa's Dyke Path approaches the town. For a pleasant walk, head along the coast to the old lighthouse at the **Point of Ayr** that marks the entrance to the Dee estuary, not an easy place for navigation: Ayr derives from a Norse word for sandbank. Coal seams run under the sea here and the colliery was active until 1996.

A golden rule along the north Wales coast, as in so many similar locations, is to explore just a few kilometres inland. The history of the hillside village of **Whitford** was written by its most famous son, Thomas Pennant, the naturalist and antiquary. The house in which Pennant was born, Downing, set in the wooded glen of Nant-y-bi, a kilometre east of the village, was tragically destroyed by fire in 1922 and subsequently demolished, but there are monuments to his memory in the south aisle of St Mary's church. Against the north wall of the churchyard is the tomb-chest of Pennant's manservant and the illustrator of his books, Moses Griffith (1747–1819). The neighbouring estate to Downing is that of **Mostyn**, the name of a family that dominated the life of Flintshire for centuries. The drive down to Mostyn Hall passes through a short tunnel through the limestone that has been elaborated as the neo-Gothic Drybridge Lodge. The grounds of Mostyn Hall run down to the Dee estuary. The house is one of the largest in the county, predominantly sixteenth-century, much restored and embellished in the Victorian period by Ambrose Poynter, but dating back centuries. The Mostyn family played an important part in securing the Tudor victory on Bosworth Field and their ancestors were living here in the age of the Welsh princes.

Celia Fiennes visited **Holywell** in 1698: 'at Holly Well they speake Welsh, the inhabitants go barefoote and bare leg'd, a nasty sort of people'. Her reason for visiting was to see the curative well of Gwenffrewi (St Winefride), who was martyred in the seventh century but miraculously restored to life. It is the only Welsh shrine to have been in continual use through all the subsequent religious upheavals. Gerard Manley Hopkins wrote a poem about the well and an unfinished verse drama about the life of St Winefride. The structure protecting the holy well was erected at the end of the fifteenth century, largely financed by Lady Margaret Beaufort, the mother of Henry VII. The chapel (Cadw) has a richly carved roof; the vaulted well chamber below, leased to the Jesuits, has graffiti ranging in provenance from the sixteenth to the nineteenth centuries and a nineteenth-century statue of the saint. The last royal pilgrims to visit the well were James II and Mary of Modena who came to pray for a son, a prayer answered with fateful consequences. The volume of water to the spring was reduced after 1917 when mining operations intercepted it. The well is still in active use. The dull parish church of St James, a Victorian restoration by Wyatt, is close by; the more interesting Italianate Roman Catholic church, completed in 1912, is some distance up the hill. Frederick William Rolfe (1860–1913), who styled himself Baron Corvo, the English novelist, essayist and convert to Roman Catholicism, scandalised the town when he was commissioned to paint ten banners for the church.

Holywell was originally under the patronage of **Basingwerk Abbey** (Cadw) the substantial sandstone ruins of which lie some two kilometres to the north-east at Greenfield, on the banks of the Dee. Originally a Sauvignac foundation, the abbey passed into the hands of the Cistercians who benefited from their ownership of St Winefride's Well. Before the Dissolution the abbey was celebrated for its wine list; its last abbot was the son of his predecessor. Roman Catholicism flourishes two kilometres west of Holywell at **Pantasaph** where Pugin was called in to give a Roman finish to a church originally built by Wyatt for the Anglicans, his patron, Viscount Fielding, having been converted to Rome in 1850. St Clare's Convent and the Franciscan Friary opened within a few years of the church's completion in 1852.

Returning to the Dee estuary, **Flint Castle** (Cadw) may disappoint readers of Shakespeare by its post-industrialised setting; Courtaulds had a rayon factory and associated high-rise housing adjacent to the site. A castle was established here early in Edward's campaigns and the site consolidated with the establishment of a borough in 1284. The castle, set on a plinth of rock above the saltings of the Dee estuary and made from the same sandstone as Basingwerk Abbey, survived the depredations of Owain Glyn Dŵr but not those of the Parliamentary army in 1647. Designed by Master James of St George, the castle's exceptional feature is its free-standing Great Tower, originally surrounded by the tidal waters of the Dee. The Welsh border takes in both sides of the Dee estuary above Flint, with the sprawling site of the **Shotton** steelworks lying north of the canalised river and the associated conurbation of **Connah's Quay** and **Queensferry** on the south bank.

A parallel trajectory inland following the A55 express-way offers greater interest. **Halkyn Mountain** (294m.) owes its eerily bare and pockmarked appearance to centuries of lead mining. **Halkyn Castle** was built for the second Earl Grosvenor (later first Marquess of Westminster) with a fortune deriving from mineral rights on the mountain; he was attracted by the proximity of Holywell Racecourse. A much older human settlement is clearly visible two kilometres to the south at **Moel-y-Gaer** iron age hill fort that occupies a hilltop that recent excavation has shown to have been also inhabited in the late neolithic and bronze age periods. To the east, **Northop** (Llaneurgain) has a church with a magnificent fifteenth-century tower and good nineteenth-century stained glass. West of the village runs a good section of Flintshire's most substantial ancient monument, the long winding earthwork known as **Wat's Dyke**. Running mainly parallel to, and east of, Offa's Dyke, it may represent a preliminary Saxon frontier guarding the Cheshire Plain from the Dee to the Severn, a distance of some 45 kilometres. **Soughton Hall**, occupying extensive parkland south of the village is a wonderful confection. Originally built for Bishop Wynne of St Asaph in the early eighteenth century, it was much elaborated for Henry Bankes, who astutely married the bishop's daughter. It is now a hotel. **Ewloe Castle** (Cadw) is Welsh in origin: its tower may be the work of Llywelyn Fawr, a ruler whose power and prestige was such that he could have a castle of this magnitude constructed in close proximity to Chester. Within a generation, the balance of power had shifted dramatically against the Welsh and Flint replaced Ewloe as the centre of power.

Hawarden is also a place of castles, primarily associated with the Grand Old Man of nineteenth-century British politics, William Ewart Gladstone (1809–1898) who made it his home. Gladstone's brother-in-law was Sir Stephen Glynne, the ecclesiologist and antiquary whose father had redesigned the property in a Romantic, castellated style. Gladstone's study, the Temple of Peace, contains his axe collection. His vast personal library is housed in a collegiate building, with accommodation for researchers, designed as part of the National Gladstone Memorial. The bronze statue of the former Prime Minister that stands in front of the St Deiniol's Library was intended for Dublin but was rejected by the city fathers there in the years immediately following independence; there are complementary bronzes in London and Edinburgh. Sir Gilbert Scott completed the restoration of the adjacent church of St Deiniol in 1859, following a tragic fire. It contains numerous memorial windows to the Gladstones and the Glynnes, and the last stained glass window designed by Burne-Jones, completed as a memorial to the Grand Old Man, whose death preceded that of the artist by only a few months. The small Gladstone Memorial Chapel contains a luxuriant Arts and Crafts memorial to the former Prime Minister and his wife, Catherine.

Mold is the county town of Flintshire, its name deriving from the Norman French, *Mont Haut*; in Welsh, it is Yr Wyddgrug, also signifying a high mound, possibly the motte that survives on Bailey Hill. There has been a long history of human settlement here: one of the treasures of the British Museum is a gold bronze age ceremonial cape that was discovered wrapped around a skeleton here in 1833. Mold did not acquire an Edwardian castle and St Mary's church dates from 1485, its construction financed by Margaret, Countess of Richmond and Derby. It is a striking building, dominating approaches to this pleasant market town on the south-west bank of the Afon Alun. It has a notable sixteenth-century aisled nave and ornate eighteenth-century tower. The chest-tomb of the artist Richard Wilson, the father of British landscape painting, is situated outside the church near the north wall. There is a bronze statue of Daniel Owen (1836–1895), the nineteenth-century Welsh novelist, outside the public library, the work of Goscombe John. The author of the classic Welsh novels *Rhys Lewis*, *Enoc Huws* and *Gwen Tomos* worshipped at the Neo-Classical Bethesda Calvinistic Methodist chapel in New Street and is buried in the town's municipal cemetery. A sequence of heritage plaques linked to a town trail provides a useful introduction to the town's history. The Civic Centre, to the north of the town and completed at the same time, comprises a forbidding Shire Hall in pre-cast concrete, the County Library and the splendid Theatr Clwyd.

The countryside around Mold is ringed, at a radius of a couple of kilometres, by country houses of exceptional architectural interest. **Nerquis Hall** and **The Tower**, a fortified tower house dating from the mid-fifteenth century, lie to the south. There are early seventeenth-century properties at **Gwysaney** and **Rhual** to the north, the latter constructed in brick. Rhual also has the Alleluia Monument in its grounds, an obelisk erected by Nehemiah Griffith in 1736 which perpetuates the story of St Garmon baptising a troop of Britons in the Alun ahead of their victorious encounter with the Saxons before which he had counselled them to chant *Alleluia!* **Pentrehobyn**, to the south-east, has the unusual **Lletyau** that may have been designed as accommodation for poor travellers or for a pack of hounds. To the south, **Leeswood Hall**, built for George Wynne, the owner of a lead mine on Halkyn Mountain, has a pair of wrought iron gates that are probably the work of Robert Davies. Continuing a little upstream, **Fferm** is another early seventeenth-century house with its own brewhouse and **Plas Teg**, of the same period, a remarkably original property long attributed in the locality to Inigo Jones and wonderfully restored. It was built for Sir John Trevor (1563–1630), Secretary to Lord Howard of Effingham, whose monument is in St Cyngar's church at **Hope**, a little further upstream. The church has some good late fourteenth-century stained glass. Hope Castle, on the west bank of the river at **Caergwrle**, can be reached by crossing a fascinating five-arched fourteenth-century pack-horse bridge. It was built in the thirteenth-century by the Welsh princes on the site of an iron age hill fort, but rapidly fell into disuse following the Conquest.

Wrexham (Wrecsam) grew rapidly in the nineteenth century as the urban focus of the North Wales Coalfield with the result that the charm of a small market town has been replaced by more dreary contemporary urban realities. The grandeur of its parish church, dedicated to St Giles continues to reflect the historic importance of the town. It is reached through fine early eighteenth-century wrought iron gates made by Robert Davies, symbols of the iron industry that fuelled the growth of the town. The church contains a varied collection of monuments, including two for the Myddelton family by the baroque sculptor, L.F. Roubiliac. A classical urn commemorates Ann Wilkinson, wife of the ironmaster John Wilkinson. The church is famous for its richly ornamented sixteenth-century tower, a replica of which has been erected on the campus of Yale University, for Elihu Yale (1649–1721), the founder of that illustrious institution, is buried in its churchyard. His fanciful epitaph reads:

> Born in America, in Europe bred,
> In Africa travell'd, and in Asia wed,
> Where long he liv'd, and thriv'd; at London dead,
> Much good, some ill, he did; so hope all's even,
> And that his soul, thro' mercy's gone to heaven.
> You that survive, and read this tale, take care
> For this most certain exit to prepare:
> Where blessed in peace the actions of the just
> Smell sweet and blossom in the silent dust

His family's ancestral home, some three kilometres east of Bryneglwys, was Plas yn Iâl, Yale being the anglicised form of Iâl, a commote of Powys Fadog in the Middle Ages. Elihu Yale resided at Plas Grono, near Erddig, a house demolished in 1876. In 1999, Yale University began a lawsuit against the local Yale College over the use of the name, much to the amusement of the locals. In the town centre, the last quarter of the twentieth century saw the demolition of some of the town's better nineteenth-century chapels, including Ebenezer for the Independents and Seion for the Calvinistic Methodists, both of which have been replaced by contemporary structures. Salisbury Park, the English Congregationalist chapel, has not been replaced.

Erddig (NT), a late seventeenth-century property south of Wrexham, is far from being just another stately home, for when bequeathed by its last owner, Philip Yorke, to the National Trust in 1973 it had preserved its decoration and contents *in toto*, down to the toy collection in the nursery. The tour of the house has been imaginatively designed to bring its daily round to life from the vantage-point of the servants, a unique collection of whose portraits, executed in the 1790s, are preserved here. It begins in the estate buildings, where the joiner and blacksmith worked, before entering the house through the laundry, bake-house and kitchen. The Yorke family bicycle collection is on display in the stable block, including the tall penny-farthing on which the last owner made the rounds of his estate.

Extensive restoration work at Erddig was necessary to remedy the effects of subsistence from the workings of **Bersham** colliery directly beneath the house. The mining of coal at Bersham ceased in 1986; the pithead gear visible from the Wrexham by-pass now signals a mining museum. In the eighteenth century Bersham had an ironworks belonging to John and William Wilkinson, a partnership that ended acrimoniously at the end of the century. The centre of the Wilkinson's iron business lay some five kilometres to the north at **Brymbo**, where, in 1792, John Wilkinson bought the estate of Brymbo Hall (sadly demolished in 1973) for the coal measures that lay beneath it. Iron production survived the fraternal feud between John and William, with the Brymbo Steel Company, established in 1885, as heir to the tradition finally killed off in 1990 by globalisation. **Coedpoeth**, to the north of Bersham, which straddles a good section of Offa's Dyke, and **Rhosllanercruchog** to the south, are both former mining villages where the tradition of choral singing has happily survived the demise of the industry that gave birth to it. Rhosllanerchruchog has a Miners' Institute (*Y Stiwt*), in Broad Street, and a remarkable concentration of chapels, two institutions that moulded the character of its people, neatly encapsulated in an oft-repeated line of *cynghanedd*, '*Beibl a rhaw i bobl y Rhos*' (A Bible and a spade for the people of Rhosllanerchruchog).

Gresford is known for disasters. In 1934, 265 men lost their lives in an underground explosion here. The parish church of All Saints is one of the finest parish churches in the country; its pinnacled bell-tower with its celebrated 'Peal of Twelve' was rebuilt in the late fifteenth century. But its chief glory was tragically damaged in 1966 when a church cleaning company applied detergent to its extensive collection of early fifteenth-century stained glass. The church retains its screens and misericords survive in the choir stalls. There is an extensive collection of monuments and brasses, including work by Chantrey.

Maelor Saesneg is a curious extension of Welsh territory east of both the natural geographical frontier of the Dee and the political frontier of Offa's Dyke. Under the old county system, it was that anomalous phenomenon, Flintshire Detached. Local government reorganisation might have placed it in Cheshire – the Parisian authorities created Loire-Atlantique out of parts of southern Brittany with far less justification – but any controversy was avoided in this case by placing Maelor Saesneg in the new unitary authority of Wrexham. Culturally, Cheshire rather than Wales predominates. **Bangor Is-Coed** has a Welsh name and a notable place in Welsh religious history as the site of the Celtic monastery where Pelagius espoused a theology considered so heretical by Rome that Garmon (St Germanus) was sent to Britain from Auxerre to have its influence suppressed. No trace of the monastery remains; the monks were massacred by the Northumbrians, following the Battle of Chester in AD613. **Overton** features in a rhyme about the Seven Wonders of Wales for the splendid collection of yews that surround St Mary's church. Some ten kilometres to the east is **Hanmer**, ancestral village of the wife of Owain Glyn Dŵr, whose praises were sung by Iolo Goch (c.1320–1398), after his visit to Sycharth.

Ruabon (Rhiwabon), some six kilometres to the south-west of Wrexham, is famed for its terracotta and red pressed bricks that spread like acne across the country with the railway network. The most notable of the manufacturers of these bricks was the Penybont Works of J.C. Edwards at Cefn Mawr, above the Dee two kilometres to the south-west, where George Borrow was amazed at the sight of blast furnaces working at night. Ruabon Grammar School's most notorious pupil was Frank Harris (1856–1931), the first edition of whose pioneeringly explicit *My Life and Loves* (1922) was endorsed 'not to be imported into England or the USA'. Welsh soldiers who obtained a copy on active service imported them to Wales claiming that their country was not included in the prohibition. **Rhosymedre**, close by, will be familiar to many in Wales as the name of the much-loved hymn-tune, written by John David Edwards (1805–1885) who was the Anglican priest in this village for over forty years.

To the south-east of Ruabon are the remains of the **Wynnstay** estate, a name that recurs throughout north Wales for streets and taverns, for this was the principal seat of the greatest landed family in Wales in the nineteenth century. Originally called Watstay – Wat's Dyke runs through its grounds – its name was changed to Wynnstay when the estate was acquired by Sir John Wyn (d.1719), fifth and last Baronet of Gwydir. On his death, the estate passed to his cousin, Sir Watkin Williams (1693–1749). The 'great Sir Watkin', as he was known, was an influential Jacobite and persecutor of Methodists, ironically sharing the same fate as William of Orange by dying in a fall from his horse. He took the name Wynn and was followed by a succession of Watkin Williams-Wynns. In 1858, the original property was destroyed by fire and the present building is the work of Benjamin Ferrey, the biographer of Pugin, who chanced to travel in the same railway carriage as Sir Watkin shortly after the tragedy, thereby acquiring a lucrative contract. Subsequently, he never tired of recommending the benefits of first class travel to his pupils. Capability Brown worked on the park, which contains charming eighteenth-century features, such as the ornamental dairy and a bathhouse, although little now remains of the majestic avenue by which the estate was approached in its heyday. The house has now been converted into flats. Unfortunately, Ferrey was also given a free hand to restore the church at Ruabon, yet it remains well worth a visit both for the profusion of opulent memorials to the Williams-Wynns and for its elegant font. The latter was designed by Robert Adam and presented to Sir Watkin, on the occasion of his son's baptism in 1772.

Approached from the east, the **Vale of Llangollen** is entered beneath Henry Robertson's monumental stone railway viaduct, completed in 1848, at the height of 'railway mania', to carry the Shrewsbury to Chester railway high over the Dee. Less than two kilometres to the west, the Dee runs under one of the most famous monuments to the industrial revolution in Wales, Thomas Telford's superb aqueduct, **Pont Cysyllte**. Completed in 1805 to carry the Ellesmere Canal, it was a pioneer work in cast-iron, quickly nicknamed 'the stream in the sky'. Using the aqueduct to cross the Dee, some forty metres below, is an exhilarating experience whether by narrow boat or by walking along the towpath. The canal basin is now used for pleasure boats with the Llangollen Branch of what became the Shropshire Union Canal running west to **Llandysilio**. It was built as a navigable feeder for the Ellesmere Canal and takes its water from the Dee at the Horseshoe Falls, a graceful crescent-shaped weir of less than half a metre in height. St Tysilio's church has a fifteenth-century stained glass window depicting St James Major.

Llangollen itself may come as a disappointment to those over familiarised with its name by over a century of tourism promotion. As a centre for visiting some remarkable sites of historical interest and scenic beauty there is no doubting its usefulness but the town itself is somewhat prosaic in its faded Victorian respectability. In July each year, it comes colourfully to life when the International Eisteddfod attracts hundreds of competitors from around the world to its musical competitions, many dressed in their national costumes. Conceived in the 1940s as a Welsh contribution to the healing of post-war divisions, its motto, composed by T. Gwynn Jones, is:

> *Byd gwyn fydd byd a gano,*
> *Gwaraidd fydd ei gerddi fo*
>
> (Blessed is a world that sings,
> Gentle are its songs.)

In 1953, 'the pig-tailed angels', in Dylan Thomas's words, of the Obernkirchen Children's Choir from Germany moved post-war Europe with their rendition of a German folk-song, *The Happy Wanderer*. For the rest of the year the town recovers from the last and prepares for the next event.

Telford's post road keeps to the south bank of the river, crossed in the town centre by the Trefor Bridge, named after a fourteenth-century Bishop of St Asaph. The town is also celebrated as the home of the Ladies of Llangollen, Eleanor Butler (1739–1829) and Sarah Ponsonby (1755–1831). Of Irish aristocratic extraction, they established a *ménage à trois* with their maid Mary Carryll at **Plas Newydd**, a house that they gothicized so that it is now a popular tourist attraction. They attracted to their home a wide and fashionable circle of curious visitors, often *en route* between London and Dublin, ranging from eminent politicians such as Burke, Castlereagh and Wellington to contemporary poets such as Byron, Shelley and Wordsworth. The latter was not granted a return invitation after describing Plas Newydd as 'a low-roof'd cott' in a commemorative sonnet. St Collen's church has a monument to the ladies commissioned by Mary Gordon, feminist, disciple of Jung and author of the biographical novel about the ladies, *The Chase of the Wild Goose* (1936). Its subjects lie buried in a triangular gothic tombstone in the churchyard, erected following the death of Mary Carryll in 1809.

Dominating the town to the north-east are the remains of **Castell Dinas Bran**, a thirteenth-century Welsh castle that never recovered from the Edwardian wars of conquest, built within the ramparts of an iron age hill fort. The castle may have been built by Gruffudd ap Madoc, the son of the founder of **Valle Crucis Abbey** (Cadw), Madog ap Gruffudd Maelor. Founded in 1201 as a colony of Strata Marcella, it occupied a typically idyllic Cistercian site near the confluence of the Eglwyseg with the Dee, now shockingly compromised by a caravan site. The surviving ruins are impressive and the sepulchral slab of the founder survives with a fine heraldic shield. The west end was repaired by Sir Gilbert Scott. A little to the north, beside the Rhuthun road, is the eighth-century cross (Cadw) from which the abbey takes its name. Erected in honour of Eliseg of the royal house of Powys, its Latin inscription, now illegible, was translated by Edward Lhuyd in the seventeenth-century and records its glories. From here the Rhuthun road crosses Maesyrychen Mountain through the **Horseshoe Pass**, a favourite with bus tours, reaching a height of 417 metres before descending into the Alun valley.

South of Ruabon, **Chirk** guards the entrance to the Ceiriog valley at the Welsh border. As at the Vale of Llangollen, there are dramatic reminders of the industrial revolution with a canal aqueduct and railway viaduct, the results of the engineering skills of Thomas Telford and Henry Robertson respectively. They cross the valley side by side before the former Ellesmere Canal disappears into a tunnel, nearly half a kilometre long, taking the canal in the direction of Llangollen. **Chirk Castle** (NT), straddling Offa's Dyke to the west of the village, was built around 1300 for Roger Mortimer, the powerful Marcher baron and was continuously occupied until 1978. It passed to the Myddelton family in 1595 when Sir Thomas Myddelton, a merchant associate of Sir Walter Raleigh acquired the property. The castle is approached through a pair of magnificent wrought iron gates, completed in 1721, the masterpiece of the Robert and John Davies. Inside, the castle has a splendid

Long Gallery, with panelling carved by Thomas Dugdale, completed in 1678. There are fine eighteenth-century rooms, such as the Great Saloon with its profusely ornamented ceiling and printed wall panels. The gardens, with their distinctive yew hedges, contain a picturesque hawk house. Needless to say, St Mary's church in the village has impressive monuments. The War Memorial, at the crossroads, depicting a soldier on the look-out, is by Eric Gill.

West of Chirk and Offa's Dyke, the Ceiriog runs down from Berwyn through its lovely valley. **Pontfadog** and **Glyn Ceiriog** are former quarrying villages, the latter has the Ceiriog Memorial Institute containing a relief portrait of the poet by Goscombe John. John Ceiriog Hughes was born further up the valley at Pen-y-bryn in the village of **Llanarmon Dyffyn Ceiriog**. St Garmon's church is a model of simplicity, set in a circular churchyard containing ancient yews. Another celebrated poet from the valley was Huw Morys (Eos Ceiriog, 1622–1709). The most prolific and accomplished Welsh poet of the seventeenth century, he spent the greater part of his adult life on the family farm at Pontymeibion, a kilometre south of **Pandy**. A devout Anglican he was one of that band who 'hated no Religion but Roundheadisme'. He witnessed the desecration of the parish church of **Llansilin** where he was a churchwarden. The magnificent fifteenth-century roofs remain and the royal arms of Queen Anne, in plaster, confirm the restoration of Anglican authority. The chancel has a marble monument to Sir William Williams Bt (1634–1700), Speaker of the House of Commons and strong supporter of James II. He married the heiress of the nearby Glascoed estate and is the grandfather of 'Great Sir Watkin'. The church occupies the site of a former Celtic *clas*.

Some three kilometres south of Llansilin is **Sycharth**. There is not much to see there, save for an apparently insignificant tree-capped motte close to the English border, but the name of the place resonates in Welsh history as the principal residence of Owain Glyn Dŵr. As a court, its praises were famously if impressionistically sung by Iolo Goch, three of whose extant poems relate to the celebrated patron of bards and minstrels whose uprising he did not live to witness:

> *Na gwall, na newyn, na gwarth,*
> *Na syched fyth yn Sycharth.*
>
> (No hunger, disgrace or dearth
> Or ever thirst at Sycharth!)

The house was burnt to the ground in 1403 by a youthful Prince Henry, the future Henry V, who proceeded to march on and destroy Owain Glyn Dŵr's other residence at Glyndyfrdwy, near Corwen. A track across the hills links the two sites and makes for an attractive if challenging walk; it would make a good extension to the Glyndŵr's Way long distance footpath.

Like the Ceiriog, the Twrch and Tanat, with their numerous tributaries tumbling down from Berwyn, form nimble fingers of the old county of Denbighshire poking west into the natural territory of Montgomeryshire. **Llanrhaeadr-ym-Mochnant** is famous in Wales as the place where William Morgan, at that time rector of the parish, worked on his celebrated translation of the Bible into Welsh. The Bishop's Bible, as it became known, is commemorated in the lych-gate of the parish church of St Dogfan. At the head of the valley, down which the Afon Rhaeadr races towards the village, is **Pistyll Rhaeadr**, at 70 metres the highest waterfall in the country and one of the celebrated 'Seven Wonders of Wales'. It is a wonderful place to contemplate the greatest wonder of all: Bishop Morgan's Bible, the door through which two millennia of a distinctive Welsh cultural tradition has passed.

Appendices

Further Reading

History

John Davies, *A History of Wales* (Allen Lane, The Penguin Press: London, 1993)

Emyr Humphreys, *The Taliesin Tradition* (Black Raven Press: London, 1983)

G.E. Jones and D. Smith (eds), *The People of Wales* (Gwasg Gomer: Llandysul, 1999)

J. Graham Jones, *A Pocket Guide to the History of Wales* (University of Wales Press: Cardiff, 1990)

Jan Morris, *The Matter of Wales* (Oxford University Press: Oxford, 1984)

Gwyn A. Williams, *When was Wales?* (Black Raven Press: London, 1985)

Each of the above single volume introductions contains guidance for more detailed further reading. The last quarter of the twentieth century was a remarkably productive period for Welsh historical scholarship with a large number of books published distinguished both for their scholarship and their accessibility to the general reader.

Architecture and Art History

Peter Lord, *The Visual Culture of Wales*, 3 volumes (University of Wales Press: Cardiff, 1998, 2000, 2004)

P. Smith, *Houses of the Welsh Countryside* (HMSO: London, 1988)

Five splendid volumes of a projected seven volume series, *The Buildings of Wales*, founded by Sir Nikolaus Pevsner (www.pevsner.co.uk), are already published.

Natural History and Topography

William Condry, *A Natural History of Wales* (Collins: London, 1981)

William Condry, *The Snowdonia National Park* (Collins: London, 1966)

Frank Emery, *The World's Landscapes: Wales* (Longmans: London, 1969)

Moelwyn Williams, *The Making of the South Wales Landscape* (Hodder and Stoughton: London, 1975)

The maps of the Ordnance Survey (www.ordsvy.gov.uk) will enhance a visit to any part of Wales.

Welsh Language

Janet Davies, *Pocket Guide to the Welsh Language* (University of Wales Press: Cardiff, 1999)

Heini Gruffudd, *Welsh Talk* (Y Lolfa: Talybont, 2000)

There are several good pocket dictionaries on the market – but be warned: Celtic languages change the beginnings not the endings of words, in a system known as mutations. This can make using a dictionary frustrating for beginners.

Welsh Literature

Welsh has a remarkable continuous literary tradition dating from the sixth century. For an introduction to this precious tradition the University of Wales Press publishes a series of chronological *Guides to Welsh Literature*. One volume deals with Welsh writing in English. (www.uwp.co.uk)

Meic Stephens (ed.), *The Oxford Companion to the Literature of Wales* (Oxford University Press: Oxford, 1998) is also indispensable.

Some Practicalities: Travel, Food, Drink and Accommodation

By Air:
Wales has one international airport at Cardiff. It is linked to several of the major European hubs (including Amsterdam and Paris) but not to London. For mid and north Wales, Birmingham and Manchester airports in England are likely to be more convenient.

By Train:
For those arriving by train, which may include international visitors routed through the London airports, there are rail links to south Wales from Paddington and to mid and north Wales from Euston. There are rail links from Birmingham and Manchester airports.

By Car:
North Wales has the A55 expressway linked to the M56. South Wales has the M4 from London. Mid Wales is approached from Birmingham on the M54.

By Ferry:
Ferries from Ireland dock at Holyhead on Anglesey (from Dublin), Fishguard and Pembroke Dock in Pembrokeshire (from Rosslare) and, seasonally, at Swansea (from Cork).

Food:
As with the UK generally, when the food is good it's very, very good and when it's bad it's horrid. *The Good Food Guide*, published annually by the Consumer's Association is a sure guide to an excellent meal (www.which.net). In recent years, Wales has

been at the forefront of organic food production, in vegetables, meat and dairy products. This is reflected in markets and menus and a cheesemakers' trail has recently been devised.

Drink:

Not everyone appreciates British beer but for those who do quality has not been higher for decades nor choice wider. CAMRA, the Campaign for Real Ale (www.camra.org.uk), publishes an excellent annual *Good Beer Guide* that lists the places that dispense real ale.

Accommodation:

For hotels of distinction, a reliable selection is offered annually in *Welsh Rarebits* (www.welsh.rarebits.co.uk). From the same stable comes an annual *Great Little Places* offering guidance on smaller hotels, inns, farms and guest houses (www.wales.little-places.co.uk).

The Wales Tourist Board (www.visitwales.com) offers advice on all of the above, and more.

Calendar of Events

Late May/early June:
Hay Literature Festival (www.hayfestival.co.uk)
Urdd National Eisteddfod (www.urdd.org)
Celtic Manor Resort Wales Open (www.walesopen.celtic-manor.com)

Early July:
Llangollen International Eisteddfod (www.international-eisteddfod.co.uk)

Late July:
Royal Welsh Show (www.rwas.co.uk)

Early August:
National Eisteddfod of Wales (www.eisteddfod.org.uk)

Mid August:
Brecon Jazz Festival (www.breconjazz.co.uk)

Late August:
Bryn Terfel's Faenol Festival (www.brynfest.com)

For a fuller listing consult Gwyliau Cymru/Festivals of Wales at www.festivalsofwales.com

The Welsh Language

Welsh is an Indo-European language belonging to the Celtic language group which is in turn sub-divided into Goidelic (Q-Celtic: Irish, Scots and Manx Gaelic) and Brythonic (P-Celtic: Welsh, Cornish and Breton). For most of Welsh history, it has been the only language spoken by the majority of the country's inhabitants. In the last quarter of the twentieth century, the small number of adult monoglot Welsh speakers remaining in the rural areas died out. Wales enters the twenty-first century with a bilingual minority, less than a quarter of the population, and an English-speaking majority. To date, the latter have been generally sympathetic to the Welsh language and the education of children through the medium of Welsh has proved popular even in homes where neither parent speaks the language. In the last half of the twentieth century the status of the language has increased, with public visibility in signage and on dedicated radio and television channels. Welsh is the most widely spoken of the surviving Celtic languages.

Welsh Pronunciation

Children learn to read more quickly in Welsh than English as the alphabet is largely phonetic. There are 29 letters in the Welsh alphabet, including seven vowels (a,e,i,o,u,w,y). The stress in Welsh is almost always on the penultimate syllable.

a a (short as in cat, long as in car)
b b
c k
ch ch (as in Scottish loch)
d d
dd th (hard the as in then)
e e (short as in met, long as in beat)
f v
ff f
g g (hard as in game)
ng ng (as in hung)
h h
i i (short as in pin, long as in week)
(j j) (only in words borrowed from English, like jam or Jones! In Welsh, the sound is represented by the letters si = sh)
l l
ll ll (place tongue to say tall and then blow lightly)
m m
n n
o o (short as in gone, long as in more)
p p
ph f
r r (rolled)
rh rh (place tongue to say r and then blow lightly)
s s
t t

th th (soft as in thing)
u u (short as in pin, long as in week)
w oo (short as in pull, long as in fool)
y i (short as in pin or fun, long as in week)

Welsh Personal Names

When the English legal system was imposed on Wales, a traditional Celtic naming system was supplanted by a Teutonic one. In Wales, as in Scotland and Ireland, a child was traditionally known as the son or daughter of its father: *Siôn ab Ifan* (John, son of Evan) or *Mair ferch Owain* (Mary, daughter of Owen), for example. The English requirement to have a surname resulted in common Christian names - like Siôn (John), Ifan (Evan) or Huw (Hugh) – being fixed as surnames, hence the plethora of Jones, Evans and Hughes in any Welsh telephone directory, where help pages – such as, *How to find your Jones* – have been inserted for the uninitiated. Survival strategy for the Welsh, under this alien system, resulted in an elaborate and often humorous use of nicknames. In order that one John Jones could be distinguished from another, for example, the name of his village might be added to his name (as in John Jones, Tal-y-sarn) or of his home (as in William Williams, Pantycelyn). A bardic name will pass into common use if it serves to distinguish one man from another: Elerydd, to distinguish W.J. Gruffydd from his illustrious predecessor, for example. An occupation might serve to distinguish Dai'r Cantwr (a ballad-singer) from Dai'r Crydd (a cobbler); or an attribute might be invoked, as in 'Bungalow' Jones for a completely bald man of that name (i.e. nothing on top) or Dai 'Full Pelt', a particularly fast bus driver. A memory of the p in *ap* or b in *ab* (before a vowel) is contained in the many surnames beginning with P or B: Prichard (ap Richard), Price (ap Rhys), Pugh (ap Huw), Bowen (ab Owain), Bevan (ab Ifan), for example. To add to the confusion, the Welsh fondness for alliteration results in a surfeit of William Williams, Huw Hughes, Morgan Morgan (the first Morgan being shortened to Moc), David (shortened to Dai) Davies, John Jones and so on.

Welsh Place-name Elements

Aber, mouth, confluence
Afon, river
Allt, hillside (wooded)

Bedwen (pl. bedw), birch
Betws, oratory
Blaen (blaenau), head of valley
Bro, vale
Bron, rounded hill
Bryn, hill
Buarth, cattle fold
Bwlch (pl. blychau), pass

Cadair, chair
Cae, field
Caer, fort (Roman)
Cam, crooked
Canol, middle
Capel, chapel
Carn, carnedd (pl. carneddau), heap of stones, mountain
Carreg (pl. cerrig), rock
Cas, castell, castle
Cefn, ridge
Celli, copse
Celyn, holly
Cemais, river bends
Ceulan, hollow bank of a river
Clawdd, bank, ditch
Clogwyn, cliff

Clwyd, gate
Coch, red
Coed, woodland
Comins, common land
Cors, bog
Craig (pl. creigiau), rock
Crib, ridge
Croes, cross
Crug (pl. crugiau), mound
Cul, narrow
Cwm, valley, cirque
Cymer (pl. cymerau), meeting of rivers

Dau (f. dwy), two
Derwen (pl. derw), oak
Diffwys, precipice
Dinas, fort, city
Diserth, place of retreat
Dol (pl. dolau), meadow
Du, black
Dulas, dark stream
Dŵr, water
Dyffryn, valley

Efail, blacksmith
Eglwys, church
Eira, snow
Eithin, gorse
Enlli, tidal race

Erw, acre
Esgair, stair, slope

Ffordd, road
Ffos, ditch
Ffridd, mountain pasture
Ffynnon, spring, well

Gafr, goat
Garw, rough
Glyn, glen
Grug, heather
Gwastad, level place
Gwern, marsh
Gwyn, white, fair
Gwynt, wind

Hafod, summer dwelling
Helygen (pl. helyg), willow
Hen, old
Hendre, winter dwelling
Heol, road, street

Isaf, low

Llan, church
Llannerch, glade
Llech, slate
Llechwedd, hillside
Llethr, slope
Llety, shelter, refuge
Lluest, bothy, summer dwelling
Llwyd, grey
Llwyn, grove
Llyn (pl. llynnoedd), lakes
Llys, court, hall

Maen (pl. meini), stone
Mawn, peat
Mawr, great, big
Meillionen, clover
Mêl, honey
Melin, mill
Merthyr, martyr
Migneint, boggy hollows
Mochyn (pl. moch), pig
Moel, bare hill
Môr, sea
Morfa, coastal marsh
Mur (pl. muriau), wall
Mwyn, mineral ore
Mynach, monk
Mynydd, mountain

Nant, stream
Neuadd, hall
Newydd, new

Odyn, kiln
Oer, cold
Ogof, cave
Onnen (pl. onn), ash

Pandy, fulling mill
Pant, hollow
Pen, head, summit
Penmaen, rocky promontory
Penrhyn, promontory
Pentref, village
Pistyll, waterfall
Plas, mansion
Pont, bridge
Porth, landing place
Pren, wood
Pwll, pool

Rhaeadr, waterfall
Rhiw, steep slope
Rhos, moor
Rhyd, ford

Sarn, ancient paved road
Sir, shire

Tal, end
Tarren, knoll
Tir, land
Tomen, mound
Traeth, shore
Traws, across
Tre, Tref, town
Tri (f. tair), three

Tref, town
Troed, foot
Tŵr, tower
Twyn, hillock
Tŷ (pl. tai), house
Tyddyn, smallholding
Tywyn, sea-shore

Waun, moor

Ynys, island
Ysbyty, hospice
Ysgol, school
Ystrad, valley floor
Ystwyth, winding

Index